TEACHING MODELS IN EDUCATION OF THE GIFTED

C. June Maker
University of Arizona
Tucson, Arizona

8700 Shoal Creek Boulevard
Austin, Texas 78758

Printed in the United States of America

Library of Congress Cataloging in Publication Data

Maker, C. June.
Teaching models in education of the gifted.

Bibliography: p. 459
Includes index.
1. Gifted children — Education. I. Title.
LC3993.M293   371.95   82-1692
ISBN 0-89079-186-4   AACR2
(formerly 0-89443-682-1)

8700 Shoal Creek Blvd.
Austin, Texas 78758

10 9 8 7 6 5 4 3 2 1   88 89 90 91 92

To Steve
who has given the freedom
and support
that allows my career to grow,
with love and appreciation

Table of Contents

v

Preface

PURPOSE OF THE BOOK

This book provides a comprehensive review of teaching-learning models that can be used in the development and implementation of a curriculum for gifted students. In providing this review, the author hopes to supply enough information to teachers, prospective teachers, program coordinators, and curriculum development specialists to enable them to (a) assess critically the match of the model's assumptions with their own philosophies; (b) evaluate the model's validity for the purpose for which they intend to employ it; (c) apply the model appropriately in any situation; and, most importantly, (d) implement the model in a program for gifted students. Because of its focus on implementation, the book provides many examples of the use of different models with gifted students of several ages.

This book also serves as a companion volume to the author's first book on curricula, *Curriculum Development for the Gifted* (Maker, 1982). In the first volume, the author discussed modifications of the regular curriculum's content, processes, products, and learning environment to make it more appropriate for gifted students. The first volume also provided suggestions for curriculum development, along with several examples of appropriate curricula. To implement such a curriculum, however, more is needed, more specific teaching strategies, more examples, and more in-depth discussions of the variety of approaches available for teaching gifted students. In effect, this book provides a variety of alternatives for implementing the general principles described in the first volume.

It is highly unlikely that any model or way of teaching the gifted that is currently being used in gifted programs can provide the comprehensive curriculum needed by the students. Therefore, this book focuses on the development of a comprehensive understanding of a variety of approaches. Once these approaches have been understood, curricula can be designed that consider the following important factors: (a) the teacher's, school's, and community's philosophy regarding the purpose of education for the gifted; (b) the underlying assumptions of the theoretical and practical approaches, along with how these assumptions mesh with the philosophies of everyone concerned; (c) child characteristics; (d) parental concerns; (e) the teaching style, strengths, and preferences of the teacher; and (f) the physical setting of the school. The final product, the curriculum, may be based mainly on one model, it may use one as a framework with others as supplements, or it may integrate several of the models into a framework generated by the developer.

The models described were chosen for several reasons. The first was a concern for their demonstrated or potential success with gifted children. Each principle described in the first volume was considered in this selection process. Second, these models were selected because of their widespread use in gifted programs. A third and final concern was variety and complementarity. No one model addresses all the content, process, product, and learning environment changes necessary for a comprehensive curriculum to be established. No one model will be attractive to all teachers, and no one model will fit every situation. For these and related reasons, models were chosen that could be combined in a variety of ways to enhance their effectiveness and increase the chances that teachers will find a particular combination that will fit their preferred styles of teaching.

ORGANIZATION OF THE BOOK

The first chapter provides an introduction to teaching-learning models and discusses their role in programs for the gifted. The main body of the book consists of a separate chapter about each model. These chapters follow a consistent outline containing a discussion of the model, a teaching unit developed from it, an analysis of the unit, and a listing of additional resources. The outline for each chapter is as follows:

A. Overview of the Model
B. Assumptions Underlying the Model
    1. About Learning
    2. About Teaching
    3. About Characteristics and Teaching of the Gifted
    4. Other
C. Elements/Parts
    1. Dimensions, Thinking Levels, or Steps
    2. Modifications of the Basic Curriculum
        a. Content
        b. Process
        c. Product
        d. Environment

The final chapter consists of a discussion of how a comprehensive approach might be developed by combining and integrating more than one of the models described.

Chapter 1

The Role of Teaching-Learning Models in Curriculum Development for the Gifted

THE NATURE OF TEACHING-LEARNING MODELS

A teaching-learning model is a structural framework that serves as a guide for developing specific educational activities and environments. A model can be highly theoretical and abstract, or it can be a more practical structural framework. Regardless of how theoretical or practical, the distinguishing features common to teaching-learning models are (a) an identified purpose or area of concentration; (b) underlying explicit and implicit assumptions about the characteristics of learners and about the teaching-learning process; (c) guidelines for developing specific day-to-day learning experiences; (d) definite patterns and requirements for these learning activities; and (e) a body of research surrounding their development or an evaluation of their effectiveness.

Joyce and Weil (1979) have identified more than 80 models of teaching and have divided them into four families based on their common viewpoints about teaching and learning. The first group, social interaction models, emphasizes the relationships of the individual to society and to other groups, and focuses on the individual's ability to relate to others, engage in democracy, and work productively within society. Information-processing models, the second group, focus on the ways people handle information, organize data, sense problems, and generate solutions to problems. The third family, personal models, shares an orientation toward the development of self-concept. Behavior modification and cybernetic models emphasize changes in observable behavior based on efficient sequencing of learning tasks along with manipulation of antecedents and consequences. Most of the models presented fall into the second category, although some of them could be considered personal models.

The area of concentration or focus on the model can be very broad or quite narrow. Renzulli's *Enrichment Triad*,* for example, was developed as a total

---

*Specific references for each model can be found in the individual chapters on each model.

enrichment program for the gifted, focusing on content knowledge, a wide range of intellectual skills, and the development of an investigative attitude. The Williams model, on the other hand, was developed to enhance creative abilities, a more narrow range of intellectual and affective skills. Because it says something about a lot of things, the Renzulli model goes into each practice in less depth than does the Williams model, which is more narrow in its scope.

Although the different models have different purposes or areas of concentration, they are not exclusive in that they only focus on one aspect of learning. For example, the information processing models, such as Parnes and Taba, also emphasize the development of social relationships and an integrated, well-functioning self. However, the major route for doing this is enhanced intellectual functioning.

Each model must make some theoretical assumptions, both regarding the nature of the learner (for example, learning, motivational, intellectual, and emotional characteristics) and the nature or effectiveness of certain teaching methods. These assumptions can range from highly theoretical and complicated ones, such as Kohlberg's assumption that all individuals progress through identifiable, invariant stages in their development of moral reasoning, to one of Taylor's simple assumptions that a variety of talent exists in individuals. The stage of development or "proof" of these assumptions also varies from model to model. A related aspect of assumptions is how clearly they are stated. Some authors clearly reveal the assumptions they reject and state the ones they accept, while others describe some and leave out other critical ones. Still other authors say nothing about either their implicit or explicit assumptions, and teachers are left to their own devices in uncovering the underlying ideas.

The third and fourth aspects of models are their guidelines for development of specific learning experiences. Along with these guidelines are associated requirements or standards by which their appropriateness is judged. The Bloom and Krathwohl *Taxonomies,* for example, provide definitions of cognitive and affective behaviors to enable the educator to design activities that systematically develop behaviors at each level in the hierarchy. One requirement or standard associated with the implementation of the models is that each lower level behavior is necessary before the higher level behavior can be executed effectively. Associated with the Taba *Strategies* is a broad range of teacher attitudes and competencies that involve much more than simply knowing what sequences of questions to ask the children.

All teaching-learning models have some basis in research, either as a background for their development or as a justification for their use because of their effectiveness. There has been extensive research on the elements included in the Parnes program, for instance, along with numerous longitudinal and experimental studies of its effectiveness with various groups. The Taba *Strategies* were developed and evaluated over a period of approximately ten years. On the other hand, there has been little research on the effectiveness of Williams's strategies in achieving their stated purposes. Renzulli's model was developed out of his experience in evaluating programs for the gifted and based on reviews of research on the characteristics of gifted individuals. However, at this time there is little research showing the model's effectiveness.

THE CURRICULUM FOR GIFTED STUDENTS*

Qualitative Differences

The phrase most frequently used to describe the appropriate school curriculum for gifted students is "qualitatively different from the program for nongifted students." This phrase implies that the basic curriculum must be examined, and changes or modifications must be made so that the most appropriate curriculum is provided for the gifted students. Modifications must be quality changes rather than quantity, and they must build upon and extend the characteristics (both present and future) that make the children different from nongifted students.

According to Gallagher (1975), to make the basic curriculum more appropriate for gifted students, a person can modify the *content* (what is learned), the *process* (the methods used and the thinking processes students are expected to use), and the *learning environment* (the psychological and physical environment in which the learning is to occur). Renzulli (1977) has added *product* (the end products expected of children as a result of the processes used) as a dimension that must be considered.

Content Modifications

The content of the curriculum consists of the ideas, concepts, descriptive information, and facts that are presented to the student. It can assume a variety of forms and can differ in its degree of abstractness, complexity, the way it is organized, and the subject areas covered.

Abstractness

The major focus of discussions, presentations, reading materials, and lectures in a gifted program should be on abstract concepts and generalizations—ideas that have a wide range of applicability or that transfer both within and across disciplines

---

*The material presented in this section represents a brief review of information contained in Section I of the companion volume, *Curriculum Development for the Gifted* (Maker, 1982). Readers who are not familiar with the concepts as presented by Maker should read this more comprehensive discussion of curriculum development for the gifted.

or fields of study. Concrete information and factual data are intended as illustrations or examples of the abstract ideas rather than as the major focus.

Complexity

Usually abstract ideas are also complex, but abstract ideas vary in their degree of complexity. The abstract ideas presented to gifted students need to be as complex as possible. The complexity of an abstract idea can be determined by examining the number and complexity of concepts involved, the number and complexity of the relationships between concepts, and the number and diversity of the disciplines or traditional content areas that must be understood or integrated to comprehend the idea.

Variety

In the past year, variety has been the definition of enrichment and, in many programs, has been the only content modification made for gifted students. The concept of variety suggests that in a gifted program, ideas and content areas not taught in the regular curriculum should be taught.

Organization and Economy

Since knowledge in most areas is increasing and changing more rapidly than ever before, and since gifted students have a limited amount of time to spend in school and in the program, every learning experience must be the most valuable that can be offered. To achieve economy, content must be organized to facilitate transfer of learning, memory, and understanding of abstract concepts and generalizations. According to Bruner (1960), these results can be achieved if the content is organized around the key concepts or abstract ideas to be taught rather than arranged in some other fashion.

Study of People

Gifted students are likely to become the scholars, leaders, and creative, productive individuals of the future. They also enjoy reading biographies and autobiographies. For these reasons, along with their potential for learning to deal with their own talents and possible success, gifted students need to study creative and productive individuals. An analysis of problems these individuals faced should be included, along with the way they handled their problems, their personal traits, their career or professional characteristics, and their social interactions.

The Study of Methods

Gifted students should study the methods of inquiry—the investigative techniques—used by scholars in different disciplines. They need practice in using these methods, and they should learn a variety of techniques. Such studies can contribute to a better understanding of the content area and enhance the independence of the students.

Process Modifications

The process aspect of the curriculum involves the way new material is presented, the activities in which the students engage, and the questions that are asked. Process includes teaching methods and the thinking skills or processes developed in the students.

Higher Levels of Thinking

The methods used in gifted programs should stress the use rather than acquisition of information. Since gifted students can rapidly and almost effortlessly acquire information, they should be expected to apply it in new situations, use it to develop new ideas, evaluate its appropriateness, and use it to develop new products.

Open-endedness

Questions and activities for gifted students should include a greater percentage of open rather than closed questions and learning activities. The principle of open-endedness indicates that there is no predetermined right answer and that the questions or activities are provocative in that they stimulate further thinking and investigation about the topic. Openness stimulates more thought, permits and encourages divergent thinking, encourages responses from more than one child, and contributes to the development of a student-centered interaction pattern.

Discovery

The activities designed for gifted students should include a greater percentage of situations in which the students use their inductive reasoning processes to discover patterns, ideas, and underlying principles. Such guided discovery has several advantages for these children: (1) it increases their interest through involvement in learning; (2) it builds on their natural curiosity, their desire to figure out the ''how and why of things'' (Renzulli, Smith, White, Callahan, & Hartman, 1976), and their desire to organize and bring structure to things; and (3) it increases their self-confidence and independence in learning by showing that they are capable of figuring things out for themselves.

Evidence of Reasoning

Another important process modification for use with gifted students is to ask them to express not only their conclusions but also the reasoning that led them to these conclusions. This aspect of teaching is especially important when using a discovery approach, developing higher levels of thinking, and asking open-ended questions. Using this strategy, students learn different reasoning processes from other students, and they are encouraged to evaluate both the process and products of others' thinking. It also provides a vehicle for the teacher to assess the student's levels of thinking.

Freedom of Choice

Whenever possible, gifted students should be given the freedom to choose what to investigate and how to study. Their interest and excitement in learning will be increased by such techniques. However, not all gifted students are independent learners, so they may need assistance in making and executing their choices.

Group Interaction Activities and Simulations

Structured activities and simulation games should be a regular part of the curriculum for gifted students to enable them to develop their social and leadership skills. These activities should include following a set of rules, interacting with a small group of students, peer evaluation, and self-analysis or critique. Both peer evaluation and self-analysis will be more effective if the activity has been video-taped or audiotaped.

Pacing and Variety

The final two process modifications serve mainly as facilitators of the success of other changes. Pacing refers to how rapidly new material is presented to the students. Research (George, 1976) and experience have indicated that rapid pacing is important to maintain the interest of the students and provide a challenge. Variety simply suggests that the teacher use various methods to maintain the interest of the children and to accommodate the different learning styles of the students.

Product Modifications

Products are the "ends" of instruction. They can be tangible or intangible, sophisticated or unsophisticated. Sophisticated products involve detailed, original work, while unsophisticated ones involve paraphrasing or copying. Products can include reports, stories, plays, dances, ideas, speeches, pictures, and illustrations. The products expected from gifted students should resemble the products developed by professionals in the discipline being studied (Renzulli, 1977). These professional products will differ from typical student products in the following ways:

- *Real problems*—The products developed by gifted students should address problems that are real to them. Students can be allowed to choose a specific area of concern within a certain field of study and to design an investigation around that area.
- *Real audiences*—To the extent possible, the products developed by gifted students should be addressed to real audiences, such as the scientific community, the city council, or a government agency. These students should not be developing products that are only seen or heard by the teacher. If real audiences are not available, other students can make up a simulated audience.
- *Transformation*—Gifted students' products should represent transformations of existing information or data rather than being mere summaries of other people's conclusions. Original research, original artwork, and other such products should include the collection and analysis of raw data. If students have used their higher levels of thinking, they must produce a product that is a true transformation.
- *Evaluation*—Often, student products are only directed toward and evaluated by the teacher. The products of professionals are evaluated by the audiences for whom they were intended. Products of gifted students should be evaluated by appropriate audiences, including simulated audiences of peers. Students should also be encouraged or required to complete an extensive self-evaluation of their own products.

Learning Environment

The learning environment refers to the setting in which learning occurs, both the physical setting of the school and classroom, and the psychological climate of the classroom. There are many dimensions of learning environments that are important, and different individuals have different preferences for certain aspects (for example, amount of noise, light, or presence of color). The learning environments appropriate for gifted students resemble the environments appropriate for all children, but are different in degree. All environment modifications presented in this section were chosen because they met the following three conditions: (1) they are preferred by the gifted as a group; (2) they are necessary for implementing the content, process, and product modifications advocated; and (3) they build on the characteristics of gifted students.

Student-Centered versus Teacher-Centered

Environments for gifted students should include a focus on the students' ideas and interests rather than on those of the teacher. There should be a high degree of emphasis on student discussions rather than on teacher talk, and patterns of interaction should seldom, if ever, have the teacher as the central figure or focus.

Independence versus Dependence

This dimension of the environment refers to the degree of tolerance for and encouragement of student initiative. The focus is on having students solve their own problems rather than having the teacher solve all the problems, including those related to classroom management.

Open versus Closed

This aspect of the environment refers to the extent to which restrictions affect the student and goes beyond academic into nonacademic areas. The physical environment needs to be open to permit new people, materials, and things to enter. The same is true of the psychological environment. It must permit new ideas, exploratory discussions, and the freedom to change directions to meet new situations.

Accepting versus Judging

There are three major elements of this dimension: (1) attempting to understand students' ideas; (2) the timing of value judgments; and (3) evaluation rather than judgment. Before teachers can assess student ideas, they must accept and understand those ideas, that is, they must attend or listen actively, accept the ideas, and then request clarification, elaboration, and extensions of the ideas before challenging them. Timing refers to the stage of problem solving when evaluations occur. Idea production, for example, is one of the most inappropriate times. Judgment implies rightness or wrongness, while evaluation implies that an assessment will recognize both the good and bad aspects of any product or person. Evaluation should be emphasized rather than judgment.

Complex versus Simple

As a dimension of classroom climate, complexity versus simplicity refers to both the physical and the psychological environment. A complex physical environment, which is necessary for the gifted, includes a variety of materials, references, and books; a balance of hard and soft elements; and a variety of colors. A complex psychological environment, which is also necessary for gifted students, includes challenging tasks, complex ideas, and sophisticated methods.

High Mobility versus Low Mobility

This dimension of the environment refers to the amount of movement allowed and encouraged. To permit gifted students to develop professional products, allow freedom of choice, and permit exploration, the environment must allow movement in and out of the classroom, different grouping arrangements within and outside the classroom, and access to different environments, materials, and equipment.

Summary

The changes advocated in this section have been chosen to meet, collectively and individually, two basic criteria that are different in quality from the regular curriculum and based on the unique characteristics of gifted students. Since these elements were chosen based on the group traits of gifted students, the curriculum for each child needs to reflect the fact that not all will possess every characteristic. Thus, the curriculum must be tailored to fit the needs of each child based on an assessment of that child's characteristics.

ADAPTING AND SELECTING MODELS*

To build a curriculum that incorporates elements such as those listed in the previous section, an approach or approaches that will provide specific strategies for accomplishing these curricular changes must be identified. In choosing an approach, several factors must be considered. These factors relate to the setting (the school district, the school, the community), the students, the teacher, and the model. In effect, there must be a match between what the model has to offer and what the program needs.

Assessing the Situation

The first step in adapting or selecting models involves assessing factors related to the setting, teacher, and students that would influence the choice of a model or models. One of the factors relating to the situation, for example, is the kind of grouping arrangement used for the program, such as a regular classroom with a consulting teacher, resource rooms in each building, resource centers across the district, or a self-contained classroom. Another factor is the attitude of regular classroom teachers toward the program. If a particular approach requires the cooperation of teachers who refuse to cooperate, the program will fail unless a different choice is made. Factors relating to the students would include both their common characteristics (average) and the range of those characteristics (differences), their ages, achievement levels, interests, background experiences, and learning style preferences.

Research on the effectiveness of educational approaches shows that the single most important variable in determining success is the teacher. If the teacher does not have the necessary skills for implementing the approach and does not believe in its value, the program cannot be effective. Teacher factors to consider can be

---

*The information in this section provides a brief summary of Chapters 5 and 6 of the companion volume. This is a review for those who are familiar with those chapters. Those who have not read those sections are encouraged to do so, as the depth of coverage of the topic is much greater.

separated into three groups: philosophical, personal, and professional. Philosophical characteristics include those related to the philosophy of education for the gifted, its purpose and implementation. Personal traits include personality, intelligence, motivation, and self-confidence. Professional characteristics include the skills possessed by the teacher, educational background, and past experiences. Factors relating to the model include all those items discussed at the beginning of this chapter. All these aspects must be taken into account when selecting or adapting a teaching-learning model (or models) for a program.

Assessing the Model

The next step in choosing an approach is to assess the model's appropriateness based on the situational factors identified. Five general criteria have been selected for evaluating a model: (a) appropriateness to the situation; (b) comprehensiveness as a framework for curriculum development for the gifted; (c) flexibility or adaptability; (d) validity; and (e) practicality. Others could be added.

Following are some specific questions that can be asked during this assessment:

Appropriateness to the Situation

- To what extent do the purposes of the model match the needs of the students, the school philosophy, parental values, and teacher characteristics?
- To what extent do the underlying assumptions made in the model fit reality? (For example, if the model makes assumptions about the characteristics of gifted students, are these characteristics true of the students in the program?)

Comprehensiveness

- What content modifications are provided by the model?
- What process modifications are provided by the model?
- What product modifications are provided by the model?
- What learning environment modifications are provided by the model?
- Which of the modifications, not actually provided by the model, could easily be generated by or integrated into the approach?

Flexibility or Adaptability

- How easily can the model be adapted to all content areas or subject matter covered in the program?
- How easily can the model be adapted to the present administrative structure of the school and program?

- How easily can the model be combined with other models to provide a comprehensive program?
- How easily can the model be used with the age levels of children served by the program?
- How adaptable is the model to individual differences in gifted children?

Practicality

- What materials or services are available to implement the approach?
- What is the cost of the materials or services?
- How much training of the special teacher or regular classroom teacher is needed to implement the model effectively?
- How easily could the approach be implemented in the present situation?

Validity

- Was the model developed using appropriate methods?
- How much research is available to show its effectiveness as an educational approach?
- How much research is available to show its effectiveness as an approach to use with gifted students?
- How much evidence is there to indicate that the model is internally valid (or structurally sound)?
- Is the approach defensible as a qualitatively different program for gifted students?

Two worksheets have been designed to facilitate the process of assessing models. On the first worksheet, the criteria and questions are listed on one side, and the models are listed at the top. (See Figure 1-1.) Using the system of 1 = poor, 2 = average, and 3 = excellent, a rating should be assigned to each model on each criterion. Next, the ratings for each should be totalled to indicate its overall appropriateness.

The second worksheet assesses the criterion of comprehensiveness. (See Figure 1-2.) On this worksheet, the curricular modifications presented earlier and in the companion volume are listed as criteria, and the models are listed at the top. A checkmark is placed in the column and row if the modification is made, and the column is left blank if it is not. The totals for each column indicate the comprehensiveness of the model. Information from this worksheet can also be used to examine the different models and determine how they complement each other.

Figure 1-1 Worksheet for Overall Curriculum Design

Criteria and Questions	Bruner	Bloom	Krathwohl	Parnes	Renzulli	Taba	Kohlberg	Taylor	Williams	Guilford	Treffinger	Totals	Comment
Assign a rating to each model on each criterion question using the following code: 1 = Poor 2 = Average 3 = Average 3 = Excellent													
Appropriateness to the Situation													
1. To what extent do the purposes of the model match the needs of the students, the school philosophy, parental values, and teacher characteristics?													
2. To what extent do the underlying assumptions made in the model fit reality?													
Flexibility/Adaptability													
1. How easily can the model be adapted to all content areas or subject matter covered in the program?													
2. How easily can the model be adapted to the present administrative structure of the school and program?													
3. How easily can the model be combined with others to provide a comprehensive program?													
4. How easily can the model be used with the age level(s) of children served by the program?													
5. How adaptable is the model to individual differences in gifted children?													
Practicality													
1. What materials and services are available to implement the approach?													
2. What is the cost of these materials or services?													
3. How much training of the special teacher or regular classroom teacher is needed to implement the model effectively?													
4. How easily could the approach be implemented in the present situation?													

Validity

1. Was the model developed using appropriate methods?

2. How much research is available to show its effectiveness as an educational approach?

3. How much research is available to show its effectiveness as an educational approach?

4. How much evidence is there to indicate that the model is internally valid or structurally sound?

5. Is the approach defensible as a qualitatively different program for gifted students?

TOTALS

Source: Reprinted from J. Maker. *Curriculum Development for the Gifted.* Rockville, Md.: Aspen Systems Corporation, 1982.

Figure 1-2 Worksheet for Overall Curriculum Design

Work Sheet #6: Evaluation of Models

Rate each model on each criterion by placing a ✓ in the column if the modification is made by the model. If not, leave the space blank.

Curricular Modifications	Bruner	Bloom	Krathwohl	Parnes	Renzulli	Taba	Kohlberg	Taylor	Williams	Guilford	Treffinger	Totals	Comment
Content — Modifications													
1. Abstractness													
2. Complexity													
3. Variety													
4. Organization													
5. Economy													
6. Study of People													
7. Methods													
Process — Modifications													
8. Higher Level Thought													
9. Open-Endedness													
10. Discovery													
11. Proof/Reasoning													
12. Freedom of Choice													
13. Group Interaction													
14. Pacing													
15. Variety													
Product — Modifications													
16. Real Problems													
17. Real Audiences													
18. Evaluation													
19. Transformation													

20. Student Centered
21. Encourages Independence
22. Openness
23. Accepting
24. Complex
25. High Mobility

Totals

Modifications

Environment

Learning

Combining the Models

The final step in the process of adaptation/selection is to decide whether one approach can serve as the only model used or whether the models must be combined, used together, or used in different situations.

The models presented in this book are different in their purposes as well as in which content, process, product, and learning environment modifications appropriate for the gifted are directly addressed by the approach. For example, Bruner's approach modifies content by suggesting that it be organized around basic concepts. His approach also addresses the process of discovery, although its major modifications are in the area of content. The *Cognitive and Affective Taxonomies*, on the other hand, provide modifications only in the process area and only in one aspect of process, the development of higher levels of thinking.

Guilford's theory provides a unifying model for changes in content, process, and product as dimensions of a learning task. However, it does not make all the suggested curricular changes in any of the areas. Thus, even though this theory is more comprehensive than many others, it alone would not provide a complete curriculum.

The same is true of Renzulli's *Triad*. Although it can provide a comprehensive framework for an overall approach, other process models need to be added, such as Bloom, Taba, Taylor, Kohlberg, and Krathwohl, to guide the development of Type II activities. Treffinger's developmental approach to self-direction can provide the teacher with methods for moving students toward the development of their Type III investigations.

Some similarities should also be noted. Most of the models modify process, and few consider content changes at all. In fact, many of them make similar process changes because of their emphasis on higher levels of thinking and on development of creative or divergent thought processes. Most also emphasize the thinking skill of evaluation (for example, Bloom, Krathwohl, Guilford, and Parnes) or decision making (for example, Taylor).

If these models are combined or used separately, their similarities and differences must be considered. In other words, they must be combined so that the total curriculum is comprehensive, but the degree of overlap should also be considered. It would not be desirable to place undue emphasis on process skills simply because more methods and materials are available for use.

Chapter 2

Benjamin Bloom and David Krathwohl: The Cognitive and Affective Taxonomies

One of the most frequently used models for the development of higher level thinking is Bloom's *Taxonomy*. Most programs for the gifted, if not based entirely on this model, at least use it in some way. Although both the *Cognitive* and *Affective Taxonomies* were developed by essentially the same group of educators and psychologists, the cognitive is usually referred to as Bloom's *Taxonomy,* the affective as Krathwohl's *Taxonomy.* In this chapter, they will simply be referred to as cognitive and affective.

The purpose of the taxonomies is to provide a set of criteria that can be used to classify educational objectives according to the level of complexity of the thinking required. They are generic in that they apply to any academic subject area and level of instruction from kindergarten through adult education (including graduate school). The two taxonomies have a different focus; one is on cognitive or intellectual behaviors, while the other is on affective or "feeling" behaviors. Although their focus and levels are different, most of their underlying assumptions, their development, and their use is similar. The basic reference for the *Cognitive Taxonomy* is Bloom (1956); for the *Affective Taxonomy,* Krathwohl, Bloom, and Masia (1964) is the basic reference.*

One of the reasons for the development of the taxonomies was to facilitate communication between psychologists and educators in such areas as test construction, research, and curriculum development. The taxonomies, especially the cognitive one, have achieved this purpose and some unintended ones. At the time of their development, it is doubtful that anyone anticipated the widespread use of the classifications to develop teaching activities. However, they provide a simple,

---

*Because these are the only references used in descriptions of the taxonomies, they are not cited each time. Whenever their general development, use, and essential elements are described, the sources are the basic ones unless otherwise specified. In discussions of their use or applicability in programs for the gifted, the information and perceptions have come from the author's experience in education of the gifted.

somewhat easy-to-learn structure for developing teaching-learning activities that take students through a sequential process in the development of a concept or learning of relationships. If the major assumption of the taxonomies is valid—that each higher level includes and depends on the behaviors below—students who have been led through the process systematically should be able to think or behave more effectively at the higher levels.

ASSUMPTIONS UNDERLYING THE MODEL

About Learning

The most basic assumption made by the developers of the taxonomies is that they are hierarchical. Each higher level depends on all the levels below it. Thus, application, the third level in the *Cognitive Taxonomy*, cannot be achieved without knowledge and comprehension. If students are to be able to solve a problem they have never seen before, they must know and understand whatever principles or computational methods are necessary for its solution. The fifth level, analysis, which is often required of students on exams (for example, compare and contrast the following ideas . . .), cannot be adequately reached unless the student has applied the ideas to a situation never before encountered. Students cannot be expected to develop a system of values unless they have first considered whether they value certain things, and how two or more of their values would compare. In short, the implications of this assumption are important to the instructional process. Teachers must make certain that their students are able to perform the behaviors at the lower levels before expecting them to function at the higher levels.

Related to this assumption is the implication that all learners are capable of the thinking and feeling processes described at each level of the taxonomies. In other words, if given enough time, all children are capable of the thinking processes of analysis, synthesis, and evaluation, as well as the feeling processes of valuing, organizing values, and internalizing values. The authors state that if students are provided with proper teaching conditions and allowed enough time, 95 percent can master any learning task. Teachers must have a view of the final level to be attained and concentrate on movement toward that goal in a step-by-step fashion to help students achieve mastery.

Another underlying principle of the taxonomies is that thinking or feeling processes or teaching objectives can be defined behaviorally and, when defined, can fit into one of the classifications of the taxonomies. In other words, there are certain types of thinking that can be observed and classified. Implicit in this assumption and the methods used to develop the taxonomies is the belief that educators and psychologists working together can develop a logical classification that approximates reality.

About Teaching

Basic to the use of the taxonomies as a teaching tool, but not proposed by their developers, is that by designing activities that evoke the types of thinking at each level of the hierarchies, thinking and feeling processes can be improved. Through systematic emphasis on each of the levels from the lowest to the highest, ultimately students will be better thinkers at the higher levels. An aspect of this idea is that teaching activities can be developed that evoke certain types of thinking and teachers can be reasonably accurate about the underlying processes that go into a particular activity. For example, in designing a factual or knowledge question (the lowest level of the *Cognitive Taxonomy*), the teacher assumes a child has had prior contact with the information being requested. If the child has not, the question requires a higher level of thinking than knowledge. To answer the question, the student may have to think about some related information, put it together in a new fashion, and develop a possible answer. Similarly, when teachers design questions to evoke the higher levels of thinking, such as evaluation, which requires students to make a judgment, they must assume that when the students give their answers, they are giving their own judgments rather than simply recalling judgments made by someone else (that is, knowledge level). Often, questions of the appropriate form calling for higher levels, such as evaluation, are asked. (For example, what do you think are the advantages and disadvantages of this approach?) However, the students are really being expected to list the pros and cons that have previously been presented by the teacher. In these cases, the students are operating at the lowest level rather than the highest.

A related idea is that any learning task can and should be broken down into smaller units or steps. These smaller units are then sequenced appropriately, and students are systematically led through the process. This idea would directly oppose the belief that each individual thinks differently, therefore an appropriate sequence cannot be developed or the related view that people learn through a process of intuitive leaps rather than sequential steps.

About Characteristics and Teaching of the Gifted

The authors of the taxonomies do not make statements directly related to their use with gifted children. They believe that all children are capable of the various processes. However, educators of the gifted assume that more time should be spent at the higher levels with these children because they are already capable of high quality thinking and feeling at the lower levels. Although this observation is usually valid due to the wide range of information the children possess, the need for knowledge and comprehension often goes unrecognized, and these important steps are neglected. In attempting to concentrate on the higher levels, educators often forget to check the children's knowledge and understanding of the concepts involved. A related assumption is that gifted children *should* spend more time at the higher levels because this type of thinking is more challenging for them.

ELEMENTS/PARTS

Dimensions, Thinking Levels, or Steps

The *Cognitive Taxonomy* consists of six levels: knowledge; comprehension; application; analysis; synthesis; and evaluation. The *Affective Taxonomy* consists of five levels: receiving or attending; responding; valuing; organization; and characterization by a value complex. Although the two taxonomies are usually viewed as parts of two different domains, human behavior, especially at the higher levels, is impossible to separate into two different components. Affective processes, particularly those related to the value placed on learning, will greatly affect children's motivation to develop the thinking processes required of them.

Affective behaviors, then, can be viewed as one of the necessary means for attaining cognitive objectives. On the other hand, cognitive objectives can be seen as one of the necessary means for attaining affective objectives. In order for an individual to develop a value complex, for example, the person must be able to evaluate available choices (including, by implication, prior knowledge, comprehension, analysis, and synthesis related to these choices). More will be said about the relationships between the taxonomies after each is explained separately.

The Taxonomy of Cognitive Objectives

Knowledge

The first level, knowledge, requires no transformation of the information an individual receives. Students must only remember what has been read, told, or seen. The knowledge level consists of remembering the following: (a) *specifics,* including terminology and specific facts; (b) *ways and means of dealing with specifics,* including conventions (for example, characteristic ways of treating or presenting phenomena), trends and sequences, classifications and categories, criteria, and methodology; and (c) *universals and abstractions in a field,* consisting of principles, generalizations, theories, and structures.

Comprehension

In the second level, comprehension, an individual is at the lowest level of understanding. The person is able to make use of materials or ideas that have been translated, and can restate them in his or her own words, but is not required to relate this information to other material or ideas. Comprehension is made up of three related skills: translation, interpretation, and extrapolation. *Translation* involves paraphrasing or restating an idea without changing its meaning. *Interpretation* is explaining or summarizing a communication, and can involve reordering or rearranging its parts. *Extrapolation*, the highest level of comprehension, involves the extension of trends or tendencies beyond the given data. Immediate implications or effects are predicted on the basis of known facts.

Application

Putting abstractions or general principles to use in new concrete situations involves the third level of cognitive behavior, application. Principles or abstractions can be in the form of general ideas, rules of procedure, technical procedures, or theories.

Application can be differentiated from comprehension. Comprehension requires that the student know something well enough that its use can be demonstrated when specifically asked to do so, while application requires that when given a new problem or new situation, the student should apply the appropriate abstraction without being told which rule is the proper one. At the application level, the student is not shown how to use the principle or rule involved, but must be able to figure it out alone.

Analysis

The fourth level, analysis, involves the breaking down of a communication into its elements or parts so that the relative hierarchy of the components is made clear and the relationships between the parts are made explicit. This breaking down has as its purpose a further understanding of the underlying structure, effect, or theoretical basis. Included in this level are such behaviors as recognizing unstated assumptions (that is, analysis of elements), checking the consistency of hypotheses with existing information (that is, analysis of relationships), and recognizing the use of propaganda techniques (that is, analysis of organizational principles).

Synthesis

Synthesis is, in many ways, the opposite of analysis. It involves the putting together of parts to form a whole. These pieces or elements are rearranged or combined so that they make a pattern or structure not there before. In other words, the products of synthesis are new and unique as distinguished from the comprehension-level skill of interpretation, which simply involves reordering or rearranging the parts to demonstrate an understanding of the idea. The products of interpretation are not really new. Synthesis, however, includes the following elements: (a) producing a unique communication either through writing or through speaking; (b) producing a plan or proposed set of operations, for example, a proposal, a unit of instruction, a blueprint for a building; and (c) derivation of a set of abstract relations, including classification schemes, hypotheses, and inductive discovery of mathematical principles or abstract generalizations. One justification for the use of discovery learning is that the intellectual skills involved in discovery are at the synthesis level, whereas in a deductive approach in which principles are given and then applied, the intellectual skills involved are only at the application level.

Evaluation

According to the taxonomy, the highest cognitive skill is evaluation, making judgments about the value of something (for example, materials, methods, ideas, theories) for a given purpose. These judgments can be based on criteria chosen by the student or on criteria given to him or her, and can be either quantitative or qualitative. Also included in evaluation are judgments based on either internal or external evidence. Internal evidence consists of criteria, such as logical accuracy or consistency, while external evidence consists of comparing a work with other recognized works of high quality or with standards of excellence established in a particular field, or of assessing the worth of an idea in terms of a particular theory. Most of the critical thinking skills discussed by Ennis (1964) involve evaluation. These judgments can be made through application of internal criteria, as in judging whether a statement follows from the premises. External evaluation would be involved in judging whether an observation statement is reliable by using a set of principles from the fields of law, history, and science (that is, a statement is more reliable if the observer is unemotional, alert, and disinterested; is skilled at observing the sort of thing observed; and uses precise techniques).

Examples of Thinking Levels

To illustrate the differences between the levels of thinking in the *Cognitive Taxonomy*, consider this example of a lesson based on the taxonomy. The purpose of the lesson is to work toward the development of the following generalization: *Every society has had rules, written or unwritten, by which social control over the people's conduct is maintained.*

Knowledge

Activity: Students are presented information about three civilizations— Roman, pioneer American, and industrial American. In filmstrips, stories, and movies, they listen to and read data on these civilizations. A discussion follows.

Questions: What were or are some of the written rules in the Roman civilization? in pioneer America? in industrial America? How were these laws used to control the people's behavior? (Each of these questions can be answered directly from the information presented.)

Comprehension

Activity: Students present a sociodrama depicting their interpretation of an event about which they have read. The class is divided into three groups so that one sociodrama is presented on each of the civilizations studied. A discussion follows.

Questions: What were some of the written rules governing each situation presented? What were some of the factors contributing to the people's reactions to these laws or rules? What do you think will happen next? Why do you think this will happen next?

Application

Activity: Students are presented with a filmstrip or movie showing a trial in a different society. A discussion follows.

Questions: Based on this trial, what do you think are some of the laws in this society? Why do you think that? What do you think are some of the characteristics of this society based on what you know about other societies or cultures? What was your reasoning that led to that conclusion?

Analysis

Activity: Written assignment and then discussion.

Questions: What were some of the unwritten codes of conduct, mores, and values in the Roman civilization? in pioneer America? in industrial America? Why do you think these were unwritten codes? How were these unwritten codes different from the written laws? Why do you think so? How were the unwritten codes different in each of the civilizations? (For example, how were the unwritten codes in pioneer America different from the unwritten codes in industrial America?) What do you think contributed to these differences? How was the overall structure of these societies different? Why do you think these were the differences? How was it the same? Why do you think these were the similarities?

Synthesis

Activity: Students are divided into two teams. Each team develops its own civilization. This civilization is to be presented to the other team in some way without actually telling the other team what the laws and social codes are.

Questions: How can you show this code through a skit? Why would that be a good way? What would be another way to present that idea?

Evaluation

Activity: Students are asked to judge the consistency of the other team's presentation based on what that team has agreed is its civilization. Students are given additional criteria upon which to evaluate their own and the other team's presentation.

Questions: What did you think of the consistency of their presentation with the identified structure of their civilization? Why did you think the first scene was inconsistent? What things about it made you think they have failed to identify some codes of conduct or values? What do you think about the validity of the statement, "Every civilization has had rules, both written and unwritten, by which social control over the people's conduct is maintained?" Why do you agree with it? Why do you disagree? What could you change about it that would make you agree? Why would this increase your agreement?

Table 2-1 gives a summary of teacher and student roles and activities at each level in the model.

The Affective Taxonomy

Receiving

At this level, the learner is simply sensitive to the fact that certain things exist. Awareness and sensitivity also include a willingness to attend, although it does not imply a judgment. Each student has had experiences that will influence this willingness either positively or negatively.

Receiving is divided into three subcategories on a continuum from a passive role on the part of the learner to the point at which the learner directs his or her own attention. *Awareness*, the lowest level, includes being conscious of something and taking it into account. This level does not imply that the individual can verbalize what has caused the awareness. The second level, *willingness to receive*, involves a neutrality or suspended judgment toward the phenomenon, but the student is inclined to notice it. An individual will not necessarily seek out something and is not actively seeking to avoid it. At the highest level of receiving is *controlled or selected attention*, where the student selects a favored stimulus and attends to it in spite of competing or distracting stimuli.

Responding

The second level, responding, includes most "interest" objectives. At this level, students are so involved in or committed to a subject or activity that they will seek it out and gain satisfaction from their participation. Responding also includes three subcategories: (a) acquiescence in responding; (b) willingness to respond;

Table 2-1 Summary of Teacher and Student Roles and Activities in the Taxonomy of Cognitive Objectives

Step, Type, or Level of Thinking	Student		Teacher	
	Role	Sample Activities	Role	Sample Activities
Knowledge	passive recipient; memorizer, active recipient	Answer questions requiring recall or memory. Answer questions almost verbatim about specific facts. Pay attention to the information read or heard.	provider of information and resources; questioner; organizer of learning activities; evaluator	Provide students with information about a subject. Provide students with resources on a topic. Ask questions to check whether they know the information presented to them. Assist students in finding information they identify as necessary or desirable.
Comprehension	active participant	Answer questions or do activities requiring translation of information (e.g., Explain a metaphor). Answer questions or do activities requiring interpretation of information (e.g., What do you think was the general idea of that last paragraph?). Answer questions or do activities requiring extrapolation from existing information (e.g., What do you think will happen next in the cold war based on what has happened so far?).	provider of information and resources; questioner; organizer of learning activities; evaluator	Check to see if students have the knowledge required to do the task. Ask questions to see whether they can paraphrase, extend, and/or make inferences based on the information. Provide sequential activities that first require the student to translate, then interpret, and then extrapolate from the given information. Give students suggestions about how they can comprehend better.
Application	active participant	Use some previously learned rule or method in a new situation. Decide which method to use or which principle to apply.	provider of information and resources; questioner; evaluator	Check to see if students have the knowledge and comprehension necessary to do the task. Provide students with a new problem or situation where they can apply a principle or principles previously learned,

Table 2-1 continued

Step, Type, or Level of Thinking	Student		Teacher	
	Role	Sample Activities	Role	Sample Activities
		From an understanding of the situation and its requirements, choose an appropriate method.		Ask questions to determine their understanding of the requirements of the problem. Provide feedback to the students on their performance (i.e., if they have applied the wrong method or have used the right method but in the wrong way, tell them what went wrong).
Analysis	active participant	Break down a piece of information, plan, or proposal into its parts (e.g., recognize unstated assumptions). Identify the relationships between the parts (e.g., check the consistency of a hypothesis with given assumptions). Identify the arrangement or structure of something (e.g., recognize the pattern of meaning of a literary work).	provider of information and resources; questioner; organizer of learning activities; evaluator	Check to see if students have the knowledge, comprehension, and application skills necessary to do the task. Design sequential learning activities that will develop the component skills of identifying the elements of a communication, analyzing the relationships between elements, and recognizing the organizational principles involved. Ask questions to determine whether students have analyzed elements, relationships, and organizational principles. Give students feedback on their performance. Let them know if they have missed important elements, overlooked relationships, hypothesized the wrong relationships, or incorrectly identified the underlying principles.
Synthesis	active participant	Put together elements in a new way so that a different pattern or product is developed.	provider of information and resources; questioner;	Check to see if students have the knowledge, comprehension, application, and synthesis skills necessary to do the task.

	Student role	Behaviors	Teacher role	Teaching activities
		Write and organize statements. Develop a research proposal. Formulate and modify a theory.	organizer of learning activities; evaluator	Design sequential learning activities that will develop synthesis skills in several areas—communication, production of a plan or proposal, and development of a set of abstract relations. Provide feedback to students on their products (e.g., Can the ideas be arranged more effectively? Is the plan or proposal realistic? Is the theory consistent?), and give specific suggestions for improvement.
Evaluation	active participant	Make judgments about the value of information, materials, or methods for given purposes. Select or develop appropriate criteria for making judgments. Make judgments based on internal or external criteria. Make quantitative and qualitative judgments.	provider of information and resources; questioner; organizer of learning activities; evaluator	Check to see if students have the knowledge, comprehension, application, analysis, and synthesis skills to do the task. Provide situations where the student must evaluate based on different kinds of evidence—internal or external. Provide criteria for evaluation. Require the student to develop criteria. Devise learning activities to help in selecting or developing standards for evaluation (e.g., assist in the learning of logical principles for evaluating arguments). Provide students with feedback on their performance (e.g., identify additional criteria to be used, show inconsistencies in application of criteria).

and (c) satisfaction in response. *Acquiescence in responding* can be described as obedience or compliance. Students are passive in the sense that they do not initiate the behavior, but they do not necessarily resist or yield unwillingly. *Willingness to respond* implies that students will do something "on their own" and that they choose to do an activity or participate in the learning process. At the next higher level, *satisfaction in response,* the element of enjoyment is included. Students have a feeling of satisfaction, pleasure, or zest when participating in an activity.

Valuing

Of all the levels in the *Affective Taxonomy,* valuing has received the most attention in educational practice. It includes three levels or subcategories ranging from simply ascribing worth to making a commitment. Valuing simply means deciding that a thing, phenomenon, or idea has worth; it is important. Behavior at this level is consistent and stable, and has taken on the characteristics of a belief or an attitude. Actions resulting from values are motivated by a commitment to the underlying value rather than by the desire to comply or obey.

Acceptance of a value, the first subcategory, includes a consistency of behavior enabling the underlying value to be identified, but is at the lowest level of commitment. There is a tendency to behave in a certain way, but individuals would probably be more willing to reevaluate their position than at the higher levels. The second level of valuing is *preference for a value* and includes not only a willingness to be identified with a value, but also a commitment to the extent that an individual will seek out or want that value. *Commitment,* the third subcategory, implies beliefs that are certain beyond a shadow of a doubt. Individuals who are committed will act in ways that further the particular value, will try to convince others, and will try to deepen their own involvement with it.

Organization

As values are internalized, situations that involve more than one value arise. It then becomes necessary to organize these values, determine the relationships among them, and establish the most pervasive ones. Two subcategories are included in this level. The first, *conceptualization of a value,* is developing a view of the value that enables an individual to see how this particular value relates to other values already held or to new ones being developed. At the next level, *organization of a value system,* students bring together a set of attitudes, beliefs, and values into an ordered relationship with each other. Some of these values may be quite different or in opposition to one another in certain situations, but the individual must synthesize these into a value complex that, if not harmonious and internally consistent, is at least a dynamic equilibrium.

Characterization by a Value or a Value Complex

At this level, values have already been internalized and organized into a hierarchy and have controlled behavior long enough for the individual to adapt to behaving this way. The subcategories, developing a generalized set of values and characterization, represent two aspects of the individual's consistent behavior. A *generalized set of values* is a basic orientation, a persistent and consistent reaction to a family of related situations or things. It is usually an unconscious set that guides action without an individual consciously considering alternatives beforehand and can be thought of as an attitude cluster. At the *characterization* level, behavior is concerned with a philosophy of life, a broad range of behaviors constituting a world view. Objectives included in this subcategory are broader or more inclusive than those considered a part of the generalized set, and there is an emphasis on internal consistency.

Examples of Thinking Levels

To illustrate the similarities and differences between the categories in the two taxonomies, the same example will be used in this section as in the illustration of the *Cognitive Taxonomy*. The purpose of the lesson is to work toward the development of the following generalization: *Every society has had rules, written or unwritten, by which social control over the people's conduct is maintained.*

Receiving

Activity: Students are presented information about three civilizations: Roman, pioneer American, and industrial American. In filmstrips, stories, and movies, they listen to and read data on these civilizations. A discussion is then held.

Questions: What were some things you saw happening in the film? What were some of the reactions of the people in the film to being told that they could not move?

Responding

Activity: Further discussion of filmstrip, movie, and readings is held.

Questions: What were some of your feelings as you watched the film? When have you been involved in a situation such as this? What were some of the things that happened? How did you feel about them? In the sociodrama, what were some of your feelings? What are some of the social controls you have experienced? What were your reactions? Why do you think you reacted that way?

Valuing

Activity: An attitude or value continuum is presented to the students, and they are asked to indicate how much social control they think is needed by placing an "X" on the line:

no control   /————————————————/ strict rules and
                                            enforcement

Question: Where on this continuum would you stand? Why do you feel that way? What are some of the things that have happened to make you feel that way? In the sociodrama, what were some of the values of the people involved? Why do you think these were their values?

Organization

Activity: Brainstorm or list all the means of social control currently in effect in this society as well as the other three societies studied. By group consensus, select five of the important ones in each society, and then individually rank them according to (1) desirability and (2) effectiveness.

Questions: How are your values (as expressed in the value continuum activity) different from those of the other societies? How do you think they are similar? Why do you think they are different or similar? (That is, what experiences have you had that would contribute to the formation of values that are similar to or different from those of the other societies studied?)

Characterization by a Value Complex

Activity: After a discussion of the team presentations (see cognitive evaluation activity), each individual develops an *ideal* set of social controls for the society.

Questions: What would be your ideal society? What aspects of it would be absolutely necessary, and what aspects are just desirable? Why?

Table 2-2 gives a summary of teacher and student roles and activities in the implementation of this model.

RELATIONSHIPS BETWEEN THE COGNITIVE AND THE AFFECTIVE TAXONOMIES

It is impossible to separate the cognitive from the affective domains in any activity. There seem to be three basic kinds of relationships. The most important is that there is a cognitive component to every affective objective and an affective

Table 2-2 Summary of Teacher and Student Roles and Activities in the Taxonomy of Affective Objectives

Step, Type, or Level of Thinking	Student Role	Student Sample Activities	Teacher Role	Teacher Sample Activities
Receiving	passive recipient to active recipient	Attend to what is being presented; be aware. Be willing to take notice Choose one stimulus over others.	provider of stimuli; organizer; presenter; covert evaluator	Present learning activities or information that will capture the attention of the learner. Check to see if she is aware of the stimuli. Plan sequential activities that will lead the student through the levels of awareness, willingness to receive, and selected attending. Covertly evaluate student's receiving behavior.
Responding	passive respondent to active, pleased respondent	Comply with suggestions. Voluntarily seek out activities of interest. Enjoy activities chosen.	provider of stimuli; organizer; presenter; covert evaluator	Check to see if students have attended to the relevant stimuli. Plan activities designed to stimulate interest (i.e., pleasure in responding). Ask questions regarding student response (feelings) toward activities, ideas, people, objects.
Valuing	chooser; believer	Accept a value; be willing to be identified with it. Act consistently so that others can identify preferences as values. Choose a position and seek it out. Attempt to convince others that your value choices are important.	provider of stimuli; organizer; questioner; presenter	Check to see what students response is to a phenomenon. Organize situations where students can make value choices. Provide situations where students can exhibit and discuss their value choices. Assist students in clarifying their values by asking provocative questions.

Table 2-2 continued

Step, Type, or Level of Thinking	Student		Teacher	
	Role	Sample Activities	Role	Sample Activities
Organization	chooser; believer; organizer of beliefs	Identify the essential characteristics of the values held. Figure out the relationships between values. Synthesize parts of values into a new value complex.	provider of stimuli; organizer; questioner; presenter	Check to see what values students hold. Arrange situations where students must choose between competing values they already hold. Assist students in examining the realtionships between their values by asking questions. Assist students in developing an equilibrium in their value systems.
Characterization by a Value or Values Complex	internalizer of values	Act consistently in accordance with internalized values. Act consistently in accordance with a total world view. Develop a consistent philosophy of life.	provider of stimuli; organizer; questioner; observer	Check to see that students have examined and organized their values. Arrange situations where students can demonstrate their internalized values. Assist students in identifying the values they have internalized.

component to every cognitive objective. These components may be explicit or implicit. At every level of the *Cognitive Taxonomy,* the affective behavior of receiving or attending is a prerequisite, as is responding if the student is asked to answer a question or actively participate in an activity. At every level of the *Affective Taxonomy,* with the possible exception of the lowest level, receiving, the cognitive behavior of knowledge, is a prerequisite. A person must know to be able to respond, value, organize values, and so on. Comprehension is also a prerequisite.

A second relationship between the domains is that educators often use one of the domains to achieve objectives in the other domain. Usually, cognitive objectives are used as a way to achieve affective objectives. Students are given new information with the hope that an attitude change will result. In the example provided earlier, students were given information about other societies and people's reactions to them as a way to help them examine their own feelings and values. The relationship can go the other way, however. Affective goals can be used to achieve cognitive goals. Educators can develop students' interest in something as a way to increase their knowledge of a phenomenon. Krathwohl et al. (1964) suggest that guided discovery methods provide a way to use an individual's drive for competency (an affective behavior probably at the valuing level) to enhance the possibility that children will discover or develop necessary cognitive abilities.

The third relationship is only slightly different; affective and cognitive goals can be simultaneously achieved. Again, Krathwohl et al. (1964) refer to discovery learning as an example. For example, in Suchman's (1965) inquiry training children are presented with a puzzling event. They ask questions, in a manner similar to the 20-questions game, of the teacher, who acts only as a data-giver. Teachers observe the pattern of the students' strategies and offer suggestions for improving them. In this way, the cognitive goal of improving the child's inquiry skill is achieved in a situation where the child is interested. By providing a critique of the strategy, the teacher also builds motivation to use the skill in other situations.

According to the authors of the *Affective Taxonomy,* the closest relationships between the taxonomies can be found between receiving and knowledge, analysis/synthesis and conceptualization, and evaluation and organization/characterization. At the lowest levels, the relationship is clear: educators must attend before they will know, and they can only develop knowledge if there is a willingness to pay attention. Thus, in the example given earlier, students attended to the information in the filmstrip to develop knowledge about the reactions of people. At the higher levels of analysis/synthesis and the related affective level of conceptualization (the first level within organization), the cognitive ability of analysis is needed as students "break down" the common elements of values or of situations in which they are involved, and put the elements back together (synthesis) into a value that is important to them. In the example, students analyzed the presentations of the other team and their own, and related their own behaviors to the presentations.

The cognitive skill of evaluation is clearly involved in both the organization category of a value system and in the highest affective level, characterization by a value complex. To develop a total philosophy of life and to weigh one value or way of behaving against situational considerations require that an individual be able to make judgments. The criteria for making these judgments become internalized to the extent that the individual behaves almost automatically in some situations. In the example, students are asked to develop their ideal society, which requires them to evaluate the other societies on the basis of some criteria and to put into their ideal those aspects that are consistent with their own philosophy.

Williams (1971) presents a slightly different, although more simple, view of the relationship between the cognitive and affective domains. He relates them almost directly in the following way:

- Receiving corresponds to knowledge through information an individual wants to receive.
- Responding relates to comprehension through the willingness to understand information.
- Valuing relates to application through the appreciation of information that is relevant and useful.
- Conceptualization relates to analysis and synthesis in that an individual forms a value system by integrating bits of information into a new and unique combination.
- Internalization relates to evaluation through an individual's judging how something fits into a way of life.

Although this expression is more simplistic than the relationships described earlier, it roughly corresponds and can be used as a guide for integrating the two domains. Further support for the use of this scheme can be found in the fact that teacher and student roles (see Tables 2-1 and 2-2) roughly correspond as the higher levels of both taxonomies are reached. The student moves from the role of a passive recipient who remembers to an active learner who makes judgments. The teacher provides the information and develops the experiences, and then moves to a more facilitative role as the student takes an active part in the learning situation.

MODIFICATIONS OF THE BASIC CURRICULUM

In programs for the gifted, the *Cognitive* and *Affective Taxonomies* have been used mainly as systems for making one process modification: development of higher levels of thinking. Although they were developed as schemes for classifying objectives or specified outcomes of instruction, what is described or classified is student behavior, either thinking (cognitive) behavior or feeling (affective) behavior. As such, the taxonomies provide ways to classify process, that is, the thinking and feeling processes that children use as they participate in a learning activity or answer a teacher's question.

The taxonomies do, however, have other valuable uses in making certain curriculum modifications for the gifted. They can be used as structures for evaluating the sophistication of products, and they can be used as systems for classifying content according to its complexity and abstractness.

Content Modifications

Although it is seldom used for this purpose, the knowledge level of the *Cognitive Taxonomy* contains a scheme for classifying content according to its type, as well as its abstractness and complexity. Three types of knowledge are described: (a) knowledge of specifics; (b) knowledge of ways and means of dealing with specifics; and (c) knowledge of the universals and abstractions in a field. These categories can be used in a variety of ways in making content changes for the gifted.

Knowledge of Specifics

This category is considered to be at the lowest level of complexity and abstraction. It includes the facts or specific information about a field of study and corresponds to the data level in the Gallagher, Shaffer, Phillips, Addy, Rainer, and Nelson (1966) classification system. These specifics are the basic elements the learner must know to become acquainted with a field. They include knowledge of terminology and knowledge of specific facts. Each field contains a set of terminology that serves as the basic language of that field. This terminology includes both verbal and nonverbal symbols that have particular referents. Some examples are terms associated with work in science, definitions of geometric figures, and important accounting terms. Each field also has a large number of dates, events, people, places, and research results that are known by specialists in the field and are used in thinking about specific topics and in solving certain problems. Examples include significant names, places, and events in the news; knowledge of the reputation of a particular author; and recall of facts about a certain culture.

Knowledge of Ways and Means of Dealing with Specifics

Information in this category includes ways of organizing, studying, judging, and critiquing ideas, events, and phenomena in a field. Methods of inquiry, patterns of organization, and standards of judgment within a field would be included in this category. These are different from specifics in that they are the operations necessary for dealing with specifics. Included in this section are five subcategories: (a) knowledge of conventions; (b) knowledge of trends and sequences; (c) knowledge of classifications and categories; (d) knowledge of criteria; and (e) knowledge of methodology.

Knowledge of conventions includes the characteristic ways of treating and presenting ideas and phenomena that scholars or workers in a field use because they suit their purpose or fit the phenomena. Examples include rules of etiquette, correct form and usage of English in speaking and writing, and standard symbols used in maps and charts.

Knowledge of trends and sequences includes trends involving time sequences as well as cause-effect relationships that are emphasized by scholars and workers in a field. Some examples are the following: (a) the evolutionary development of humans; (b) effects of industrialization on the culture of a nation; and (c) trends of government in this country during the last 50 years.

The third group, knowledge of classifications and categories, includes the classes, sets, or divisions that are considered fundamental or useful in a particular field. These classification systems are used to help structure and systematize the phenomena being studied. Objectives in this group include types of literature, the classification of elements in chemistry, and the classifications of living things in biology.

Knowledge of criteria includes the standards by which facts, principles, opinions, and conduct are tested or judged. This includes such criteria as those used to judge the nutritive value of a meal, the aesthetic value of a work of art, or the validity of sources of information. Knowledge of methodology includes methods of inquiry, techniques, and procedures that characterize a particular field along with those usually employed in investigating certain problems. These include the steps in a scientific method, attitude surveys, and techniques for conducting health and medical research.

Knowledge of Principles and Generalizations

The most abstract and complex of the groups, this category of knowledge includes the major ideas, schemes, and patterns that dominate a field. They correspond to generalizations in the Gallagher et al. (1966) classification scheme and, as such, serve as organizing themes for the other information available in a field. These universals and abstractions bring together a large number of facts and events, and describe the relationships between them. The category includes two subgroups: (a) knowledge of principles and generalizations; and (b) knowledge of theories and structures. Knowledge of principles and generalizations includes abstractions that summarize observations of phenomena and are valuable in explaining, describing, or predicting. These include such items as fundamental principles of logic, generalizations about cultures, biological laws of reproduction and heredity, and principles of learning.

Knowledge of theories and structure differs from knowledge of principles and generalizations in that it includes a body of principles and generalizations that are interrelated to form a theory. This subcategory corresponds to the "thought systems" described by Taba (1962), which are the characteristic modes of thinking employed by scholars in a particular field. Some examples of theories and structures are philosophic bases for judgments, a formulation of the theory of evolution, and major theories of the development of cultures.

Abstractness and Complexity

To use this classification system in providing the content modifications of abstractness and complexity, the major emphasis or focus would be placed at each level of the taxonomy on the third category, principles and abstractions. Of course, knowledge and understanding of specifics are important to the understanding of the more abstract ideas, but the *focus* should be on the principles and abstractions. At the knowledge level, specifics would perhaps be as important as the generalizations and abstractions, but as an individual moves up the levels of the *Taxonomy,* specifics assume much less importance.

Variety

The curricular modification of variety can also be provided by using this scheme for classifying knowledge. As described by Maker (1982), in a gifted program it is important to sample systematically from a variety of types of knowledge to make certain that students have been exposed to a range of ideas in a particular field or across several fields. Bloom's system could be used as a scheme for viewing the knowledge in each field of study and for making certain that gifted students have received exposure to all types of knowledge available in each field, that is, the specifics, the methods, and the theories.

Methods of Inquiry

The classification scheme proposed by Bloom brings attention to the fact that within each field of study there are a variety of conventions, techniques, and strategies that may be unique to that field of study. When teaching gifted students methods of inquiry, this system can be used to suggest methods that might otherwise have been forgotten.

The Affective Taxonomy

Because of its concentration on an aspect of behavior that is traditionally considered only a small part of the educational process, the *Affective Taxonomy* could also be considered a vehicle for making content changes by suggesting that affective components be included in the curriculum. This idea relates especially to the content change of variety. However, there is not a system of classification of affective content in this taxonomy like the one contained in the cognitive one.

Process Modifications

One critical point should be made clear. Even though the taxonomies have enjoyed widespread use as schemes for making process modifications for the gifted and for seriously considering process in the regular curriculum, the developers did not intend them to be used in this way. As they developed the systems, they were attempting to make each description neutral. They did not suggest, for example, that everyone should develop activities at all levels of the taxonomies or that specified amounts of time be spent at the various levels. The developers did not even suggest that learning objectives or activities be arranged sequentially according to the levels of the taxonomies, although such a sequential arrangement would logically follow from their statement that the *Cognitive Taxonomy* is arranged from the most simple to the most complex intellectual behavior. All these uses and implications have been added by those who have subsequently applied the taxonomies to their educational situations.

The *Cognitive Taxonomy* provides a useful way for educators of the gifted to develop learning activities that require higher levels of thinking or more complex intellectual activity, which is one of the most basic goals of curriculum modification for the gifted. The implication that follows is that more time is spent at the higher levels with the gifted, when perhaps an equal amount of time would be spent at all levels with average students. With slower students, who need much more time to decode and thus remember, more time may be needed at the lower levels.

The *Affective Taxonomy,* though not particularly intended for this purpose, can be used as a means for making process changes emphasizing greater complexity or higher levels. Since intellectual activity cannot be entirely separated from its affective components, this taxonomy can be incorporated into the methodology as a way to develop "higher levels of feeling." Although the concept of complexity was not used as an explicit organizing principle in this taxonomy as it was in the cognitive one, the behaviors are arranged in a developmental order (for example, a person must be aware of something before developing a preference for it or before it can become a part of a total world view). Since the behaviors are arranged in this way, the taxonomy can provide a framework for devising learning activities that systematically develop affective processes.

Product and Learning Environment Modifications

Because it is based on an arrangement of thinking behaviors ranging from simple to complex, the *Cognitive Taxonomy* can be used to evaluate the complexity of student products, particularly in the area of assessing whether they involve a mere summary of prior information (comprehensive level) or a higher level involving a new product resulting from reordering, reinterpreting, and recombining information (synthesis level). Students can be taught to use the taxonomy in evaluating their own products.

Neither of the taxonomies provides specific guidelines for the development of appropriate learning environments. However, as one of the few classifications of feelings that considers developmental aspects, the *Affective Taxonomy* provides the teacher with some suggestions for developing an effective psychological climate, particularly in the dimensions of student-centeredness and independence. By keeping in mind that students must go through each of the levels in learning situations, teachers can structure their own behavior toward the students in such a way that the students can reach the higher levels. Teachers must respect the learner's prior level of feeling about a situation and build upon these feelings in the learning process.

MODIFYING THE APPROACHES

In addition to the curricular changes directly suggested by the taxonomies, other modifications important in gifted programs can be made either by combining the taxonomies with other models or by using them in ways other than those suggested by the authors.

Content Changes

Abstractness, Complexity, and Organization/Economy

Both taxonomies easily lend themselves to being combined with Bruner's ideas related to ''teaching the structure of a discipline.'' To combine the models, the first step would be to identify or develop the abstract, complex generalizations that the children will learn. These generalizations and the key concepts contained in them will serve as the content organizers. The specific information and facts to be taught are then selected as examples of the concepts. When designing learning activities, the data or specific facts pertaining to the concepts and generalizations serve as the basis for the lowest levels of the taxonomies, and the concepts and generalizations become more important at the higher levels.

In the examples presented earlier in this chapter, a generalization was used as the content organizer. At the knowledge and receiving levels, students were presented with data about three different civilizations. The questions they were asked were designed to check their memory of this information, in other words, to check whether they ''attended'' and ''received'' the information they would need to use later.

At the responding level in the *Affective Taxonomy* and at the comprehension level in the *Cognitive Taxonomy,* the data continue to be important, but concepts begin to enter into the process. For example, when students are presenting the sociodrama, they are demonstrating their understanding of some of the underlying concepts, such as written rules and people's reactions to rules, and they are predicting what might happen next based on this understanding. At the responding level of the *Affective Taxonomy,* the students are asked to indicate their responses to some of the concepts and to describe their personal experiences with these aspects of social control. At the valuing level, concepts are also important, particularly the value placed on the concepts.

At the application level of the *Cognitive Taxonomy,* generalizations begin to assume importance as the students apply a rule or principle in a new situation. This rule or principle can be a concept (category) or a generalization that states a relationship between certain concepts. Analysis can include examining different aspects of concepts, along with examining several concepts and how they relate to each other to form a generalization. Of course, students are dealing with infor-mation, but they are using it as examples or proof for ideas. Synthesis involves developing new generalizations or new products based on combining the ideas encountered in a new way. Usually content would be mainly at the generalization level. At the evaluation level, all types of content would be important. Students would be judging the accuracy or appropriateness of information and the validity of concepts and generalizations. In the two highest levels of the *Affective Tax-onomy,* the major emphasis is on generalizations, with some focus on concepts and how they are related.

In both examples presented in this chapter, the element of complexity is included, since both the affective and cognitive processes are used. Complex ideas or thought systems as described by Taba (1962) consist not only of facts, prin-ciples, and concepts, but also of methods and characteristic ways of thinking about things, including value systems. To aid in fully understanding others' feelings about an idea, method, or phenomenon, students can be led through a process of examining their own affective behavior related to the same idea, method, or phenomenon.

To achieve economy, in addition to organizing content around key concepts and generalizations, an educator could begin the learning process at the application level as a way of discovering what is not known and thus needs to be taught. In this way, previous learning would not be repeated. The same process could be used with the *Affective Taxonomy* by beginning at the valuing level.

Variety

Because of its emphasis on affective content, Krathwohl's *Taxonomy* suggests the incorporation of content not usually taught in the regular curriculum. To achieve variety of content with the *Affective Taxonomy,* the suggested procedure and worksheet presented in the discussion of Bruner's approach would be appropriate. (See Exhibit 3-1.)

Study of People

To incorporate this content modification, the taxonomies could be used as a structure for studying about the lives and accomplishments of eminent individuals. A teaching approach that uses the taxonomies concurrently would be especially appropriate in this context. Students could be led through a process of examining the people and their characteristics, and then they could study the reactions of other people. The gifted students could then examine their own lives, including value systems, and compare themselves with the individuals being studied.

Methods of Inquiry

The taxonomies can be used easily as structures for studying different methods of inquiry. The taxonomies themselves are methods and, as such, can be taught to the students. The taxonomies are classification systems to facilitate communication between professionals in the behavioral sciences. Students can use them in the same way that professionals do.

Process Changes

Open-Endedness and Proof/Reasoning

These two process modifications are easily incorporated into teaching strategies that use the taxonomies as a basis. To achieve open-endedness, an educator should simply design all questions and learning activities so that they will encourage varied perceptions and be provocative. Stimulating, divergent activities and questions can easily be designed at the higher levels of the taxonomies, but may be more difficult at the lower ones. Asking students to explain their reasoning or cite examples as evidence to support their conclusions is easily incorporated by asking for these explanations when answers are given at the higher levels of the taxonomies. Such explanations are not necessary at the lowest levels, although they may be appropriate at the responding and comprehension levels, depending on the content and activities.

In the examples presented earlier in this chapter, all questions were designed to be open-ended and to stimulate further activity or thought. The examples also included questions calling for explanations of reasoning or logic when appropriate. For instance, one question at the responding level was: ''What are some of the social controls you have experienced? What were your reactions?'' After this second question, a question calling for support is appropriate: ''Why do you think you reacted that way?''

Discovery

Incorporating discovery learning into the use of the taxonomies is difficult if they are used as a strict hierarchical model. If the assumption is accepted that activities must be presented at each level of a taxonomy, beginning with knowledge and receiving, and then progressing to comprehension and responding, the learning sequence would be deductive rather than inductive. With the *Cognitive Taxonomy,* for example, students are given the information needed to solve a problem (that is, the rule or principle) at the knowledge level, are shown how to use the principle at the comprehension level, and are given a new problem and expected to apply some rule or principle in solving the problem at the application level. Following this, they analyze or break down the problem or solution, create something new, and then evaluate. This is essentially a deductive learning sequence.

To incorporate an inductive or discovery approach, then, it is necessary to reject the assumption that activities must be presented sequentially at each level of the taxonomies and make a major adaptation of the approach. Since there does not seem to be adequate research data to indicate that sequential presentation is necessary, and there is support for the idea that inductive approaches work well with gifted stuents, such an adaptation seems justified. One way that the taxonomies can be adapted for the gifted is by presenting the first activities at the application level rather than beginning at the knowledge level.

One obvious advantage of this approach is that the teacher does not reteach anything the students already know. A new problem or situation is presented to the students, and they attempt to solve it. If they do solve the problem, the teacher asks them to explain how they arrived at the solution. If they can explain the principle involved, as well as the process, further activities can be presented at the higher levels of the taxonomy. When students are unable to solve the problem, the teacher has several options. He or she can change to a deductive approach and present some applicable rules and principles, show how they are used, and then present more new problems. The teacher can also continue with an inductive approach and present several new problems that illustrate the rules or principles to be taught and, through questioning, lead the students to discover these underlying principles.

Another use of both taxonomies in discovery learning situations is as a model for students to use in structuring their own investigations after a situation has been presented to them for a solution. However, they should not be required to use this method.

Freedom of Choice

With regard to students' freedom to choose learning activities and topics of study, the *Cognitive* and *Affective Taxonomies* can be used effectively. The teacher can design a variety of learning activities at each level and allow the students to choose from the ones that are of the most interest. The taxonomies could also be presented to the students and used as a structure for designing their own learning activities. Students could choose their own topics of study, but be required to structure their learning about the topic so that mastery of each level of the taxonomy is demonstrated.

Group Interaction and Variety

To use the taxonomies in providing the curricular modification of group inter-action, an educator can simply design activities for group interaction situations using the taxonomies as the structure. Activities can be designed at the higher levels so that they will be challenging to students. Analysis activities are suited to the examination of tapes or other observational data, while synthesis activities are appropriate for designing plans for improving an individual's or a group's inter-action patterns. Evaluation is particularly appropriate for assessing individual and group participation, and the plans for improvement.

The *Affective Taxonomy* is particularly helpful as a procedure for examining each individual's participation in the group activities. Observers can, for example, examine and discuss the differing values of the individuals involved and how these values may have influenced their interaction in the group. In this same context, this taxonomy could be used as an observation tool. Observers could look for behaviors and statements that indicate the stage of development of certain values in the individuals being observed. In other words, does a person's behavior indicate that the individual has incorporated a particular belief to the extent that it has become a part of his or her philosophy of life? Also, does he or she always behave consistently with that belief (that is, characterization by a value or value complex)? Or is the person simply willing to be identified with that belief (that is, valuing level)?

To provide the curricular modification of variety, the taxonomies, adaptable to a variety of situations and types of learning activities, can be used to develop a variety of activities. The taxonomies can be used to develop a structured series of questions for use in a class discussion that would lead students gradually through the levels of thinking. They can be used to design learning center tasks that would lead students to higher levels of thinking, they can be used in designing games, they can be a part of contract learning, and they can be the basis for auto-instruc-tional programs. Creative readers can generate many more uses for these adaptable classification systems.

Pacing

The most important aspect of pacing with regard to the taxonomies is that movement through the lower levels must be as rapid as possible since these students can acquire the needed knowledge quickly and learn to put it to use rapidly. They *must* be allowed to move to the next level as soon as they have demonstrated mastery of a particular level.

Product Changes

Neither of the taxonomies provide specific suggestions for product modifications, except that the *Cognitive Taxonomy* provides a useful way of assessing whether a product is a transformation of existing information or merely a summary. With regard to the evaluation of products, however, both classifications can be used by the students in self-evaluation and can be used by other audiences to evaluate the products. When using them as evaluation schemes, the product is examined in two ways. First, the evaluator attempts to determine whether the student who produced the product used all levels of thinking in the development process or whether the person only used the lower levels. In other words, the product as a whole is evaluated to determine its level in the taxonomy scheme. The next assessment attempts to determine the quality and accuracy of the product with regard to each level. For example, at the knowledge level, "Does the product contain accurate and complete information?" At the comprehension level, "Are the trends and implications that are presented valid?" And at the characterization level, "Are the values presented consistent with the attitudes and behaviors described?" These are questions that can be asked to determine the quality and accuracy of the product.

Learning activities at the analysis level can be valuable in helping students decide upon problems to investigate or narrow an area of study so that a solvable problem or researchable question is investigated. Teachers can assist in this process by designing activities for each student, or the students can be taught how to design their own activities for use in this context.

The evaluation level of the taxonomy can be used as a guide for developing criteria for simulated audiences to use in evaluating the product. Activities at this level can also be used to generate possible criteria that a real audience would use in its evaluation.

Learning Environment Changes

All the learning environment changes advocated for gifted students are important facilitators of the successful use of the taxonomies as they would be modified. If students are to achieve the objectives of reaching the highest levels, the environment must be centered around their ideas and interests. They must be encouraged to be independent; the environment must be open and must include complex tasks and materials. If students are allowed the freedom to choose activities at all levels, they will need high physical mobility.

One aspect of the environment that is particularly critical in the development of higher levels of thinking is the accepting versus judging dimension. If students do not believe they are free to express their ideas, they will only respond at the lower levels by repeating what the teacher or someone else has said, rather than take a risk by generating their own ideas. Since expressing feelings is riskier than expressing ideas, this dimension of the environment is more important with the *Affective Taxonomy* than with the cognitive one. The hierarchy of teacher behaviors presented by Maker (1982) that moves from attending through accepting, clarifying, and challenging is especially critical.

The authors of the taxonomies do not make suggestions about the kind of learning environment that should be established when the taxonomies are used. Their comments do not address the environment dimensions important at different levels of the classification schemes.

Summary

By combining the *Cognitive* and *Affective Taxonomies* with Bruner's content suggestions, and by using the taxonomies differently (for example, not rigidly progressing through each level), many of the content, process, and product modifications appropriate for the gifted can be made. Two major adaptations of the models have been suggested: (1) teaching the taxonomies to gifted students so they can apply the ideas to their own investigations; and (2) beginning each learning sequence at the application level rather than at the knowledge level so that learning is not repeated and inductive learning is facilitated.

DEVELOPMENT

In 1948, at an informal meeting of college examiners attending the American Psychological Association (APA) convention (Bloom, 1956), the idea for developing a theoretical framework for classifying educational objectives was proposed. This meeting became the first of a series of informal annual meetings of college examiners. The members were not always the same, but a core group was usually present. Early in the process, the group decided that the major purpose of the taxonomy should be to facilitate communication between educators. To fulfill this purpose, it would need to have at least the following four characteristics:

1. It should be an educational taxonomy and, whenever possible, should be closely related to the decisions educators must make.
2. The classification system should be logical; it should define terms as concisely as possible and should use them consistently.
3. It should be consistent with psychological theories and principles that are widely accepted and relevant.

4. It should avoid value judgments, being neutral about principles and philosophies so that objectives from many different orientations could be
classified.

The committee of approximately 30 people began its work by collecting a large
list of educational objectives, dividing each objective into intended behavior and
content of the behavior, and then attempting to group the behaviors according to
their similarities. In an attempt to develop an order from simple to complex, the
committee looked for a psychological theory that could be used as an overall
framework. They found none, so they developed their own logical system. After
developing the categories and definitions of the categories, the committee members attempted to classify additional objectives independently using the system and
to compare their separate classifications. In this way, they could clarify ambigui-
ties and further refine the system.

At the outset, the committee's intent was to develop taxonomies in three
domains: (a) cognitive; (b) affective; and (c) psychomotor. Since the cognitive
domain was most central to their work, it was the first area to be developed and was
the only taxonomy completed by the basic committee. A subcommittee responsible for the affective domain finally completed its work and published that
taxonomy without submitting it to the original committee for review (Krathwohl et
al., 1964). Thus, the *Cognitive Taxonomy* has been subjected to more critical
reviews both by the committee and by other educators.

After the committee completed its work, a preliminary edition of 1,000 copies
was published and sent to college and secondary teachers, administrators, and
research specialists, who were asked to read and offer suggestions. Their critiques
and ideas were incorporated into the final version of the *Cognitive Taxonomy*. The
Affective Taxonomy, although read by a wide variety of educators, has not received
the same depth of criticism.

RESEARCH ON EFFECTIVENESS

With Nongifted

Research on the use of the taxonomies, because of their nature as hierarchies,
must concentrate on three related issues: (a) the validity of the hierarchical
arrangement (that is, Are they actually arranged from simple to complex? Do the
higher levels actually include the lower levels?); (b) their clarity and comprehensiveness (that is, If two or more independent observers classify an objective or
a question, will they put it in the same category? Can every educational objective
be classified according to the taxonomy?); and (c) the effectiveness of the taxonomy's use with students (that is, By participating in learning activities designed

according to the taxonomies, are students more capable of behaving competently at the higher levels?). Most research to date has concentrated on the first two issues, although some evidence is available on the third.

Whether or not the *Cognitive Taxonomy*'s hierarchical arrangement is valid is a question that still has not been resolved. There is some evidence (Bloom, 1956; Chausow, 1955; Dressel & Mayhew, 1954; Stoker & Kropp, 1964; Ayers, Note 1) that the complex behaviors at the higher levels are more difficult than the simple ones at the lower levels. In other words, fewer students will perform as well on tests of the higher abilities. Each individual's performance will decrease as the tasks become more complex. The level that usually seems out of place, however, is evaluation. It does not appear to be the most difficult intellectual behavior (Stoker & Kropp, 1964).

In general, the research supports the *Cognitive Taxonomy*'s comprehensiveness and clarity when used both by practitioners and researchers (Bloom, 1956; Buros, 1959; Dressel & Nelson, 1956; Lessinger, 1963; McGuire, 1963; Morris, 1961; Stanley & Bolton, 1957; Stoker & Kropp, 1964; Tyler, 1966). The first test of the taxonomy's clarity and comprehensiveness was made by its developers when they independently classified additional objectives using their system. They only identified a few objectives that could not be classified. In subsequent studies of its use, there is also considerable agreement among raters attempting to classify objectives, as well as conclusive evidence that almost no objectives exist that do not fit into the system. Factor analytic studies of its structure (Stoker & Kropp, 1964; Milholland, Note 2; Zinn, Note 3), however, indicate that the categories are not mutually exclusive—a student's general ability and motivation appear to be the factors determining his or her achievement of objectives at all levels.

Relative to the use of the *Cognitive Taxonomy* as a basis for developing sequential learning activities, there has been some empirical support from studies of the effectiveness of asking higher level questions before, during, and after a student reads a passage of material. In most of these studies, subjects are given questions at some or all levels of the taxonomy to guide in their reading or recall of the information, and they are tested later to see how effective their learning has been. Hutchins (1969), for example, had sixth-grade students study materials containing either knowledge level or evaluation level materials. He then tested their performance by asking questions at all levels of the taxonomy and found that students who had received evaluation questions during instruction did better on evaluation questions on the posttests. Although this study provides some support for the use of the taxonomy, the same effect that was present for evaluation questions was not found for the knowledge questions.

In a long-term study, McKenzie (1972) had eighth-grade students take weekly quizzes that required either recall of given facts (knowledge level) or drawing inferences about the political interests of groups discussed (the highest level of comprehension). After eight weeks, the subjects were given posttests requiring them to: (a) recall facts (knowledge level); (b) make new inferences about the groups studied (comprehension); and (c) make new inferences about new groups (application). The results were interesting. The type of question asked in quizzes did not influence either recall of facts or the making of new inferences about new groups, but did influence making new inferences about old groups. Those who had been given inferential questions did better overall and significantly better on the questions calling for new inferences about old groups than did those given factual questions. Interpreted in the light of Hutchins's (1969) study and other research using classifications of cognitive questions other than the taxonomy (Felker & Dapra, 1975; Watts & Anderson, 1971; Dapra & Felker, Note 4), these results indicate that when students have practice at a certain level, they do better on posttests at that level. Practice at the lower levels does not seem to improve performance at the higher levels, however. Other studies (Holland, 1965; Andre, Note 5) however, have not provided support for this idea.

In research of a different nature, results indicate that certain types of learning activities improve performance at the higher levels. McKeachie (1962), in reviewing studies on lecture versus discussion, states that knowledge objectives may be learned equally well under both conditions, while performance at the higher levels seem to be facilitated by discussions and laboratory experiences where students are engaged in problem solving and are helped to see how their skills can be improved. Since discussions and laboratory experiences usually require learning activities similar to those designed to develop the higher levels, while lectures do not really encourage their use, this research provides some indirect evidence for the use of the *Cognitive Taxonomy* in designing learning experiences.

Relative to the *Affective Taxonomy,* no studies have been identified that address any one of the three issues identified earlier. Perhaps this lack of research is due to a general lack of interest in affective outcomes. It could also be due to the ambiguity often found in affective objectives or the emotional aspects of dealing with values or value-laden subjects. Regardless of the causes for this lack of research, the widespread use of this taxonomy implies a need for some tests of its validity.

With Gifted

When searching for information about the possible effectiveness of curricula based on the *Cognitive* and *Affective Taxonomies* with gifted children, the picture is even more bleak. Although programs with curricula based on the *Cognitive Taxonomy* have generally been effective as evidenced by their evaluations, there is absolutely no way to determine the role of the taxonomy in producing these results. Their effectiveness could simply be due to the fact that gifted students are identified, thus enhancing the students' perceptions of themselves as capable individuals. Similarly, programs based on or using the *Affective Taxonomy* have shown success, but the program evaluations have not shown that this success is attributable to the use of the taxonomy. Perhaps the development of the *Ross Test of Higher Cognitive Processes* (Ross & Ross, 1976), based on the *Cognitive Taxonomy,* will contribute to better research in the cognitive area.

JUDGMENTS

Advantages

The most obvious advantages for use of the taxonomies, particularly the cognitive one, stem from their widespread use and acceptance in educational circles. The taxonomy project certainly has achieved its goal of facilitating communication through developing a useful system of classification. Because the system is known, understood, and used in numerous classrooms as a part of the regular curriculum, it is easy to build on this regular curriculum by concentrating on a greater number of experiences at the higher levels. Communication with other teachers and the administration is enhanced by having the same language. Also due to this widespread use, many classroom materials based on the *Cognitive Taxonomy* are available.

A second advantage of the taxonomies is their relative simplicity and applicability. They are not difficult for teachers to learn and use, and they can be applied in all content areas and at all levels of instruction. They are comprehensive enough to include most objectives that have been developed. The research shows that the hierarchy is valid except for the possible misplacement of the evaluation level.

In addition to its use as a way to develop learning activities that improve students' higher levels of thinking and feeling, the taxonomies have certain related uses (Limburg, Note 6). First, they help teachers develop more precise, measurable objectives. If teachers have in mind a general objective, such as "understands concepts involved in . . .," the *Cognitive Taxonomy* can be used to suggest a more quantifiable statement of the objective. Second, the taxonomies can be used as guides for the development of better teacher-made tests, tests that will sample a variety of levels of thinking or feeling. A related use is evaluating standardized tests for measuring the success of gifted programs. Often, even though the program is designed to facilitate the higher levels of thinking, achievement tests that merely assess recognition and recall are the only instruments used to evaluate their success. In construction of evaluation measures, the taxonomies provide a useful way of matching the instructional emphasis according to levels with the emphasis in evaluative procedures.

Important to the effective use of the taxonomies is the availability of a practical reference source for the teacher. Both systems have comprehensive handbooks available that describe the various categories, relationships among the categories, and numerous specific examples of items included in each category. The handbooks also include self-assessment sections to aid the reader in learning the system.

Disadvantages

On the negative side, the most important considerations are the lack of research on effectiveness with children, particularly the gifted, and the limited scope in providing a structure for curricular modification for the gifted. The review of research has not uncovered evidence that the use of the taxonomies will have the hypothesized effect of improving higher levels of thinking. There has been no research even touching on the validity of the categories or the hierarchical arrangement of the *Affective Taxonomy,* and the research on one level of the *Cognitive Taxonomy,* evaluation, suggests that it may not be placed at the right level.

The second disadvantage, a limited scope, was discussed earlier, along with the description of curricular modifications suggested by the models. Curricular adaptations made possible through use of the taxonomies are mainly in the areas of process (for example, the development of higher levels of thinking and feeling) and content (for example, developing objectives that focus on the principles and abstractions in a particular discipline). Use of the *Affective Taxonomy* facilitates content changes by suggesting ways to integrate "feeling" content into academic areas and providing a structure for doing so. Some psychological environment modifications are also facilitated by the use of the *Affective Taxonomy.* The taxonomies must be combined with other models or used differently to provide a framework for a total approach to curriculum development for gifted students.

CONCLUSION

The *Taxonomies of Educational Objectives* cannot be defended as a total approach to curriculum development for gifted children and are sometimes difficult to justify at all due to their widespread use in regular education. However, they can be used as one aspect of a program, particularly to show the relative emphasis on higher versus lower thinking and feeling processes in gifted programs. Associated uses (that is, evaluation, development of teacher-made tests, evaluation of standardized tests, construction of more quantifiable objectives) and modifications of the taxonomies can make them more defensible as models to be used in programs for the gifted.

RESOURCES

Background Information

Bloom, B.S., ed. *Taxonomy of educational objectives: The classification of educational goals. Handbook I: Cognitive domain.* New York City: Longmans, Green & Co., 1956. Determining the success of achieving educational goals has often been a vague and unscientific process. The *Taxonomy of Educational Objectives* grew out of the need to develop a more accountable method of classifying educational goals. Facilitating communication is the major purpose of the taxonomy. In this book the cognitive domain is the emphasis. Part I of the book is an introduction and explanation to the taxonomy, its history, development, relation to curriculum, and the problems in writing it. Part II discusses each level of the taxonomy in detail: knowledge, comprehension, application, analysis, synthesis, and evaluation. In each section there are sample test items of each level to illustrate the descriptions.

Drumheller, S.J. *Handbook of curriculum design for individualized instruction: A systems approach.* Englewood Cliffs, N.J.: Educational Technology Publications, 1971. Designing curriculum materials using strictly defined behavioral objectives as a base is the purpose of the book. Bloom's *Taxonomy* of the cognitive domain is the author's base for the design models presented here. The taxonomy offers a strictly defined communication system for professionals interested in designing curricula based on the six levels. The book relates how a person can identify a well-defined objective and sequence a series of objectives into an educational program. Chapters include "A System's Approach to Curriculum Design," "Stating Objectives in Terms of Student Behavior," "Identifying Learning Outcomes," "A Model for Curriculum Design," "Implementing the Design Model," "Using the Model in Curriculum Design," and "Specific Guidelines for Using the Design Model." It is a step-by-step manual for how to develop curriculum materials using objectives from Bloom's *Taxonomy*. References and foldouts are included.

Krathwohl, D.R., Bloom, B.S., and Masia, B.B. *Taxonomy of educational objectives: The classification of educational goals. Handbook II: Affective Domain.* New York: David McKay Co., 1964. The *Taxonomy of Educational Objectives* for the affective domain, described in this handbook, is the companion volume to the *Cognitive Taxonomy*. In comparison, determining a classification system for the affective domain is a much more difficult and challenging task, as the authors readily admit. Affective education has been neglected or ignored because of the difficulties involved. This is one of the first attempts to define systematically a classification system for affective feelings and reactions. Like its companion volume, there are two parts. The first describes the need for a taxonomy, its basis, and the relationship between the affective and cognitive domains. The second part describes each of the five levels: receiving, responding, valuing, organization, and characterization by a value or value complex. Sample test items based on each level are given.

Instructional Materials and Ideas

Eberle, B., and Hall, R.E. *Affective education guidebook: Classroom activities in the realm of feelings.* Buffalo, N.Y.: D.O.K. Publishers, 1975. There are five levels in the taxonomy of affective domain described in this book. Receiving, willingness to respond, valuing, organizing a value system, and characterization are the five levels that are based on Krathwohl's *Taxonomy.* The central purpose of this book is to emphasize the teaching of these levels. There are two introductory chapters explaining the instructional model, but the major proportion of the book centers on instructional activities for each level. Each of the five levels has a series of activities to promote its specific development. The activities are detailed with objectives and instructions. Most are applicable to all age groups. There are appendixes describing group discussion dynamics and how to make your classroom into a community.

Eberle, B., and Hall, R. *Affective direction: Planning and teaching for thinking and feeling.* Buffalo, N.Y.: D.O.K. Publishers, 1979. This helpful book provides teaching suggestions based on the integration of the *Cognitive* and *Affective Taxonomies.* It outlines the taxonomies, provides reasons for emphasizing affective education, and provides many suggested activities for encouraging development at all levels. This is a working book and is not intended as something a reader should "thumb through" with a cursory review.

Sanders, N.M. *Classroom questions: What kinds?* New York City: Harper and Row, 1966. The art of questioning requires skills teachers often lack. The purpose of this book is to help a teacher develop the ability to ask questions based on the levels of Bloom's *Taxonomy.* The book briefly describes each level in the first chapter. Subsequent chapters deal with each level individually and the types of questions a teacher might ask to encourage that specific level of thinking. More emphasis is spent on the higher levels of analysis, synthesis, and evaluation as they are more complex and difficult to develop. Each chapter provides practical suggestions for the teacher to use in the classroom. Also, each chapter ends with a helpful self-evaluation with questions for the reader to judge acquisition of the material.

Treffinger, D.J., Borgers, S.B., Render, G.F., and Hoffman, R.M. Encouraging affective development: A compendium of techniques and resources. *Gifted Child Quarterly,* 1976, *20,* 47-65. The authors have compiled a comprehensive bibliography of methods, techniques, materials, and references concerning the development of affective education in the classroom. It is intended as a resource directory for teachers who are interested in incorporating affective education into their classrooms. Books, pamphlets, games, simulations, filmstrips, organizations, and journals are included. The item, the publisher and address, the price, and a brief annotation are given. The authors have 31 categories for the resources covering such topics as general references, affective education activities, classroom management, gestalt therapy, values clarification, group dynamics, and communication. This bibliography offers a wide range of materials.

Chapter 3

Jerome Bruner: The Basic Structure of a Discipline

Of all the teaching-learning models discussed in this book, Bruner's is the most philosophical. In fact, his is not actually a framework, but a way of approaching the development of a framework. Bruner's ideas have contributed to many of the other models presented, and to the author's overall view of curricular modifications appropriate for the gifted. From the author's point of view, the "basic concept" idea assumed greater importance through the success of the new curricular approaches based on these ideas (for example, new math, Biological Sciences Curriculum Study (BSCS), and Elementary Science Study (ESS), *Man: A Course of Study* [MACOS]) with gifted students.

At the same time, many of these curricula were not enjoying the same degree of success with average students. One school district in Illinois, for example, attempted to implement the *Leppert Social Studies Curriculum* in all its regular social studies classrooms because of its success as an innovation in the gifted program. Much to the educators' disappointment, the curriculum had to be "watered down" so much that much of the original form was lost. As an aside, they also felt that to teach the curriculum effectively, the teacher needed to be gifted. Gallagher (1966), who was greatly involved in the development of the Illinois program, also notes the value of Bruner's approach for the same reasons.

Taba, in the development of both her theory of curriculum development (1962) and her *Teaching Strategies* program (1964, 1966) draws heavily upon the concept of teaching the "basic structure" of a discipline as a way to organize and structure the content to be taught. Teaching the methodology and "thought systems" of the various disciplines, an associated idea attributed to Bruner, also influenced Taba, as it did Renzulli in the conception of his "Type III Enrichment" activities. Students acting as "real inquirers" is another Brunerian concept influencing curricular practices in education of the gifted.

Many ideas in this chapter are actually a result of the now-famous "Woods Hole" Conference on education in science, sponsored by the National Academy of

Sciences and directed by Jerome Bruner. In the report from the conference, The Process of Education (Bruner, 1960), five areas of education are discussed: (a) the importance of structure; (b) readiness for learning; (c) intuitive and analytic thinking; (d) motives for learning; and (e) aids to teaching. Although four of these areas will be discussed, the importance of structure is of most interest in this book because of the influence these ideas have had on practices in the field of education of the gifted. The basic reference for the ideas is Bruner (1960), and the implications for curriculum development for the gifted are the author's unless otherwise noted.

ASSUMPTIONS UNDERLYING THE APPROACH

About Teaching and Learning

One assumption has formed the basis for most of Bruner's ideas: "Intellectual activity anywhere is the same, whether at the frontier of knowledge or in a third-grade classroom." The difference is in degree, not in kind, and the best way to learn history is to do it by behaving the way a historian would. Thus instead of focusing on the conclusions in a field of inquiry, the focus should be on the inquiry itself. Most of Bruner's ideas follow from this basic conviction. A person more nearly approximates an inquirer if the basic ideas of that discipline are understood and are of concern, if concepts are "revisited" as understanding increases, if there is a balance between intuition and analysis, and if there is a long-term commitment to intellectual activity and the pursuit of knowledge.

The Importance of Structure

The theme underlying Bruner's approach is that the aim in education should be to teach the basic structure of academic disciplines in a way that this structure can be understood by children. This basic structure consists of certain concepts (for example, biological tropisms in science; revolution in social studies; supply and demand in economics; and commutation, distribution, and association in mathematics) and the important relationships between them. Such concepts and relationships, when understood, enable the learner to understand most of the phenomena in that discipline. Understanding the basic structure means that an individual not only has learned a specific thing, but also has learned a model for understanding similar things that may be encountered. A phenomenon is recognized as a specific instance of a more general case. Carefully developed understandings should also permit the student to recognize the limits of applicability of the generalizations.

In developing this theme, several assumptions were made. These beliefs have varying degrees of acceptance or proof in the psychological and educational literature. The first assumption is that the first object of learning is service in the future; whatever people learn should allow them to go further more easily. Learning serves persons in the future through both specific and general transfer. By definition, Bruner argues, basic concepts or ideas have wider applicability and thus greater transfer to future situations. By learning underlying ideas, the student can master more of the subject much quicker, and since there is little time and much to teach, these basic ideas will go much further.

Related to this idea is that memory is facilitated if a structure is learned. Bruner states that research on memory has shown that unless details (for example, facts, data) are placed in a structured pattern, they are easily forgotten. Once the structure is learned, these facts or details can be remembered more easily or at least reconstructed if necessary. Another underlying assumption is that by teaching basic structure the gap between basic and advanced knowledge can be narrowed. One difficulty encountered often from elementary school through graduate school is that much has to be relearned, because the elementary curriculum lags so far behind new developments in a field of study.

In order for the teaching of structure to be effective, the curriculum must be rewritten and materials devised so that the most basic ideas are taught. This can best be done by scholars and competent persons in their respective fields. The second requirement is that the materials and presentation must be matched to the abilities of children at different grade levels. This can only be done by those familiar with and experienced in working with children.

Certainly there are problems involved in these two assumptions. A major problem is difficulty in achieving agreement among scholars about what constitutes the structure or the most basic ideas that should be taught. Indeed, several attempts to define these basic ideas have resulted in the development of thousands of ideas due to the lack of agreement.

Readiness for Learning

The theme of this section can be summed up in Bruner's bold statement that ". . . any subject can be taught effectively in some intellectually honest form to any child at any stage of development" (1960, p. 33). This statement implies that the form in which the basic structure is taught must be matched to the level of intellectual development of the child and that the basic concepts involved should be "revisited" as time goes on and the child is capable of understanding more of the complexities of the concept.

Underlying the ideas about readiness for learning is the basic assumption that Piaget and other developmentalists are right in saying that at certain stages of development children have a characteristic way of viewing and explaining the world. A young child learns through direct sensory and motor experiences, while children in the next stage—concrete operations—no longer need direct trial-and-error experiences. They can now learn through mentally carrying out activities. At the concrete operational stage, internalized cognitive structures or "schema" are developed that guide the child's perception of reality. However, at this stage the child still must deal only with present reality or direct experiences from the past. Only after children have reached the stage of formal operations can they deal with hypothetical propositions.

The obvious implication of a developmental view of learning readiness is that in the stage of concrete operations, for example, understanding of a basic concept would need to be developed by providing the child with direct concrete experiences. Learning can be accomplished through exercises in manipulating, classifying, and ordering objects, but it would be futile to attempt a formal, logical explanation of the principles involved. After students have reached formal operations, they are able to understand a formal logical proof or explanation and to develop it themselves.

One assumption that Bruner makes, however, is somewhat different from Piaget's emphasis. Although Piaget recognizes the role of the environment in the learning process, he does not encourage manipulation of the environment. Instead, he suggests that the normal course of development be allowed to occur. Bruner, on the other hand, suggests that children be "tempted" into the next stages of development by presenting them with challenging and useable opportunities to move ahead.

When educators consider what concepts to teach a child using the idea of a spiral curriculum, in addition to the methods used and the consideration of the act of learning, they must consider whether, when fully developed, this concept would be valuable for an adult to know. This requirement underlies the idea of a spiral curriculum. As time goes on, the child returns to these basic concepts, building on them and making them more complex. The child also relates them to more complex stimuli, so the concepts must be valuable to know.

In his discussion of readiness, Bruner also includes the assumption that learning a subject involves three almost simultaneous processes. First, the learner must acquire information. The information may replace, enhance, contradict, or refine present knowledge. Then comes transformation, the process of manipulating knowledge to make it fit new tasks. Learners transform knowledge in a way that will enable them to go beyond it. A third process is evaluation, a process of checking to see whether manipulation or transformation of information was adequate. In each learning "episode," which may be brief or long and contain many or few ideas, all three processes are present. What is not known, and Bruner makes no assumptions about, is the amount of emphasis there should be on each process in a learning episode, the length and intensity of an episode, the kinds of techniques that can increase motivation to learn in each episode, and how to achieve a balance between intrinsic and extrinsic rewards to enhance learning in each episode.

Intuitive and Analytic Thinking

Although the nature, predisposing conditions, and techniques for measuring intuitive thinking are unknown or undeveloped, intuition is an important complement to analytic thinking and should be developed to the fullest extent possible. The two thinking processes are almost direct opposites. In contrast to analytic thinking, intuitive thinking does not proceed in a step-by-step order with full awareness of the information and operations needed. Rather, it involves maneuvers based on implicit perception of the total problem with little or no awareness of the process used. An individual who uses intuition makes seemingly careless, big leaps instead of smaller, measured steps.

According to scholars in various academic fields, the effectiveness of intuition lies in an individual's knowledge of a subject. By being familiar with the subject, individuals feed their intuition or give it something with which to work. After making an "intuitive leap" and coming up with a solution or hypothesis, the individual can then check or prove its validity through more careful analytical means. The nature of intuitive thinking, ways of measuring it, factors affecting it, or possible predisposing characteristics that enable a person to be a good intuiter are all areas that need further study since little is known about these important aspects. Bruner does make some observations about them but does not assume he is correct. He believes, for example, that effective intuitive thinking requires self-confidence and courage on the part of the student. Mistakes can easily be made by relying on intuition, so a certain willingness to take risks is important. In drawing a parallel with business and industry where the increasing importance and novelty of a situation causes a decrease in the tendency to think intuitively, Bruner suggests that the present system of rewards and punishments (usually in the form of grades) may actually discourage intuitive thinking.

When considering the development of this process of thinking, the problems involved must also be recognized. Teachers must be sensitive enough to differentiate between an ignorant answer and an answer from an interesting wrong leap. They must have a thorough knowledge of subject matter, and they must be able to give both approval and correction to a student at the same time.

Motives for Learning

Motivation, an important step toward a pursuit of excellence, must be a happy medium between frenzied activity and apathy. One of the important goals of education must be to arouse long-term interest or a continuing commitment to learning and the world of ideas, rather than a commitment to capturing the short-term interest of children necessary for learning a "lesson." Bruner believes that the pursuit of excellence should be emphasized through education and that one way to facilitate this pursuit of excellence is through a continuing interest in learning. Along with interest will be a high regard for intellectual activity.

Students have varied and mixed motives for learning, including approval of parents, teachers, and peers, along with their own sense of mastery. To foster the development of interest, educators can develop better exams, counseling techniques, improvement of teaching methods, and improvement of subject matter.

About Characteristics and Teaching the Gifted

In his book, Bruner makes several references to the gifted that are interesting in the light of subsequent application of his ideas to the education of gifted children. The first statement he makes is: "Good teaching which emphasizes the structure of a subject is probably even more valuable for the less able student than for the gifted one, for it is the former rather than the latter who is most easily thrown off the track by poor teaching" (1960, p. 9). By this statement he does not mean that the content or pace of courses should be the same, but that if there is good teaching, even the slowest students can achieve. What he did not take into account with this statement, however, is that not all students would be able to handle or learn the basic concepts identified. Many concepts important to the understanding of a discipline are abstract and highly complex, requiring reasoning powers beyond the level of average or slow students.

From this statement, along with the members of the committee who developed the ideas in his book, one assumption seems clear: the conference participants, who were themselves scholars in academic disciplines, were assuming that all learners could profit from the kind of inquiry activities that they themselves profited from. Indeed, they stated their central conviction that "intellectual activity anywhere is the same, whether at the frontier of knowledge or in a third-grade classroom" (1960, p. 14). What literary critics or students studying literature do in reading a literary work is the same if they are to achieve understanding. This assumption may be true for all learners, but perhaps it is only true of those who are able to achieve a complete understanding of the basic abstract concepts that form the structure of an academic discipline.

Bruner should also consider his requirement that each concept taught to students be subjected to the test of whether it will be useful to them as adults. It is doubtful that any slow students or many average students, for example, will need a deep understanding of algebraic principles, the principles of logic, or even the idea of biological tropism. Only those who choose to pursue further study in a field will be interested in these ideas or use them as adults.

A second reference to the gifted is in the speculation that new improvements in the teaching of science and mathematics may accentuate the gaps between children of differing ability levels. This possibility, though, should not deter educators from making modifications that will allow students to develop their reasoning powers fully. Democracy and leadership will have a better chance of surviving if the top quarter of this nation's students are not neglected as they have been in the past.

Bruner states that the pursuit of excellence should not be limited to gifted students. On the other hand, teaching should not simply be aimed at the average. The curriculum should contain something for everyone. The challenge is to develop materials that are difficult enough for the most able learners without destroying the confidence of those who are less able—an almost impossible task!

Although not made by Bruner, an assumption made by those who implement his ideas is expressed in the above discussion related to which children need to learn (or will use as adults) the basic ideas or concepts in academic areas. Basic modes of inquiry, the "thought systems," and certain abstract ideas necessary for complete understanding of a field of study will most likely be of use to potential scholars. These scholars are usually gifted.

ELEMENTS/PARTS

Rather than explaining how an individual can implement each of the five themes expressed by Bruner, which would require volumes, the parts of his approach appearing to have the most potential for success with gifted children are selected and explained. Selection of the ideas to be explained is based not only on the author's experience but also on the recommendations of other educators of the gifted (for example, Gallagher, 1975; Renzulli, 1977; Ward, 1961).

Modifications of Content

The most important curricular suggestions made by Bruner are changes in content or what is taught. His major theme is that what should be taught is the "basic structure" of a discipline. Incorporated into his definition of basic structure are several of the recommended content modifications: abstractness; complexity; economy; organization; and the teaching of methods of inquiry in each discipline. In fact, the only content modifications not addressed in his approach are variety and the study of people. The first four concepts (i.e., abstractness, complexity, economy and organization) are, from Bruner's point of view, implications resulting from the teaching of basic structure and necessary requirements for its successful implementation. All of these will be discussed together since they are related. The recommendation for teaching methods of inquiry will be discussed as a process or method modification, since his suggestion is that students learn history the way a historian would or learn science the way a scientist would.

The first suggestion Bruner makes is related to the first task in curriculum development: what should be taught? In other words, what are those basic ideas that form the structure of a subject? Which ideas or concepts, when understood, will have the widest applicability to new situations? Which concepts will be needed by students as adults? The people qualified to make these decisions are the scholars in various disciplines. Only they have a complete enough understanding of their discipline to decide what is basic. Since the problem involves not only what concepts should be taught but also how they can be translated into a form that children at different levels of development can understand, Bruner suggests committees made up of both scholars and child development specialists. These committees can address both questions simultaneously.

A problem with this suggestion is the apparently erroneous assumption that scholars can agree upon the basic concepts that should be taught. Some of the earlier curriculum development projects that grew out of this suggestion compiled lists of as many as 3,500 generalizations in the social sciences. This phenomenon defeated the purpose of the project since teachers still had to make the major decisions about what was most important. There was no way all of these general ideas could be taught. It is possible, however, to force the issue and get at least a majority opinion. Those ideas agreed upon by the majority can constitute the basic or required curriculum, while those with lesser degrees of agreement can make up the optional or extending curriculum.

The idea of economy is also a significant one in implementing a basic concept approach. Since children only have a limited amount of time in school and an almost unlimited number of things to learn, educators must make each learning experience a valuable one and each concept an important one. As a guiding principle for implementing this idea, Bruner suggests as criteria the following dual consideration: (a) when fully developed, is it worth being known by an adult? and (b) having known it as a child, does a person become a better adult? According to Bruner: "If the answer to both is negative or ambiguous, then the material is cluttering the curriculum" (1960, p. 52).

A related principle, implicit in Bruner's discussions but not stated as such, is that of organizing the content so that it will facilitate the discovery or development of a basic idea. Using the methods of a scholar and studying phenomena with the potential to increase the chances that a basic idea will be discovered is at the heart of this approach. By structuring activities so that discovery is facilitated, the teacher also develops the interests of students and capitalizes on their curiosity and excitement.

One example of the organization of content or learning experiences to facilitate discovery is Bruner's classic example of a "basic concept" in the area of biology. Presented as an example of a basic idea and how it can transfer to a new situation, it also illustrates how content can be organized:

Take first a set of observations on an inchworm crossing a sheet of graph paper mounted on a straight line. We tilt the board so that the inclined plane or upward grade is 30°. We observe that the animal does not go straight up, but travels at an angle of 45° from the line of maximum climb. We now tilt the board to 60°. At what angle does the animal travel with respect to the line of maximum climb? Now, say, he travels along a line 75° off the straight-up line. From these two measures, we may infer that inchworms "prefer" to travel uphill, if uphill they must go, along an incline of 15°. We have discovered a tropism, as it is called, indeed a geo-tropism. It is not an isolated fact. We can go on to show that among simple organisms, such phenomena—regulation of locomotion according to a fixed or built-in standard—are the rule. There is a preferred level of illumination toward which lower organisms orient, a preferred level of salinity, of temperature, and so on. Once a student grasps this basic relation between external stimulation and locomotor action, he is well on his way toward being able to handle a good deal of seemingly new but, in fact, highly related information. The swarming of locusts where temperature determines the swarm density in which locusts are forced to travel, the species maintenance of insects at different altitudes on the side of a mountain where crossbreeding is prevented by the tendency of each species to travel in its preferred oxygen zone, and many other phenomena in biology can be understood in the light of tropisms. (Bruner, 1960, pp. 6-7)

First, the student can be asked to make observations of the behavior of the inchworm when the board is horizontal. Next, the student should observe under the conditions of a 30°, 45°, 60°, and 75° angle and record the behavior of the inchworm. Students can be asked to make similar observations about preferences of animals for environmental conditions, such as illumination, level of salinity, and temperature. In this way, the teacher has organized the content or the specific facts and data to be used around a concept. By having experiences arranged within a definite time period, the teacher facilitates discovery of the underlying principle of tropism. Organization around basic ideas also facilitates selection of the data to be used. Economy is achieved at the same time, since fewer experiences would be needed if arranged closely together to facilitate more rapid transfer.

Process Modifications

Although mainly a theory suggesting content changes, Bruner's ideas include the three following process modifications that would be appropriate for gifted students: (a) higher levels of thinking; (b) discovery; and (c) open-endedness. Underlying the development of the concept of teaching basic structure is the idea that all intellectual activity is the same regardless of the level and that the best way to learn is to act the way a scholar would act or "create" knowledge in the way that someone on the frontier of knowledge would create it. Even though this underlying assumption contributed to the development of Bruner's basic structure theme, it also suggests a method for the effective teaching of structure. The suggestion is an obvious one: methods of teaching should put the learner in the role of a scholar or inquirer in each subject area being taught.

In the physical sciences, the child should behave as a physicist, chemist, or engineer. In the natural sciences, the child should behave as a biologist, herpetologist, or geologist. In literature he or she should act as a poet, a short story writer, a literary critic, or a playwright. Teachers not only need to be familiar with the data and basic ideas of a discipline, but also must know its characteristic methods of inquiry. In addition to giving children feedback on the accuracy of their information, teachers must provide them with suggestions for improving their methodological skills. When a child acting as a sociologist is conducting an attitude survey, for example, the teacher must be prepared to give specific suggestions for designing better questions, analyzing the data, conducting interviews, scaling, and other data collection or evaluation methods.

Because of Bruner's emphasis on putting the learner in the role of a scholar or inquirer, the three process modifications are made. When children behave as scholars, they will use rather than simply acquire information. Information gained will be applied in practical situations, evaluated, and used to form products new to the students. While using professional methods, the students are also participating in open-ended activities that are provocative in nature. Aspects of open-endedness not included as part of Bruner's approach, however, relate to the questions asked of students while engaged in inquiry. Discovery is an integral part of Bruner's approach, and he makes many suggestions for implementing it, in addition to the student behaving as a scholar or professional.

The following are three important aspects involved in implementing guided discovery: (a) organization and selection of data to be used in facilitating the child's discovery of some basic idea; (b) the use of teacher questions or activities that will guide students in their process of inquiry; and (c) ways of teaching that will develop in the child an excitement about learning that will translate into an "inquiry attitude." Bruner does not give specific suggestions for implementing the approach, but he does provide general guidelines. First, there needs to be a balance between an approach where the generalization is first stated by the teacher with students providing the proof (a deductive approach), and an inductive or discovery approach. Presenting all of what a student needs to know through a discovery approach would be too time-consuming. However, with gifted students the approach does not take nearly as much time as with average or slow students. If an inductive approach were used exclusively, though, it no doubt would get boring. Students would not have practice in a deductive approach either. In short, there should be a balance between the two types of approaches, but just what constitutes balance is as yet unknown. Bruner makes no assumptions about the relative emphases.

Discovery approaches need not be limited to formal subjects such as mathematics. They can and should be used in social studies, language arts, and the sciences.

Related to the use of a discovery approach is the theme of intuitive versus analytic thinking. Intuitive thinking, which proceeds by a series of "jumps" rather than in an analytical step-by-step fashion, is often the scientist's or scholar's way of making an important new discovery. In mathematics, for example, individuals are said to think intuitively when they suddenly achieve a solution, but still have not provided the formal proof. Another example of intuition in mathematics is the ability to make good, quick guesses about the best possible approaches to take in solving a problem. The phenomenon of intuition as described by Bruner is similar, if not identical, to the "Aha!" experience described by Parnes (see Chapter 6). In an "Aha!" experience, an individual suddenly understands, suddenly has a great idea. This experience usually comes after a period of incubation in which the person has subconsciously been working on a problem. Suddenly things click, and the person knows the answer, but has no idea how the idea came.

According to Bruner, little is known about the nature of intuition and the factors affecting it. Most of his comments on this topic are related to a justification for attempting to develop it and an outline of needed research. He does, however, speculate on its possible nature and the factors affecting it. He was of the opinion that solid knowledge of a subject helps a person become a good intuiter, but that not all people who are familiar with their subject areas are good intuiters. Thus, a good background in the basic ideas of the subject may be necessary but not sufficient for intuition to occur. Other conditions that may be necessary or at least increase the probability that intuitive thinking will be developed include: (a) intuitive teachers who can provide a model of effective intuition or at least a willingness to use intuition; (b) emphasis on the structure or connectedness of knowledge; (c) encouragement of guessing; and (d) a change in grading practices so that there is less emphasis on getting the right answer in certain situations.

One way to increase the possibility that intuitive thinking will occur is to use a discovery approach. Discovery, if true to its definition, should more nearly approximate the inquiry process of a scholar. In their own fields and day-to-day work, scholars often make intuitive leaps. Thus, by using an approach that ensures that the learning situation in school is more like the true inquiry process, the probability of intuitive thinking may be increased. In the day-to-day work of a scholar, intuitive thinking is often used to come up with an hypothesis that can be tested by analytical means. When using a discovery approach, this aspect of the inquiry process can also be incorporated. Students can be encouraged to make guesses about the underlying principles through intuition and then to check these guesses. Grading can be based on methods of proof regardless of the accuracy of the hypothesis, with only constructive criticism on the child's use of intuition in forming the hypothesis.

Product and Learning Environment Modifications

Although Bruner does not specifically address curricular modifications in the areas of product and learning environment, modifications of products are implied by (and, in fact, required by) his approach. Because students are acting as real inquirers and scholars, their products address real problems and involve transformations rather than summaries of existing ideas or information. The involvement of real audiences and the realistic evaluation of products are ideas not implied or addressed by his approach.

With regard to the learning environment, Bruner makes no specific suggestions. Some of his comments imply that the environment would need to resemble the environments professionals have. This idea is related to the dimensions of student-centered, encouraging independence, complexity, and high mobility. However, since no mention is made of the environment, these modifications are not really addressed.

To provide a way for the reader to integrate the underlying themes expressed in Bruner's book with the following example of the use of his approach, the basic ideas relating to curriculum development for the gifted are summarized in Table 3-1. In this table, student roles and activities and teacher roles and activities are related to each major theme.

Examples of Teaching Activities

A prime example of Bruner's activities and strategies is found in *Man: A Course of Study* (MACOS) (Education Development Center, 1970). Through this social studies curriculum, children learn a set of key concepts, the *acquisition of new information,* and then are led to *generalize* from these newly assimilated facts and to *evaluate* their generalizations. Through a series of films that simulate field study and a set of 30 booklets, the children assimilate information about animal and human behavior arranged around a few basic themes. Much of the learning comes from the work of Irven DeVore, Jane Goodall, and Niko Tinbergen, all admired scientists, specialists in their fields who devoted their energies to long-term investigation. By studying the works of such people, children develop an understanding of and appreciation for ongoing scientific investigation. Through independent and small group study and through group discussion, children arrive at generalizations about the essence of being human.

The most basic theme of MACOS is "What makes man human?" This conceptual question forms the basis for organizing the course, which is concerned with the nature of humans as a species and the forces (for example, tool making, language, social organization, management of prolonged childhood, and the urge to explain

Table 3-1 Summary of Teacher and Student Roles and Activities in Bruner's Basic Structure of a Discipline Approach

THEME	STUDENT		TEACHER	
	ROLE	SAMPLE ACTIVITY	ROLE	SAMPLE ACTIVITY
Basic Concepts	Inquirer; data gatherer, analyzer, synthesizer	Using primary sources, study some phenomemon by collecting "raw data." Using secondary sources, study the conclusions or ideas of others about some phenomenon. Acquire, transform, and evaluate new information	Organizer; facilitator; methodological consultant; resource.	Choose those concepts or basic ideas identified as most important to the disciplines by the scholars in a field; if these ideas are not already available in a discipline, form a committee made up of scholars and child development specialists to develop these ideas as well as suggestions for how they can best be learned by children. Subject each concept to be taught to the tests of usefulness to an adult. Select the data and plan the learning experiences that are the "richest" and most economical in developing these ideas.
Inquiry as a Scholar	Inquirer; data gather, analyzer, synthesizer	Be a scientist, mathematician, physicist, writer, playwright.	Organizer; facilitator; resource; methodological consultant	Provide students with constructive feedback on their inquiry skills. Provide students with feedback on the accuracy of their conclusions and/or logic in reaching them.

Table 3-1 continued

THEME	STUDENT		TEACHER	
	ROLE	SAMPLE ACTIVITY	ROLE	SAMPLE ACTIVITY
Discovery	Inquirer	Try to figure things out. Make hypotheses and test them.	Organizer; facilitator; resourse; interest stimulator	Organize the content and plan the learning experiences that will facilitate student discovery of basic concepts. Provide a balance between discovery and deductive approaches. Develop discovery techniques in all content areas.
Intuitive Thinking	Hypothesizer; risk-taker	Make guesses intuitively and then check them by analytical methods. Guess about solutions as well as about the best approaches.	Supporter; facilitator	Assist children in developing a good solid knowledge of a subject that will enable them to become good intuitive thinkers. Model the use of intuition by making hypotheses. Encourage students to make hypotheses. Emphasize the structure or connectedness of knowledge. Change grading practices so that wrong bunches are not unnecessarily punished.

the world) that shape and have shaped humanity. Nine conceptual themes are explored through both primary and secondary data sources using the inquiry methods of scholars in the major fields that are associated with the themes: biologists, psychologists, sociologists, and anthropologists. (See Table 3-2.) Table 3-2 gives a summary of conceptual themes, data sources, classroom techniques, and learning methods used in the MACOS curriculum.

One of the introductory lessons suggested to teachers, shown in Exhibit 3-1, concerns how an anthropologist studies behavior.

MODIFYING THE APPROACH

Bruner's model does not suggest curricular modifications appropriate for the gifted in the following areas: (a) *content*—variety and the study of people; (b) *process*—evidence of reasoning, freedom of choice, group interaction, pacing, and variety; (c) *product*—real audiences and appropriate evaluation; and (d) *learning environment*—no changes are made. Since his approach is such a comprehensive one, it can almost be used as a total approach. However, it would be more appropriate if the elements described in the following sections were added.

Content Changes

Variety

To add the element of variety, a person simply needs to assess the regular curriculum to determine what is being taught and make certain that the content in the gifted program is different. In so doing, however, the organization of content around key concepts needs to be continued as Bruner suggests. To illustrate this process, Maker (1982) has developed a worksheet for assessing content plans. (See Figure 3-1.) The generalization to be discovered is written at the top of the worksheet, and the concepts contained in the generalization are listed below it. Each concept is analyzed separately. On the left, the data and information pertaining to the concept that is taught in the regular curriculum are listed. On the right side, the teacher lists what additional data need to be taught for the students to achieve a full understanding of the concept's use. In the example, the generalization and concepts pertain to the scientific method and its use. Two concepts—observation and organization of data—are analyzed. The process should be continued until each concept contained in the generalization is analyzed.

Table 3-2 Summary of Conceptual Themes, Data Sources, Classroom Techniques, and Learning Methods in *Man: A Course of Study*

CONCEPTUAL THEMES	DATA SOURCES	CLASSROOM TECHNIQUES	LEARNING METHODS
Life cycle (including reproduction)	1. Primary Sources	Examples	Learning Methods
Adaptation	Student experiences Behavior of family Behavior of young children in school Behavior of animals	Individual and group research, e.g. direct observation or reading of texts	Inquiry, investigation (problem-defining, hypothesizing, experimentation, observation, interviewing, literature searching, summarizing and reporting)
Learning			
Aggression	2. Secondary Sources	Large and small group discussion	
Organization of groups (including group relationships, the family and community, division of labor)	Films and slides of animals and Eskimos Recording of animal sounds	Games	Sharing and evaluating of interpretation
		Role Play	Accumulating and retaining information
Technology	Recording of Eskimo myths, legends and poetry Anthropological field notes	Large and small group projects such as art and construction projects	Exchange of opinion, defense of opinion
Communication and language			Exploration of individual feelings
World view	Written data on humans, other animals and environments	Writing of songs and poems	Exposure to diverse aesthetic styles
Values			

Source: Adapted from J.P. Hanley, D.K. Whitla, E.W. Moo, and A.S. Walter. *Man: A Course of Study.* © Education Development Center, Newton, Mass., 1970, p. 7.

Exhibit 3-1 Lesson B: The Study of Human Beings from an Anthropological Perspective

Materials
A selection from:

lipstick	road map	note pad
aspirin	magazine	pencils or pens
address book	photographs	spoon
newspaper	calendar	eyeglasses
tissues or handkerchief		wallet with some contents
letter from a friend		candy bar or gum

I. Introducing the Task

Before class, fill a pocketbook, briefcase, or desk drawer with several of the items listed above and/or other common items. In a brief introduction to the class, explain that the students are to pretend that they have just discovered these items and do not know anything about the person to whom they belong or the place or time the person lived in. What can they learn about the person's way of life from these belongings? What can they guess about the society the person lives in? What does the person seem to care about? Which items seem necessary for survival? What questions would they like to ask this person?

After examining one item together, small groups can take other items and examine them in light of some of the questions raised on the previous page. (You might reproduce the questions for each group; the class could then compile their guesses on a chart.)

II. Focusing on Ways of Studying Human Beings

After students have discussed what they think they know about the owner of the items and the society to which he/she belongs, you can explain that, in some ways, they have been acting as anthropologists, scientists who study human beings. They have been using available evidence to inquire into the nature of human beings and the societies in which they live. Students should think about some of these questions:

• What would you have to know about another group of people to understand their culture?
• How would you keep records of what you learn?
• Are some of the ways you study about human beings similar to the ways you study other animal species?
• How is the study different?

In response to the last question, it should be clear that we can observe human beings to try to see what is important to them, but we can also ask them questions and ask them to give their opinions. What can be learned through observations? What cannot be learned through observation alone? To focus on these questions, students can list their responses and develop a chart similar to the one that follows. The chart points out the different kinds of things we can learn about human beings, based upon our ability to speak with each other.

Exhibit 3-1 continued

Learned through Observation	*Learned through Talking*
What they look like	What they did yesterday and will
How they meet basic needs	do tomorrow
How they act toward one	How they like what they do
another	What their favorite color is
How they play	What they think or feel about an
How the young act with the	event in another part of the
old	world
How parents act with offspring	What they believe in
What they do not like to eat	What they think is funny

III. A Visit from an Anthropologist

Students may be interested in learning more about anthropology as a field of study and about what anthropologists do. The teacher might make a statement such as the following:

Some anthropologists look mostly at the physical structure of human beings; others examine traces of human beings from the past. Still others are what we call cultural anthropologists; they look at what a group of people share in common: their beliefs, their tools, the ways they define their relationships with each other, their language, the way they raise their children, and so on. Anthropologists call all the things that people share their culture. Cultural anthropologists often study groups of people who share a culture, such as the Netsilik Eskimos, the people whose way of life is the focus of the course.

Students might think about what an anthropologist visiting their classroom would observe. How does an anthropologist decide what to record? Would every anthropologist record the same things? This question can lead to a discussion of the bias of different anthropologists. How might a woman's view differ from a man's? Suppose one anthropologist was an artist as well as an anthropologist, and another was a school teacher as well as an anthropologist. How might this affect the way they look at a group of people? How would you feel about having your customs recorded by a person taking notes on your activities and talking with you? (Possible conflict over individual privacy versus scientific study could come out of a discussion of this question. How does a real anthropologist answer that question?)

Students will better understand anthropology as a professional field if they indeed meet and speak with an anthropologist. Frequently, colleges and universities have departments of anthropology with professors or graduate students who enjoy talking with young people about their field. You could probably locate such a person through a call or note to the head of a nearby anthropology department.

Source: Education Development Center, 1976, pp. 45-47. Reprinted by permission.

Figure 3-1 Worksheet for Overall Curriculum Design (Worksheet #6b: Building Content Plans upon the Regular Curriculum)

Generalization # ___1___ : The growth of knowledge in science occurs through questioning, observation, experimentation, manipulation of materials, observation of results, and revision of original theories.

Key concepts To Be Developed:

Observation*	Organization of Data*	Control Groups
Prediction	Classification	Hypothesis
Environment	Inferences	Energy
Scientific Method	Contamination	Variable
	Raw Data	Brainstorming

Data Taught in the Regular Curriculum	Data Needing to Be Taught in the Special Curriculum
Observation	*Observation*
Ways to observe and record changes in temperature	Different types of observations that can be made: checklists, coding schemes, timed observation, use of microscope, changes in color from use of chemicals
The importance of careful observation	Types of measurement of observations: weight, length, color, density, temperature
	Experimental and control observations
	Examples of incorrect inferences resulting from careless observations
Organization of Data	*Organization of Data*
Keeping records of observations in notebooks	Types of graphs: bar, line
	Choosing units for graphs
Grouping like observations together	Separating experimental from control observations

* Concept(s) developed in this work sheet

Source: Reprinted from J. Maker. *Curriculum Development for the Gifted.* Rockville, Md.: Aspen Systems Corporation, 1982.

Study of People

This content modification would be interesting and fun as an adjunct to Bruner's model and is easy to incorporate. When considering each key concept to be developed, the teacher could, as a part of the process of deciding what data to teach, also choose a person or persons who have contributed significantly to the development of understanding of that concept. The students could examine the ideas and methods of those individuals and attempt to trace the evolution of their ideas. At the same time, they can examine how these individuals' methods differed and how the different methods may have contributed to the development of different theories or ideas.

As students are using the methods of scholars and investigators, they can engage in discussions of the different investigative techniques and examine the lives of eminent individuals who developed and used these methods. In addition they can discuss the creative/productive accomplishments of these individuals and others' reactions to these discoveries or accomplishments.

Process Changes

The most effective way to modify Bruner's approach would be to combine it with the Taba *Strategies* and with Treffinger's *self-directed learning* model. The Taba *Strategies* could be used to guide class discussions of key concepts and methods, and Treffinger's model could be used to assess the students' levels of self-direction and move them toward greater independence.

Since many of Taba's ideas were influenced by Bruner, the two approaches are compatible. For example, in planning a Taba discussion, the teacher could begin with a concept or generalization and plan a series of focusing questions to stimulate the students' interaction with each other, through which they eventually will reach their own statement of a generalization or organization of information around a concept.

Treffinger's model is also compatible with Bruner's approach. Bruner suggests that children use investigative techniques; however, in many cases, the teacher tells them what techniques to use and what problems to study. With gifted students, a more effective approach would be to assess their level of self-direction, and either guide their investigations or serve as a resource for their study of a problem of interest to them. The teacher can retain the organization of content around key concepts by encouraging investigations related to a particular concept. The teacher can also suggest that students attempt to use a variety of methods selected from the many investigative techniques available to them.

With the use of Taba's techniques, the teacher would be certain of the systematic development of higher levels of thinking, use of open-ended questions, and the use of questions calling for explanations of reasoning and logic. An element of variety (class discussions) would be added, and specific suggestions for pacing would be included. If Treffinger's suggestions are followed, freedom of choice would be added, as would other elements of variety.

Pacing

In addition to the pacing of discussions, when using Bruner's ideas or the curricula developed from his ideas, teachers must realize that gifted students need fewer examples (or specific facts) to enable them to discover a principle or understand a concept. Thus, an important aspect of implementation is to select only a few examples and to move quickly from one concept to the next, depending on how quickly the students grasp the ideas, rather than teaching everything contained in the curriculum.

Variety

In addition to the variety added by Taba discussions and varied investigative techniques, the teacher should include field trips to observe scientists, poets, or other professionals at work. Methods can also include learning centers for investigations as well as lectures, demonstrations, and simulation games.

Group Interaction

It would be interesting to add simulation games and structured interaction techniques to the basic methods suggested by Bruner. In fact, such an addition would not represent a great amount of deviation from his suggestions. For instance, the example in which students behave as anthropologists is similar to the activities contained in the simulation game *Dig,* in which two teams of students develop a culture, create the artifacts of the culture, and bury them. The teams then uncover and analyze the artifacts developed by the other team, and attempt to re-create the culture. This sort of activity is the type that would satisfy Bruner's requirements for learning situations.

This game offers many excellent opportunities for structured interaction and for self- and peer-analysis of the process. The digging process, the analysis, and many other activities could be videotaped, and the students could analyze their own and others' performances, looking not only at their interactions with each other, but also critiquing the scientific (or unscientific) methods being used. If videotaping equipment is not available, observers can serve the same purpose. All the students can take turns observing and recording their observations of interactions or methods being used.

Product Changes

Although the problems being studied when using Bruner's approach are "real," they may not be of interest to the child. However, Treffinger's model would provide the structure for student selection of problems to investigate.

Real Audiences

Adding this element to Bruner's approach is also easy. Since the emphasis in his method is on use of the techniques of professionals, the teacher can simply extend this idea by asking Renzulli's (Note 1) "Key Question" about the research: What do anthropologists do with the results of their research? What do creative writers do with their poems, short stories, novels, or plays? The answers to these questions suggest what the students should attempt to do with their products. This aspect of product development can mesh well with the study of people, as the students can use these people's products and audiences as a way to stimulate their own ideas.

Appropriate Evaluation

Building on the previous example, students can be asked another Key Question: How are the anthropologist's products judged? How do different audiences view these products? A study of eminent individuals can also provide answers to these questions. The products and the reactions of different audiences to the products can be examined. At the same time, it would be valuable to examine the way the eminent individual reacted to or handled the audiences' assessment of his or her product.

Learning Environment Changes

Even though Bruner does not directly address the question of what kind of learning environment a teacher should establish, environments similar to those described for gifted students are essential if Bruner's ideas are to be implemented effectively. For example, for students to function as real inquirers, the focus must be on student ideas and student activities, and there must be a low percentage of teacher talk. The environment must permit a high degree of mobility to enable students to carry out their investigations. The following techniques can be used to make the environment more appropriate.

Student-Centered

If Bruner's approach is combined with the Taba *Strategies* as suggested earlier, discussions will be student-centered. There will be little teacher talk, the teacher will not be the center of a discussion, and the teacher will not serve as an authority figure. The classroom can become even more student-centered if Treffinger's suggestions are followed; student ideas and topics of investigation will be emphasized rather than those of the teacher.

Encouraging Independence

This aspect of classroom climate extends the emphasis on independence into the nonacademic realm as well as the academic one. Bruner's objectives of having students learn as professionals can be achieved simultaneously with this one. If, for example, the teacher has been having difficulty with classroom management, but does not want to impose solutions on the students (an important aspect of this dimension), the next topic of study could become "government," and the students could begin to learn how government works by establishing their own classroom government, electing their own officials, and developing and enforcing their own laws. Thus, they learn the system, while at the same time they solve their own problems.

Openness

The classroom environment must be open to allow students to make "wrong" intuitive leaps during the discovery process, to make their own hypotheses, and to test them with experiments. The teacher must let them make their own mistakes and learn from them. Other people, including content experts, should be brought into the classroom. There must be few restrictions on the areas of study and the methods used.

Accepting

This dimension of the classroom climate is particularly important in the discovery process. The teacher must be careful to avoid both positive and negative judgments of student ideas during the discovery process. If one student has developed a hypothesis that the teacher knows will "work," the teacher should avoid praising the student until after the hypothesis has been "proven." This gives that child the opportunity to explore his or her own ideas, and other children the equal opportunity to develop and test their own ideas, rather than using the hypothesis praised by the teacher. Acceptance does not imply nonevaluation. In fact, evaluation is necessary to the process. Students must be assisted in examining their hypotheses to determine both the accurate or valid aspects and the inaccurate ones. They must also examine the appropriateness of their methods.

Complexity

To enable gifted students to learn as a scholar does and to facilitate their discovery of abstract, complex ideas, the classroom must include a variety of references, equipment, and environments. They need environments that simulate those used by professionals in as many ways as possible.

High Mobility

A high degree of mobility is also necessary. If reference materials are not available in the classroom, students must be allowed to leave the class to find them. They must also be allowed to leave the classroom and school to conduct their investigations. Such provisions are essential if the approach is to work.

Summary

Bruner's approach is mainly a content model, although his suggestions for discovery and the use of techniques used by professionals are pervasive, important processes. His ideas can be combined effectively with the strategies of Taba and Treffinger to achieve a comprehensive complementary program. They could also be combined with Renzulli's, Bloom's, and William's models.

DEVELOPMENT

After the conference in Woods Hole, Jerome Bruner began his massive task of synthesizing the major points made by the conferees after their ten days of discussion and debate. Since the members of the conference had been divided into five work groups and each of these groups had prepared a lengthy report to present to the rest of the participants for debate, his task was not easy. In an attempt to reflect as accurately as possible the major themes, conclusions, and disagreements, the chairman of the conference first prepared a draft report based on the conference papers. Copies were then sent to all participants for their comments and critiques. The final draft, which incorporated as much of the flavor of the meetings and comments as possible, became a classic book in curricular reform.

Bruner's ideas have continued to develop along the lines suggested in the conference report. Subsequent writing and research have extended and refined many of them. In the massive project, MACOS, he has incorporated these ideas into an exciting effective curriculum for children.

RESEARCH ON EFFECTIVENESS

With Nongifted

In a comprehensive evaluation of MACOS, Hanley et al. (1970) found the curriculum to be highly effective in achieving its goals with children and in effecting desirable changes in the teachers who used it. In the teachers, there was a noticeable shift from didactic to interpersonal modes of teaching and learning. After teaching the course, teachers talked less and were less dominating. They allowed students to give longer responses, raise more issues for discussion, and engage in more student-to-student interaction. In comparisons of control and experimental groups, there were several differences in favor of the classes using MACOS. Following are some of the desirable outcomes for children:

- There was an increased desire and ability to work independently.
- The wide range of course materials seemed to modify students' views of traditional data sources.
- Children learned a lot of information and methods of investigation. They began to understand the meaning of serious investigation.
- Children were personally involved in and reflective about the course ideas.
- Interdependence of species members was a concept that began to be fully understood.

Evaluation of the course materials and relative effectiveness for achieving the goals of the course yielded the following results:

- The materials and methods were enjoyable, exciting, and interesting to the students.
- Children tended to become much more aware of the similarities between humans and animals than they did of differences.
- Ability to master and use the concepts in the course correctly seemed to depend heavily on the quality and number of examples given.
- Students became impatient with obvious repetition in material, but also were disturbed when ideas were not presented in a thorough manner.
- The Netsilik unit (the section on humans) was the favorite of the majority of the children.
- The hunting games were highly successful teaching devices, but youngsters must reflect on their play to learn much from it.

In addition to MACOS, many other curricula have been based on Bruner's approach. Most were developed and evaluated in the 1960s, some of them quite extensively.* In a large scale evaluation of the University of Illinois Committee on School Mathematics (UICSM) math program involving almost 2,000 students,

---

*For a list of some of these projects, along with names and addresses, see the resource list at the end of this chapter.

Tatsuoka and Easley (1963) found significant gains in the experimental over the control group on a traditional test of algebraic concepts. Others (Begle & Wilson, 1970; Grobman, 1962; Wallace, 1962) found that when progress was measured by traditional tests of achievement, which usually measure factual information, curricula built on Bruner's approach were not as successful as traditional curricula. On tests constructed by the developers of the curricula, however, the experimental groups were similar. Most of this research says what a person would logically predict. The traditional approaches are better at doing what they intend to do, while the new approaches are better at doing what they intend to do.

With Gifted

There has been some research comparing the achievement of different ability levels of children when using Bruner-type curricula. Generally, however, these comparisons have been more or less afterthoughts except for two well-designed studies. In another evaluation of the UICSM material stressing the discovery method, Lowman (1961) compared this method with a traditional algebra class. He found that there was a significant difference favoring the UICSM materials for students in the top third in ability, but not for the middle and lower thirds. In a three-year study of six curricular approaches with over 1,500 gifted junior high students, Goldberg, Passow, Camm, and Neill (cited in Gallagher, 1975) found that the ranking of these programs was as follows: (1) School Mathematics Study Group (SMSG)—accelerated (four years of SMSG in a three-year period); (2) UICSM—normal; (3) UICSM—beginning earlier; (4) SMSG—normal; (5) traditional accelerated; and (6) traditional enriched. Thus, the new curricular approaches were superior to traditional ones, and the most superior was one of the new approaches taught in a more concentrated period of time.

In other evaluations, there has been evidence that gifted and high-ability students profit more from learning abstract concepts and using a discovery approach. In evaluations of Biological Sciences Curriculum Study (BSCS) materials, Wallace (1962) and Grobman (1962) concluded that high ability was an important factor in the mastery of the concepts presented and that low intelligence was a negative factor. Others (Mayor, 1966; Proviss, 1960; Suppes, 1969) have concluded that modern math students do as well as students in traditional programs in arithmetic fundamentals and do better at conceptualization.

For the gifted, the difference in conceptualization is even greater. The MACOS evaluation showed that intelligence quotients (IQs) made no difference in the amount of learning from pretest to posttest in the animals unit, but did make a difference in the Netsilik unit. Some of the important differences between the two units include: (a) in the animal unit, there is much more repetition of the basic ideas and concepts through returning to them each time a new animal is studied; (b) more inferential skill and transfer of concepts is needed in the Netsilik unit because children compare humans with all the animals studied to "discover" important similarities and differences; and (c) the unit on humans requires the most speculation and reflection upon how all the learned concepts contribute to and affect personal lives.

Throughout all these evaluations, a consistent trend emerges. Gifted students enjoy dealing with abstract, complex ideas and can handle them more easily than slower students. They need fewer examples to learn the concepts, and they need to "revisit" the ideas much less frequently in the learning process. In fact, when there are too many examples and too many returns to the ideas, they get "turned off" and do not achieve as well as when the content is accelerated or economically chosen.

Characteristics of Gifted

Added to their high ability are two other characteristics that indicate the reasons for the success of Brunerian-based curricula. One is that gifted and creative people *prefer* to use their intuition in searching for deeper meanings rather than using direct sensory data in forming impressions and making decisions. Another is that they tend to learn in a series of intuitive leaps.

Support for the idea that gifted persons prefer to use an intuitive mode for gathering information and making decisions comes from research with the *Myers-Briggs Type Indicator* (Myers & Briggs, 1971), a personality assessment tool based on Karl Jung's (1923) theory of psychological types. According to the theory, a major dimension of personality is an individual's preferred way of gathering information. The two opposite psychological types are called sensing and intuitive. A sensing person prefers to get information directly through the five senses and to stick with the verifiable facts. An intuitive person relies on the deeper meanings and possibilities obtained through intuition, based on hunches and perceptions rather than verifiable facts. Although in the general population there are fewer intuitive than sensing types (that is, approximately 75 percent are sensing, while 25 percent are intuitive), an extremely high percentage of intellectually gifted and creative individuals can be classified as intuitive types (Myers & Briggs, 1971). In fact, in MacKinnon's (1962) studies of creative people, 90 percent of the creative writers, 92 percent of the mathematicians, 93 percent of the research scientists, and 100 percent of the architects were classified as intuitive types.

Studies of concept formation (Osler & Fivel, 1961; Osler & Troutman, 1961) have provided the basis for saying that the gifted tend to learn through a series of intuitive leaps. The learning curves of the higher ability subjects showed a series of dramatic increases interspersed with an almost flat progression. Lower ability subjects showed a steady progression over a series of trials. Osler and her associates interpreted the results to mean that the high ability subjects were forming hypotheses and then testing them. When they hypothesized correctly, their performance increased dramatically. The periods when learning curves were flat occurred while subjects were operating on the basis of incorrect hypotheses. Another finding in the study was that the high ability subjects were more distracted by certain kinds of irrelevant cues than were those of lower ability. The interpretation of this finding was that those of higher ability were attempting to use all of the situational cues in forming their hypotheses, while the trial and error learning of the other subjects did not require their use of these cues.

JUDGMENTS

Advantages

Bruner's approach has a number of important characteristics to recommend its use with gifted students. First, it is a total approach that provides a framework for most if not all the curricular modifications suggested earlier. The majority of the adaptations are addressed directly by the approach (for example, content changes of abstractness, complexity, economy, organization, methodology; process changes of varied methods, higher levels of thinking, discovery), while others are suggested indirectly (for example, process modifications of pacing, open-endedness, expressing logic or reasoning, product changes of real problems, use of raw data; learning environment changes of available resources and equipment, free expression). Those not addressed, such as freedom of choice of topics, choice of method, real audiences, and self-evaluation, can easily be incorporated into the approach and would no doubt enhance its effectiveness.

A second major advantage is that evaluations have shown its effectiveness with gifted children. Since many approaches do work with these children, an added bonus of this approach is that, although it works well with gifted students, its effectiveness with average and slow students is less consistent. They seem to be unable to handle the abstract concepts without numerous examples that are often repeated. The advantage to educators, then, in answering the tough question, ''But isn't that good for *all* children?'' is that in this case, for once, the answer is ''no.'' Some of the other methods are good for all children, to some degree, so the ''no'' answer given in other situations must be endlessly qualified.

Another practical advantage is that a variety of materials and comprehensive curricula are built on this approach. Although some have been revised so that average and slow learners can be successful in using them, some are still available in their original forms. It is possible also to use the materials selectively. Usually, in using commercial materials with the gifted, the teacher must add to the materials by introducing higher level content, more challenging ideas, and so on. However, since the problem with some of the Bruner-based curricula is that there are often too many examples and activities for the abstract concepts, teachers have an easier task, leaving out rather than making up activities. Another way to be selective is to "revisit" each concept less often or fewer times. This helps avoid the unnecessary repetition that causes boredom in gifted students.

Building on the unique characteristics of gifted students while preparing them for the roles they will be likely to assume in society is one final advantage of the basic structure approach. Gifted students will need the inquiry skills and the abstract concepts. Most importantly, the attitude toward discovery—a love of learning—can carry over into their lives as adults, regardless of whether they become scholars or leaders.

Disadvantages

The major disadvantage in using Bruner's approach is that teachers have a tough role. They must not only keep up on the latest informational and theoretical developments in a field, but also must be knowledgeable enough in the methods of inquiry to be able to give children assistance in their investigations. To teach these high-level concepts adequately, the teacher must understand them. Many, if not most, elementary teachers are not knowledgeable enough about the academic areas because child development and teaching methods (for example, techniques for individualizing instruction) have been viewed as a more important part of teacher education than academic understanding. This is probably true in most cases. However, teachers of the gifted must be special persons. They may need to go back to school or in some way develop this understanding before teaching in the way Bruner would suggest. Of course, there is no way one person can be an expert in every academic area or even all the major ones, no matter how much he or she studies or how gifted a teacher he or she is.

Another problem is that even the scholars in a field have difficulty deciding what are the basic concepts that should be learned. Certainly, if scholars disagree, it will be difficult for others to reach a consensus.

CONCLUSION

Based on the available research, the basic structure approach combined with teaching methods emphasizing inquiry and discovery rather than didactic ones can be highly successful with gifted students. Although the teaching of structure and abstract concepts is a difficult task for the teacher, materials and comprehensive curricula are available as aids. With Bruner's approach, the advantages greatly outweigh the disadvantages.

RESOURCES

Background Information

Womack, J.G. *Discovering the structure of social studies.* New York City: Benziger Brothers, 1966. In the 1960s there were many efforts to explore alternative teaching methods. In the social studies field there was a movement away from isolated pieces of content toward the teaching of broad, interdisciplinary generalizations which could be applied to a variety of different situations. Bruner was one of the forerunners of this type of approach; his theory lays the groundwork for Womack's book. Womack has written both a theoretical and practical book on how to teach social studies using interdisciplinary generalizations and concepts. The first half looks at generalizations: what is a generalization, what is the function of a generalization in social studies, and what is the relationship between generalizations and concepts. Chapters include "Four Types of Social Studies Generalizations," "The Functions of Generalizations," "Testing Students on Generalizations," and "An Interdisciplinary Approach to Generalizations." The second half of the book presents model units for the classroom based on the theories of Womack. Each unit has a provocative or leading question to establish the unit, generalizations to be developed, disciplines to be studied, activities, and a reference list. Newspapers, Andrew Jackson, the desert environment, and Latin America's relationship with the United States are some of the sample units offered. These model units are by no means complete but do offer teachers a comprehensive outline. More importantly, this part of the book shows the theory in practice, and can help explain how an individual can use an interdisciplinary approach to the teaching of social studies through an actual curriculum. Although this book was not written specifically for teachers of the gifted, the benefits of using generalizations in a classroom for the gifted has been discussed by Maker (1982).

Instructional Materials and Ideas

Martin, C.I. *Elementary school social studies. Part II: The children's program.* Using generalizations in teaching gifted students is an economical and effective approach; both Bruner and Taba stress this in their models. Womack (1966) wrote a theoretical and practical book about the use of interdisciplinary generalizations in the social studies classroom; here is another practical book on the same subject. There is no theory in Martin's book, just ample and developed ideas for teachers to use. The book explains how a generalization could be taught through the elementary grades, K-6. The format is simple: a large generalization is given (i.e., People of all races, religions, and cultures have contributed to the cultural heritage. Modern society owes a debt to cultural inventors from other places and times) and then the teaching of this generalization is traced through each grade level. The content that should be taught, related generalizations, activities, and materials (books, films, filmstrips) are given for each grade. This idea is a good example of Taba's and Bruner's theories of returning to a generalization repeatedly over the years, increasing in sophistication and knowledge, until one achieves mastery of the generalization. Only two generalizations are developed in this extensive format; however, with the book as a guideline a group of teachers could easily design their own. Teachers are encouraged to add or modify the activities based on the characteristics of the gifted students in their classrooms. The book was not written specifically for gifted students but is easily adaptable.

Chapter 4

J.P. Guilford: The Structure
of Intellect

J.P. Guilford's (1959, 1967) theory of the structure of human intelligence has no doubt had a greater influence on the field of education of the gifted than any other theory or model. Its influence has been felt in all areas of programming, including definition, philosophy, identification, and testing, as well as curriculum development and teaching strategies. Indeed, the theory is used as the sole basis of many gifted programs. Perhaps its most important influence has been in expanding the concept or definition of giftedness. Prior to Guilford's work, the concept of giftedness was almost synonymous with IQ, but after his ideas spread into the educational community, the multifaceted or multidimensional conception of giftedness began to form the basis for programs.

In addition to its influence on the actual operation of programs for the gifted, Guilford's model had a great deal of influence on several of the theorists and leaders in education of the gifted. For example, Parnes, Taylor, and Williams were all stimulated in some manner by the ideas in Guilford's theory. Taylor's and Williams's approaches were actually developed as educational counterparts to Guilford's psychological model.

It is important at this point to make a distinction between the work of J.P. Guilford and the work of Mary N. Meeker. Guilford, a psychologist and theorist, spent most of his professional life conducting research on human abilities, their structure and function, and the various means of testing them. Using factor analytic statistical techniques, he attempted to identify or isolate the basic abilities that are a part of human intelligence. After several years of measuring and analyzing various tests of ability, Guilford developed a morphological model to describe what he had found through his research. After developing the model, he continued his attempts to isolate abilities predicted by the model but not yet identified by psychological tests.

Mary Meeker, an associate of Guilford's, became interested in the more practical psychological and educational implications of the model. She developed extensive testing materials, test item "mapping" procedures for development of *Structure of Intellect* ability profiles using existing test data, workbooks for use with children, computer programs for analyzing ability profiles and developing prescriptions, and materials for training teachers and others to use the model. In addition, Mary Meeker (1969) conducted research on the unique ability patterns of various cultural and clinical groups, as well as on the effectiveness of her training materials on the development of specific abilities.

One final distinction should be noted. When referring to the theoretical model, Guilford uses the abbreviation SI for the *Structure of Intellect*, while Meeker uses SOI to refer to her educational applications of the theoretical model. The same abbreviations will be used in this chapter.

Because of the extensive nature of this theory, the amount of research validating or attempting to validate it, and psychological literature written about it, this chapter can only contain an introduction to the model. It will provide a description of the basic principles of the theory and elements, but will focus mainly on the uses of the SOI model for curriculum development in education of the gifted.

BASIC ASSUMPTIONS UNDERLYING GUILFORD'S MODEL

About Intelligence

According to Guilford (1959, 1967), intelligence has three facets or dimensions: (a) content or information; (b) mental operations; and (c) products. Every human ability has these three dimensions and can be classified according to the sub-categories within each dimension. These abilities are related, but are identifiable as 120 separate entities. The best model a person can construct to explain graphically the structure and relationships among these postulated abilities is a three-dimensional cube or morphological model. (See Figure 4-1.) Each of the facets is one dimension of the cube, and each separate ability is one cell that can be identified by the intersection of the three dimensions. For example, the cell in the lower left corner would bear the identification CFU because the operation involved is *C*ognition, the content is *F*igural, and the product is *I*mplications.

Each individual may not possess all of the abilites, but in a large population of people, Guilford believes that all of the abilities could be identified. Also, this is a model of adult or mature intelligence; young children would not be expected to demonstrate all of the abilities.

Perhaps the most basic idea underlying the model is Guilford's multidimensional, multifaceted view of intelligence. Essentially he believes that there are many "intelligences" rather than a unitary trait of general intelligence. His view of intelligence does not consider creativity as separate from intelligence; rather, it is an aspect of intelligence. Creative abilities seem to be concentrated in the

Figure 4-1 The Structure of Intellect Model

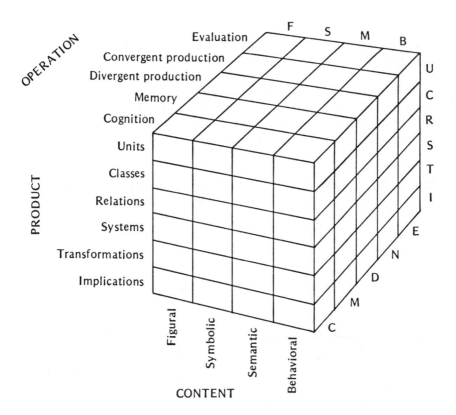

Source: Reprinted with permission from J.P. Guilford, *The nature of human intelligence,* New York: McGraw-Hill, 1967.

operation of divergent production and the product of transformations. In the past, tests of intelligence, which are largely scored according to "correctness" of answers, have tapped only the operations of cognition, memory, and convergent production. Tests of creativity, however, have measured divergent production because scores are derived from quality and quantity of answers rather than correctness. This has led to the view that intelligence and creativity are different constructs since they have a low relationship in some people. On the basis of Guilford's (1967) model and his research, a low relationship would be predicted, however, because divergent production as an operation is very different from cognition and convergent production.

A fuller understanding of the significance of Guilford's model (Maker, Note 7) can be gained by comparing the model with the conceptions of intelligence underlying the two most commonly used tests of intelligence, the *Wechsler Scales* and the *Stanford-Binet*. (See Figures 4-2 and 4-3.*) Wechsler recognizes a natural division of abilities: verbal and performance. Verbal ability is measured by information, comprehension, arithmetic, digits, similarities, and vocabulary subtests, while performance ability is measured by picture completion, picture arrangement, object assembly, block design, and digit span subtests. Verbal ability is more general than vocabulary and thus is of a higher order. A vocabulary test measures abilities more like those measured by comprehension tests than those measured by a block design test, so these tests are clustered together. Verbal and

Figure 4-2 Illustration of Wechsler's Theory of the Nature of Human Intelligence by Using a Hierarchical Model

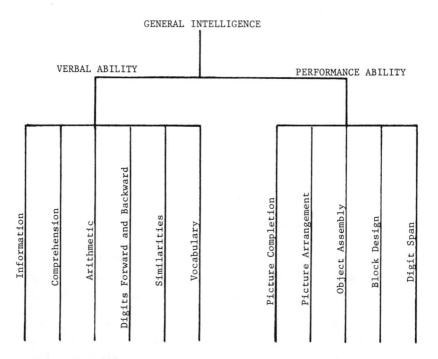

Source: J. Maker. *Intelligence test construction–A comparison of methods*. Unpublished paper, 1974. (Available from Dr. J. Maker, Department of Special Education, University of Arizona, Tucson, Arizona.)

*The models were derived from this writer's understanding of their theories and not from any graphic models in their writing.

Figure 4-3 Illustration of Binet's Theory of the Nature of Human Intelligence by Using a Hierarchical Model

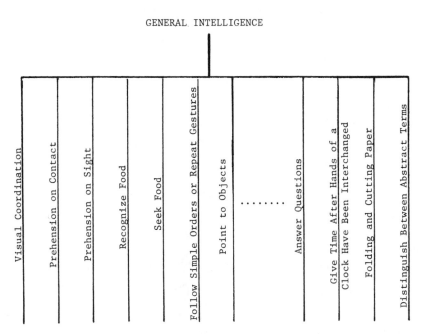

Source: J. Maker. *Intelligence test construction–A comparison of methods.* Unpublished paper, 1974. (Available from Dr. J. Maker, Department of Special Education, University of Arizona, Tucson, Arizona.)

performance tests are related in that they both measure general intelligence. Binet, on the other hand, sees all the tests in his scales as being equal measures of general intelligence; therefore, there is one general aspect and a number of specific ones that are related, in that they all measure part of the same construct.

Guilford, however, does not feel that hierarchical models such as these two are sufficient to explain the interrelationships in human abilities. A model of this type, for example, cannot explain why certain verbal tests, such as information, correlate highly with certain performance tests, such as block design, while certain other verbal tests have a low correlation with some of the performance tests.

Guilford's morphological model explains such phenomena in this way. Each cell in the cube is related to all other cells in the row and column in which it appears. For example, a test involving cognition of figural implications (CFI) is related to implications involving all content, all operations performed on figural content, and all products resulting from cognition of figural content. Figure 4-4 shows the section of Guilford's model that illustrates these relationships.

Figure 4-4 Section of the Structure of Intellect Model Illustrating Relationships between Abilities

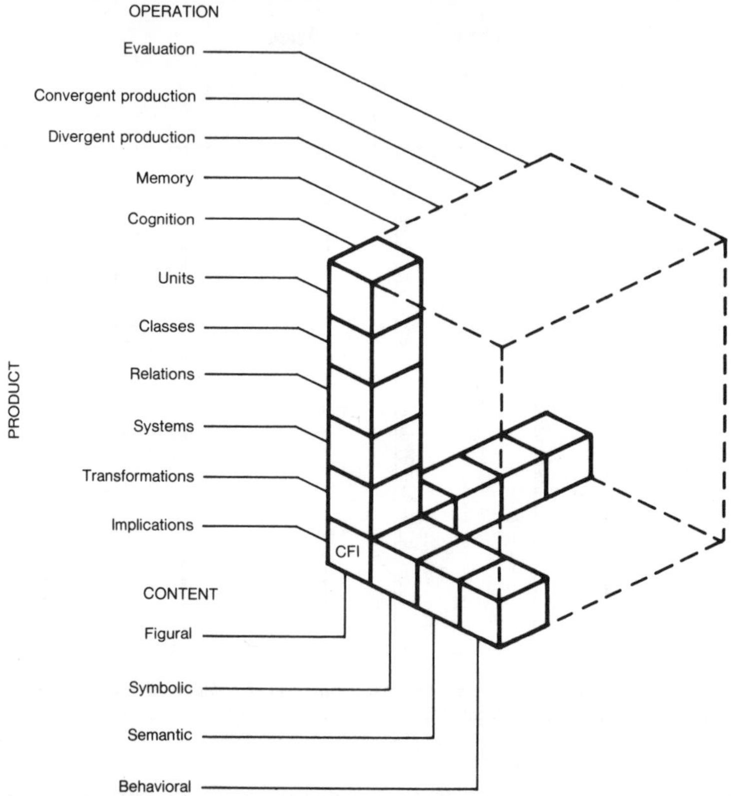

OPERATION

Evaluation

Convergent production

Divergent production

Memory

Cognition

Units

Classes

PRODUCT

Relations

Systems

Transformations

Implications

CFI

CONTENT

Figural

Symbolic

Semantic

Behavioral

Source: Adapted from J.P. Guilford. *The nature of human intelligence.* New York: McGraw-Hill, 1967.

In summary, two major philosophical differences between Binet, Terman, Wechsler, and Guilford have influenced their development of tests of intelligence: general intelligence and rate of intellectual development.

General Intelligence

Binet and Terman believe that even though intelligence is many-faceted, the parts are not separate and an individual's general level of intelligence is determined by the combined functional capacity of these separate abilities. In contrast, Guilford believes that the parts are separate and can be differentiated, there is a definite kind of relationship among groups of abilities, and there is no "general intelligence factor" that is present in all these separate abilities. Guilford (1972) does suggest, however, that there may be some underlying abilities that correspond roughly to certain of the dimensions (that is, memory, semantic, transformation) along with some lesser general abilities (that is, visual memory, behavioral divergent production, or symbolic cognition). Although Wechsler leans more toward the position of Binet and Terman, he recognizes that the assessment of separate abilities and combination of the results is not enough to explain intelligent behavior adequately.

Rate of Intellectual Development

Binet, Terman, and Wechsler seem to agree that general intelligence increases with age, each individual's rate of development is relatively stable, and a more intelligent person's rate of development will be more accelerated than that of an average person. Although Guilford does not address the issues directly, he seems to be saying that there is no single rate of development for each ability that is the same for all individuals. It would be impossible to determine which person would be the most intelligent without specifying "most intelligent in what." In determining intellectual capacity, rather than being concerned about the rate at which certain abilities are acquired, Guilford is interested in the number and kind of abilities that were ultimately acquired, or the number and kind possessed by a person at a given time.

Another difference between Guilford's (1967) theory and the psychometric conceptions of intelligence is his focus on the *nature* of intelligence rather than *level* of intelligence. In most conceptions of intelligence, the level of ability is determined by comparison of one individual with age-level peers and with those who are younger. Those who, at one age, can perform just as well as individuals who are one or two years older are considered more intelligent than those who perform at the same level as others of their own age. Thus, giftedness implies accelerated intellectual development.

Guilford (1972, 1975), on the other hand, considers those who possess a greater number of abilities in general or who possess a greater number of abilities from a particular cluster to be gifted. For example, talented artists, sculptors, and mechanics are high in abilities involving figural content, while talented mathematicians are high in abilities involving symbolic content. Creative individuals are high in the abilities involving the operation of divergent production and in the product area of transformations. The implication, then, is to identify these clusters and choose children for special programs based on their profiles within these clusters.

About Learning and Teaching

In any discussion of intelligence and its development, the haunting question of the role of heredity and environment in the development of abilities must be addressed. Guilford (1967), in summarizing the research, concludes that both heredity and environment establish upper limits for development. However, an individual rarely reaches those upper limits. Guilford indicates that no statement can be made about the lower limits, and he recommends that educators accept the possibility that every intellectual factor can be developed to some extent by learning. If education has the goal of developing the intellect of students, then each factor or ability is a potential goal. However, since not all SI abilities are equally important for all people, some value judgments have to be made to determine the emphasis for each person. Guilford suggests that a balance is needed in developing the whole intellect and all dimensions. Once decisions have been made about the emphasis on abilities, a particular curriculum and teaching method can be designed to develop these abilities.

According to Guilford (1959) most learning probably has both specific and general aspects. The general aspects are along the lines of the dimensions and factors, while the specific aspects pertain to individual tasks. It is important to note (Guilford, 1972) that different kinds of abilities from the SI model are involved in different kinds of school learning. For example, obtaining information through reading (that is, reading comprehension) depends most on the SI ability cognition of semantic units, while the act of learning to read involves mainly cognition, memory, and evaluation of figural units. Other memory abilities, such as memory of symbolic and semantic transformations, are related to reading achievement at later stages of elementary school. Thus, the educator must be aware of the types of abilities necessary for certain kinds of learning so that these underlying abilities can be developed to facilitate a child's school learning in certain areas. Since the SI abilities are considered general influences on learning (because they are *classes* of abilities), training in these abilities will transfer readily to different kinds of tasks within the same category.

One final assumption Guilford (1972) makes is related to the value of instruction in developing intellectual abilities. Because of his belief that knowledge of the range of intellectual characteristics and their value in all types of learning enhances performance, he recommends that educators teach children about their abilities as early as they can understand them. Children should be taught the nature of abilities in general and they should be given information about their own strengths and weaknesses in abilities and about areas of achievement. Self-knowledge related to both abilities and personality traits, he notes, may reduce the likelihood that young people will complain that "they do not know who they are" (1972, p. 184).

About Teaching the Gifted

Although he does not address the issue directly, Guilford (1972) suggests that after children are selected for a special program because of their particular kind of intelligence, educators should attempt to develop all their abilities within that cluster. For example, he recommends that in the selection of children as potential leaders, educators should pay particular attention to their "social intelligence" indicated by abilities that involve behavioral content. Leaders need to be able to communicate more fully with others and need to develop skills in managing others. These recommendations imply that children should be given training in all of the operations as applied to behavioral content.

Guilford also makes similar recommendations for the development of creative talent. For these children, the educational program must concentrate on the development of divergent production, transformations, and evaluation. The two operations—divergent production and evaluation—should be separated, though, because evaluation puts a damper on productivity. Because creative individuals are independent and often inattentive to criticism of their performance by others, they should be taught the process and value of self-evaluation.

A somewhat different recommendation relates to the development of creative-productive abilities in children with high IQs. In making this suggestion, Guilford (1972, 1975) departs somewhat from the position that educators should try to develop the cluster of abilities in which the individual shows a particular talent. Although he states that when children are selected because of their high IQs educators should expect a high proportion who are superior in divergent production abilities, he also notes that many children with high IQs are low in divergent production. With these children, he says that the development of creative capacities promises "the greatest payoff for individuals and for society" (Guilford, 1972, p. 240). This idea reveals the implicit assumption that concentration on a set of abilities different from their identified strengths would be more valuable than development of the cluster in which they have already shown high potential.

The recommendation of developing creative potential in children with high IQs also seems, at first glance, to conflict with an assumption Guilford makes about the relationship of motivation to abilities. He proposes the idea that "an individual high in an ability has also an urge to use it" (1972, p. 181). If this assumption is correct, those who are high in the convergent production abilities required for performance at a gifted level on an IQ test but who are low in divergent production would be motivated to perform in convergent production tasks but not in those requiring divergent production. Thus, an educator who attempts to develop the child's divergent production abilities will encounter a motivational problem as well. Guilford notes that the only clear example of an interest or motivational factor is a definite preference in many people for either divergent or convergent production. The only resolution of this apparent contradiction seems to be the additional assumption that if the abilities can be developed, the motivation will result, and these individuals will become productive adults in both the convergent and divergent processes.

ELEMENTS/PARTS

The SI model (Guilford, 1959, 1967) depicts human intelligence as consisting of three "faces" or dimensions: (1) an *operation* is performed on a particular kind of (2) *content,* yielding a certain type of (3) *product.* There are four types of information or content of thought: (1) figural; (2) semantic; (3) symbolic; and (4) behavioral. There are five types of thinking processes or operations: (1) cognition; (2) memory; (3) convergent production; (4) divergent production; and (5) evaluation. When the intellect acts upon a particular type of content, the result is one of the six types of products: (1) units; (2) classes; (3) relations; (4) systems; (5) transformations; and (6) implications. The intersection of each of the three dimensions results in a unique ability or a component of intelligence. This means that there are potentially 120 separate human abilities ($4 \times 5 \times 6 = 120$).*

Content

The first and most primitive type of content is *figural* (F). It includes concrete objects or forms that are perceived visually, auditory elements such as rhythms and simple sounds, and tactual or kinesthetic materials. Figural content has sensory character. *Symbolic* (S) information includes signs and other materials that have no meaning in and of themselves, but that represent something. These codes can be combined in many ways and include such items as letters, numbers, musical notations, and universal traffic signals. The third type of information, *semantic* (M), differs from figural and symbolic in that it has meaning. Usually these meanings are external. For example, the word "house" is semantic content, because it relates to an image in a person's mind. It is somewhat abstract in that one person's image of its meaning may be different from another's image. *Behavioral* (B) content is nonverbal information pertaining to human interactions. The actions, emotions, intentions, and moods of people are interpreted without the aid of verbal cues. Behavioral information includes body language and facial expressions that are evidence of some affective state. See Figure 4-5 for examples of each of these types of content.

---

*In Meeker's educational applications of Guilford's theory, each of these abilities is represented by a trigram symbol containing a letter from the content, process, and product dimensions. This letter is usually the first letter from each type within each dimension. For example, the ability involving the operation of Cognition, Figural content, and the product area of Units is referred to as CFU. The operation is listed first, the content second, and the product last. In this chapter, the same system of notation will be used. In the first explanation of abilities, the whole names will be listed. However, in subsequent references, only the trigrams will be used.

Figure 4-5 Examples of Types of Content in Guilford's Structure of Intellect Model

Figural Information

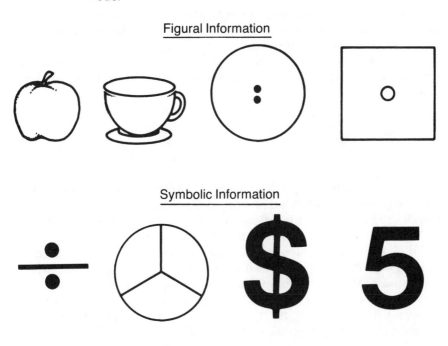

Symbolic Information

Semantic Information

tree   pencil

pest   ruler

animal   paper

Behavioral Information

Operations

The operations or thinking processes in Guilford's (1967) model are not hierarchical. They are simply different abilities. *Cognition* (C), the most basic of the operations, is recognition or perception of a stimulus. It is the immediate discovery of various forms of content. For example, in one of Guilford's (1977) tests called "disemvoweled" words, the task is to recognize familiar words without their vowels:

p-ct-r-	(picture)
s-lf	(self)
c-l-br-t--n	(celebration)

This involves cognition of symbolic units (CSU). Another example of cognition is the familiar test item in which sets of items are given along with one item belonging to each of the sets. The task is to figure out which of the extra items belongs with each set. This involves cognition of figural classes (CFC).

The second operation is *memory* (M) or remembering any type of information. It includes ways of storing information and the ability to retrieve the information when needed. Most of the items testing memory require the individual to study some information and then reconstruct that information on a test page. In one test, Monogram Recall (Guilford, 1977), several different arrangements of three letters are given on the study page, such as:

On the test page, only the three letters, C J M, are given and the task is to reconstruct the arrangements seen earlier. This item tests memory of figural systems (MFS).

Convergent production (N) is generating answers when there is a correct answer and when the solution requires more than just retrieval or recognition. The first component of the definition, the availability of a conventionally accepted best or correct answer, distinguishes convergent production from divergent production. The second component requires more than recall and distinguishes it from memory. In convergent production, new information is generated from given information. For example, a well-known item from the *Wechsler Intelligence Scales for Children–Revised* (WISC-R) requires the person to put a series of pictures into their correct order. This Picture Arrangement Test taps the ability of convergent production of semantic systems (NMS). Another example involves convergent production of semantic relations (NMR) (Guilford, 1977, pp. 115-16):

> What word is related to both words in each pair?
> 1. nonsense .... bed
> 2. recline .... deceive
> 3. hit .... fruit drink
> 4. tiresome .... drilling
> 5. sphere .... dance.

The answers are bunk, lie, punch, boring, and ball.

Divergent production (D) is generation of information when the emphasis is on variety, quantity, and quality rather than on a best or correct solution. In divergent production, more information is usually generated than was initially given. For example, an item measuring divergent production of semantic units (DMU) requires a person to generate titles for a story. In another item (testing divergent production of semantic systems (DMS)), the task is to generate several analogies from one given pair:

> SLEEP is to BED as _____ is to _____ .
> SLEEP is to BED as _____ is to _____ .
> SLEEP is to BED as _____ is to _____ .
> SLEEP is to BED as _____ is to _____ .
> SLEEP is to BED as _____ is to _____ .

Evaluation is decision making or making judgments about something. It requires decisions on the basis of known or understood standards. For example, in one item, a principle for a number series is given (for example, contains odd numbers and skips two numbers each time), and a group of series, some of which follow the principle and some of which do not is also given. The task is to decide which series follow the principle. This item tests evaluation of symbolic systems (ESS).

Products

The product dimension is concerned with the way figural, symbolic, semantic, or behavioral content is organized. The product dimension can be considered hierarchical or at least inclusive in that later products subsume earlier ones (for example, systems include relations, relations include classes, classes include units). *Units* (U) are the simplest form of product. A unit is a single item, for example, one figure, one symbol, or one idea. *Classes* (C) are categories or classifications of items grouped together because they have certain properties in common. *Relations* (R) are connections between items of information or between classes of information. *Systems* (S), complex types of information, are composed of more than two interconnected units. Systems are organized or structured complexes of interrelated parts, such as melodies and rhythms (auditory), numbers in a series, sequences of events, or cartoon strips. *Transformations* (T) are modifications of existing information so that a new item is created. Some examples of transformations are rotation of an object, reading words spelled backwards, and substitutions of meaning of words, as in making puns. *Implications* (I) are predictions made from the given information. They include generalizations or expectations that are extended beyond what is given. The most common example of implications is in the semantic area in the form of prediction of future events based on past or present events or conditions. Figure 4-6 contains some examples of each type of product. In the examples, only two types of information are illustrated, figural and symbolic. Since this information is the most concrete, these items are more simple than items containing semantic or behavioral content. In addition, the items chosen were selected because of their simplicity so that the reader can quickly understand them. Many similar items can be designed that are more difficult.

According to Guilford (1972), teachers who wish to apply SI theory in their classrooms need not memorize each of the 120 abilities and their descriptions. Knowledge of the 15 basic types of content, processes, and products, and an understanding of how they can be combined is sufficient for the curriculum planner. Mary Meeker, however, has recognized the need for developing a series of aids for the teacher including tests, computer analysis of profiles, workbooks, worksheets, and educational games. The following sections draw mainly upon her extensive work in the application of the SI theory to educational practice through the SOI materials and principles.

Curriculum Planning Based on the SOI

The general approach advocated by Mary Meeker (1969) is an individualized one based on the analysis of a student's intellectual profile of strengths and weaknesses in the ability areas identified in the SI model. This profile can be developed through an analysis of existing psychological test data or through testing with instruments designed to assess abilities included in Guilford's model. When a profile has been developed, an individualized education plan is designed for each child. Depending on the student, this prescription will be based on development of strengths, weaknesses, weaknesses through strengths, or a combination of strengths and weaknesses. Meeker's general guidelines for the gifted without handicaps focus on a balance between development of strengths and remediation of weak areas. Work on individual SOI prescriptions should result in significant gains if approximately 20 minutes is spent on the activity three times a week

Figure 4-6 Examples of Types of Products in Guilford's Structure of Intellect Model

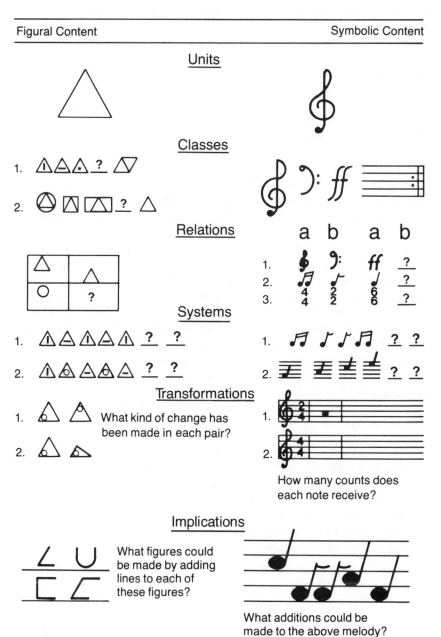

Figural Content	Symbolic Content

Units

Classes

1.

2.

Relations

a b   a b

1.
2.
3.

Systems

1.

2.

Transformations

1. What kind of change has been made in each pair?

2.

1.

2.

How many counts does each note receive?

Implications

What figures could be made by adding lines to each of these figures?

What additions could be made to the above melody?

(Meeker, 1969). Student gains in all abilities, especially the target areas, should be evaluated periodically by administering the pretests again or by administering any of Guilford's tasks used for identifying the ability. To provide a concrete example of the application of the SOI to curriculum planning, the following example shows how an individualized plan was developed for a highly creative, highly intelligent boy, David M.*

David had been referred for testing to determine whether he should be served by a gifted program, but had not scored above 130 on the WISC-R. His teacher noticed his creative writing and drawing ability along with his superior achievement and felt he needed some extra services. He came to the author's attention when his mother, a student of the author, brought in some of his stories and drawings, explaining that she could not understand why a boy who could write these stories would not score high enough on an IQ test to be placed in a program for the gifted. His work was truly remarkable, so the author encouraged her to do some further testing in an attempt to determine David's intellectual strengths and weaknesses, and plan some teaching strategies that could be implemented by his classroom teacher.

David was first given the *Structure of Intellect Learning Abilities Test* (SOI-LA), and it was sent to Mary Meeker for analysis. David's profile was interesting, showing a great deal of strength in divergent thinking, semantic content, and units, with some specific weaknesses in classes, implications, convergent production, and evaluation. (See Table 4-1.) Based on what was known about David, some supplementary information was needed from at least one more test. To detect a possible strength in transformations or implications because of his creativity, he was given both the figural and verbal forms of the *Torrance Tests of Creative Thinking* (TTCT). His responses were so amazing (see Figure 4-7) that neither of the test givers felt competent enough to score his test, so it was mailed to Paul Torrance for scoring by the experts. Torrance's (Note 8) reply included the following evaluation:

> When I evaluated his figural test, I thought he may share a lack of flexibility with other highly creative learning disabled children. However, he shows an extraordinary flexibility on the verbal tests. Even his low flexibility score on the figural test is due to a creative kind of behavior which does not characterize most creative learning disabled youngsters. His low flexibility score resulted from his hitchhiking and interrelating the incomplete figures and the related figures.
>
> From both sets of performances, it is clear that this boy possesses a rich store of information and images. In many ways, he is quite sophisticated in this thinking.

---

*The information presented here is only part of David's profile presented by Maker (1982).

Table 4-1 David M.'s SOI-LA Profile

SOI DIMENSION	ADJUSTED SCORES			SUMMARY SCORES % of DIMENSION	STRONG/WEAK INDEX (1=Weakest 9=Strongest)
OPERATIONS:					
Cognition	54.96	of	72	0.76	4
Memory	25.42	of	32	0.79	4
Evaluation	23.17	of	32	0.72	3
Convergent	22.90	of	32	0.71	2
Divergent	24.01	of	24	1.00	9
CONTENTS:					
Figural	55.50	of	72	0.77	4
Symbolic	66.53	of	88	0.75	3
Semantic	28.44	of	32	0.88	7
PRODUCTS:					
Units	58.08	of	64	0.90	7
Classes	15.20	of	24	0.63	1
Relations	17.80	of	24	0.74	3
Systems	36.37	of	48	0.75	4
Transformations	11.88	of	16	0.74	3
Implications	11.11	of	16	0.69	2

Source: M. Meeker and R. Meeker. SOI learning abilities test (rev. ed.). El Segundo, Calif.: SOI Institute, 1979.

Figure 4-7 A Sample of David M.'s Responses on the Torrance Test of
Creative Thinking—Figural Form A

Activity 2. PICTURE COMPLETION

By adding lines to the incomplete figures on this and the next page, you can sketch some interesting objects or pictures. Again, try to think of some picture or object that no one else will think of. Try to make it tell as complete and as interesting a story as you can by adding to and building up your first idea. Make up an interesting title for each of your drawings and write it at the bottom of each block next to the number of the figure.

Source: E.P. Torrance. *The Torrance tests of creative thinking.* Lexington, Mass.: Ginn and Co., 1972.

Figure 4-7 continued

The scores indicated that David certainly does have strengths in transformations and implications, as evidenced by his "creativity index" of 176 on the figural form and his T score of 200+ on the verbal form. His WISC-R scores were also quickly reviewed to see what information from this test would support or change the test givers' perceptions of strengths and weaknesses based on the SOI-LA test. From this rather cursory review, it was noted that he scored much lower on the similarities subtest than would be expected given his high verbal ability. This supports the information from the SOI-LA showing a definite weakness in classes.

Armed with the data from Meeker's computer analysis (including a prescription based on the results of the SOI-LA test), supplementary information from the TTCT, SOI workbooks on each of the operations, and Meeker's general instructions for the development of individual curriculum programs, David's evaluators sat down to figure out a plan for him. The general procedure (Meeker, 1969) calls for two types of strategies: (1) remediation of specific weaknesses and development of specific strengths through concentration on individual "cells" targeted for work; and (2) remediation of general weaknesses and development of general strengths by combining a strength with a weakness. For example, if a student shows a weakness in one of the operations, the strategy is to look for a strength in one of the content and/or product dimensions to combine with it. If there is a deficit in one of the contents, then the strategy would be to look for a strength in one of the operations and/or products to match with the weak area. In certain instances, particularly if the student has a low self-concept or is sensitive to failure, two strengths should be combined with one weakness. When the student has a long history of failure or is extremely sensitive, the teacher should begin with only strengths and work toward combining one weak area with two strengths, and eventually combining two weaknesses with one strength.

To implement the first strategy, working on specific strengths and weaknesses, the evaluators consulted David and discussed the areas of weakness, asking for his input into decisions about what cells should be the targets for remediation and development. The weak areas chosen for remediation were the following: *EFC*, *NFU*, *MSS*, *CFS*, *CSS*, and *ESS*. The strengths chosen for development were the following: *CFU*, *CFT*, *DFU*, *DMU*, *DSR*, *CMR*, and *MSU*. After identifying the target cells, the next step was to select activities at the appropriate level from the SOI workbooks. David's prescription provided an analysis of his scores by grade level, so the identification of specific lessons was quite simple. (See Table 4-2.) Some of his weaknesses are as low as grade two and three, while others are at grades four and five. All his strengths are at grade eleven and above. An example of an exercise chosen to remediate his weakest area (EFC) is the activity in Exhibit 4-1 from the basic workbook for evaluation (Meeker, 1976).

To remediate David's strongest area, DFU, the activity in Exhibit 4-2 from the advanced workbook for divergent production (Meeker, 1969) was chosen.

Table 4-2 Graph of Obtained Scores for David M. on the SOI-LA Test

CELL	Grade 1	Grade 2	Grade 3	Grade 4	Grade 5	Grade 6		Grade 11
CFU							*	.14
CFU					.6		*	
CFS				18			*	
CFT							*	16
CSR						..6	*	
CSS					5		*	
CMU							*	24
CMR							*	24
CMS							*	20
MFU							*	19
MSU							*	18
MSS			14				*	
MSI							*	13
EFU						..22	*	

Source: M. Meeker and R. Meeker. *SOI learning abilities test* (rev. ed.). El Segundo, Calif.: SOI Institute, 1979.

Table 4-2 continued

CELL	Grade 1	Grade 2	Grade 3	Grade 4	Grade 5	Grade 6	Grade 11
EFC	7					*	
ESC						*	24
ESS				6			
NFU			19			*	
NSS					6	*	
NST						*	175
NSI			14			*	
DFU						*	92
DMU						*	118
DSR						*	96

Exhibit 4-1 Sample Activity to Remediate David M's Weakest Area (EFC)

ABILITY: Evaluation of Figural Classes

SUBJECT: Conceptualizing

OBJECTIVE: The student will be able to develop the ability to judge whether figural units are properly classified; the task for the student is to analyze how units are classified and then judge how other units are similarly classified in another group of figures or forms.

MATERIALS: Scissors
See Exercise Sheet EFC-2

INSTRUCTIONS:
Discuss the meanings of these words before beginning this lesson: triangle, float, living plants, initials, frame.
General:
This kind of exercise prepares students for understanding analogies. Reproduce Exercise Sheet EFC-2 for each student.
Specific:
1. Present frame one and explain to students how they are alike—both are triangles. Present frame two and help students see that these are different—one is a toy and the other is not, only one has a triangular shape.
2. Look at the other cards. Mark the ones that are *not* alike because they *do not belong to the same group.*
3. Now see which ones match.
Possible matches;
1 & 8 (shape)
4 & 6 (shape)
5 & 9 (nature) and so on (p.11)

To complete the program prescription, general strategies involving the combination of strengths and weaknesses had to be developed. Since David does not have anxiety about failure and is a strong person, the strategy of combining one strength with two weaknesses would have been no problem. However, the evaluators also wanted to emphasize the development of strengths, and in most cases, two strong areas would be combined with one weak one. The general strategies suggested in the prescription received from the SOI Institute are shown in Exhibit 4-3 and Exhibit 4-4.

As seen from the recommendations in Exhibit 4-4, David's weakness in the product area of classes would be remediated through his strength in the operation of divergent thinking and the semantic content area, which emphasizes the DMC cell. His weakness in symbolic content would be remediated through his strength in divergent thinking and his strength in the product area of units. Since additional information showing that David really does have strengths in transformations and

Exhibit 4-2 Sample Activity to Remediate David M's Strongest Area (DFU)

ABILITY: Divergent Production of Figural Units (DFU)

OBJECTIVE: The student will be able to develop the ability to produce many figures conforming to simple specifications.

MATERIALS

Put these shapes on the board:

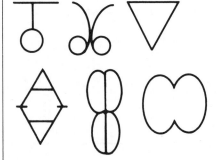

INSTRUCTIONS

SPECIFIC:
1. Ask: What is the next symbol in this series? Allow 15 minutes before the end of the period. Give a weekend for time to solve the problem.
2. What is the next letter in this "a" series? "b" series?

a   J F M A M J
       J A S O N

b   OTTFFSSE

Answers:
Mirror images of numbers
First letter of months
First letter of numbers

Exhibit 4-3 Strategy 1: Target Specific in SOI Workbooks

Single Cell Discrimination:	Subtest Weakness	Cells to be Remediated
		DMU
		CFU
		CMU
		CFS
		CFT
		CMS
		DSR
		CSR
		MSS
		MSI
		EFU
		CFC
		EFC
		ESC
		CSS
		ESS
		NSS
		NST
		NSI
		MFU
		NFU

Exhibit 4-4 Strategy 2: Strengths through Weaknesses

Summary Discrimination:	Dimensional Weaknesses	Cells to be Exercised
Weakness: Classes		
Remediate Through Strength In:	Divergent.....	And Semantic... ...DMC
Weakness: Convergent		
Remediate Through Strength In:	Semantic....	And Units ....NMU
Weakness: Implications		
Remediate Through Strength In:	Divergent....	And Semantic ... ...DMI
Weakness: Evaluation		
Remediate Through Strength In:	Semantic...	And Units ....EMU
Weakness: Symbolic		
Remediate Through Strength In:	Divergent....	And Units ....DSU
Weakness: Relations		
Remediate Through Strength In:	Divergent...	And Semantic... ...DMR
Weakness: Transformations		
Remediate Through Strength In:	Divergent....	And Semantic ... ...DMT
Weakness: Memory		
Remediate Through Strength In:	Semantic....	And Units ....MMU
Weakness: Figural		
Remediate Through Strength In:	Divergent....	And Units ....DFU

figural content had been gathered, based on his performance on the *Torrance Tests of Creative Thinking*, the prescription was modified somewhat, and the following general strategy was developed:

- His weakness in *classes* would be remediated through his strengths in divergent production, semantic content, and figural content, leading to the exercise of DMC and DFC cells.

- His weakness in *convergent production* would be remediated through his strengths in semantic and figural content, and through his strengths in units, transformations, and implications. This leads to the exercise of NMU, NMT, NMI, NFU, NFT, and NFI.

- His weakness in *evaluation* would be remediated through the strength in semantic and figural content and through his strength in units, transformations, and implications. This would lead to the exercise of EMU, EMT, EMI, EFU, EFT, and EFI.

- The *symbolic* weakness would be remediated through strengths in divergent production, units, transformations, and implications. In this case, DSU, DST, and DSI would be the cells receiving exercise.

- The weak area of *relations* would be reached through strengths in divergent production, figural content, and semantic content. Thus, there would be concentration on DFR and DMR.

- *Memory* would be reached through his strengths in figural and semantic content and his strength in units, transformations, and implications. The MMU, MMT, MMI, MFU, MFT, and MFI cells would be the areas of concentration.

With this general plan, activities from the workbooks designed to develop the particular SI abilities to be exercised could be selected. General types of learning activities could also be developed to suggest to his teacher. His teacher would be given an individualized prescription in the form of a booklet containing exercises for David to do for certain periods of the day. He would work on these for an average of a half hour every day, but the amount of time spent each day would depend on his other activities and his free time during that day. In addition, it was recommended that the *New Directions in Creativity* program (Callahan & Renzulli, 1977) be used with the class since all children would profit from the divergent thinking exercises. Activities from this program that would be particularly important for David are Words with Feeling (DMC), Sames and Opposites, Comparisons, Word Trees, Crunch-Munch (DMR), Fun With Words, Time to Rhyme, Making Words with Prefixes and Suffixes, Building Words (SUD), Wandering Words (DST), Figure Families (DFC), Say it with Symbols, and Make a Character (DFR). Other activities in the program would continue the development of his strengths in divergent production.

As an overall strategy for dealing with these activities it was recommended that in brainstorming or listing activities, such as Alternate or Unusual Uses of Common Objects, David should be encouraged to evaluate his own ability to produce different classes or categories of answers. This could be done through Taba's *Strategy of Concept Development*, which has students generate a list; make groups or categories of answers; and then label, subsume, and regroup. (See Chapter 8.) The task should also be modified at step four, Subsuming, by having David concentrate on generating additional items for the categories he develops and at steps three and five, Grouping, having him concentrate on generating categories that were not included in the original list. He could also generate items from these categories. This modification of Taba's concept development strategy would strengthen his weakness in classes, while at the same time build his retrieval from memory and strengthen his divergent production.

Another helpful program suggested for David was the *SOI Group Memory Test and Training Manual* (Meeker, 1973), which includes exercises for training visual memory, visual-sequential memory, auditory memory, and auditory-sequential memory for both figural, symbolic, and semantic content. To develop his evaluative abilities and as an overall strategy, *Creative Problem Solving* was recommended with emphasis on strategies for solution-finding, using the grid and other similar methods. (See Chapter 6.) Critical thinking skills as described by Ennis (1964) were also recommended for emphasis.

After this program is used with David for three or four months, his progress in each of the target cells will be evaluated to determine whether changes should be made in the program. At the end of the school year, he will be evaluated again. These evaluations can be done formally by readministering the SOI-LA test or by informal evaluations using some of the practice exercises.

Table 4-3 summarizes the process for developing individual prescriptions for gifted and talented students. It provides a summary of teacher and student roles and activities at each step in the process of implementing an individualized program based on the SOI approach. In this model, the teacher's role is primarily that of a diagnostic-prescriptive specialist except in the planning of general strategies (step four) for development. Students generally follow the prescription except for their involvement in decisions about targeted areas.

MODIFICATIONS OF THE BASIC CURRICULUM

Content Modifications

The Guilford model with Meeker's applications suggests some modifications of the basic curriculum in all four areas. One content change is directly recommended by the model, while two are suggested indirectly. The major content modification,

Table 4-3 Summary of Teacher and Student Roles and Activities in the Implementation of the SOI Approach

Step, Type, or Level of Thinking	Student		Teacher	
	Role	Sample Activities	Role	Sample Activities
Assess level of functioning on SI Abilities	test-taker	Take tests administered by the teacher, psychologist or counselor.	tester	Administer informal tests on individual abilities. Locate or administer other ability tests that can be analyzed for the purpose of developing a profile of SI abilities Administer formalized tests of SI abilities, including choice of any of all of the following instruments: 1. SOI-LA 2. Guilford Creativity Tests for Children

Develop a profile of SI Abilities	none	Students are not really involved in this step.	diagnos-tician	3. SOI Screening Form for Gifted 4. SOI Reading Readiness Test 5. SOI Reading Test 6. SOI Math Test 7. SOI Figural-Symbolic-Semantic Memory Test 8. SOI-LA Career and Vocational Form Organize test information to facilitate interpretation. Develop classroom, school, program, or intra-individual norms to facilitate comparison.

Table 4-3 continued

Step, Type, or Level of Thinking	Student		Teacher	
	Role	Sample Activities	Role	Sample Activities
				Develop tables of expected scores and ranges.
				Send test protocols to SOI institute for analysis of the basic profile and also the career and vocational analysis.
				Using templates, develop an SOI profile using existing tests of abilities such as the WISC-R, Binet, CTBS, Hiskey-Nebraska, Slosson, Detroit, and the Porch Index of Communicative Ability in Children (PICAC).
				Develop graphs or other graphic displays of profiles for easy interpretation and explanation to parents and students.

| Develop a plan for specific remediation of weak areas and development of strong areas | assistant in deci- sion making | Review profile of intellectual strengths and weaknesses and decide which weak areas are important to work on. Decide which strong areas to develop. Review career and vocational analysis to determine abili- ties needing development for careers of interest | instructional planner | Share results of testing and test interpretation with students and parents. With input from the student and parents, develop a list of specific SOI cells needing remediation and development, Select activities from SOI work- books or worksheets at the student's level of functioning in each ability. Develop activities other than workbooks and worksheets based on descriptions in Meeker's (1969) and Guilford's (1967, 1977) books. |

Table 4-3 continued

Step, Type, or Level of Thinking	Student		Teacher	
	Role	Sample Activities	Role	Sample Activities
Develop a plan for remediation and enhancement by combining strong and weak areas	assistant in deci-sion making learner	Help to decide on areas of general concentration. Assist in deciding whether to work mainly on strengths or weaknesses. Assist in deciding what combination of strengths and weaknesses is best. Do activities from indi-vidualized workbooks and those planned by the teacher.	instruc-tional planner	With input from the student and parents, decide on general areas of concentration. Decide whether to work only on strengths, whether to concen-trate on 2 strong and 1 weak or 2 weak and 1 strong. Select specific SI cells to emphasize based on the above decision. Choose activities from workbooks or worksheets that will exercise these targeted abilities. Develop individualized booklets for each child containing these activities and worksheets.

Evaluate the progress of students in the targeted areas	test-taker	Take tests administered by the teacher, counselor, psychologist, or diagnostician.	tester	Select activities from other instructional materials that will develop the targeted specific or general areas. Examine Meeker's list of instructional games classified according to the abilities and choose games for small groups, large groups, or individuals. Readminister any of the pre-tests to determine progress in the targeted areas. Administer informal tests at regular intervals to determine the effectiveness of the program.

Table 4-3 continued

Step, Type, or Level of Thinking	Student		Teacher	
	Role	Sample Activities	Role	Sample Activities
				If not effective, develop a different overall strategy, such as combining more strengths with a weakness or combining different areas.

which is a part of the SI model, is that of variety. *Structure of Intellect* theory points to the existence of four basic types of information, ranging from the most concrete, figural, to the most abstract, behavioral. These types of content assume equal importance in general, but have differential importance based on individual needs. Indirectly, the theory provides a framework for viewing the abstractness of information in that the basic types of information range from concrete to abstract. However, it does not suggest any particular level of abstraction for gifted students. In fact, there are no overall suggestions related to content except that the ability to deal with all types of content is important, and certain types of content may be important to people in certain kinds of occupations (or with certain kinds of talents). Complexity of content is suggested, somewhat indirectly, by the product dimension of the SI model. Products are essentially ways of organizing or combining types of content, and they range from simple units through the more complex classes, relations, systems, transformations, and implications. Since the theory states that content serves as the input, a process is performed on the content, and a product results, the implication is that the elements in the product dimension are always the output and never the input or stimulus. However, if the items used to identify abilities involving the product dimension are examined, the stimulus is often the same type as the product expected from the respondent. (See Figure 4-6.) For example, in the test of convergent production of symbolic systems (NSS), the input is a particular symbolic system. The task of the respondent is to produce two more items that belong in the system. Thus, both the input and output are systems.

Although Guilford and Meeker do not specifically recommend complexity of content for intellectually gifted individuals, the model provides a useful framework for viewing content in terms of its complexity. Of all the product types, a system is the most complex organization of content. The next two product types, transformations and implications, can actually result from the initial input of a system. By organizing abstract content (that is, semantic or behavioral) into systems, transformations, and implications, content would be both complex and abstract.

Process Modifications

Process modifications are also suggested by the SI model. Although Guilford (1959, 1967) states that the processes of cognition, memory, convergent production, divergent production, and evaluation are not hierarchical, Meeker (1969) believes that learning flows from cognition to all the other processes. In other words, information must first be recognized before it can be evaluated, new information can be produced from it, or it can be stored in memory for later retrieval. Thus at least one of the operations is a prerequisite to the others.

The same is true of memory. Even Guilford (1972, 1975) recognizes the role of memory in convergent and divergent production. He quotes creative individuals as saying that having a store of information on a particular topic ready for easy access is important to their creative production in that area. Thus, memory and cognition can be viewed as prerequisites or lower processes, and convergent production, divergent production, and evaluation as higher processes. In Bruner's (1960) terms, cognition and memory would be considered *acquisition* of information, while the other processes would be considered *use* of information. Taken together, these ideas lead to the conclusion that SI theory and the SOI applications of the theory do recommend or at least provide a framework for the process modification of "development of higher levels of thinking."

The process modifications of open-endedness and variety are more directly recommended by the model. Divergent production is by definition open-ended in that no "correct" answers are sought or intended. Emphasis on divergent production in programs for the gifted is recommended by both Guilford (1972, 1975) and Meeker (1969). The principle of variety is also provided for by the SI theory because of the recommendation that educators provide training in all intellectual abilities. This recommendation at least ensures that a variety of thinking processes would be developed by using the model. Use of a variety of teaching methods, however, is a different matter. Even though teaching activities of all kinds can be designed for developing most of the SI abilities, because of the readily available SOI workbooks, worksheets, and prescriptions in the form of workbooks, many individuals who use the model tend to overemphasize this method of teaching.

Product and Learning Environment Modifications

Product modifications recommended by Guilford (1972) for the gifted and the creative are transformations and realistic evaluation, with particular emphasis on self-evaluation. Emphasis on transformation is recommended, as a result of interviews with creative producers who rated transformations higher in importance in their work than the process of divergent production. Guilford suggests self-evaluation because of the resistance of creative individuals to criticism of their work by others.

None of the learning environment changes recommended for use with the gifted are directly addressed by Guilford or Meeker, although the idea of deferred judgment (an aspect of acceptance) is viewed as an important strategy by Guilford when dealing with divergent production abilities. He states that a person should not attempt to develop the ability of divergent production at the same time as evaluation because evaluation tends to inhibit divergent production.

MODIFYING THE APPROACH

It is strongly recommended that the SOI approach be used in conjunction with other models in the development of a comprehensive curriculum for gifted students. Many modifications of process, content, and environment are not addressed by the model and would be difficult to incorporate into the system as it is designed. The most effective use is as a system for assessing intellectual strengths and weaknesses in the students, and providing for the development and remediation of these abilities in a somewhat isolated fashion. Guilford's model and Meeker's practical applications would also be useful to assist students in career planning and development of abilities needed for a selected career.

Content Changes

To make the content changes appropriate for gifted students, the SOI approach would need to be used in conjunction with Bruner or Taba, and Williams. Bruner's or Taba's models would provide a curriculum in which the content is organized around abstract, complex generalizations to produce economy of learning experiences. Guilford's product dimensions of transformations and implications could be used to judge the generalizations developed to determine their level of complexity. By using the SOI approach in conjunction with Williams, the study of creative people, creative processes, and methods of inquiry would also be included.

The content modification of variety could be developed using Guilford's categories of content and/or his categories of products. To ensure that a variety of content in each discipline or area of study is in the program, the information could be examined to determine how much is figural, how much is symbolic, how much is semantic, and how much is behavioral. Obviously, certain content areas will have a majority of one or two types of content, but there would be some important information of all types. The same kind of analysis could be done using the product dimensions. After analysis, the major task would be to incorporate the under-represented or missing types of information.

When using the SOI with Williams's strategies (for example, the study of creative people and creative processes, organized random search, and skills of search), the SI categories in all dimensions can be used by students in examining people, processes, and methods. This would necessitate teaching Guilford's theory to the students. Although it would not be easy to teach children the descriptions of 120 abilities, they could apply what they have learned in many different instances in addition to this one. Many materials are available for teaching the SOI to teachers, parents, psychologists, and other interested persons. The materials available for parents would be the most useful with children since they tend to be free from educational jargon.

Process Changes

The SOI approach could be used in conjunction with the *Taba Strategies* to ensure that all process modifications are made. It could also be used with Bruner and Parnes, which would increase the number of process modifications made. It would be difficult to ensure that all changes would be made if only the SOI were used and a teacher attempted to modify the approach. However, following are some ways teachers can make modifications of the SOI model to integrate some of the needed elements.

Discovery

- When students have completed an activity, have them identify the intellectual abilities involved.
- Use many activities involving convergent production of (a) figural, symbolic, semantic, or behavioral content; and (b) relations, systems, transformations, and implications. These seem to be some of the most important abilities involved in discovery learning.

Proof/Reasoning

- When doing activities involving convergent production or evaluation and when appropriate, have students explain how they arrived at the answers they gave.
- When complex information or products are involved in an activity, have students provide support and explain their reasoning for responses.

Freedom of Choice

- Allow students to choose from a variety of activities that have been developed to exercise different abilities. This allows the students to indicate through their choices or expressions the talent areas or abilities they prefer to use.
- Provide students information on the intellectual abilities required by different careers, and allow them to choose the SI abilities they would like to develop and to what extent they would like to develop them. In other words, explain the theory, and allow students the freedom to choose how much time and effort they will spend on the development of their strengths and weaknesses.
- As in the example of David, allow the students to participate in making decisions about the instructional program designed for them.

Group Interaction

- Use categories in the behavioral dimension as a structure for the organization of observations of group interaction.
- Use the behavioral dimension as pre- and postmeasures of the effectiveness of group interaction activities in developing the ability to interpret and use behavioral information.

Pacing

- Allow students to work on many activities individually so that they can move at their own rate through the materials.
- After group activities, ask for student feedback on the appropriateness of the pacing of the lesson.

Variety

- Avoid the tendency to "take the easy way out," and use only the SOI workbooks as curricular materials.
- Analyze games and other learning activities to determine the SI abilities involved, and use these when needed to develop particular abilities in children.
- As an aspect of learning the model, have students create activities and games to develop the different abilities. These can be kept in the classroom for use with other students.

Product and Learning Environment Changes

The most effective way to ensure that product and learning environment modifications are made for gifted students would be to use the SOI approach in conjunction with Renzulli or Parnes. Both of these approaches emphasize the product and environment elements missing from Guilford's model.

In the development of products that address real problems, are directed toward real audiences, are evaluated appropriately, and are transformations rather than summaries, Guilford's model can be a useful complement to either Parnes's or Renzulli's models. Several SI abilities can be identified that are important in developing certain types of products. After the strengths and weaknesses of students' products have been identified by the teacher, student, or audiences, the teacher or student can identify which SI abilities are involved and which ones need further work by the student, either to continue development of a strength or to remediate a weak area. For example, if a student is having difficulty or wants to work on making transitions between ideas, it may help to work on the SI abilities of divergent production of semantic relations or convergent production of semantic relations. If the difficulty is in developing original products, the student could practice activities involving transformations using all the operations and products.

Students could enhance their ability to evaluate their own products by practicing the SI operation of evaluation using all content and product categories. The SI abilities involving evaluation could also be used to develop instruments or procedures for use by everyone who participates in the evaluation of a student's product.

In addition to combining Guilford's approach with Renzulli and Parnes to make appropriate changes in the learning environment, some of the procedures suggested earlier can be useful in making this model more comprehensive for use with the gifted. For instance, by teaching students the theory and suggesting that they use it in self-evaluation, the teacher is developing a more student-centered approach. Also, when students participate in decisions about their own instructional programs, the classroom is on its way toward becoming more student-centered and encouraging independence. Teachers must maintain an open, accepting environment and permit a high degree of mobility if they are to implement or allow this high level of student involvement in the planning process.

When conducting activities that develop the SI operation of divergent production, the teacher should review Parnes's rules for brainstorming and other suggestions for conducting group activities. His recommendations at the idea-finding step would be of particular importance. The teacher should also review some of the research on use of the Parnes *Creative Problem Solving* model before implementing divergent production activities.

Summary

Since the SOI approach lacks many of the content, process, product, and learning environment modifications necessary for a comprehensive curriculum for the gifted, it should not be the only basis for curriculum development. It can be used effectively in assessing individual profiles of intellectual strengths and weaknesses, and in providing the structure for their development. Using the SOI approach in this way provides an important complement to any curriculum development model used in a program for the gifted. Although the SOI may be used with Bruner, Taba, Williams, Renzulli, and Parnes to ensure a comprehensive approach, the model could certainly be used with any other curriculum development process.

Gifted students can also be taught the SI theory and encouraged to apply it in many of their activities. This adaptation of the model, along with the others listed for process changes, can make the SOI approach a more comprehensive curriculum model for the gifted.

DEVELOPMENT

The SI Theory

Guilford (1967) began his research on human abilities in the Aptitudes Project at the University of Southern California. Along the lines suggested by L.L. Thurstone's work on primary mental abilities, he gathered tests of special aptitudes, achievement, intelligence, and cognitive processes; administered them. Then he analyzed the results by factor analysis. After almost 40 separate factors of ability had been demonstrated through factor analysis, Guilford (1959) organized these into a system that would serve as a way of explaining the interrelationships and provide a basis for further empirical study.

In his earlier research, Guilford began collecting all items or types of items that had been shown through research to measure particular abilities. He then constructed additional items that measure a particular aspect of an ability so that there are at least two specific tests for each aspect of the ability he had hypothesized. An example from one study should serve to illustrate these methods further.

In an investigation of factors involved in flexibility of thinking, Guilford and others (Frick, Guilford, Christensen, & Merrifield, 1959) hypothesized that two kinds of flexibility—adaptive and spontaneous—are qualities that directly oppose two forms of rigidity—persistence and perseveration, respectively. They first defined the four qualities in a general way, and then developed subhypotheses regarding the abilities involved. For example, spontaneous flexibility was hypothesized to consist of (1) "the ability to shift mental set freely, making it possible to get away from more obvious and more trite responses," (p. 472); and (2) "the ability to react in a relatively unstructured situation in divergent channels or directions" (p. 473). From these subhypotheses, specific tests were either selected or designed because they seemed to measure logically the ability hypothesized. For the first aspect, ability to shift mental set freely, two tests, Riddles (requiring the subject to explain riddles in a clever manner) and Rhyming Definitions (requiring the subject to produce two-word rhyming definitions of objects) were developed to test the ability. Two other tests, Remote Consequences and Unusual Uses, were selected because they had previously shown relation to the ability to shift mental set freely.

In his later work, Guilford's hypotheses about the existence of specific abilities were based on his SI model. He selected or developed items (usually at least three separate tests) that utilized a particular type of content, required a certain operation, and resulted in a particular kind of product. If he perceived that a test that had been included to measure a particular kind of ability also required a different kind of ability (for example, in the study mentioned, Guilford and his colleagues suspected that certain nonflexibility factors, such as verbal comprehension, general reasoning, logical evaluation, originality, and ideational fluency, would also be involved in the tests they devised), in order to remove the influence of such factors, Guilford included marker tests in the battery that required a different ability that was not currently being investigated. In this way, he "removed the variance" due to the abilities not being measured so that the "structure" of that ability as well as its relationship to other abilities became more clear.

To assist the reader unfamiliar with statistical procedures, a brief and somewhat simplistic explanation may be helpful. Factor analysis is a well-known statistical technique used to identify clusters or groups of things that are related to each other. The commonalities between these related items are called "factors," and the individual items are said to "load" on a particular factor. The loading of an item on a factor is essentially the amount of the commonality it shares with other items that load on the factor. Factors can also be related to each other if the experimenter uses the kind of factor analytic methods that permit them to be correlated. This aspect of the statistical technique is much more difficult to explain, but it is important in understanding the differences between Guilford's methods and those employed by some psychologists in their studies of human intelligence.

In one part of the process of factor analysis, a procedure called rotation is used. One method of rotation, orthogonal, assumes that the factors are at right angles to each other, that they are not correlated. However, a second method, oblique rotation, allows the factors to be correlated either negatively or positively. There is considerable controversy among statisticians regarding factor analytic procedures and their validity, including disagreements about the appropriateness of orthogonal rotation versus oblique rotation. Guilford (1961) is of the opinion that orthogonal rotation provides the most pure or clear picture of the phenomena being observed. For this reason, he uses this procedure in his research on human abilities. In contrast, Cattell (1971) believes that oblique rotation provides an accurate description of the phenomena being observed because it allows the factors to be correlated if they actually are related.* A further discussion of the pros and cons of both methods is beyond the scope of this chapter, but a knowledge of the basic issues is important to understanding some of the criticisms of Guilford's methods.

The SOI Approach

Beginning about 1962, Mary Meeker (1969), an associate of Guilford, developed procedures for analyzing test items (beginning with the *Wechsler* and *Binet* IQ tests) according to the abilities in the SI model. The procedure, called "mapping," consists of guidelines for deciding which SI abilities are tested by items or subtests in the instruments. Using the SI model as the theoretical structure, Meeker designed an entire system of procedures, tests, instructional materials, toys, and inservice training materials to facilitate educational applications of the theory. Her research concentrated on the following educational applications: (a) determining whether there are general patterns of strengths and weaknesses in certain clinical types (for example, gifted, educationally handicapped, blind, deaf, mentally retarded) or certain cultural groups (for example, Mexican American, Navajo, Black); (b) evaluating the effectiveness of using individual prescriptions to remediate deficits and build on strengths; and (c) developing procedures for using

---

*Readers interested in pursuing the debate over orthogonal versus oblique rotation can consult the major writings of two theorists with opposing viewpoints (Cattell, 1971; Guilford, 1961, 1967).

SOI profiles in identifying different types of giftedness. Some of the research on effectiveness is summarized in the following section, and some of the research on profiles is summarized by Maker (1982).

RESEARCH ON EFFECTIVENESS*

Most of Guilford's SI research (from 1944-1966) has been directed toward validating the major assumptions of the model and its theoretical base. Since this research and its critiques would fill volumes, space does not permit even a quick review that would do justice to the topic. The research reported here is limited to studies of the effectiveness of the SOI approach with both gifted and nongifted students. Although a number of studies on its effectiveness have been reported, many of them have serious methodological difficulties or are presented in incomplete form. The studies cited here were selected on the following basis: (a) use of a control group for comparison; (b) lack of serious methodological difficulties; and (c) availability of complete tables of results.

Most research on the effectiveness of SOI-based training programs has concentrated on their use in improving either reading or creativity. Most of the training programs have been relatively short, although one project lasted for three years and another for four. Hess (Note 9) randomly assigned incoming first graders to an experimental or control group. The two control classes were given regular instruction in beginning reading, while the two experimental classes received instruction based on SOI profile analysis in their weak areas along with all the SOI abilities identified in an earlier study by Feldman (1971) as necessary for success in beginning reading. After 4½ months, the control group showed no gains, while the experimental group's gains in reading were significant at the .05 level.

In a second study, Hays and Pereira (1972) found that their experimental group, which had received training for 15 minutes a day for 50 days, had made significantly more gains in reading accuracy than a comparable group. In this study, the children only received training in *one* cell or one specific ability from Guilford's model, Memory for Figural Units, using the visual mode (MFU-V). Although these children showed significant gains in reading accuracy, they did not show overall gains in memory. The results of this study indicate that this particular ability has a great influence on reading accuracy, certainly greater than its influence on memory.

In an evaluation of the effectiveness of a language arts program based on the SI model and designed to enhance creativity, Callahan and Renzulli (1977) measured the effect on creative thinking and self-perception of sixth graders. Activities in the

---

*Those who are interested in further reading on the validity of the model or research on its effectiveness are encouraged to request bibliographies, reading lists, and/or reprints from the SOI Institute, 343 Richmond Street, El Segundo, CA 90245.

New Directions in Creativity Program (Renzulli, 1976) are classified according to the type of information involved (content) and the ways that information is organized (products). All activities require the operation of divergent thinking. The 22 classrooms of 660 children were randomly assigned to an experimental or control group, and the children were ranked by IQ as being in the top, middle, or bottom third of their classes. The experimental groups used the program for 2½ hours each week for eight weeks, while the control group simply continued its regular language arts program. Using a posttest-only design with the TTCT and a self-perception inventory of their own design as the criterion measures, they found no significant differences between experimental and control groups. They did find a great deal of variability between experimental groups, however, showing the importance of the teacher variable in implementing this educational program. The *authors* suspect that the lack of significance was due to the amount of variability between experimental groups. The experimental groups did have higher average scores on six of the seven subscores obtained from the TTCT, but none were significant. Class rank did not have a significant effect on the scores. With regard to self-perception, 75 percent of the students in the experimental group felt that their thinking abilities had improved as a result of the program.

An interesting evaluation of a four-year program using SOI training (SOI Institute, 1979) showed it to be highly effective with Mexican American students. The classroom program concentrated on only those abilities involved in arithmetic learning, and evaluation consisted of (a) pre- and posttest assessment of the SI abilities involved in arithmetic and (b) pre- and posttest assessment of student achievement in arithmetic and reading. A control group receiving no treatment was also assessed using the same measures. Results were very positive, showing significant gains in both SI abilities and arithmetic achievement and significant gains for experimental over control groups. No significant gains were found in reading scores—a result that was expected because no training was given in SI abilities associated with reading.

Even though the SOI approach has been popular in programs for gifted children and has been evaluated in a number of projects, only two studies of gifted children were located in which control groups were used. Hoepfner (Note 10) evaluated a three-year experimental project involving mentally gifted students in grades one through eight. All students (241 in the control group and 249 in the experimental group) received instruction using the SOI approach of developing strengths and remediating weaknesses. However, with the experimental group, the first year emphasis was placed on the abilities involved in creativity, that is, the whole operations area of divergent thinking and in the product areas of transformations and implications. In the second year evaluation training was added. When tested with both the figural and verbal forms of the TTCT and the Meeker rating scale, all experimental groups showed greater gains than the control groups. Most differences were significant at the .01 level of confidence. In effect, this study showed that training in the SOI abilities involved in creative thinking increases creative thinking as measured by the TTCT more than no training in creative thinking. In addition, the study showed higher SAT scores for the experimental group than for the control group.

Summarizing these results is difficult since all are different in their curricular emphasis, training time, and methods of assessment. There is, however, a trend indicating that use of the SOI approach can be successful in developing SI abilities and in improving academic achievement. Results show that the approach can be successful with students regardless of their overall level of ability and does not seem to have a differential effect on gifted children. Only one study was reviewed that could have showed a different effect. Further studies must be done before any conclusions can be reached.

This review of research has raised many questions: What is the optimum time needed for training in each ability? How should this training be arranged (that is, how often, for what length of time)? Which abilities are important to train at what age? What are the long-term effects of training (that is, do the differences between trained and untrained groups persist over a long period of time)? Is the approach more effective with gifted students than with educationally handicapped children? Which is the most effective approach: remediating weak areas, developing strong ones, or some combination of strengths and weaknesses? None of these questions has been answered definitively, since the SOI method is an approach that can be assessed much more easily than others commonly used in education of the gifted because of the clear definitions of the abilities being measured and developed. More efforts must be focused on such research by those who advocate its use.

In a second study, Meeker (1979) evaluated the effectiveness of a gifted program based on the SOI for children in grades three through six using the SOI-LA test. He assessed growth in three areas of creativity—figural, semantic, and symbolic—and found that the gains were significant for experimental groups in all areas. The control groups showed significant gains in some areas. When comparisons were made, there were significant differences in experimental over control group gains in figural creativity for all grade levels, in semantic creativity in grades four and six but not five, and in symbolic creativity for only grade six. Although significant differences were not found for all grade levels in all areas, the program effects were positive.

JUDGMENTS

Advantages

One of the most important advantages of the SOI approach is its usefulness in diagnosing and developing appropriate programs for gifted students who are having problems learning. It is usually difficult to identify the causes of these problems without a model of intellectual abilities, such as the *Structure of Intellect*. Often, these children have unusual discrepancies between separate abilities. These discrepancies are not identified by traditional means of testing since the child has developed strategies for compensating or masking the disabilities. A model such as the SI offers a way to separate intellectual abilities into small definable units. Using the well-developed approaches of specific remediation combined with more general remediation of weaknesses through strengths, individualized education programs (IEPs) can be developed easily. Parents who wish to assist in their child's education can use the workbooks and activities at home.

A second advantage is the ease of individualization when using the tests, computer analysis, and workbooks. All the materials and systems are readily available at a price affordable by most schools. The development of IEPs is made simple by the availability of SOI tests and materials. In addition to its value in individualized curriculum planning, the SOI offers support to the teacher through career and vocational analysis based on individual intellectual profiles. The task of counseling students on career choices is easier because of this service.

Indirectly related to curriculum development but an important prerequisite, the SI model is useful in helping teachers, parents, children, psychologists, and others understand the multidimensional nature of giftedness and talent. Gifted children (because they are gifted) are often expected to be superior in everything they do. Educators and parents are often disappointed or feel the child is different if a few weak areas are identified. Use of a model such as the SI helps to show graphically why these children should not be expected to excel in everything and provides a framework for viewing talented children as individuals. Perhaps in the future because of models such as this, educators will develop valid profiles of *types* of giftedness and talent based on particular clusters of intellectual abilities and will build individual programs for every child that can develop the entire cluster of abilities necessary for the talent to be realized.

Disadvantages

Although the availability of tests and materials for remediation/development is considered a major advantage of Guilford's model, it can also be a disadvantage. Because of the ease in using a cookbook approach where specific cells are targeted and the workbooks are keyed to these cells, there is a tendency to use only these workbooks and paper-and-pencil tasks. Not as much creativity is required on the part of the teacher as with some other approaches, so not as much creativity is used. Teachers often complain that their gifted students get bored with their SOI workbooks day after day. This is not the fault of the model, because many exciting non-paper-and-pencil tasks can be designed to develop the SI abilities. However, their availability makes them easy to fall back on. Perhaps a related reason for using what has already been developed is a feeling of insecurity based on the lack of knowledge about various abilities and how they can be developed.

Another disadvantage is the lack of research on the validity and reliability of some of the procedures advocated. One big problem involves the "mapping" of test items from existing instruments into an SOI profile. No factor analytic studies have been conducted showing that particular SI abilities have actually been assessed by the items added to obtain a score in a particular cell. There is no research showing the effectiveness of the recommended specific versus general remediation strategy. It is not clear which approach is best to use with what children and under what circumstances. It is also not clear (although humanistically appealing) whether the approach of combining strengths with weaknesses is more effective than concentrating directly on the weak areas or the strong ones. Many other questions need to be addressed by solid research to determine the validity of the model for curriculum development.

The SI model does not provide a total framework for curriculum development, although it does provide for curricular modifications in several areas. It should be combined with a good content model so that the modifications relating to abstractness, complexity, economy, and organization can be incorporated. As often used, the SOI approach contributes to a fragmentation of the content areas rather than the integration of ideas into abstract thought systems.

A big concern of critics is the validity of methods used to identify the SI factors. By using only orthogonal rotation, many feel that Guilford is trying to make reality fit his model rather than fitting his model to reality. It seems clear from his writing and that of Meeker, along with some of the data from factor analysis, that certain abilities are prerequisites to others. For example, an ample and readily available memory store on a particular topic is a necessity in divergent production and often in convergent production. Cognition is even a more basic operation. In the product dimension, there is also a hierarchy or at least a sequence of abilities with units being the simplest, and transformations and implications the most complex. Because of Guilford's use of marker tests in an attempt to identify pure abilities, he may actually be partialling out the variance caused by one of the prerequisites or underlying abilities. In other words, the basic problem is that his methods have limited his results and also the theory because of their restrictiveness.

CONCLUSIONS

J.P. Guilford's SI model can be used effectively in planning IEPs to develop the intellectual abilities of gifted children. Research has shown that the approaches designed by Mary Meeker can be effective in enhancing specific abilities. These approaches are also practical and easy to implement. However, this approach is not recommended as a total framework for curriculum development. Perhaps the most important drawback in this respect would be the tendency toward fragmentation. The SOI approach needs to be combined with another model (for example, Bruner, Taba, or Renzulli), which would provide the important elements that are lacking.

RESOURCES

Background Information

Guilford, J.P. *The nature of human intelligence.* New York: McGraw-Hill, 1967. In *The Nature of Human Intelligence,* Guildford attempts to establish, in detail, a comprehensive theoretical foundation for the concept of intelligence. Guilford's *Structure of Intellect* (SI) theory is the result of 12 years of extensive research. There are three introductory chapters, outlining the SI theory. The second section outlines the five operation categories of the structure: cognition, memory, divergent production, convergent production, and evaluation. The implications for psychological theory are contained in the third section, with further ramifications and apparent applications of the SI concepts covered in the final section. The book presents a highly theoretical and technical explanation of a theory that has had a major impact on both present and past theories of intelligence.

Guilford, J.P. *Way beyond the IQ.* Buffalo, NY: Creative Education Foundation, 1977. In Guilford's theory of *Structure of Intellect,* intelligence is not defined solely by one's IQ, but includes five diverse abilities. In *The Nature of Human Intelligence,* Guilford outlines his theory. In this book, published ten years later, he demonstrates how these concepts can be used in improving creativity and intelligence in the classroom. After three opening chapters, in which the content and structure of intelligence are discussed, there are five chapters covering the five components of the SI theory. Each ability is illustrated with tasks for the readers, offering a chance to concretely understand each concept. There are also practical ideas as to how an individual might develop and utilize these abilities. The five abilities in Guilford's theory do not always work in isolation; the author believes they work best together in the processes of problem solving and creative thinking. Consequently, problem solving and creative thinking, and how they reflect the workings of the entire SI model, are discussed in the final chapters.

Meeker, M.N. *The structure of intellect: Its interpretation and uses.* Columbus, Ohio: Charles E. Merrill, 1969. The main purpose of this book is to discover how Guilford's SI theory can be utilized to benefit students in a school curriculum. Suggestions for planning curricula and organizing teaching experiences are included. Meeker discusses the various intelligence tests used and their relationship to the *Structure of Intellect* and includes diagrams of individual test profiles. There are three parts to the book: An Overview of the *Structure of Intellect,* Operations and Descriptions of Components, and Interpretation and Uses for Curriculum Planning.

Instructional Materials and Ideas

Karnes, M.B. *Structure of the intellect based model lesson plans*. Urbana-Champaign, Ill: Institute for Research on Exceptional Children, 1973. Over 200 activities designed to develop the SI components are presented. The introduction outlines Guilford's theory, but the bulk of the material centers on a variety of practical teaching suggestions to encourage memory, cognition, divergent production, convergent production, and evaluative thinking. The latter three particularly are emphasized. Each activity is classified by the component it is designed to develop. A behavioral objective, prerequisites, materials, and procedure for each exercise is delineated, and worksheets for many of the ideas are included. The book provides an extensive resource of activities for the classroom teacher.

Meeker, M.N. *The creative learning workbook*. El Segundo, CA: SOI Institute, 1973. This is a workbook for encouraging creative learning based on Guilford's SI theory. It is specifically for use with preschool children. The workbook consists of over 100 various games and exercises designed to help train the five SI components. There are five sections, one for each component, and each section is printed on a different color paper for easy reference. In the introduction, the author stresses that the activities are not passive, require teacher-student interaction, and need teacher imagination. The glossary at the end defines the specific intellectual abilities of the Guilford model.

Meeker, M.N. *How the alphabet doubled*. El Segundo, CA: SOI Institute, 1976. This book is for use with children learning the alphabet. It is a story the teacher reads to the students about each letter in the alphabet. During the story there are numerous activities and games to involve the students and promote the learning of individual letters. The book is designed so that as the teacher reads, he or she can show the class illustrations. Also included are extra copies of the ''letter characters'' so they can be duplicated, enlarged, or utilized in other ways for the learning process.

Meeker, M.N. *Using SOI test results: A teacher's guide*. El Segundo, CA: SOI Institute, 1979. As its name implies, this booklet provides guidelines to assist teachers in interpreting the results of SOI-LA testing, whether analyzed by the individual or the institute. Educational recommendations are made for the development of specific as well as general abilities. Also provided are useful charts showing the relationship of SI abilities to academic subjects as well as methods for matching teaching methods with student learning styles. A bibliography of references and SOI-approved curriculum materials is included.

Meeker, M., & Maxwell, V. *Advanced and gifted convergent production: A structure of intellect abilities workbook* (rev. ed.). 1975.

Meeker, M. *Memory: An SOI abilities workbook and manual for teachers.* (rev. ed.). 1973.

Meeker, M. *Learning to plan, judge and make decisions, basic: A structure of intellect evaluation workbook.* 1976.

Meeker, M. *Learning to plan, judge and make decisions, advanced: A structure of intellect evaluation workbook.* 1976.

Meeker, M. *Advanced teaching comprehension skills: An SOI cognition workbook.* 1976.

Meeker, M. *Basic learning how to comprehend: A structure of intellect cognition workbook* (rev. ed.). 1973.

Meeker, M., & Maxwell, V. *Convergent production, basic: A structure of intellect abilities workbook* (rev. ed.). 1975.

This is a series of workbooks, published by the SOI Institute, designed to encourage the growth of memory, cognition, convergent production, and evaluation, four of the five major components in Guilford's *Structure of Intellect* theory. The basic format for each workbook is the same. Each one contains numerous exercises focusing on the development of one of the four major abilities and their related aspects. Cognition, convergent production, and evaluation have two volumes, one basic and one advanced. All the activities, regardless of the topic, outline the related curriculum subject, a behavioral objective, materials to use, and instructions. Grade levels are given in some of the workbooks, and there are exercise sheets included for use with some ideas. In the cognition volumes, bibliographies on materials about images of minority cultures are found. The author encourages the use of an SOI profile to identify the specific deficiencies the workbooks are designed to remedy.

Chapter 5

Lawrence Kohlberg: Discussions of Moral Dilemmas

The development of values, moral reasoning, ethical behavior, and virtuous action has been a concern of educators of all children. Educators of the gifted have been interested primarily in the development of values and assisting children to clarify their values through the process of values clarification advocated by individuals such as Raths (1963) and Raths, Harmin, and Simon (1966). Educators and parents are often concerned about developing ethical behavior in children and, in the past, they attempted to do so through such vehicles as religious education, Boy Scouts, Girl Scouts, and other approaches emphasizing to children that the virtuous person is honest, loyal, reverent, just, and altruistic. If they acquire these virtues, children are told, they will be happy, well-respected, and fortunate.

In contrast to the attempts to develop ethical behavior is the approach of values clarification, the position that the school's and teacher's responsibility is not to indoctrinate children as to what values they should hold, but to assist them in following a process whereby they think seriously about what values they hold and what values they should hold. The teacher's role in the process is a nonjudgmental one, and involves posing questions and planning activities that will lead children through the processes of *choosing* (for example, choosing freely, choosing from alternatives, choosing after thoughtful consideration of the consequences of each alternative), *prizing* (for example, prizing and cherishing of oneself, affirming publicly), and *acting* (for example, acting upon choices, repeating the action in a pattern over time) (Raths et al., 1966). A fundamental idea behind this approach is that of "ethical relativity;" there are no universal ethical principles, because values and ethics are relative. As long as a person has followed the processes of choosing, prizing, and acting, all values developed are equally valid.

Kohlberg's (1966) theory of the development of moral reasoning and his approach to moral education is a response to the failure of indoctrination programs

137

and disagreement with the idea of ethical relativity as a basis for values education (Kohlberg, 1971). In the late 1920s, a classic study of children's cheating and stealing by Hartshorne and May (1930) shocked the educational community by showing that indoctrination approaches were ineffective. Children who attend Sunday school, participate in Boy Scouts and Girl Scouts, and whose parents emphasize ethical behavior do not behave more ethically than children who do none of these things. Other results of this study, also confirmed by later research, are that: (a) the world cannot be divided into honest and dishonest people since almost everyone cheats at some time; (b) if a person cheats in one situation, whether the person will cheat in other situations cannot be predicted (in other words, cheating seems to be situationally determined); and (c) the moral values expressed by people have nothing to do with how they act; people who express extreme moral disapproval of cheating will cheat as much as those who do not verbally express disapproval of cheating.

Perhaps the values clarification approaches were formulated as a reaction to the ineffectiveness of indoctrination or as a 1960s reaction to adults' attempts to manipulate children through developing certain moral values advocated by the "educational establishment." However, Kohlberg rejected the most fundamental idea behind this approach, ethical relativity, on a philosophical basis. His key idea (Kohlberg, 1971), which is in part based on the writings of Kant (1929, 1965) and the contemporary moral philosopher John Rawls (1971), is that, although different values relating to personal choice (for example, what clothing to wear, the most appropriate way to spend time) are equally appropriate, different values relating to basic moral questions (for example, the sanctity of life, the equality of all people) are *not* equally appropriate. In other words, there *are* certain universal ethical principles. For example, even though an individual arrives at the decision that all blacks should be slaves because they are an inferior race through the seven-step process of values clarification, this conclusion is not as appropriate as the conclusion that slavery is wrong for everyone. A conclusion such as this would be based on such universal ethical principles as the worth of every person and the equality of every person relative to certain rights and freedoms. Such ethical principles as respect for the worth of all individuals, justice and liberty for all, and "inalienable rights" are firmly imbedded in and necessary to a democratic way of life. As educators and individuals participating in a democracy, teachers can and should assist children in developing moral reasoning that will consider these higher philosophical principles in decisions involving basic moral questions.

Relative to this philosophical position, Kohlberg (1966) studied the development of moral reasoning by interviewing 50 boys over a period of time. He posted moral dilemmas to them and asked them to tell first what would be morally right for the individual to do and, second, why this action would be right. He found that children's reasoning about moral issues proceeds through certain stages in a sequential order and becomes more sophisticated at each stage. Subsequent to the research on these developmental stages, numerous individuals including Kohlberg, his colleagues, and his students have studied how this development can be facilitated. They have concluded that educators can encourage the development of higher levels of moral reasoning through methods emphasizing class discussion of moral dilemmas. The techniques used in moral dilemma discussions have been continually refined over a period of several years and are still being developed in several experimental projects.

Although Kohlberg and his colleagues do not write specifically about the gifted, educators of the gifted have long been concerned about the moral and ethical development of bright students. If these children are to become future leaders, they should serve as models of the highest ethical behavior in addition to being models of intellectual/productive behavior. Many educators of the gifted have accepted the idea of ethical relativity and advocated the use of values clarification as the most effective means for dealing with moral/ethical principles in schools. Ward (1961), however, is convincing in his argument that intellectually superior individuals have a greater capacity than average individuals to develop consistency between their ethical ideals and their actual behavior. Many of the characteristics of the gifted (for example, their ability to foresee consequences of their own behavior, their ability to choose long-term benefits over short-range consequences, and their greater capacity to generalize learning from one situation) suggest that a concentration on moral reasoning and the development of an understanding of ''universal ethical principles'' would be an effective approach to the development of ethical behavior.

Ward (1961) suggests that the gifted should be instructed in ''the theoretical bases of ideal moral behavior and of personal and social adjustments'' (p. 202). In further explanations of this idea, he suggests that gifted individuals should examine critically the historical development of societal philosophies and values, and that they should study the effects of these ideas on the development of societies. This examination should also include the analysis and classification of values with an emphasis on the individuals' development of their own ''reasoned synthesis'' of values. Such an approach differs from values clarification in that individuals have examined high ideals and considered their appropriateness rather than simply looking within themselves for these ideals. The approach is similar to values clarification in that individuals must go through a process of self-examination and develop personal conclusions.

Kohlberg's approach fits well with these ideas since the emphasis is on ''reasoning,'' with the objective of ultimately reaching a level at which certain universal ethical principles or ideals guide behavior. An analysis of the philosophical and theoretical bases of the ethical principles being discussed should be added to Kohlberg's approach.

ASSUMPTIONS UNDERLYING THE MODEL

About Learning

Kohlberg's (1966) most basic assumptions form a comprehensive theory of moral development and are based on Piaget's theories and research on the development of thinking. Kohlberg's stage theory complements and extends Piaget's (1948) work in moral development. Basic to the understanding of Kohlberg's theory is the realization that it is a cognitive approach. He is studying and suggesting that educators attempt to develop moral *reasoning* rather than moral *behavior*. Sophisticated moral reasoning usually leads to ethical behavior, and educators should be concentrating on reasoning. Several aspects of the developmental stage theory must be understood before the teaching methods can be implemented: (a) the general assumptions of developmental stage theories; (b) the nature of an individual's thinking at each stage; (c) the general structure of the progression of thinking from lower to higher stages; and (d) how an individual progresses (for example, transition from one step to another, facilitators of progress, inhibitors of progress, necessary conditions, rate).

General Assumptions of Developmental Stage Theories

The first assumption usually made in stage theories of development is that there are identifiably different stages characterized by a particular type of thinking. These stages are qualitatively different from one another; an individual progresses naturally through them in the process of maturing. The sequence of stages is invariant; individuals do not skip stages, and they always begin at the lowest level and progress to the highest attainable stage. Inherent in the approach is the perception that higher stages are better because they reflect more maturity. In other words, quality of thought improves rather than deteriorates as a person grows and matures.

The Nature of Kohlberg's Stages of Moral Reasoning

In his theory, Kohlberg identifies six stages that fall into three levels. The following dilemma—the story of Joe—will help explain these levels and stages and is used during Kohlberg's longitudinal study of moral development:

> Joe is a fourteen-year-old boy who wanted to go to camp very much. His father promised him he could go if he saved up the money for it himself. So Joe worked hard at his paper route and saved up the $40 it cost to go to camp and a little more besides. But just before camp was going to start, his father changed his mind. Some of his friends decided to go on a special fishing trip, and Joe's father was short of the money it would

cost. So he told Joe to give him the money he had saved from the paper route. Joe didn't want to give up going to camp, so he thought of refusing to give his father the money. (Porter & Taylor, 1972, pp. 37, 38)

Preconventional Level. At this level, the individual interprets the labels of good and bad in terms of their physical consequences or in terms of the physical power of those who enforce the rules. The power of authority figures and the physical or hedonistic consequences of action, such as reward, punishment, or exchange of favors, determine moral decisions.

Stage One: Obedience and Punishment Orientation—At this stage, the physical consequences of an action determine whether it is good or bad regardless of the human meaning or value of the consequences. Often, an individual's wrong act is not considered bad unless it is punished, and degrees of badness are determined by the amount of physical pain inflicted as punishment. *Rules are obeyed to avoid punishment, and "right" is what is not punished.*

In response to questions about Joe's dilemma, a stage one person feels that the boy has no choice but to give up the money, either to avoid punishment or because "he is his father." The father's authority lies in his power—age and strength—rather than his moral or intellectual qualities. The son wants the money, but he does not own it, and even though the father promised, the son can go another year. (Sample student responses to specific examiner questions can be found in Porter and Taylor [1972].)

Stage Two: Instrumental Relativist Orientation—The stage two individual makes moral judgments based on the principle of reciprocity in the sense that a person's needs will be satisfied if he or she behaves in certain ways. Elements of fairness are often involved, but the reasons are pragmatic rather than a reflection of a sense of justice or loyalty. The idea, "You scratch my back, and I'll scratch yours," is basic. *Rules are obeyed to gain something for oneself, and "right" is what satisfies a person's needs.*

In response to questions about Joe's dilemma, a stage two person usually believes that the boy should not give his father the money because the boy earned it. That means the money is his. It is unfair of the father even to ask, because he has promised the boy that he can go to camp. The father should earn his own money. At stage two, there is neither real respect for the authority of the father nor is there concern for pleasing him. According to a person at this stage, promises should be kept for motives of self-interest (for example, so people will keep their promises to you; so people will believe you).

Conventional Level. At this level of moral reasoning, an individual is concerned with maintaining the social order for its own sake regardless of the immediate consequences. People at this level show loyalty to the social order (for example, family, cultural group, nation) and not only conform to its expectations and rules, but actively work to maintain or support it through justifying it and identifying with other people or groups who are involved.

Stage Three: Interpersonal Concordance or "Good Boy-Nice Girl Orientation"—At this stage, the primary concern is for the approval of others. Behavior is often judged by intentions and conforms to stereotypical ideas of what would be agreeable to others in the group. A person earns approval by pleasing others and by being "nice." *Rules are obeyed to gain the approval of others, and "right" is what pleases or is approved by them.*

In response to Joe's dilemma, some stage three individuals will decide that Joe should keep the money, while others will decide that he should give it up. It is usually difficult for people in this stage to decide what is right, and they will often decide on a compromise solution, such as splitting up the money or suggesting that the son get his father to promise that he will pay the money back. The conflict over the boy's right to the money and the boy's desire to please his father is a difficult one for stage three individuals to resolve. The boy earned the money, and the father promised his son that he could go. However, the father has a right to ask for the money since he raised his son and constantly looks after him. The son should be a "good" son and show appreciation for this past care. The father has his son's interests at heart. At this stage, individuals suggest that it may be worse for the father to break his promise to the son because he should set an example. Breaking promises may cause a lack of respect and a loss of friends, and may let down those who are depending on the person.

Stage Four: "Law and Order" Orientation—The stage four individual is concerned about authority, fixed rules, and maintaining the social order. Doing personal duty is important. *Rules are obeyed because that is what the law says, and people must do their duty and uphold the law. "Right" is doing personal duty, showing respect for authority, and maintaining the social order for its own sake.*

At this stage, typical responses to Joe's dilemma will focus on two issues in the story: (a) the son's right to keep the money because he earned it and has the right to do with it as he pleases; and (b) the father's right to the money as an authority figure in the situation. Individuals who decide that the son should give up the money will concentrate on the father's authority and suggest that sons should respect and obey their fathers even when they feel their fathers' actions are unfair or unjustifiable. A lack of obedience or respect implies disrespect for the social order, and, if this practice is continued in all phases of people's lives, anarchy results.

Those who decide that the son should not give up his money concentrate on the son's property rights. An authority figure such as a father is seen as a moral teacher or an example, so the father, in breaking his promise, is setting a bad example. People at this stage may also recognize the son's indebtedness to his father for raising him and may suggest that the son give up the money as a part of this debt.

Postconventional, Autonomous, or Principled Level. At this highest level, there is a clear effort to define certain moral principles that have validity apart from the particular groups or persons holding them. These principles are valid in themselves regardless of the particular individual's identification with a group.

Stage Five: Social Contract Legalistic Orientation—At this stage, people recognize certain general individual rights that have been critically examined and agreed upon by society. Examples of these rights can be found in documents such as the *Declaration of Independence* and the *Bill of Rights*. However, rather than unquestionably accepting the authority of the law or those who enforce the laws, a stage five individual will suggest that if laws are not accomplishing what they were intended to do, they should be subjected to critical review and perhaps changed. At this stage individuals recognize the relativism of personal values and opinions. There is an emphasis upon procedural rules for resolving differences if neither of the positions conflicts with what is constitutionally and democratically agreed upon by society. Outside the legal realm, free agreements and contracts are binding upon people. *Rules are obeyed to maintain the respect of an impartial judge and because they reflect certain agreed-upon principles of the society.* If, however, a particular rule conflicts with these principles and basic human rights, the rule should be changed. *"Right" is what has been critically examined and agreed upon by the society.*

The individual at stage five who is faced with making a decision about Joe's dilemma will respond that the father has no right to ask for the money and that the son should refuse to give it to him. The individual recognizes the father's legal right to his son's money, but the father has given up that right by making a promise or contract with the son. By breaking the agreement, the father relieves his son of the responsibility to obey him.

As a general response to questions relating to a promise, stage five individuals will usually discuss the value of a promise as a form of contract, which leads a person to make plans and base expectations on the fulfillment of the promise.

Stage Six: Universal Ethical Principle Orientation—At this stage, moral decisions are made on the basis of certain self-chosen ethical principles that satisfy criteria such as logical comprehensiveness, universality, consistency, and abstractness. These include principles related to justice, reciprocity, equality of human rights, and respect for the dignity of human beings as individuals. *Rules are obeyed to avoid self-condemnation, and "right" is what is universally ethical and respects human worth, individuality, reciprocity, and other similar abstract concepts.*

In decisions about Joe's dilemma, people at stage six see the situation in much the same way as a person in stage five, but they are usually more clear in the belief that the father has absolutely no moral right to the son's money, even though he may have a legal right. The focus is not so much on the contractual agreement in the form of the father's promise to the son, but on the destruction of the underlying bond of trust that was established by the promise.

Each of these stages represents an organized system of thought, a system with an underlying structure that is independent of its content. In other words, answers to questions about a moral dilemma may differ in the behavior recommended. For example, in response to Joe's dilemma, some individuals at stage three recommended that Joe keep the money, while others believed he should give it to his father. The specific reasons were also different. For example, Joe should not give the money up because he did a lot of work to earn it, or he should give it up because his father had been good to him in the past. The underlying patterns of thought, however, emphasize doing things to please other people and win their approval.

The Structure of Progression of Thinking from Lower to Higher Stages

As a person can see from these descriptions and examples, progress through the stages is characterized by cognitive differentiation (for example, the value of property is distinguished from the value of human life); more integration of ideas (for example, the values of trust, life, law, property are put into a hierarchy); and more universal (for example, they appeal to principles or ideas that are more universally accepted) than the lower stages. The higher stages, in effect, are better for these and other reasons.

One argument for the idea that higher stages are better is that more problems can be resolved by using reasons or solutions from higher stages. Take, for example, a conflict between two ethnic communities (Guidance Associates, 1976a). Members of each community who are at stage three define what is right according to what is approved by the majority of the people in their group. If the members of the two groups endorse a different way of life, they may come into conflict when an issue arises, such as busing to achieve racial integration of schools. For individuals at stage four, the conflict would be resolved because those in both groups would be oriented toward maintaining the social order through obedience to authority. This kind of thought pattern could lead to a fair solution for both groups.

The sequence of development of moral thinking roughly parallels the development of abstract thought as outlined by Piaget (1948). The individual moves away from egocentric thought and objective judgment based on consequences, toward an ability to take the roles of others along with subjective judgment based on the intent and motivations of the individual involved in an act.

How an Individual Progresses through the Stages

Individuals reason predominantly at one stage of thought but use contiguous stages as a secondary thinking pattern (Kohlberg, 1966). For example, a person who is in a transition between stages three and four may express stage three reasoning 60 percent of the time and stage four reasoning 40 percent of the time.

Everyone moves through the stages in the same sequence, beginning with stage one, but people do so at different rates and may stop at different stages. Most people do not achieve higher than stage four, and an extremely small number reach stage six. A young child reasons at stage one. Most people then move to stage two and stay there until early or middle adolescence, when they enter stage three. Toward middle or late adolescence, some enter stage four. If it occurs, the transition to stage five takes place when people are in their late teens and early twenties, or even later in life. Few attain stage six, but those who do are over thirty. According to the theory, people do not regress to lower stages once a higher level is attained.

Movement through the stages requires and is facilitated by (a) the development of abstract thought; and (b) the development of perspective-taking ability (Selman, 1971). As a person's cognitive abilities increase, he or she is able to comprehend more sophisticated reasoning, reasoning that takes into account more viewpoints and more factors, which enables moral reasoning at a higher level. Selman (1971) has examined the development of a broadened social perspective or role-taking ability. He defines role taking by the way individuals differentiate their own perspective from the perspectives of others and by the way people relate these perspectives to each other. On the basis of his research, Selman has defined four stages of perspective-taking ability that parallel Kohlberg's stages of moral development. The ability to take the point of view of another person, according to Selman, is a necessary but not sufficient condition for achieving high levels of moral reasoning.

The Preconventional Level (Stages 1 and 2). At this level, people have the perspective of an isolated individual rather than of a person who belongs to a group or social system. This level has the following two stages:

Stage 1	*Stage 2*
At this stage, people focus only on their own interests and do not think of themselves as people with responsibilities to others or as people who belong to a group.	At this stage, people still want to serve their own interests, but are able to anticipate another person's reactions. Here, there is a willingness to make a deal to get what one wants.

The Conventional Level (Stages 3 and 4). At this level, people assume the perspective of a person who is a member of a group or of a society. This level has the following two stages:

Stage 3	*Stage 4*
Here people can see things from the point of view of shared relationships, such as caring, trust, and respect between two or more individuals who know each other.	Here people can take the point of view of a member of a social system or a society as a whole. People are able to see a situation through the eyes of many, including people in the society whom they do not know (Guidance Associates, 1976a, Handout 10, p. 6).

Movement upward through the stages identified by Kohlberg occurs for two related reasons: (a) people prefer the highest stages of reasoning they can comprehend; and (b) when reasoning from a higher stage is understood, it conflicts with the individual's existing point of view. This cognitive conflict causes a dissonance or discomfort that must be resolved.

About Teaching

Following from these assumptions about progress through the stages is the idea that an educator's role is to establish a setting where students are exposed to moral dilemmas and encouraged to discuss them with each other. In other words, if situations are set up in which cognitive conflict can occur and students are continually and systematically exposed to reasoning at a higher stage than their own, students may move through the stages more rapidly and ultimately achieve higher stages than if educators sit back and allow the normal course of development to occur (Kohlberg & Mayer, 1972).

A second underlying idea is that teaching should concentrate on developing higher levels of moral judgment rather than moral behavior. High levels of moral judgment are necessary for ethical behavior, but do not ensure that ethical behavior will occur. How individuals will behave cannot accurately be predicted based on their reasoning at the preconventional and conventional levels. At the principled level, however, the structure of thought often leads to one solution based on universally accepted ethical principles, so behavior is more predictable. In addition to moral reasoning, at least three other factors influence moral behavior: (1) situational stress including emotional factors; (2) diffused responsibility; and (3) the complexity of moral issues involved (Guidance Associates, 1976a). It is difficult to predict the results of these influences.

About Characteristics and Teaching of the Gifted

Although Kohlberg's moral learning theory is used as a model for education of the gifted, Kohlberg and his followers have not generally commented on the gifted. Characteristics of the gifted student and teaching strategies useful with them are not addressed specifically. With Kohlberg's emphasis on increasing abstraction in moral thought and what is known about the development of gifted children, it is possible to define some implicit assumptions of the model on these issues.

First, gifted children are capable of abstract thought sooner than their peers. If moral thinking involves increasing abstraction, this would lead to more rapid passage through the stages by gifted children, given the proper environmental stimulus. This implies earlier presentation of certain dilemmas in the education of the gifted and increased activity to induce cognitive uncertainty, thereby causing maximal growth.

Gifted children also tend to be more interested in humanitarian issues than their peers, and they develop this interest at an earlier age. This reinforces the notion that the moral dilemmas discussed as part of the Kohlberg educational programs would be interesting and helpful to gifted students.

A third implicit assumption made by those who employ the Kohlberg approach is that the gifted, who are more likely to attain the highest levels of abstract thought, have the potential to achieve the highest levels of moral reasoning. Because of this potential, it is educators' responsibility to provide an environment where optimal development can occur.

ELEMENTS/PARTS

Dimensions, Thinking Levels, or Steps

The most important aspect of Kohlberg's approach to the development of moral reasoning is the *Discussion of Moral Dilemmas*. These dilemmas are chosen or created on the basis of several criteria: (a) a central character must decide between alternative possibilities for action; (b) there is at least one moral issue involved; and (c) society lends some support for any of several actions that could be taken by the protagonist. Dilemmas are presented to students, and a discussion follows. Moral discussions follow a six-step process and may be accomplished in several ways to avoid boredom with the process (Guidance Associates, 1976a).

Step One: Present the Dilemma

Moral dilemmas can be presented in several ways. Sound-filmstrips are available, as are written materials. Students can also be asked to role-play conflict situations.

Step Two: Have Students Clarify the Facts of the Situation and Identify the Issues Involved

At this step, the teacher asks for information about what happened in the story. Students summarize the events, identify the principal characters, and describe the alternatives open to the protagonist. This part of the discussion will take a short period of time.

Step Three: Have Students Identify a Tentative Position on the Action the Central Character Should Take and State One or Two Reasons for That Position

At this step, students are asked to choose from the identified alternatives what the character *should* do and the major reason for their choice. This can be done in writing to ensure that children will think for themselves and develop a position. While students are writing, the teacher can walk around the room to get an idea of how the class is thinking. After each student has developed a written opinion, the teacher then asks for a show of hands on the various alternatives to get an idea of the differences or similarities that exist. This information is also used to guide in the organization of the next step.

Step Four: Divide the Class into Small Groups

In this setting children have the chance to share their reasons for the positions they have taken. Shy children and those who may feel threatened by the teacher's presence should find this setting comfortable for sharing their ideas. Small group discussions with four to six members should take approximately 10 to 15 minutes. To organize these small groups for maximum effectiveness and interaction among students, the teacher should divide them differently depending on how the class is split on the issue. If the class splits unevenly on the issue, students can be divided into groups that have taken the same position. They can discuss their reasons and decide on the two best reasons for the position. If the class splits evenly on the issue, students can be divided into groups with an approximately even number that agree with each position. In groups, these students discuss both positions and choose the best reasons for each. If the class agrees about one position, the students can be divided into groups based on the similarity of their reasons for supporting a position. Each group can then decide why the reason they prefer is the best one. In this situation, students can also be divided according to differences in reasons. The small groups then discuss their reasons and decide on the best two or three to support their decision.

During these small group discussions, the teacher should move around the class to make certain that students understand the task and that they focus on reasons rather than argue about the facts or some aspect of the situation. While observing the groups, the teacher can get some ideas for opening the discussion in a large group.

Step Five: Reconvene the Class for a Full Class Discussion of the Dilemma

This part of the process should take the majority of class time. The class should be seated in a circle, with the teacher included, to encourage a maximum amount of student-to-student interaction. Although student interaction is the most important aspect of this discussion time, the teacher's role is crucial in encouraging interaction among students with different points of view, establishing an atmosphere where students feel free to express different ideas, and keeping the discussion focused on the reasons and positions rather than side issues or facts of the situation.

A full class discussion can be initiated in several ways: (a) having each group write its position and supporting reasons on the board, and then asking opposing groups to respond to each other; (b) asking for oral reports from each group, beginning with those who seemed to function well in the small group setting, and then asking for comments from those with opposing viewpoints after each report; or (c) opening the discussion to all, asking the general question, "What should the central character do? Why?" and keeping the discussion going with teacher questions when needed.

During this part of the discussion, teacher questions are crucial for keeping the conversation focused on reasons, encouraging shy students to participate, encouraging interaction among students who are reasoning at different stages, and encouraging students to think about reasons at stages higher than their own. Following are some examples of the types of questions teachers can ask at this step of the discussion:

- *Perception-checking questions* determine whether or not other students understand a statement that an individual has made: "Mary, will you tell me in your own words what Sheila said?"
- *Interstudent-participation questions* ask one student to respond to the position of another student: "Mary, what do you think of what Charles said?"
- *Clarifying questions* ask students to make the meaning of their own statements clear: "What do you mean by justice?"
- *Issue-related questions* focus attention on one or more moral issues: "Is it ever all right to break a law?"
- *Role-switch questions* ask a student to look at a situation from the point of view of another character in the dilemma: "Jill would want her to lie, you say. Would the storeowner want her to lie?"

- *Universal-consequences questions* ask a student to imagine what would happen if everyone behaved in a certain way: "What would our lives be like if everyone broke laws when it pleased them to do so?"
- *Seeking-reason questions* ask for the reasoning behind the statement of a position: "Why?" (Guidance Associates, 1976a, Handout 11, p. 5)

As the teacher listens to the discussion, he or she should identify reasoning at a particular stage and then encourage a student to respond who has previously expressed reasoning at a higher stage. The teacher should also prepare questions that force students to consider reasoning that is at a higher level than anyone in the class has expressed. If the teacher knows from past discussions the levels of reasoning usually employed, such "provocative" questions can be prepared in advance.

Step Six: Ask Students to Reevaluate Their Original Positions Individually

After the large group discussion, the teacher should ask students to review the discussion and answer the following two questions privately: (1) "Now what do you think the main character should do?" and (2) "What is the most important reason for this action?" The teacher should not attempt to get the group to reach consensus about the dilemma or to suggest that one reason or position may be better than another, but the reevaluation is important. The teacher can collect these responses along with the original written position of the student to see if any significant changes occurred. These individual responses should be evaluated according to their stage so that growth over a period of time can be assessed.

To keep the process interesting and stimulating, teachers can and should vary their methods of presenting and discussing moral dilemmas. In the *Values in a Democracy* and *Values in American History* series edited by Fenton and Kohlberg (Guidance Associates, 1976b, 1976c), the following different ways of presenting dilemmas are used: (a) a list of statements about an issue, each followed by "agree," "disagree," or "can't decide," with instructions for students to indicate their position and then write the most important reason for it; (b) one or two paragraphs about an issue, with four reasons supporting an action and four opposing it, with instructions for students to choose their preferred reasons; (c) a short description of a dilemma with a list of five arguments at each of five stages supporting an action, which students rank according to their preference; and (d) three arguments supporting a different position on an issue from which the students choose a preferred argument and expand upon it.

With these varied presentations of a dilemma, teachers would need to modify the six-step process. In all of them, however, there should be an opportunity for students to discuss their reasons. The teacher should set up the situation so that students are interacting and being exposed to reasoning at higher stages than their own. In the first presentation, where students respond to statements indicating their agreement or disagreement, only steps five and six are appropriate, and the procedures at step five should be modified. A way to facilitate discussion in this situation would be to consider each of the five statements in turn, asking students who have taken each position (agree, disagree, can't decide) to state their reasons for the position. As the discussion proceeds, the teacher can ask questions in the same manner outlined previously for this step. Step six is much the same except that students should be asked to choose the statement they prefer and write the major reason for this preference. Suggestions for modification of the process based on other ways of presenting dilemmas are given in the material developed by Guidance Associates (1976a). The major part of each, however, is whole-class discussion of the issues and reasons (step five), with small-group discussions at different times to encourage more interaction among students.

MODIFICATION OF THE BASIC CURRICULUM

Kohlberg's *Moral Dilemma* discussions suggest mainly content and process modifications that are appropriate for the gifted. To implement these changes effectively, however, the psychological learning environment must be centered on student ideas, permit independence, be open to new ideas and new viewpoints, and be accepting rather than judgmental.

Content Modifications

Discussions of Moral Dilemmas suggest content modifications appropriate for the gifted due to their focus on moral/ethical issues rather than the usual subject matter content. Because the content is different, the principle of variety is met. However, more important modifications are suggested in the areas of abstractness and complexity. Because the ultimate goal of these discussions is to encourage students to consider ideas at higher stages, which are by definition more abstract, more complex, and more universal, and because gifted children are capable of reaching these stages more quickly, discussions should concentrate on these abstract ideas. Guidelines are also given for selecting dilemmas that have no simple solution, dilemmas whose solutions must take into consideration several complex issues with no clear-cut societal solution.

Process Modifications

Process modifications suggested by the method include emphasis on higher levels (stages) of thinking, concentration on reasoning, group interaction, and variety in methods. There also should be some emphasis on open-endedness. Kohlberg suggests a step-by-step procedure for accomplishing these purposes during a discussion. Since the emphasis is on presenting reasoning at levels higher than the students' predominant ones and there are specific descriptions of the type of thinking at each stage, the goal of developing higher levels of thinking should be achieved.

Although Kohlberg's discussion procedures do not emphasize the asking of open-ended questions, the element of provocativeness is included in the entire method. The whole approach is designed to promote cognitive conflict and further thought about a moral issue to cause positive change or movement through the stages. At step five, there is also a great deal of emphasis on provocative questions, especially "issue-related" questions, "role-switch" questions, and "universal-consequences" questions. Teachers should use these questions to stimulate further and higher level thought from students.

Almost by definition, the procedure makes the process modifications of proof/reasoning and group interaction. The approach focuses on encouraging students to express moral reasoning at higher levels than before the method was introduced, and a basic assumption of the method is that this reasoning reaches higher levels because students have interacted with each other. Those at a lower stage have listened to the reasons presented at higher levels, and since they tend to prefer higher level reasons, they will adopt this other reasoning. The teacher's major task at steps four (small-group discussion) and five (full-class discussion) is to keep the group's attention focused on a discussion of reasons for actions. Several types of questions recommended at step five are designed to force students to listen and react to the ideas presented by other members of the group (for example, perception-checking questions and interstudent-participation questions).

Variety of methods is accomplished through varied means of presenting and discussing dilemmas. In each different method, the six-step process needs to be modified.

Product and Learning Environment Modifications

The *Moral Dilemma* discussion strategy does not suggest product modifications appropriate for the gifted, but does provide one learning environment change. The method makes provisions for developing a student-centered process. Because the class is divided into small groups for a portion of the time (step four), student talk must be emphasized without the teacher as the center. There is also no opportunity for the teacher to talk during a discussion of this type. Teachers must exercise care, however, to avoid becoming the center of the discussion during step five. The central position can be avoided by (a) liberal use of "perception-checking" and "interstudent-participation" questions to encourage student reaction to student ideas; and (b) avoiding a response to every student idea.

Other suggestions for changes in the learning environment are made by Kohlberg's newest experiments, the experiments in development of "communities" that govern themselves (Muson, 1979). In these communities, the emphasis is on having group members develop their own rules of government, solve their own problems, and enforce their own rules. According to Kohlberg, the principles of democracy cannot be taught in an autocratic school or institution. These principles must be practiced on a daily basis and developed in a setting where individuals can observe the effects of their decision making. In most schools, rather than learning democratic principles, students learn obedience to authority and to arbitrary rules made and enforced by adults.

These communities have been developed in several high schools and prisons as an experiment in rehabilitation. Members discuss solutions to their problems based on "fairness and morality." In other words, instead of discussing hypothetical dilemmas, such as the ones used to study moral development, the communities discuss their own real problems. Although the communities have not escaped criticism, Kohlberg views them as a success, especially those operating in high schools. Students have been able to develop a sense of community and govern themselves responsibly. They have their problems, especially when the wishes of the group conflict with state or federal rules, and when they conflict with school policy.

Regardless of the criticism, the basic idea of the community directly applies to the development of learning environment changes appropriate for the gifted, especially in the dimension of independence and in the areas of openness and acceptance. With regard to independence, students are encouraged to develop their own management and government rather than relying on the teacher to develop and implement solutions to their problems. The element of openness is present since the students are free to develop and implement their own procedures and to express themselves freely. Teachers present their ideas, but as equal members of groups. The teacher, according to the theory, should present moral reasoning at a higher level than the students so they can be exposed to the highest levels.

Certainly, acceptance is an important part of the process since the teacher must be one of the group and model the kind of behavior expected from students. This behavior includes attempting to understand another person's perspective and ideas, acceptance of the ideas, clarification of the ideas (an important aspect of the *Moral Dilemma* discussions), and challenging the ideas. This challenging is valuable in the Kohlberg strategy since the theory states that growth occurs through cognitive conflict. Since the communities operate for a long period of time and a significant aspect is development of mutual trust, the challenging of ideas should be easily integrated.

EXAMPLES OF TEACHING ACTIVITIES

To provide an example of the use of Kohlberg's techniques, the classic story of Heinz will be used. This dilemma has been used as one of the stimuli for Kohlberg's interviews with subjects in his longitudinal studies to establish the developmental stages. In the following example, the six-step process is followed as a model. However, to make the process more appropriate for the gifted and to increase the likelihood that the purposes will be accomplished, elements of Hilda Taba's (Institute for Staff Development, IV, 1971d), *Resolution of Conflict Strategy,* have been added. A short discussion of the process after its presentation will identify those elements and provide a rationale for their inclusion.

Step One. Presenting the Dilemma

Heinz's Dilemma

In Europe, a woman was near death from a special kind of cancer. There was one drug that the doctors thought might save her. It was a form of radium that a druggist in the same town had recently discovered. The drug was expensive to make, but the druggist was charging 10 times what the drug cost him to make. He paid $200 for the radium and charged $2,000 for a small dose of the drug. The sick woman's husband, Heinz, went to everyone he knew to borrow the money, but he could only get together about $1,000, which is half of what it cost. He told the druggist that his wife was dying, and asked him to sell it cheaper or let him pay later. But the druggist said, "No, I discovered the drug and I'm going to make money from it." So Heinz gets desperate and considers breaking into the man's store to steal the drug for his wife. (Muson, 1979, p. 53)

Step Two. Listing the Facts of the Situation

In a large group, the students should list the facts in the story. They should concentrate on actions of people and things people said, rather than on subjective perceptions of what happened. Questions to be asked include the following: What happened in the story? What things did Heinz do? What did the druggist do? What did Heinz say to the druggist? What did the druggist say to Heinz? If students make inferences such as "the druggist didn't care about Heinz's dying wife," ask for specific data through questions such as "What did the druggist do or say that made you think he didn't care about Heinz's wife?"

Step Three. Exploring the Perspectives of the Different Characters

At this step, each important action of each individual involved in the dilemma should be explored, and students should be asked to make inferences about (a) the reasons for behavior; (b) the feelings of the people involved; and (c) the reasons why people felt a certain way. At this step, a particular action should be chosen, then a series of questions should be asked about that action. Next another action should be selected and the same questions asked. This should continue until the important facts have been explored. For example, in this story, important facts are the following:

- Heinz could not borrow or raise enough money to buy the one drug his wife needed to cure her cancer.
- Heinz's wife would die without the drug.
- The druggist was charging ten times what the drug was worth.
- The druggist would not sell the drug cheaper or let Heinz pay later.
- Heinz considered breaking into the store to steal the drug.

To explore one of these facts, for example, the druggist charging ten times the worth of the drug, the teacher would ask the following questions:

- Why do you think the druggist charged so much for the drug? (The teacher should elicit a variety of reasons.)
- How do you think the druggist felt about doing this? (A typical answer may be that he felt justified.)
- Why do you think he felt justified in doing this?
- How else do you think he felt? (The answer may be that he felt a little guilty.)
- Why would he feel this way?

After eliciting a variety of possible feelings of the druggist, the teacher should concentrate on Heinz's feelings.

- How do you think Heinz felt about the druggist charging so much? (One answer is angry.)
- Why would this make him angry?
- How else might Heinz feel?

The teacher should elicit a variety of possible feelings for Heinz and then explore another fact of the story, following the same sequence of questions: (a) reasons for actions; (b) feelings of action and a reason for each feeling; and

(c) feelings of person receiving the action and a reason for each feeling. The teacher should ask for a variety of reasons for actions, a variety of feelings for each person, and support for each inference about feelings.

Step Four. Identifying the Two or Three Major Alternatives of the Protagonist

In this situation, in order to focus the discussion on the moral issue of stealing to save a life, the discussion must be limited to Heinz's two alternatives of stealing or not stealing. Although Taba's *Resolution of Conflict Strategy* and many other strategies for problem solving emphasize the development of many alternatives at this step, a good Kohlberg *Moral Dilemma* discussion does not avoid the dilemma by developing a compromise solution. Kohlberg stresses discussing the moral issues in a situation where two ethical positions are competing. In some cases, there may be as many as three alternatives. In most dilemmas, however, the focus should be on two choices.

Step Five. Exploring the Consequences of the Identified Alternatives

Each alternative should be explored separately in the following manner. First, the teacher should have the students predict what would happen by asking, "What do you think would happen if Heinz steals the drug?" The teacher should ask for a variety of predictions (for example, What else do you think might happen? How would Heinz's wife react? What would Heinz do?). After a variety of predictions have been made, the teacher should go back to each prediction and ask the students why they would predict that this would happen.

Next, the other alternative should be explored: "What do you think will happen if Heinz does not steal the drug?" After a variety of predictions have been made, the teacher should go back and ask for reasons for each of the predictions.

Since this is essentially a brainstorming strategy, it is more effective to make predictions and then discuss reasons later. Asking for reasons immediately after predictions often inhibits the flow of ideas.

Step Six. Identifying a Tentative Position

The students should identify individually what they think Heinz should do and write down why they think he should do this. It should be emphasized that this is only a tentative position for the purpose of discussion and small-group divisions. After asking for individual decisions, the teacher should take a poll of the class, asking for a show of hands on each identified alternative.

Step Seven. Dividing the Class into Small Groups for Discussion*

After polling the class, the students should be separated into small groups based on their division on the issues. If the class is equally divided, each small group can have participants who hold opposing positions. They should discuss each position and choose the best reason for each. If there is a definite minority opinion, the small groups should be made up of those who share the same position. These students should then discuss the position and reasons, and select the two best reasons to justify the position. If the class agrees on the action Heinz should take, they can be divided according to their reasons, either put together because they have the same reasons or different ones. If the reasons are similar, they should decide why this reason is best, but if the reasons are different, the students should discuss the various reasons and decide on the best two or three.

Step Eight. A Full Group Discussion of Conclusions and Reasons

At this step, students from each of the small groups should report their decisions, and the teacher should encourage students to react to the ideas of those who hold opposing viewpoints. The teacher has several objectives at this step including (a) exposure of students to reasoning at higher levels than their own; (b) encouraging students to consider and react to reasoning that is different from their own; (c) focusing on the moral issues involved; and (d) encouraging students to consider the universal consequences of their solutions. The sequence of the discussion, at this point, is to first ask students to state what they think Heinz should do and then to give their reasons. After this, teachers should use their own judgment to decide when to ask a particular kind of question.

To aid in designing discussion plans for this part of the lesson, Table 5-1 provides a sample plan. The format includes behavioral objectives, focusing questions to achieve the objective, and support procedures (Institute for Staff Development, 1971). Support procedures are essentially teacher behaviors other than focusing questions that are necessary for achieving the objective. These are the teacher behaviors involved in establishing an appropriate learning environment.

Step Nine. Reevaluating Original Student Positions

Now that students have discussed each of the alternatives and their consequences, have listened to a variety of reasons for each position on what Heinz should do, and have considered the moral issues involved, they are ready to think back about their original position and reevaluate it. They should do this activity

---

*This step is only appropriate if the group is large. If there are less than ten children, there is no need for these small-group divisions.

Table 5-1 Objectives, Focusing Questions, and Support Procedures for Step Eight of a Moral Dilemma Discussion

Behavioral Objectives	Focusing Questions	Support Procedures*
(a) Students will state what they think Heinz should do.	What do you think Heinz should do? Based on our discussions about the possible consequences of each of the alternatives, what do you think Heinz should do?	Since students have already written their answers and discussed this question, each group can report its decisions. Have students write these selected solutions on the board along with their reasons
(b) Students will state why they think that is what Heinz should do, and will consider reasons at higher levels than their own.	Why do you think Heinz should steal the drug? What were the most important reasons your group gave for saying that he should not steal the drug?	When students are expressing their reasons, listen carefully to determine the level or stage of reasoning they express. As students are discussing their reasons and reacting to the reasons of others, listen carefully for opportunities to introduce them to reasoning at a level higher than

that expressed by anyone in the group. Since there will usually be someone in the group at least at stage 3, have prepared questions that will expose them to reasoning at stages 4 and 5. For example, at stage 4 people are concerned with law and order and obedience to laws. Some questions that would focus on this kind of reasoning would be: "But there are laws against stealing from someone. How does caring about his wife make it OK to steal? As a husband, Heinz has a duty to his wife. What is it not his duty to try his best to save her life even if he has to steal?" At stage 5, people usually express conflict over whether to uphold the

Table 5-1 continued

Behavioral Objectives	Focusing Questions	Support Procedures
		law, since it was developed for our protection, or whether to try and save the life of his wife. They recognize the sacredness of life, but also recognize that an impartial judge for the sake of consistency would have to convict Heinz. Some sample questions would be: "Which would be more wrong, letting his wife die or stealing? What do you think would be the reaction of the judge if Heinz is brought to trial for stealing? Do you think a judge would sentence or convict a man for trying to keep his wife from dying?

(c) Students will react to the reasoning of students that is different from their own.

Bill, what do you think about what Diane just said?

Ray, how are your reasons different from Jan's?

Encourage students who have an opposite point of view or reasons at a higher stage to react to another student's ideas. As students are discussing their reasons of others, listen carefully for opportunities to introduce them to reasoning at a level higher than that expressed by anyone in the group.

(d) Students will respond to questions regarding the moral issues involved.

When is it all right to break a law?

When is it all right to steal?

When is it all right to make an unreasonable profit?

How would the situation be different if the woman were not Heinz's wife?

As students give their answers to all questions, look for references to moral issues. Pinpoint the issue and ask a question that will require a direct response.

Table 5-1 continued

Behavioral Objectives	Focusing Questions	Support procedures
(e) Students will consider the universal consequences of their solutions.	What would the world be like if everyone broke laws? What do you think would happen if everyone stole drugs to save someone in their family?	Encourage consideration of the consequences of several people making the same decision.

* At all steps in this phase of the lesson, make certain that students clarify their statements so that all understand their meaning (for example, What do you mean by "fair?" Explain what you mean by "right to life.").

individually and write their reevaluation on a second sheet of paper. They should write what they think Heinz should do and why he should do this.

Analyses of Sample Activity

For the purpose of analyzing this lesson and explaining which parts are based entirely on Kohlberg's techniques and which parts are based on Taba's *Resolution of Conflict Strategy*, it will be helpful to compare the sample lesson plan with Table 5-2. Table 5-2 provides a summary of the steps in a Kohlberg *Moral Dilemma* discussion along with student and teacher activities. In making this comparison, three steps have been added after step two by combining this strategy with Taba's *Resolution of Conflict Strategy*. At step two, Kohlberg only suggests having students clarify the facts, identify the issues, and discuss the alternatives for action. There is no sequence to the questions, and students are not asked to consider reasons for the actions of people, their possible feelings, and the reasons for their feelings.

The addition of a discussion of each alternative—its possible consequences and the reasons for these consequences—also goes beyond what is suggested by Kohlberg. The addition of these questions at steps three, four, and five is extremely important to the discussion for two related reasons: (a) practice in perspective taking and (b) resistance to closure. The questions asking students to consider reasons for actions, feelings, and reasons for feelings of all the people involved give them needed practice in taking into account the perspectives of others, which Selman (1971) has identified as a prerequisite to advanced moral reasoning. Considering these perspectives before making even a tentative judgment about what Heinz should do is important because students have not already made a judgment and will be more open to alternative considerations at this point. Remaining open to new considerations and resisting cognitive closure is the most salient reason for adding a discussion of each alternative and its consequences at this point. There is a considerable amount of research in the creativity literature showing the benefits of resisting early closure or judgment on an idea. Some of the best cognitive growth can occur when students are forced to keep an open mind about an issue until they have adequately considered all the alternatives and their consequences. This is when the process of "disequilibrium" or cognitive discomfort can begin. According to both Kohlberg and Piaget, this is the way cognitive growth happens. After considering the alternatives carefully, the students should take a *tentative* position (step six). This is Kohlberg's step three, which is not modified in the previous lesson. His step four (new step six) is also the same.

At the seventh step (Kohlberg's fifth), the full class discussion, elements of Taba's strategy have again been added to bring some structure and sequence to the discussion and to emphasize perspective taking and resistance to closure. At this step, Kohlberg suggests that the teacher get the discussion started and that he or she

Table 5-2 Summary of Teacher and Student Roles and Activities in Kohlberg's Moral Dilemma Discussions

Step, Type, or Level of Thinking	Student		Teacher	
	Role	Sample Activities	Role	Sample Activities
Step 1: Present the dilemma	observer	Read, listen to, or watch the presentation of a situation in which a main character is involved in a moral dilemma.	presenter	Develop or select an interesting story about a main character faced with a moral/ethical choice. Develop a role-playing situation in which characters act out a situation in which there is a moral dilemma.
Step 2: Have students clarify the facts and issues involved in the dilemma	summarizer; clarifier; identifier of issues	Summarize the events and facts in the dilemma presented. Identify the major issues. Recall the names of the characters. Identify the possible alternatives for action open to the main character.	questioner; facilitator	Ask the students questions which will elicit student summaries, identification of issues, and recall of facts. Ask students to generate alternative courses of action for the protagonist.
Step 3: Have students identify a tentative position with reasons	active participant	Take a tentative position on what action the protagonist should take. Write the position and the reasons.	questioner; observer	Ask students to identify a tentative position individually and justify that position. Observe what the students are writing.
Step 4: Divide the class into small groups	active participant	In a small group, discuss the positions taken and the reasons for taking them. Select the favored positions and the best reasons to justify them.	facilitator; observer; supporter	Take a quick poll of the class to see how it splits on the issue. Divide the class into small groups of 4–6 students. Divide them in a way that will facilitate maximum discussion of issues and reasons. Encourage discussion of and provide support for minority viewpoints.

Step		Student Role	Student Activities	Teacher Role	Teacher Activities
Step 5:	Reconvene the class for a full-class discussion of the dilemma	active participant; reporter; discussant; active listener	In a large group, present the decisions of the small group. React to and challenge the reasoning of other students. Actively try to understand their reasons and see their viewpoints when different from own.	facilitator; questioner; active listener; presenter	Observe small-group discussions and keep the groups focused on reasons. Observe small groups to get ideas for opening questions or comments that will encourage maximum discussion and interaction in the large group. Request a report from each group that gives their position and agreed-upon reasons supporting it. Ask questions that encourage student interaction. Ask questions that require students to understand or summarize the viewpoints of others. Ask questions that require students to consider universal consequences of actions. Ask questions that require students to consider reasoning at stages higher than their own. Ask students to clarify their statements. Ask students questions which require them to look at a situation from a different viewpoint. Ask students to explain their reasons for all statements. Foster a climate of free expression, openness, and respect for all points of view.
Step 6:	Ask students to reevaluate their original positions	reevaluator	Think carefully about all ideas expressed—particularly the suggested reasons—and reevaluate the tentative position taken and the reasons. Decide what action the character should take and the major reason for doing so.	questioner	Ask students to carefully think about the discussion and reevaluate their original positions. Have them individually write answers to the question "Now what do you think the protagonist should do? What is your major reason for thinking this?".

encourage student interaction, pose universal-consequences questions, pose issue-related questions, and pose questions that will force students to consider reasoning at higher levels than their own.

The addition of a particular sequence and structure to this questioning process is based on Taba's strategy. First, the small groups are asked to report what they decided Heinz should do and why. Next, students who have a different point of view or different reasons are asked to comment on or react to the positions and reasons. During this time, the teacher asks students to indicate their understanding of the other person's point of view. During these discussions of what Heinz should do and why, the teacher should listen for references to moral issues and ask students to respond to a direct question pinpointing the issue involved. During this part of the discussion, the teacher should also be listening and looking for opportunities to introduce students to a higher level of reasoning by asking them questions that will force them to consider this line of reasoning.

During this time, the teacher should also ask questions that require students to consider the consequences for everyone involved (not just Heinz) and to consider the universal consequences (for example, what would happen if everyone broke laws). Finally, students should reevaluate their original position and write what they now think Heinz should do and why—Kohlberg's step six.

The addition of elements from Taba's *Resolution of Conflict Strategy* may make Kohlberg *Moral Dilemma* discussions longer than they would be otherwise, but the discussions will be more sequential and more likely achieve the purposes identified by Kohlberg. Taba's (1966) research has demonstrated the effectiveness of her sequencing of questions. (See Chapter 8 for a discussion of the research on the *Hilda Taba Strategies.*) Also, there is no comparable research on the appropriate sequencing of questions in Kohlberg's approach.

MODIFYING THE APPROACH

In addition to the reasons listed above, elements of the Taba *Strategy* were combined with Kohlberg's discussion strategy to make the approach more appropriate for use with the gifted. As the needed content, process, product, and learning environment modifications are discussed below, the sample lesson will be examined to illustrate how this approach makes the strategy more appropriate for use with the gifted.

Content Changes

Kohlberg's approach does not make curricular modifications appropriate for the gifted in the following areas: (a) organization and economy; (b) study of people; and (c) methods of inquiry. However, adding strategies for incorporating such changes would be easy. In a curriculum where the content to be taught is organized around key concepts and generalizations, dilemmas that illustrate the moral/ethical side of a concept can be chosen for discussion. For example, the Heinz dilemma could be discussed when dealing with the human side of scientific advances, both from the perspective of the patient and of the scientist who is making a break-through. The dilemma could also be integrated into social studies by considering the consequences of crimes and their effect on punishment. The addition of a moral dilemma discussion in both these instances adds an element of complexity into the study of such concepts.

The study of people could be integrated by studying the moral/ethical issues faced by the famous people and identifying how they resolved the conflicts they faced. Students could discuss whether the famous person's decision was morally right or wrong, and students could consider whether they would make the same decision when faced with such a choice. In these cases, students have the benefit of knowing the real consequences of the actions taken. They can also compare the consequences of a decision made now with a decision made during the lifetime of the person being studied.

Moral Dilemma discussions can also be combined with the study of methods of inquiry. Scientific and other investigations always involve ethical decisions of some kind. A *Moral Dilemma* discussion provides an excellent way to consider such issues.

Although the general approach advocated by Kohlberg and his colleagues modifies the curriculum in the content areas of abstraction and complexity, the concepts of abstractness and complexity should provide guidelines for selecting the moral issues and dilemmas to be discussed. Gifted students should be involved in discussions of dilemmas involving the most abstract and complex moral/ethical issues they can understand at a particular age.

Process Changes

Higher Level Thought

Although the focus of Kohlberg's approach is moving students from lower to higher levels of reasoning, the strategy proposed by Kohlberg and his colleagues does not provide for the structured movement of a discussion from lower to higher levels of thinking. The general progression of discussions is from concern with facts to a concern with moral issues and how they should be resolved. However, students are expected to move from a discussion of the facts of the situation to identification of the moral issues and selection of a tentative position without any intermediate steps. Adding elements of the Taba *Strategy* provides these needed intermediate steps in the discussion. With these new steps, students can look at actions, reasons, and feelings of the people involved and consequences of actions before taking a tentative position. These added elements should provide needed perspectives for making decisions in situations involving other people.

Open-endedness

The Kohlberg strategy incorporates the element of provocativeness in all aspects of the approach. However, there is little attention to the asking of open-ended questions. The Taba questions provide models for integrating the concept of open-endedness in questioning.

Discovery

In some ways, Kohlberg *Discussions of Moral Dilemmas* could be considered inductive or discovery approaches, since students must identify moral issues and decide for themselves how these issues should be resolved. However, the actual discussion strategy is so unstructured that the teacher lacks some important guidelines for implementing the approach effectively. To make the strategy a completely inductive one, the teacher must avoid any role other than that of questioner after the initial presentation of the dilemma. Students must identify the moral issues, identify the facts and alternatives, and infer the consequences of actions on their own. Adding Taba's structured questioning sequence provides needed guidelines for the teacher in making these discussions completely inductive.

At one step in the discussion, the teacher may need to be directive in order to accomplish the goals of the strategy. As indicated earlier, when identifying alternatives, most problem-solving strategies (including Taba's *Resolution of Conflict*) require that a variety of alternatives be identified for solving the problem. When this aspect of the Taba *Strategy* was incorporated into Kohlberg *Moral Dilemma* discussions, teachers in the author's classes found that attention was diverted from the moral issues involved. Students tended to discuss the pros and cons of the alternatives and to combine alternatives so that the moral issues did not really have to be confronted. If the focus were on the development of solutions acceptable to everyone, such an approach would be highly appropriate. However, since the purpose is to develop cognitive conflict, two opposing alternatives must be the focus of the discussion. Thus, the teacher may need to simply say: "These are Heinz's two alternatives."

Evidence of Reasoning

Since much of Kohlberg's strategy focuses on the reasons for action, this curricular modification is very much a part of the approach. However, three additional steps provide other opportunities for discussing reasons: (a) reasons for actions; (b) reasons for inferences about feelings; and (c) reasons for predictions about consequences.

Freedom of Choice

The element of freedom of choice could be incorporated by giving students the opportunity to identify moral issues or dilemmas they would like to discuss. Gifted students could also be given the freedom to develop and conduct their own discussions of moral dilemmas.

Pacing

Kohlberg and his colleagues do not provide suggestions for appropriate pacing of discussions for gifted students. Taba does suggest, however, that the teacher must be sensitive to the needs of the group and move students to the next level of thinking when they are ready. The structure of the discussions provides an excellent setting for making such decisions. In addition, the discussion must be paced so that the majority of time is spent on the later steps rather than in clarifying the issues and facts. Higher levels of thinking and reasoning are involved in these later steps than in the earlier ones.

Product Changes

The only products required in a Kohlberg *Moral Dilemma* discussion are student ideas that are verbalized and their written positions on the issue, both tentative and reevaluated. To incorporate product modifications recommended for the gifted, the teacher should suggest that students develop essays, research papers, presentations, or other original products that are directed toward real audiences. Such products could be further developments of student ideas or positions, or could involve research on other people's attitudes toward a particular moral issue that was the subject of a discussion. A student might also become interested in tracing the historical development of attitudes toward a particular ethical issue. If the development and presentation of these products involve investigation of problems perceived as important by the students, involve presentation to real audiences (for example, submitting essays for publication, presenting research to a sociological group), are evaluated appropriately, and involve the use of raw data in the development of original conclusions, the products are appropriate for gifted students.

Learning Environment Changes

The two learning environment changes that are not suggested by any of Kohlberg's methods are complexity and high mobility. These changes are not as important to the implementation of his basic approach as the other environment dimensions. However, if product changes appropriate for the gifted are to be implemented, a complex environment that permits high mobility is necessary. To permit and provide the setting for conducting research and presenting it to real audiences, students must have access to high-level references, have a variety of types of working spaces, and be permitted to move in and out of the classroom to conduct their investigations. A variety of grouping arrangements within the classroom must also be provided.

With regard to grouping, to facilitate maximum interaction about moral and ethical issues, students at various levels of moral development need to be included in the group. The process is facilitated and the discussion is livelier if the students do not agree on the solutions or on the reasons for solutions. Thus, the grouping arrangements must be flexible enough for the teacher to mix students who will express different types of reasoning after he or she has been able to observe their participation in such situations.

DEVELOPMENT

Kohlberg's (1966) theory of moral reasoning both complements and extends the earlier work of Piaget (1948) in the area of moral development. To establish his stages, Kohlberg interviewed 75 boys between the ages of 10 and 16, using moral dilemmas as a stimulus and asking the boys to respond to questions about what the central character should do and why. He then looked for patterns of similarity in their responses and classified them into stages. The first work was presented in his doctoral dissertation (Kohlberg, 1958). In subsequent years, he has interviewed the same people every three years to determine movement through the stages. Most of these people are now in their thirties. Others have conducted similar research in different cultural settings to determine whether the stages are universally applicable.

Kohlberg's recent research has concentrated on how movement upward to the highest levels can be facilitated. In several experimental programs around Boston, Pittsburgh, and Scarsdale, New York, and in several prisons (Guidance Associates, 1976a; Muson, 1979), Kohlberg, his associates, and his students have studied the effects of *Moral Dilemma* discussions on an individual's rate of advancement through the stages and on the highest level of attainment. These discussions focus not only on contrived dilemmas, but on the dilemmas and conflicts faced by students every day as they attempt to govern themselves in their "just community."

RESEARCH ON THE MODEL

About the Stages of Reasoning

Since the theoretical background of Kohlberg's approach depends on the validity of his assumptions about the development of moral reasoning, including the sequence and hierarchy of the stages, research on this aspect of his theory will be examined first. There has been considerable controversy over the stages proposed by Kohlberg, especially the highest, the principled level or stages five and six.

In general, the outcomes of research have supported Kohlberg's ideas about the progression of types of reasoning from stages one through four (Gibbs, 1977). People do seem to progress upward through these types of reasoning as they mature and grow older. In his follow-up studies of the original subjects, Kohlberg (1971) has found that movement is upward, following the invariant sequence he identifies.

Crosscultural studies in Turkey, Mexico, Taiwan, Israel, India, and Canada indicate that the developmental stages are present and follow the same sequence in cultures other than the United States. Sullivan (1975), for example, has done extensive work in establishing norms for the Canadian population. In studying students of various age levels in elementary and secondary schools, he has found that 9- and 10-year-olds usually respond with stage one and two judgments and a small number of stage three judgments. There are no stage four, five, or six responses. At the age of 11, more stage three answers are found, and with 12-year-olds there are few stage one responses. In the 15 through 18 age ranges, there is a predominance of stage three thinking, with the beginning of some stage four and five reasoning found.

Critics have argued that the stages are not valid because, in some studies (Muson, 1979), it has been impossible to place the majority of the subjects in a particular stage. In these studies the majority of people have been classified as in a transition from one stage to another. Others have argued that subjectivity in scoring answers has contributed to low reliability in measurement (Kurtines & Greif, 1974). Still others have achieved high (.90) interscorer reliability (Guidance Associates, 1976a; Sullivan, 1975). A manual with a detailed scoring guide completed in 1979 should assist in the standardization of measurement, as will Rest's (1972) objective instrument, the *Defining Issues Test.*

Although research seems to support Kohlberg's assumptions about the first four stages, there is much less support for the validity of the principled level (stages five and six) (Muson, 1979). Kohlberg himself has questioned the existence of a sixth stage. So few people ever attain this level that it is difficult to conceive of it as a valid natural developmental stage. It has been left out of the new scoring guide. Questions about the existence of stage five, although present, are not as strong, but there does seem to be some cultural bias. In the crosscultural studies, for example, about seven percent of 16-year-olds in America and Mexico used stage six reasoning, while less than one percent of the same group in Taiwan employed this level of reasoning. None of those studied in Turkey or Yucatan had even reached the fifth stage.* Such research lends support to the criticism that Kohlberg has developed a theory based on a liberal philosophy and democratic ideals.

---

*Sample student responses to specific examiner questions can be found in Porter and Taylor (1972).

Moral Reasoning and the Gifted

Only one study has been identified that investigated moral reasoning in gifted students. Karnes and Brown (1981), using the *Defining Issues Test,* found a significant correlation (.31) between intelligence measured by the *Stanford Binet* and the presence of Level III (stages five and six) moral judgments. The correlation between WISC-R verbal scores and principled moral reasoning was also significant (.25). Students in the study ranged in age from 9 to 15, with a mean of 11.5. In a further analysis of the responses, the majority (74%) were at stages four and five, with most at stage four. Most research has shown that children under age 11 are functioning at stage one; those of ages 11-14 are usually at stage two; those of ages 14-17 are at stage three; and those 19 and over are usually reasoning at stage four. In many studies, however, results show a relationship between level of reasoning or Selman's levels of perspective-taking ability (Selman, 1971) and intelligence.

These results indicate that gifted students will progress through the stages more rapidly and that the gifted are capable of attaining the higher, principled stages while in school.

The Relationship of Moral Reasoning to Moral Behavior

One criticism of Kohlberg's approach is that, as a description of stages of moral reasoning, it has no bearing on moral behavior; therefore, of what benefit is an educational approach that will not cause any changes in ethical behavior? Little research has been done in this area, but at least two studies have been reported (Guidance Associates, 1976a) in which there was a strong relationship between high levels of moral reasoning and ethical behavior. In one experiment, only about 30 percent of the individuals who reasoned at stages two and three behaved ethically in an experimental situation, while 70 percent of the people at stage four and 100 percent of those at stage five were ethical. In a second study, about 70 percent of the people who were reasoning at stages one and two cheated in a situation where they knew they would not be caught, while only 55 percent at stages three and four, and only 15 percent at stage five did so. There are obvious situational factors, such as lack of emotional stress and a simple moral issue, that would contribute to clear experimental results. In a more realistic setting, however, these factors would combine with moral reasoning to determine moral behavior, which would reduce the accuracy of predictions of moral behavior based on the level of moral reasoning.

Effectiveness of the Approach

In 1968, one of Kohlberg's students (Blatt, 1969) conducted a one-year project to study the effect of *Moral Dilemma* discussions on upward movement through the stages. He found that the average gain in one year of the experimental over the control group was one-third of a stage. In addition, movement was upward; stage three's moved toward stage four, four's toward five, and so on. Since that time, many educators and psychologists have initiated programs attempting to stimulate moral development using discussions of moral dilemmas.

Rest (1974), in a review of these educational approaches, concludes that they seem to be effective, although not spectacularly so. Certain elements are emphasized in the programs: structural organization; developmental sequence; and interactionism. However, they receive a different amount of emphasis in the various programs, and their practical implementation is considerably different. Current research does not provide data on what aspects of the approaches are essential to success. (For example, is it important for there to be a mixture of students at different stages, or is it more important to have a homogeneous group? Should the teacher provide modeling at the higher stages?) Current research does not provide answers to questions about the most effective implementation strategies: What is the best arrangement for teacher-student interaction? What is the curriculum? (For example, what should be the content of the dilemmas? Are there certain dilemmas that are important to discuss at particular stages? What about sequencing? Should certain issues be discussed before others?) What is the teacher's role? In short, there are no definite answers to the practical questions relating to the various elements of the approach in an applied setting. Hopefully, some of the research currently in progress will provide answers to these pressing questions.*

The effectiveness of Kohlberg's approach with the gifted has not been evaluated, even though it seems that the attainment of Piagetian levels of abstract thought are essential to reaching the highest stages of moral reasoning, and the gifted are more likely to be functioning at these high levels while in school. Kohlberg's assumptions about the prerequisites for stage changes—abstract thought and perspective-taking ability—suggest that the approach should be more effective with the gifted than with nongifted, but this idea has not been investigated.

JUDGMENTS

Advantages

Advantages of the Kohlberg approach seem to be in the area of content changes suggested by the discussion of abstract, complex moral issues. The concentration on ideas and issues of the type suggested by Kohlberg's approach should be not only interesting and stimulating, but also valuable in producing the kind of

---

*For a review of research on the effectiveness of *Discussions of Moral Dilemmas,* the reader is referred to Rest (1974) and Sullivan (1975).

cognitive conflict or disequilibrium that causes growth to occur. Encouraging students to consider these big ideas as early as possible should contribute to higher quality thought about them in the future.

A second advantage is in the possibilities for combining discussions of moral dilemmas with other areas of the curriculum to achieve economy and effective organization. In social studies classes, for example, when studying some of the abstract ideas that form the basis of the democratic system, discussions of historical and current moral dilemmas involving these ideas can bring an added dimension to the student's understanding of the abstraction. The story of Heinz and the druggist could even be used with science lessons when considering the value of research and the ethics of certain acts in the light of advancement of science. It could be argued, for example, that the druggist was justified in charging so much for his miracle drug because, when perfected and produced in mass quantities, it might have the potential to save countless lives and if he continued to sell it at a low price, he would never be able to refine it or develop techniques that would enable it to be mass-produced.

The Kohlberg approach to moral education certainly presents a better alternative than the two previous ones of indoctrination and values clarification for use with gifted children. The indoctrination approach, often seen in the form of behavior modification, has little effect on the ethical behavior of these children and no effect on their moral reasoning. Values clarification, on the other hand, with its emphasis on a process of examining values, is an important technique to use with gifted children and can help them develop valuable critical thinking skills. However, it is not enough; it does not go far enough in the areas of examination of moral and ethical issues. In the area of personal choice, there is no problem with the approach or the underlying philosophy of values clarification. However, in the area of moral and ethical issues, the underlying philosophy of ethical relativism is difficult to accept. The Kohlberg approach goes one step further in recognizing that there are certain universal ethical principles that students should develop.

Disadvantages

The major disadvantages of this approach lie in the process and how *Moral Dilemma* discussions are implemented. As outlined earlier, the use of discussions or moral dilemmas facilitates growth in moral reasoning. However, the results are mixed and rather unspectacular. It is not clear what elements cause positive change. A related weakness is that there is no structure or sequence to follow in the discussions. Through extensive research on the development of children's abstract thinking, Taba (1966) found that both the type and sequence of teacher questions are important in achieving growth in cognitive abilities. Not only the question immediately preceding a child's answer, but also the whole sequence of teacher questions and acts leading up to the question determined the quality of thinking exhibited by the answer. This research suggests that there is also a particular sequence that is most valuable for questioning in a Kohlberg discussion. However, none has been identified.

A related disadvantage is in the lack of guidelines for selection of dilemmas. If Kohlberg is right about the developmental sequence of moral reasoning, it follows that certain dilemmas would be more appropriate for discussions at particular stages. There may also be an optimum sequence of issues (for example, discussing stealing before discussing killing).

CONCLUSIONS

Since the major advantages of the Kohlberg approach are in the area of content modifications and its major disadvantages are in the process area, it would seem to be a valuable approach to use in gifted programs when combined with one of the process models, such as the *Taba Strategies*. It could also be combined effectively with a *Creative Problem Solving* approach if moral or ethical problems were selected as the focus of *Creative Problem Solving*. Although the research is inconclusive about the validity of Kohlberg's stages five and six as natural developmental stages, the model does provide a valuable goal for programs for the gifted: the development of sophisticated moral reasoning.

RESOURCES

Background Information

Porter, N., and Taylor, N. *How to assess the moral reasoning of students.* Toronto, Ontario: The Ontario Institute for Studies in Education, 1972. As the title suggests, the major purpose of this pamphlet is to describe a method for assessing the degree of moral development of students from fourth grade through university age. Briefly, the book outlines Kohlberg's six stages and how to assess the stages described. The body of the book presents five moral dilemma stories, including the infamous Heinz story, with questions to ask following the stories. Detailed possible answers for each stage of moral development are included for each question. Teachers can present the stories and, by using the detailed outlines of answers, roughly determine the moral development of their students. Knowledge of how students view moral questions can be useful to teachers in a variety of curriculum areas, including social studies, English, and science.

Instructional Materials and Ideas

Blatt, M., Colby, A., and Speicher, B. *Hypothetical dilemmas for use in moral discussions.* Moral Education and Research Foundation, 1974. One of the problems in using Kohlberg's approach will be solved by purchasing this collection of more than 50 moral dilemmas. Each dilemma is presented, usually in two to three paragraphs, with several discussion questions following the dilemma. The dilemmas are sophisticated and relevant. Issues, such as abortion, homosexuality, artificial heart, racial segregation, the My Lai massacre, and lying, are presented. Most of the dilemmas can be used just as they are, while others need some modifications to make them more specific. Even if they cannot be used as they are, these dilemmas may spark the creativity of the teacher of junior and senior high students.

Mattox, B.A. *Getting it together: Dilemmas for the classroom based on Kohlberg's approach.* San Diego, Cal.: Pennant Press, 1975. The major bulk of this book contains moral dilemmas based on Kohlberg's theory. The dilemmas are written with contemporary issues at their base, which makes them more applicable for students today. There are different dilemmas for different age groups. The book also includes a description of Kohlberg's theory and the six stages, a justification for its use by teachers, and suggestions for leading discussions through simulation and role-playing techniques. Helpful guidelines for writing original dilemmas are also included.

Bryne, D.F., and Selman, R.I. *How can you work things out?* (Teacher's guide for sound filmstrip). New York: Guidance Associates, 1974. The set contains a guide, background material, and a two-part filmstrip, *How can you work things out?* The filmstrip is based on Bryne's and Selman's research on the ability of an individual to view the world from other perspectives. Their theory is a developmental one consisting of four levels. The development of sophisticated perspective taking is considered basic to the development of moral judgments. Consequently, this theory is intricately related to Kohlberg's. The two-part filmstrip presents two dilemmas that encourage students to view the problems from others' perspectives and stimulate development through the levels. There are suggestions for discussions and related activities. The two scripts are included. The material is nonsexist; however, no audience age level is given.

Chapter 6

Sidney Parnes: Creative Problem Solving *

One approach that has been widely used in programs for the gifted is the *Creative Problem Solving* model developed by Sidney J. Parnes, director of the annual Creative Problem Solving Institute (CPSI) held at the State University of New York (SUNY) at Buffalo. Influenced greatly by the work of Alex Osborn (1963) in applying imagination to the practical problems encountered in the business and professional worlds, Sidney Parnes attempted to develop the most comprehensive process possible for stimulating the use of imagination in practical situations. He used his own applied research on the development of creative thinking in the program at SUNY, along with the applied and theoretical research of others, to come up with a process that would be comprehensive, theoretically sound, and above all, effective. He is continually involved in the modification of this process as new information becomes available. His institutes are attended yearly by many of the most widely known researchers and theorists in creativity development and by individuals just beginning to be interested in their own or others' creative development.

The Parnes *Creative Problem Solving* model provides a structured method for approaching problems in an imaginative way. It is different from the usual problem-solving methods in its emphasis on the generation of a variety of alternatives before selecting or implementing a solution. In each of the five steps of the process, the problem solver defers judgment during ideation or generation of alternatives to avoid inhibiting even the wildest possibilities, which may turn out to be the best ideas. Judgment is then exercised at a more appropriate time.

Purposes of the model are twofold: (1) to provide a sequential process that will enable an individual to work from a ''mess'' to arrive at a creative, innovative, or effective solution; and (2) to enhance an individual's overall creative behavior.

---

*Appreciation is expressed to Patricia Kerr, teacher of the gifted in Albuquerque, New Mexico, for her assistance in preparing the first section of this chapter.

Creative behavior, according to Parnes, is "a response, responses, or pattern of responses which operate upon internal or external discriminative stimuli, usually called things, words, symbols, etc., and result in at least one unique combination that reinforces the response or pattern of responses" (Parnes, 1966, p. 2). Creative behavior is a function of knowledge, imagination, and evaluation, and results in a product that has both uniqueness and value to an individual or group. In other words, through participation in a process such as that developed by Parnes, individuals apply their own knowledge, imagination, and evaluation to both internal and external "stimuli," and as a result develop a product (for example, plan, idea, performance, report) that is both unique and valuable. These definitions of creative behavior, although precise and rather dry, provide clear and measurable guidelines for a program's development and evaluation.

The need for creativity training in all phases of education can no longer be ignored. The current state of the educational process, with its emphasis on "the right way," together with the necessity of dealing with massive amounts of information, a constantly and rapidly changing world, and pressing social concerns, make the development of creative problem-solving skills imperative. Parnes cites Maslow's (1970) "need for self-actualization" as a goal that can be met through education for creativity. Thus, the kind of education developed from a creative problem-solving perspective would meet both individual and societal needs.

Of the many teaching-learning models currently used in programs for the gifted, the Parnes model provides the most "hard data" showing its effectiveness. It also demonstrates the most versatility based on successful practical application in business, government, the health care professions, and education. The process is taught to university students, teachers, young children, adolescents, parents, artists, managers, scientists, city planners, architects—anyone who is interested—through the Creative Problem Solving Institutes (CPSI). Participants are almost unanimous in their response to these institutes: "It was the most valuable personal and professional experience I've ever had. It's fun and it also works!"

ASSUMPTIONS UNDERLYING THE MODEL

About Learning

A major assumption made by Parnes is that creativity is a behavior or set of behaviors that can be learned. Creativity is not an inborn, fixed characteristic, but is present to varying degrees in all individuals. It can be deliberately manipulated and cultivated. Since creativity is learned, the model also assumes that examples and practice will strengthen it and that the methods used in a creative problem-solving course are generalizable to new situations. In other words, all persons can become more creative, and they can apply this creativity in all facets of their lives.

A related assumption is that creativity is positively related to other characteristics of individuals, such as ability to learn, achievement, self-concept, and intelligence. These characteristics, when combined, contribute to a "wholeness" of objective (factual-logical) and subjective (sensing-feeling) aspects of an individual. Inherent in this assumption is the belief by Parnes that knowledge is important in creative productivity. Although factual knowledge must be manipulated and transformed into useable ideas, a person cannot be creative without first having an available store of knowledge. This knowledge, however, can be used more creatively and effectively if initially learned with a "creative" set than if initially learned with a "memory" set.

About Teaching

Since Parnes believes that creative behavior can be learned, he obviously believes that educators can and should teach creative behavior. According to Parnes, when his sequential problem-solving process is taught to students in school or to adults in an institute, a set of skills is developed that can be applied to all kinds of practical problems, for example, improving relationships with others, making decisions about activities or programs, managing resources, and planning personal or career goals. He believes that by participating in the process, creative leaders can learn to use *Creative Problem Solving* (CPS) successfully with groups ranging from elementary school children through adults. In short, Parnes feels that CPS is simple to learn, easy to teach, and highly transferable.

Parnes (1967) makes an important distinction between creative teaching and teaching for creativity. A teacher who is creative will be imaginative in the use of materials (films, posters, tapes) and strategies (demonstrations, unique experiences), while a teacher who teaches for creativity will stimulate the children to develop their own productivity, allow children to express themselves, and listen rather than talk. Individuals who teach for creativity do not need to be creative in their methods of imparting information. In developing an atmosphere conducive to the learning of creative behavior, a teacher must: (a) establish a climate of psychological safety for the free expression of ideas; (b) encourage playfulness; (c) allow incubation; and (d) seek quantity as well as quality of ideas.

About Characteristics and Teaching of the Gifted

Although not stated, an implicit assumption made by Parnes is that individuals who are intellectually gifted have the potential to be more creative than those who are of average or below average intelligence. These gifted people can also benefit from learning how to use the creative problem-solving method in artistic, social, and scientific areas. Following from this assumption is the recommendation that in teaching the gifted, educators should use a method such as CPS much more frequently and/or earlier because of the greater potential of gifted students to benefit from its use. Following this line of reasoning, the gifted also have greater amounts of information that they must organize, manipulate, and evaluate, which causes them to need the process much more often.

ELEMENTS/PARTS

Dimensions, Thinking Levels, or Steps

Since he first encountered Alex Osborn's program in 1953, Parnes has worked toward the establishment of the most comprehensive program possible for nurturing creative behavior. Using Osborn's model as a base, he added parts of existing theories and programs he could uncover, as well as the new approaches recently developed. Parnes feels that the resulting process is easy to follow, and he maintains that to be properly effective the steps must be followed in sequential order. Each new step relies on the previous step for further development. The steps (Parnes, 1977), along with activities at each step, are described in Table 6-1.

Figure 6-1 illustrates movement through the five steps. The diamond in Figure 6-1 represents the divergent and convergent thinking that occurs again and again while moving through the steps or returning to an earlier step to try a different approach. After listing a variety of ideas (divergent), for example, in step three, the problem solver selects a few that seem the most important (convergent) and puts them into a grid like the one shown in Figure 6-2. The problem solver needs to decide on the criteria to be used and should add this to the grid. At this point, a rating scale is devised (for example, a rating of 1 for poor, 2 for fair, 3 for good). The rating is done in the boxes of the graph and is totaled. This is the solution-finding step. Then the final step (step five) is accomplished, that is, is this plan acceptable? If it is, the problem is solved, and the problem solver has an acceptable plan, an acceptable action, or possibly a new challenge. If the plan is not acceptable, the problem solver goes back to step three, selects different ideas, and once again sets up the grid. The criteria usually stay the same, but they can be changed or rearranged in the same way that the ideas can be changed.

Movement through the steps of the process is aided by some proven techniques for stimulating idea output and development, for example, deferred judgment, elimination of fears, extended practice, forced relationships, brainstorming, hitchhiking, checklists, attribute listing, morphological analysis, synectics, and incubation. These are all strategies to assist in getting data out of memory storage and relating it to current situations that require problem solving. Deferred judgment, for example, is a cardinal principle in allowing the expression of as many

Table 6-1 Steps in the Parnes Creative Problem Solving Process

Steps	Activities
1. Fact-finding	Analyzing what is known about the "mess"
	Collecting data about the problem
	Acting as a camera, observing carefully and objectively
	Exploring the facts of the situation
2. Problem-finding	Looking at possible problems from several viewpoints
	Speculating on possible problems
	Narrowing down to the major problem
	Restating the problem into solvable form
	Using the phrase "In what ways might I" (IWWMI) to encourage ideation and elaboration
	Changing the verb when restating the problem
	Trying out the plan on a pilot basis to see if it works
	Making contingency plans in case the first plan doesn't work
3. Idea-finding	Generating many ideas and possible solutions
	Producing ideas to solve a problem

Table 6-1 continued

	Brainstorming for ideas or alternative solutions Listing as many ideas as possible
4. Solution-finding	Choosing those alternatives with the greatest potential for solving the problem Developing criteria for the evaluation of alternatives Objectively applying the criteria to each alternative Evaluating alternatives on the basis of criteria appropriate to the needs of the problem Listing the criteria using either a convergent or divergent process
5. Acceptance-finding	Developing a plan of action Considering all audiences who must accept the plan Brainstorming the concerns of all these audiences

Figure 6-1 Illustration of the Steps in Creative Problem Solving

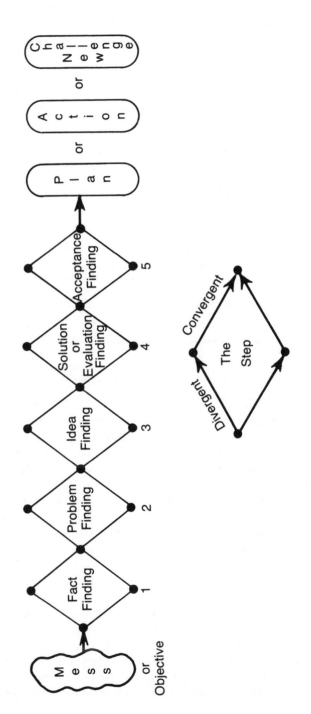

Source: Adapted from R.B. Noller, S.J. Parnes, and A.M. Biondi, *Creative actionbook: Revised edition of creative behavior workbook.* New York: Charles Scribner's Sons, 1976.

Figure 6-2 Grid for Use in Selecting and Evaluating Alternative
Solutions

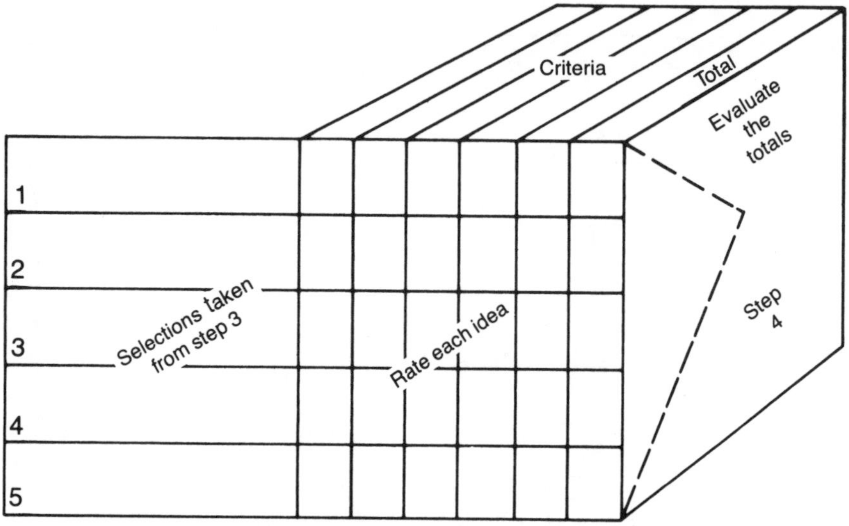

Source: Adapted from R.B. Noller, S.J. Parnes, and A.M. Biondi. *Creative actionbook: Revised edition of creative behavior workbook.* New York: Charles Scribner's Sons, 1976.

ideas as possible. When used in a group, the principle is called brainstorming. Supplemental to this process is the procedure of hitchhiking, or building upon and elaborating on the ideas of others. In order to hitchhike, students can add to another's idea during the conversation by merely snapping their fingers. This allows the discussion to keep moving.

Synectics, another example, is a process that involves two basic activities, making the strange familiar and making the familiar strange. It consists of the mental activities of analysis, generalization, and model seeking or analogy. According to Wilson, Greer, and Johnson (1973), synectics is a powerful tool for use with the gifted, as it enables them to "keep pace with the requirements of a rapidly changing world where traditional methods fall glaringly short" (p. 261).

To facilitate movement through the steps, another required skill is asking creative questions that can lead to unconventional solutions. Parnes feels this skill takes critical thinking and practice, but once acquired it enables creative problem solving to be accomplished in a minimum amount of time. As John Dewey has said, "A problem well put is half solved." Einstein continued, "The formulation of a problem is often more essential than its solution, which may be merely a matter of mathematical or experimental skill. To raise new questions, new possibilities, to regard old questions from a new angle, requires creative imagination and marks real advance in science.''

J.W. Getzels, who along with P.W. Jackson (Getzels & Jackson, 1962) started the continuing controversy over the creativity-intelligence distinction in the gifted, observes that there are two types of problem situations, the presented problem situation and the discovered problem situation. A presented problem situation is a problem that has a known formulation, a known method of solution, and a known solution. A discovered problem situation is a problem that does not yet have a known formulation, no known method of solution, and no known solution. This latter type stimulates creative problem solving.

Getzels (1975) gives examples of the two types; the story that illustrates them briefly is of a car being driven along a deserted road when its tire has a blowout. The occupants discover they have no jack, and their question is, ''Where can we get a jack?'' They remember a gas station several miles back and begin walking. Another car is driving on the same road, and it, too, has a blowout and no jack. The occupants of the second car ask the question, ''How can the automobile be raised?'' It just so happens they see a deserted barn nearby, and in the barn is an old pulley for lifting bales of hay to the loft. The car is raised, the tire changed, and the occupants are on their way again, while the other people are still walking to the service station.

Getzels concludes:

> In effect, the first group dealt with the dilemma as a ''presented problem situation'' akin to type-case 1: a known problem, a known method of solution, a known solution. The second group dealt with the dilemma as a ''discovered problem situation'' akin to type-case 3: a situation which could be defined in terms of a variety of problems (1975, p. 12-18).

In a discussion of the development of creativity in the gifted, Gallagher (1975) indicates that one of the general principles for encouraging a person to be more creative is to ''remove the brakes that stop his associative mechanisms from functioning naturally'' (p. 244). He continues by observing that gifted children, who are often concerned about pleasing the teacher and giving a quick answer to questions, will find it difficult to inhibit this first reaction, think about the problem, and allow their associative thoughts to flow. While this is an important observation to make, it is also crucial to consider Parnes's principle of deferred judgment. ''Removal of the brakes'' includes not only inhibiting the first reaction, but also problem solvers freeing themselves from the natural tendency to judge an idea as good or bad before saying or writing it. If the idea gets a bad rating in a student's mind, he or she may decide not to say it because others might laugh or think he or she has stupid ideas. This ''wild'' idea may be much better than any of the conventional ones that pass the spur of the moment test of value. According to

Parnes, it is much easier to tame a wild idea than to "beef-up" a conventional one. Thus, with gifted children who have been successful in school by pleasing the teacher, appearing smart, and not having "stupid" ideas but who have the potential to create the most unique and original ideas of all, practice in using the principle of deferred judgment is essential.

Another related idea important in the development of creative thinking in gifted children is developing and maintaining a balance between the more freewheeling playful side of a person and the logical, judgmental, analytical side. In describing the program at SUNY (and this also applies to Parnes's institutes taught in other parts of the United States), he concludes:

> In adapting all of the evolving programs that we have been able to synthesize with our creative problem-solving courses and institutes, we have been trying always to develop a balance in individuals—a balance between the judgment and the imagination—between the open awareness of the environment through all of the senses and the deep self-searching into layer upon layer of data stored in the memory cells—between the logic and the emotion—between the deliberate creative effort and the incubation—between the individual working with the group and his working alone. The longer I work in this field the more the underlying problem seems to become one of developing this balance between these extremes, by strengthening the weaker aspect, not by stunting the stronger side (Parnes, Noller, & Biondi, 1967, p. 154).

MODIFICATION OF THE CURRICULUM

Although the Parnes model provides a setting for modification of content and product, the most significant (and direct) modifications suggested are those of process and learning environment. The approach itself is a process model. Therefore, by using this process or by teaching children to use it, the usual process of learning is modified. Learners are active rather than passive; teachers are facilitators rather than information disseminators; and learners must separate their use of divergent and convergent thinking so that the flow of ideas is not inhibited while evaluations are made. Each sequential step in the process initially requires divergent thinking and ends with convergent thinking.

Content Modifications

The CPS process suggests content modifications of variety and methods that are appropriate for gifted students. Variety is suggested because the problems that are identified and solved are those practical problems not usually considered in a school curriculum. The CPS method is used to identify and solve a variety of personal, social, and academic problems. The process itself is a method of inquiry, so it is easy to see how this content modification is made. Gifted students should participate in the process in group situations and should be taught how to apply it to the solution of their own problem situations.

Process Modifications

Process modifications appropriate for the gifted are made in the following four areas: (1) higher levels of thinking; (2) open-endedness; (3) freedom of choice; and (4) variety. The development of higher levels of thinking (for example, the use rather than acquisition of information) is facilitated by the five-step process, which proceeds from the identification of facts about the situation through defining the problem, developing ideas for solving the problem, evaluating the ideas, and finally, developing a plan for implementing the solution. Although these steps are sequential rather than hierarchical, they progress from recalling facts (that is, Bloom's knowledge level) to analysis of the situation, creating new ideas (that is, Bloom's synthesis), and evaluation (that is, solution-finding), and then "back" to synthesis (that is, acceptance-finding). Open-endedness is also an important process modification made by CPS. Both teacher and student questions at all steps of the process must be open-ended to facilitate divergent answers. The process even includes components that assist participants in devising their own open-ended questions at the problem-finding step. As shown in Figure 6-1, each step in the process contains both a divergent and a convergent aspect. Participants are taught through the process when each type of thinking is appropriate for problem solving.

The CPS process encourages freedom of choice and suggests the use of a variety of methods at different steps in the process. With regard to freedom of choice, participants are usually encouraged to choose a problem of interest to them. Although they are expected to follow the basic approach, there is room for individual variations, especially at the problem-finding and idea-finding steps. For example, at the idea-finding step, a variety of idea-stimulating questions and techniques are presented, and individuals can later choose those that work best for them in a particular situation. Since a variety of methods are available and are suggested at each step, the principle of variety is also incorporated.

Product Modifications

Parnes's method suggests product modifications in all areas that are appropriate for the gifted. Addressing problems that are real to and interesting for gifted students is very much a part of this method. Although some teachers may be directive in their use of the method with children, the first two steps are designed to assist participants in identifying and stating a problem as they see it. If this product modification is not made, the problem is in the implementation, not the process itself.

A second modification, directing products toward real audiences, is made through the acceptance-finding step. At this step, the problem solver attempts to anticipate how those who must accept the solution will react to it. Based on this analysis, a plan is developed implementing the solution. Some detailed suggestions are given for assessing audiences, developing plans, and implementing solutions.

Another product modification concerns appropriate evaluation. The process teaches both teacher and student how to develop criteria for evaluating products and how to apply this criteria to the selection of solutions. In developing criteria for evaluation, for example, problem solvers should consider the problem from the viewpoint of many individuals and judge the possible solutions on criteria other than whether they themselves like the solution. Often decisions and evaluation depend very much on this subjective aspect of judgment. This and other suggested techniques help students develop skills in making appropriate evaluations. The techniques also provide methods for peers and audiences to use in evaluating products presented to them.

The final product modification, transformation rather than summary, is made easily through application of CPS. Throughout the process in solving problems, students must manipulate information, seek a variety of new data, combine information in new ways, and view situations from new perspectives. Particularly in the idea-finding step, development of original ideas is emphasized, that is, combining old ideas to form new ones, substituting parts of one idea, and other similar techniques.

Learning Environment Modifications

To facilitate movement through the problem-solving process, the leader must establish and continue an environment that is similar to that recommended for the gifted in most of the dimensions. The dimensions of particular importance are student-centered, independent, open, and accepting.

The environment must be student-centered. The students should identify the problems to be solved and generate the ideas for solving them. Selecting solutions and developing plans for implementation are also the responsibility of the students. Appropriate implementation of CPS requires that the leader serve as a facilitator of the process rather than as a person who instructs or "leads" the process. Thus, the teacher does not talk, but rather asks questions, plans activities to stimulate idea-production, and enforces the rules of brainstorming. Since the teacher is not offering ideas, he or she does not become the center of the discussions. When CPS is implemented in other than a group setting, there is absolutely no danger of the teacher assuming control or dominating the group.

Independence is fostered by encouraging individuals and groups to apply the process on their own and to use it as a procedure for solving everyday problems as well as academic ones. Since the ultimate goal of those who teach the process is to see it used by individuals to solve their own problems, this modification is an important aspect of the creative problem-solving process.

Specific guidelines are given by Parnes for the development of an open and accepting environment. For example, the rules of brainstorming should be strictly enforced at all times when generating ideas or when the activity requires divergent production. As a way to assist in the idea-finding step, Noller, Treffinger, and Houseman (1979) provide the following instructions for conducting and participating in brainstorming. These instructions illustrate the learning environment suggestions for implementing CPS.

The teacher must foster a climate of appreciation and understanding of the creative process. For example, the teacher must encourage and appreciate the need for incubation, allowing subconscious concentration on the problem. As students focus on a problem and search for ideas, they will consciously defer judgment and allow free flow to the associative mental processes. These associations may also occur in the preconscious, before a student is aware that they are being formed. By detaching from direct involvement in a problem, preconscious activity occurs, where links that may otherwise be inhibited are allowed to form (Parnes, 1967). Individuals often become consciously aware of these subconscious associations in an "aha!" experience; a new idea suddenly appears when they are not consciously thinking about the problem. Teachers must not only provide for incubation, but also encourage and appreciate the need for it even when it does not fit into the daily lesson plan.

Examples of Teaching Activities

One student used the following steps in solving an everyday problem using CPS (Keisel, Note 11).

Fact-Finding: Collect all data surrounding the problem.

In an attempt to solve his problem, Arnold first developed a chart to help in the gathering of data related to his situation. (See Exhibit 6-1.)

Problem-Finding: Restate the problem in a more solvable form.

As Arnold thought about his situation, he decided that the problem seemed to center around ways to get the information to write the paper rather than how to put the words down on paper. He tried the following restatements of the problem:

Exhibit 6-1 Arnold's Problem: "How Will I Write My Research Paper?"

Known	Like to Know	Sources
• There is only one book published on my subject.	• Are any articles published?	• Author of technique
• I have the book.	• Are other people's lecture notes from the author around?	• People predominant in the field who will know about the model
• I'm not to ask my teacher directly about my paper.	• Are there any people in the city who know about my subject?	• ERIC search
• I have access to a Wide Area Telephone Service WATS line.		• Other professors at the university
• I have notes from two sessions I attended about my subject.		• Author's secretary
• I have only one week to accomplish this.		
• I need to find more information.		

Source: S. Keisel. *The creative problem solving model.* Unpublished paper, 1979. (Available from J. Maker, Department of Special Education, University of Arizona, Tucson, Arizona.)

- In what ways might I write this paper?
- What is the best way to write my research paper?
- How can I get rid of the teacher who is making me write this paper?
- Who will help me write this paper?
- What information will I use to write this paper?
- In what ways might I get the information to write this paper?

He finally selected the last question as the most appropriate problem to solve.

Idea-Finding: Brainstorm and defer judgment in an attempt to develop as many ideas as possible for solving the problem.

Arnold tried asking himself the question, "In what ways might I get the information to write this paper?" He came up with the following ideas:

- Call the author of the technique.
- Call his secretary.
- Call predominant people in the field.

He then tried a few of the idea-spurring concepts suggested by Alex Osborn (1963)—magnify, minify, rearrange, combine, substitute, put to new uses—and applied these to the ideas he had and to the questions resulting from the fact-finding process. He was happier with this result, which follows:

- Reread the book I have.
- Go through all class notes on my subject.
- Go through workshop notes.
- Conduct an ERIC search, and look for articles.
- Talk to university professors who might know.
- Talk to people who have researched the author's ideas previously.
- Call one of the author's students.
- Write to one of the author's students.
- Cry, and give up.
- Go to the university where the author teaches, and hang around.
- Read the American Psychological Association (APA) manual.
- Read any article on information gathering.
- Check the *Education Index*.

Solution-Finding: Select criteria for evaluating solutions, and then apply the criteria to each possible solution. Choose the best solution.

Arnold first thought about some possible ways to judge his ideas. He could consider time, cost, effectiveness, safety, acceptability to the teacher, and uniqueness. Based on what he knew about the situation, Arnold decided that the most important criteria were *time* (he had only one week to finish the paper), *effectiveness* (it had to work), and *acceptability to the teacher* (he wanted a good grade). He then developed a grid for rating his possible solutions from the idea-finding step. (See Figure 6-3.) He assigned a point value of 1 for the bad ideas, 2 for those in the middle, and 3 for the good ideas. Each idea was rated on each criterion, and the points were totalled. According to this rating, there were several good solutions, including the following: call the author; reread the book I have; go through class notes; go through workshop notes; conduct an ERIC search; and call one of the author's students.

Acceptance-Finding: Present the solution to all parties involved to decide if it will be workable. Plan, implement, and evaluate the solution.

Since conducting an ERIC search and calling one of the author's students seemed to be the most promising solution, Arnold decided to implement these first. Since the only individuals involved would be Arnold and his teacher, he

Figure 6-3 Rating of Arnold's Ideas on Selected Criteria

POSSIBLE SOLUTIONS	Time	Effective-ness	Accept-ability	Total
Call the author	3	2	3	8
Call his secretary	3	1	2	6
Call predominant people in the field	2	2	3	7
Re-read the book I have	3	2	3	8
Go through all call notes	3	2	3	8
Conduct an ERIC search	3	3	3	9
Talk to university professors	2	2	3	7
Talk to people who have researched his ideas previously	1	2	3	6
Call one of his students	3	3	3	9
Write to one of his students	1	2	3	6
Cry and give up	3	1	1	5
Go to the university where he teaches & hang around	1	1	3	5
Read the APA manual	3	1	3	7
Read an article on information-gathering	1	2	3	6
Check the Education Index	1	2	3	6

Source: Reprinted with permission from R.B. Noller, S. Parnes, and A.M. Biondi. *Creative actionbook.* New York: Charles Scribner's Sons, 1976.

quickly checked with her to determine the acceptability of these solutions. After her approval, he began to develop his plan for implementing the solutions. He would first call a student of the author to get as much information as possible, then he would get a friend to show him how to conduct an ERIC search. After retrieving the available articles, he would decide whether additional information was needed. If so, he would call the author, go through his notes, and reread his book.

In Arnold's situation, as in many others, the most crucial aspect is the statement of the problem. The problem must be stated in an open-ended, solvable way, and must be focused on the aspect of the situation that is actually causing a problem. The teacher was not involved in this process at all. She had initially taught Arnold the process, which he had transferred to the new situation.

Table 6-2 provides a summary of teacher and student activities and roles for each step in the CPS process.

Table 6-2 Summary of Teacher and Student Roles and Activities in the Parnes Creative Problem Solving Model

Step, Type or Level of Thinking	Student		Teacher	
	Role	Sample Activities	Role	Sample Activities
Fact-finding	active participant; fact-finder	collect information about the situation. act as objectively as possible differentiate what is known from what needs to be known. observe carefully	facilitator; resource	develop or select exercises to lead students through a process of finding out the known and unknown facts about a situation. lead students through exercise, both individually and as a group. help students identify new sources of information about their situation or "mess".
Problem-finding	active participant;	look at the problem from several viewpoints. restate the problem in more solvable form.	facilitator; resource	develop or select exercises that will assist students in narrowing the problem, stating it in solvable form, and looking at it from different viewpoints. lead students through exercises both individually and as a group. provide examples of verbs that provide a more solvable statement of the problem. encourage students to use the phrase "In what ways might I..." (IWWMI). help students speculate on possible problems.
Idea-finding	active participant	generate as many ideas as possible defer judgment until all ideas are out. hitchhike on own ideas as well as ideas of others. strive for quantity rather than quality. "incubate" on the problem for an extended time period.	facilitator; resource	develop or select exercises that will assist students in generating a wide variety of useful and original ideas. lead students through the exercises both individually and as a group. provide idea-spurring questions (i.e., magnify, minify, rearrange, combine) to help students generate as many ideas as possible.

Table 6-2 continued

Step, Type, or Level of Thinking	Student		Teacher	
	Role	Sample Activities	Role	Sample Activities
				enforce the rules of brain-storming (i.e., quantity over quality, no evaluation of ideas, hitchhiking is desired). maintain an evironment that is psychologically safe for the free expression of ideas.
Solution-finding	active participant	develop criteria for evaluating solutions. objectively apply criteria to selected ideas. choose alternatives with the greatest potential for solving the problem.	facilitator; resource	develop or select exercises needed to enhance the student's ability to (a) generate criteria for judging a solution (b) select the relevant and (c) objectively apply the criteria to selected ideas. lead students through exercises either individually or as a group. assist in identifying possible criteria for evaluating ideas. show students how to use the grid. encourage students to try and make their "strange" ideas into useful ones
Acceptance-finding	active participant	develop a plan of action. consider all audiences. try out plans on a pilot basis. brainstorm ways to gain acceptance of ideas.	facilitator; resource	develop or select exercises that will help students formulate plans of action to implement solutions. lead students through exercises either individually or as a group. help students identify all audiences concerned with the solution. enforce the rules of brainstorming maintain a psychologically safe environment.

MODIFYING THE APPROACH

In modifying the Parnes CPS approach to make it more appropriate for the gifted, the changes are made mainly in how the approach is used rather than in the method. The majority of suggestions are in the content area, with a few in the area of process. To make these changes one effective method is to combine Parnes with Bruner, while another would be to make each separate change as described below.

Content Changes

As it stands, the CPS method does not make content changes appropriate for the gifted in the following areas: abstractness; complexity; organization and economy; and study of people. It can be combined with other approaches to achieve several of these changes. The first content changes, abstractness and complexity, suggest that the problem areas selected for problem solving by gifted students should involve complex, high-level problem situations rather than mundane or simple problems. Some examples of complex problems involving abstract concepts would be the following: the current energy situation; the current economic situation; talent development in an egalitarian society; rising populations and shrinking land availability; and industrialization or exploitation of underdeveloped countries by world powers. In all of these situations, information or facts would need to be gathered from a variety of sources and traditional disciplines in both the definition and solution of problems. No one viewpoint or set of information would provide the necessary background. In addition, the concepts involved in understanding the situations and in devising possible solutions would certainly be abstract.

The addition of the process of CPS to any area of study would add an element of complexity. Since the process encourages integration of a variety of information from several points of view in the identification of problems and development of solutions, complexity is automatically introduced. Creative solutions to problems often require that information from seemingly remote fields be brought together in an original way.

The modifications of organization and economy are not suggested by Parnes's approach, but can be readily incorporated. If the content is already arranged around key concepts or generalizations, the problem situations to which CPS is applied can directly involve these concepts. For example, in Chapter 2, activities were developed around the following generalization: *Every society has had rules, written or unwritten, by which social control over the people's conduct can be maintained.* Students can, of course, identify many problem situations that are related to this idea and should be encouraged to do so. However, the teacher can also present problem situations for further examination through CPS. Some problem situations related to this generalization are prison riots, the death penalty, government intervention in crisis situations, rehabilitation of prisoners, moral and ethical development through education, the present court system, the juvenile justice system, the development of appropriate parent-child relationships, and society's changing values.

If the content is not already organized around key concepts and generalizations, it could be organized around problem situations. The CPS process could then be used as the overall method for gathering information, identifying subproblems for study by small groups of students, and combining old information with new ideas to form new, creative solutions. Complex problems involving abstract concepts would need to be selected as organizers; most current local and national problems would be excellent organizers. The students could identify with the problems, could select subproblems of interest to them, and could develop end products (for example, solutions, research reports) that are directed toward real audiences and represent their creative thinking and original research about a problem area.

The study of creative, productive people can certainly be accomplished through the use of CPS. Students can identify problems faced by these individuals and use CPS to develop solutions for them. They can then compare their solutions with the ones actually developed and implemented by the individual being studied. This comparison should definitely include a look at the differences and similarities between the individual being studied and the gifted students themselves, along with similarities and differences in the social situation now and during the life of the individual being studied.

Process Changes

Process changes that are not directly suggested by the Parnes model are discovery, proof/reasoning, group interaction, and pacing. The problem of pacing does not seem relevant to the implementation of CPS with gifted students since new material is not being presented and participants have much opportunity for setting their own pace in solving problems. If the process is being used in a group setting, however, the teacher should attend to the appropriate pacing of discussions during most of the steps. At idea-finding, the teacher should be careful to allow plenty of time for thought since students are producing rather than acquiring or remembering information.

Discovery

Although CPS is not a strategy for discovery learning in the sense that discovery is defined by this writer, it is closely related. The methods employed in the first four steps of CPS can also be used by students in structuring their process of discovery or inquiry. For instance, fact-finding would be important as a way to gather information from the situation that is relevant to the generation of hypotheses. The problem-finding step would assist in sifting through the information to identify those aspects that are most relevant, and the idea-finding step would be used for the generation of hypotheses. Solution-finding would provide a framework and methods for evaluating and selecting hypotheses.

Evidence of Reasoning

Asking students to explain their reasoning or provide evidence for their inferences would be easy to incorporate into the CPS process. However, questions such as these must be asked only at certain times. Otherwise, the idea-production phases of each step would be inhibited. During brainstorming, fact-finding, and phases of the process involving divergent thinking, questions calling for explanations of reasoning would be completely inappropriate. During selection of problem statements, selection of criteria for evaluation, and development of action plans, however, such questions are highly appropriate and will facilitate understanding of the process and its use in solving problems.

If teachers fear that the asking of "why" questions will inhibit the process, they can always use the procedure in Taba's *Application of Generalizations Strategy*. In this strategy, students brainstorm their predictions without any interruptions by the teacher except to clarify ambiguous ideas. After the ideas have been listed, the teacher goes back and asks for reasons why each prediction was made. This strategy would not be appropriate at the idea-finding step, but would work well at solution-finding and acceptance-finding.

Group Interaction

If the CPS process is used in a group setting, it can provide a situation for observation and analysis of group interaction. To implement this curricular modification, the teacher should tape the process or appoint observers willing to stay out of the discussion. Through this method, however, only one type of group interaction could be observed, that is, participation in group problem solving. The process could also be used as an adjunct to the observation of group interaction by using it as a method for developing solutions to interaction situations that have been observed.

Learning Environment

Learning environment changes not suggested by the CPS method are complexity and high mobility. These aspects of the environment become important when students are developing sophisticated products and conducting original research. They can also be crucial at the fact-finding step of the process if students need to gather information from a variety of sources in the solution of certain types of problems. In other words, depending on the type of problem to be solved, these environmental dimensions assume more or less importance.

Although independence has already been discussed as a learning environment modification made by the Parnes approach, a few more ideas must be discussed. The CPS method provides an excellent process for use by students in solving their own problems and in developing solutions to classroom management problems. Students need to be taught the methods thoroughly, however. This includes working through several sample problems, discussing the process and how it is implemented, and learning a variety of techniques that can be employed at each step to facilitate the process. Finally, they need supervised practice in using the method both individually and in group situations.

DEVELOPMENT

Sidney Parnes was greatly influenced by Alex Osborn's techniques, which are presented in *Applied Imagination* (Osborn, 1963). Parnes extended and elaborated on Osborn's work through research on identifying and nurturing creativity. He developed a course and later a programmed text that has been highly effective in developing the creative behavior discussed by Osborn. Since developing the Interdisciplinary Center for Creative Studies and beginning the Creative Problem Solving Institute, Parnes has continued to incorporate new ideas and research into the process.

RESEARCH ON EFFECTIVENESS

With Nongifted

The CPS model has been the subject of extensive research. This research has focused on two different but related issues, creativity and problem solving (James, Note 12). The two terms are often used interchangeably, which leads to confusion and inconsistency in research. Parnes uses CPS to produce a set for solving problems, then evaluates its effectiveness using measures of general creativity. Parnes assumes that creativity enhances the whole problem-solving process. Others (see Mansfield, Busse, & Krepelka, 1978) evaluate the effectiveness of the solutions and find that other problem-solving methods are just as effective as the Parnes process. For example, some studies have shown that other methods, such as the use of Program Evaluation and Review Technique (*PERT*) charts and conventional (nondeferred judgment) methods of problem solving are just as effective in developing ability to solve problems as the Parnes process. However, these other programs do not seem to cause increases in performance on measures of creativity.

In 1957, Parnes began an extensive research effort to evaluate the effectiveness of his program. For the first ten years, the research was concentrated in the following four areas:

1. the effects of a semester course in stimulation of creativity
2. the relative effects of a programmed course used alone or with instructors and class interaction
3. the effects of extended effort in problem solving
4. the effectiveness of the principle of deferred judgment

In general, the results of several studies indicate that the program is highly effective. Some of the major findings were as follows (Parnes, 1975):

• The semester programs resulted in increases in both quantity and quality of ideas produced. These increases (over a control group) held up even when students were tested from one to four years after taking the course.

• The results of research on the effectiveness of the programmed course were also positive. The instructor-taught groups were superior to the other two groups, while the group using the programmed materials alone was superior to the control group receiving no creativity training.

• Extended effort in idea-production results in a greater proportion of good ideas among those produced later.

• Individuals instructed to defer judgment during idea production produce significantly more good quality ideas (criteria included uniqueness and usefulness) than did individuals instructed to judge concurrently with idea production. In addition, subjects trained to use the principle of deferred judgment produced significantly more good quality ideas under the deferred judgment condition that did subjects who were not trained. Groups also produce more and better ideas when using this principle than do either groups or the same number of individuals working independently while using concurrent evaluation.

After these initial studies, which concentrated heavily on development of the process, Parnes and his associates began a longitudinal investigation, *The Creative Studies Project*. They hypothesized that students who complete a four-semester sequence of creative studies courses will perform better than students who are otherwise comparable but do not take the courses on: (a) measures of mental ability, problem-solving capability, and job performance; (b) tests measuring the creative application of academic subject matter; (c) achievement in other than academic areas calling for creative performance; and (d) measures of personality characteristics associated with creativity. Parnes (1975) provides the following brief summary of the results to date:

• Students in the courses are significantly better able to cope with real life situational tests, including production, evaluation, and development of useful ideas.

- Students taking the courses are significantly better at applying their creative abilities in special tests given in English courses.
- In the semantic and behavioral half of J.P. Guilford's *Structure of Intellect* (SI) model of intelligence (Guilford, 1967), students in the courses perform significantly better on three out of five mental operations: cognition, divergent production, and convergent production. Students show significant year-to-year gains over comparable controls and perform similarly to the controls on two of the operations—memory and evaluation—and also in the symbolic and figural half of the model.
- Most of these students believe they have become more creative and productive, and that the program has been helpful in other college courses and in their everyday lives. Those continuing for two years in the program feel that this improvement is shown in their more active participation in class discussions and in their ability to cope with everyday problems.
- In nonacademic areas calling for creative performance, these students show a growing tendency to become more productive than students not enrolled in the program.
- Measures of personality characteristics show that students taking the courses are changing in ways that make them more like highly creative persons.
- Based on the gains of students so far, the differences between the two groups are expected to continue.
- Since the students in both the experimental (Creative Studies Program) and control groups are similar to students at most colleges and universities, the results of this research should generalize to many other situations.

In a review of research on the effectiveness of creativity training programs, Mansfield et al. (1978) report that of all the creativity programs reviewed, the Parnes program is the most effective. They are not as positive as Parnes about the results, as they believe that several of the studies showing gains suffer from serious methodological flaws. Some of the problems include confounding of instructor effects with program effects, massive sample attrition, and volunteer subjects for the instructed but not for the control groups. Parnes and his colleagues, however, do not agree with this assessment except in the case of volunteer subjects in experimental, but not controls, in the first study. These concerns were dealt with in other studies. One extensive, well-designed study, however, showed very positive results: high school students in an instructor-taught course performed significantly better on all ten verbal tests of divergent thinking (four of fluency, two of flexibility, two of originality, and one each of elaboration and sensitivity) than did students in the control group. In the same study, students using the programmed text without an instructor were inferior to the instructor-taught groups but superior to the controls who had no instruction.

Torrance (1972) also reviews studies testing the effectiveness of programs designed to develop creativity in children. Approaches were separated into nine categories, including CPS and other disciplined approaches, including training in general semantics, complex programs involving packages of materials, the creative arts as vehicles, media and reading programs, curricular and administrative arrangements, teacher-classroom variables, motivation, and testing conditions. Of all these approaches, the Parnes *Creative Problem Solving Process* and other disciplined approaches showed by far the highest percentages of success. These approaches achieved 91 and 92 percent success rates compared to the next highest percentages—81 percent for the creative arts as vehicles and 78 percent for the media and reading programs.

In summary, the program does seem to be effective in improving performance on tests of divergent thinking, which may be an important aspect of creativity. Certain specific principles, such as deferred judgment and extended effort, are also effective in producing more and better ideas.

With Gifted

Although gifted students are included in the groups studied by Parnes and his associates, no research has concentrated on the effectiveness of CPS with only the gifted. A significant body of research related to the topic is concerned with relationships between creativity and intelligence. However, since a review of this literature could fill volumes, only a few of the more significant results will be presented.

In a classic study of the creativity-intelligence relationship, Getzels and Jackson (1962) found a low correlation between IQ scores and performance on tests of creativity in gifted students (average IQ 132). They also found that those who scored highest on tests of creativity, but not highest on IQ tests (average IQ 132), scored just as well on achievement tests as did those who were highest on IQ tests (average IQ 150), but not highest on tests of creativity. A later study by Wallach and Kogan (1965) also measured the performance of those who were highest on measures of both creativity and intelligence. They found, as did Getzels and Jackson, that the "high creatives" did just as well on achievement tests as did the "highly intelligent." However, they also found that the highest achievers and most versatile individuals were those who were *both* highly creative and highly intelligent. Another important finding of this study is that those who scored high on IQ tests but not on tests of creativity have a "disinclination" rather than an "inability" to perform well on tasks calling for divergent thinking. The subjects appeared to be reluctant or fearful of being original rather than unable to be original.

The results of these studies have important implications for the use of CPS or other such techniques with gifted children. If intellectually gifted but not necessarily creative children have the potential to be more original than they are, and if these children can be more effective achievers when they use both their intelligence and their creativity, then teachers must provide experiences that will increase these children's use of *all* their potential abilities.

JUDGMENTS

Advantages

The major advantages of the Parnes model in programs for the gifted are its versatility and validity. The CPS process can be used in any content area, both as a method for learning about the content area and for arriving at creative solutions to significant problems proposed by scholars in that field. The process can also be used to solve the practical problems encountered in business, industry, and daily life. The skills are easily transferable from one situation to another and can be taught to children of all ages. For the teacher, the advantages also include a wide variety of materials that are readily available, teacher training that is available, fun while using the process, and a personally rewarding experience. Its goals are easily explained and justified to parents or school personnel, and gifted children enjoy participating in the process.

With regard to its validity, although comparative studies have not assessed the effectiveness of the method with gifted students, the Parnes model is consistent with the characteristics of gifted learners. It builds on their capability for developing unique products and at the same time provides for the development of the "inclination" to use their creative potential. The model defines creativity in specific behavioral terms and provides a structure and process for increasing these behaviors. Thus, the goals, procedures, and evaluative measures are clear. Research indicates that when this process is followed, the results are positive. Continuing research and evaluation of the process by Parnes and his associates ensure that new developments will be incorporated into the process to enhance its effectiveness.

Disadvantages

The major disadvantage of the model is that it was not designed specifically for use with the gifted (and in fact, may be equally effective with those who are not gifted). For this reason, a gifted program based only on the Parnes model may be difficult to justify as "qualitatively different" from the basic school curriculum. There is not even a rationale for concentrating on particular aspects of the process with gifted students, as there is with certain other models (for example, Bloom's and Krathwohl's *Taxonomies*). The use of these approaches in gifted programs can be justified by the rationale that the educator is concentrating on the higher rather than lower levels of thinking. In this way, the program is qualitatively different for gifted students. On the other hand, with CPS, each step is equally important for all learners. Thus, when used by itself, CPS does not provide a comprehensive, qualitatively different program for gifted students.

Although the program is supported by extensive positive research, there are methodological problems in several important studies. The major problem is in measurement of creativity. Most studies equate divergent thinking with creativity, even though this type of thought process may be only a small part of creative behavior. A related problem is that most studies use standardized measures of creativity as the criterion rather than long-term assessment of transfer effects. For example, a critical question involving the transfer effect of risk taking might be: "Will students who engage in creative problem solving exhibit fluency, flexibility, and originality in situations in which their ideas may be subject to criticism?" (Bodnar, Note 13, p. 4).

Another disadvantage discussed by Bodnar (Note 13) is that the model tends to overemphasize the inspiration and imagination required in the idea-finding phases of creativity and tends to neglect the actual implementation phase, which requires a high degree of motivation, discipline, conviction, self-criticism, and hard work. If the model is used alone in a gifted program, this could become a major disadvantage, but if the Parnes process is one of several approaches in a total program, the emphasis on inspiration and imagination adds a positive dimension to the program.

CONCLUSION

As a total approach to curriculum development for the gifted, the Parnes (CPS) model is difficult to justify as qualitatively different or comprehensive. However, it can easily be combined with other approaches in a way that can minimize or eliminate its disadvantages. Teachers can also emphasize *different uses* of the process, along with application in a variety of areas to make it more appropriate as a strategy in program development for the gifted.

RESOURCES

Background Information

Feldhusen, J.F., and Treffinger, D.J. *Teaching creative thinking and problem solving*. Dubuque, Iowa: Kendall/Hunt Publishing Co., 1977. This book aids teachers in helping children think creatively and solve problems. Chapters include "Teaching Children to Think," "Special Needs of Disadvantaged Children," "Methods of Teaching Creativity and Problem Solving," "How to Get Projects

Started," and "Review of Instructional Materials and Books for Teaching." The bulk of the book is directed toward giving ideas and suggestions to teachers for encouraging creative thinking. There is a review of a variety of instructional materials and books, elementary through high school. Information in this chapter includes title, publisher, where to order, description, target audience, materials provided, subject matter, and teaching strategy and rationale. Filmstrips, games, and books from various publishers are listed.

Feldhusen, J.F., and Treffinger, D.J. *Creative thinking and problem solving in gifted education.* Dubuque, Iowa: Kendall/Hunt Publishing Co., 1980. This book is almost identical to an earlier book (Feldhusen & Treffinger, 1977). It has a more recent copyright, but most of the materials are similar. One chapter is a discussion of recent developments in education of the gifted: "Teaching Creative Thinking and Problem Solving to the Gifted, Creative and Talented." It includes a discussion of enrichment models and IEPs. This book contains an updated review of instructional materials, including more contemporary materials and books, and lists the same information as the earlier book.

Instructional Materials and Ideas

Castle, D. *How to write a saleable story.* Buffalo, N.Y.: D.O.K. Publishers, undated. Using a technique called "morphological synthesis," the author describes a method for writing a story that will be potentially publishable. Information is provided on how to outline and create a plot and then actually write the story. Also included is technical information on titles, as well as how to type and submit a manuscript. The book uses "tooltables"—individual charts which allow an author to organize and generate ideas for the various elements of the book, such as characters, time, and plot. The tooltables also allow a prospective author to organize systemically the writing of a story and to use a creative problem-solving approach to generate original ideas.

Eberle, R.F. *Scamper: Games for imagination development.* Buffalo, N.Y.: D.O.K. Publishers, 1977. This is another D.O.K. publication to encourage creativity. The purpose of the book is to assist children in maintaining and improving their imaginative ability. It takes at least two to *scamper* (run playfully through one's mind)—a child older than three and a young adult. The book contains ten games. One example is "New Zoo," where children imagine new animals by combining parts of familiar ones. There are appendixes for scampering alone or with adults.

Eberle, B., and Stanish, B. *CPS for kids: A resource book for teaching creative problem solving to children.* Buffalo, N.Y.: This is a publication for encouraging the development of *Creative Problem Solving* in grades 3 through 9. There are seven levels to the process as outlined by the authors. The levels are sensing, problems and challenges, fact-finding, problem-finding, idea-finding, solution-finding, and acceptance-finding. There are five exercises for each of the seven levels. For teacher use, there is a description and overview of each level with directions for use of the material. Teachers can determine the best instructional uses for the material. A variety of options exist. There are worksheets included which can be duplicated. The exercises are relevant to children and primarily involve real-life situations.

Fearn, L. *Teaching for thinking: 311 ways to cause creative behavior*. San Diego, Cal.: Kabyn Books, 1977. This book is concerned primarily with ideas for developing creative thinking talents. It is based on the author's own process model in creative thinking, based on the assumption that creative thinking is a process, not a product, and an individual cannot think creatively without information. Components of the model are described and specific classroom exercises given in reading, math, vocabulary, and geography. Also reviewed are five other models: Bruner, Piaget, Guilford and Meeker, Williams, and Bloom. Although the ideas are good, the book needs a more interesting format to improve its readability.

Koberg, D., and Bagnall, J. *The universal traveler: A soft-systems guide to creativity, problem solving, and the process of reaching goals*. Los Altos, Cal.: William Kauffman, 1976. *The Universal Traveler* is a guide to improving problem-solving and creative-thinking skills logically and systematically. The format is one of a 'travel guide' because the authors see the creative process as a journey that can be planned carefully. The book is divided into three parts. The "Expedition Outfitter" discusses the necessary information for one's journey—the background on what creativity and the design process entail. The bulk of the book, the "Universal Travel Agency," outlines in detail the necessary steps in the creative problem-solving process. Finally, "Side Trips," contains supplementary activities. The theme, illustrations, and layout are unique, and offer an unusual teaching tool.

Land, V.A., and Fletcher, N. *Making waves with creative problem-solving*. Buffalo, N.Y.: D.O.K. Publishers, 1979. The emphasis is on developing problem-solving skills by utilizing a series of activities that emphasize a variety of skills. There are seven steps in the process. The material is designed so that students can work through the entire problem-solving process in a step-by-step fashion or work on individual steps separately using the activity cards. Several cards are included for each step. The final section of the book allows students to go through the entire process of problem solving, from the definition of the problem to an evaluation of their CPS process.

Mohan, M., and Risko, V. *Perception stimulators*. Buffalo, N.Y.: D.O.K. Publishers, undated. This is a set of 94 exercises designed to encourage imagination, curiosity, and observation techniques. The authors believe that in order to stimulate the ability to acquire knowledge, one should be confronted with exercises in perception, observation, curiosity, and tolerance of ambiguity and complexity. The 94 exercises attempt to do this. Most of them are in the form of puzzles (for example, Does England have a 4th of July?). There are math problems, optical illusions, and mazes. The exercises are entertaining and challenging, and are in the form of cards which can be handled easily.

Noller, R.B., Heintz, R.E., and Blaeuer, D.A. *Creative problem solving in mathematics*. Buffalo, N.Y.: D.O.K. Publishers, 1978. This book focuses on a problem-solving approach to mathematics. It utilizes the basic components of the CPS approach: fact-finding, problem-finding, idea-finding, solution-finding, and acceptance-finding. The authors believe the usual type of math students know can be essentially creative, if approached through the CPS method. A large percentage of the book explains the process in detail using various examples. At the end, the authors list other math problems for the reader to solve using CPS.

Noller, R.B., Treffinger, D.J., and Houseman, E.D. *It's a gas to be gifted or CPS for the gifted and talented*. Buffalo, N.Y.: D.O.K. Publishers, 1979. The pamphlet uses a simulation problem to encourage the development and use of creative problem-solving skills by students. The simulation, concerning the Froop Oil Company, involves students in determining the best use for a gas station that is being closed by the oil company. The major purpose is to develop a wide variety of creative thinking processes such as observation, seeing new relationships, sensitivity to problems, and the discovery of new ideas. The booklet outlines the major steps for the CPS process and guidelines for the simulation, which should take approximately three hours.

Uraneck, W.O. *Booster box for imagination and self development*. Buffalo, N.Y.: D.O.K. Publishers, undated. These 24 creative learning experience cards designed for grades 7 through 12 can be used individually, with a small group, or with the entire class. Each card has a separate creative exercise. Examples include thinking of unusual uses for a sweater, different ways to travel, dreams, places to visit, "what if" games, and fears at night. The author suggests that a point system for numbers of answers on the various exercises could be recorded as motivation. There are no wrong or right answers, an element that is essential when encouraging creativity.

Chapter 7

Joseph S. Renzulli: The Enrichment Triad[*]

Several teaching-learning models have been developed for education and used in programs for the gifted, but few have been developed specifically for teaching gifted children. One of the most popular is Renzulli's (1977) *Enrichment Triad.* Educators of the gifted and critics of special provisions for the gifted have long been concerned about providing "qualitatively different" learning experiences for these children; therefore, Renzulli presents an enrichment model that can be used as a guide in developing defensible programs for the gifted, that is, programs that are qualitatively different.

Qualitatively different, according to Renzulli, means more than freedom of choice, lack of pressure, absence of grading, and individualization of rate or pace, although all of these are important in gifted programs. Modifications also need to be made in areas such as content, learning style, and teaching strategies. With these in mind, Renzulli developed a model for moving the student through awareness, the learning of process, and the development of a product using three different but interrelated types of learning activities. Type I and II enrichment activities lead to Type III, which is considered especially appropriate for gifted students.

The simplest form of enrichment, sometimes referred to as vertical enrichment or acceleration, consists of introducing gifted students to advanced courses early. This practice takes care of the student's need to be challenged and to interact with equally advanced peers and a more specialized instructor. Thus, through accelerated placement the advanced ability of the learner is considered. However, according to Renzulli, there are two other dimensions of learning in enrichment activities that must be respected: the student's content interest and preferred style of learning. These are important components of Renzulli's model.

*Appreciation is expressed to Anaida Pascuale-Sosa, teacher of underachieving students in Puerto Rico, for her assistance in preparing the first section of this chapter.

There are two main program objectives that Renzulli (1977) recommends for guiding the education of gifted and talented students and that are incorporated into the *Triad* approach:

1. For the majority of time spent in the gifted programs, students will have an opportunity to pursue their own interests to whatever depth and extent they so desire; and they will be allowed to pursue these interests in a manner that is consistent with their own preferred styles of learning. (p. 5)
2. The primary role of each teacher in the program for gifted and talented students will be to provide each student with assistance in (1) identifying and structuring realistic, solvable problems that are consistent with the student's interests, (2) acquiring the necessary methodological resources and investigative skills that are necessary for solving these particular problems; and
3. finding appropriate outlets for student products. (p. 10)

Superior intelligence, or an extremely high ability score on a test, has been the major criterion for admitting students to gifted programs in the past. This model offers a rationale for using more than one criterion. According to Renzulli, there are three clusters of characteristics that students must have in order to benefit from his model: (1) above average intelligence; (2) above average creativity; and (3) task commitment (motivation-persistence). There is a definite interaction among these three, which results in superior performance.

ASSUMPTIONS UNDERLYING THE MODEL

About Teaching and Learning

In developing his model, Renzulli (1977) states that he has made major assumptions about the regular curriculum and about enrichment activities. Inherent in his approach and following from his stated premises are implicit and important assumptions that must be recognized and accepted before his approach can be appropriately implemented.

The following six assumptions are clear from discussions of the model's development:

1. "There are . . . certain basic competencies that all students should master in order to adapt effectively to the culture in which they are growing" (p. 14-15).

2. ". . . the mastery of these competencies should be made [as] streamlined, exciting, and relevant as possible" (p. 15).
3. Enrichment consists of "experiences and activities that are above and beyond the so-called 'regular curriculum' " (p. 14).
4. ". . . enrichment activities (with the possible exception of some Type II activities) must show complete respect for the learner's interests and learning styles . . ." (p. 16).
5. ". . . the point-of-entry for all enrichment must be an honest and sincere desire on the part of the student to pursue a particular topic or activity of his or her own choosing" (p. 16).
6. There are ". . . no predetermined notions about the physical circumstances under which enrichment experiences should take place" (p. 16).

Most of these assumptions are concerned with the educator's concept of providing "enriching experiences" for their gifted students. All children participate in the regular curriculum, but gifted students need experiences designed specifically for them that are above and beyond those experiences provided for all children. Renzulli assumes that gifted children should participate in the regular curriculum for some part of their school experience, or they should at least demonstrate the minimum competencies that are required as a part of this regular curriculum. An implication of this assumption, very important for those planning to implement Renzulli's ideas, is that the *Triad* model may need some major modifications if it is to be used as a basis for curriculum planning in a self-contained program for the gifted.

The last assumption about the physical setting carries with it some important considerations that go beyond the usual concerns in a classroom setting. To implement appropriately the model and its requirement that ". . . if a particular student has a superior potential for performance in a particular area of sincere interest, then he or she must be allowed the opportunity to pursue topics therein to unlimited levels of inquiry" (p. 317) means that administrative flexibility is absolutely essential. Enrichment activities could take place in the regular classroom, in a special resource room, in an independent study carrel in the library, or in the community. They could involve one child or several children. However, these enrichment activities *must not be limited* to any one place. For example, students should be able to study with a college professor if this is the best way for them to pursue their topics to "unlimited levels of inquiry."

About Characteristics and Teaching of the Gifted

The major assumption Renzulli (1978) makes about the characteristics of the gifted follows from his reviews of the research on characteristics of successful or eminent individuals. He reviews the research of Ann Roe (1952), Wallach (1976),

Terman and Oden (1959), Hoyt (1965), and MacKinnon (1965) to reach his conclusions about the characteristics of the gifted. From these and other studies, he concludes that gifted individuals possess three interlocking clusters of traits, which he calls the "three-ring conception" of giftedness. The clusters are: (1) above average though not necessarily superior general ability; (2) task commitment; and (3) creativity. He points out that the interaction among the clusters, not one single cluster, is what is necessary for creative/productive accomplishment. Each cluster is an equal partner in an individual's achievement. Following are some examples of behaviors included in the three clusters.

Above Average Ability

Renzulli includes in this cluster those characteristics usually referred to as IQ and achievement, measured by grades and/or standardized tests. He discusses the overreliance on superior scores in this area to select children for gifted programs, and he reviews an extensive volume of research showing the low relationship between, for example, grades in school and success in a job. Although he does not discuss exactly what he means by "above average ability," an individual must have knowledge of academic areas as well as some mental facility to be able to use knowledge creatively.

Task Commitment

Of the three clusters, task commitment is the newest concept and seems to be the most misunderstood by individuals attempting to implement the *Triad* model. Educators seem to equate the concept of task commitment with either a global concept of motivation or a more specific concept of a child who is "motivated" to do a teacher-chosen task. What Renzulli has in mind is different. The kind of motivation he discusses is a refined or focused commitment and ability to "involve oneself totally in a problem area for an extended period of time" (p. 183). Some of the characteristics included in this cluster are the following: persistence in the accomplishment of goals; integration toward goals; drive to achieve (Terman, 1959); enthusiasm; determination; and industry (MacKinnon, 1965). It is important to emphasize that these characteristics were observed when the individuals were involved in work of their own choosing—their life work—not a *teacher-designed task* that might be boring to them.

Renzulli's task commitment cluster seems similar to the concept of continuing motivation (CM) discussed by Maehr (1976). Continuing motivation is defined as "the tendency to return to and continue working on tasks away from the instructional content in which they were initially confronted" (p. 443). Included in this definition are several important ideas, for example, *returning* to a task in *different* circumstances *without external pressures* and when other alternatives are available. In justifying the value of this concept, Maehr cites some research suggesting that some classroom practices designed to increase performance on classroom tasks may, for children who have the most intrinsic interest in the activity, actually decrease the probability that they will exhibit continuing motivation. Therefore, educators must be careful in assessing these motivational traits in a regular classroom setting. Maehr's approach offers some promising ways to approach the assessment problem.

Creativity

Included in this cluster of characteristics are such traits as "originality of thinking and freshness of approaches," ingenuity, and "ability to set aside established conventions and procedures when appropriate" (Renzulli, 1978, p. 184). As with motivational traits, however, caution must be exercised in assessing creativity in students. Creative performance on a test of divergent thinking may have little or no relation to creativity in a person's life work. Educators may be able to observe some characteristics in children that would lead them to believe that these children have the potential to become creative adults, but the persistence required to return to an idea again and again, and the creativity necessary to generate relevant solutions to a pressing problem day after day may be something entirely different.

Renzulli seems to be right about the importance of the interaction of these three traits in the achievement of eminence. Again and again, research on successful adults supports the conclusion that high ability alone does not predict an individual's success in a career. What educators must all remember, however, is first, that most of this research was done on adults, and second, that the purpose was to identify the characteristics of those who had *achieved success* in a socially recognized manner. In Terman's (1959) study, for example, the "gifted" sample, identified by IQ tests, was divided into groups according to degree of success in life accomplishments. Terman then attempted to determine the characteristics on which the most and least successful groups differed most widely. He found that the groups differed most in their motivational traits and their self-concept or confidence in themselves. Maker, Redden, Tonelson, and Howell (1978) have also identified the same pattern of traits in successful handicapped adults. From this research, as with other research on successful adults, it is impossible to determine whether these characteristics were the result of the individuals' success or whether the characteristics were actually the antecedents of success. If these motivational characteristics were indeed the antecedents or causes of success, then educators would be justified in selecting students for participation in gifted programs based on their motivation. However, if these traits actually were results of the individuals' success, children should be chosen on other characteristics and motivation should be developed through an interesting, exciting program and through successful experiences.

The achievement of success in a socially recognized manner is also an important aspect of many of these studies. What about those individuals who have achieved success by becoming self-actualized individuals, but who have not become eminent or recognized for superior accomplishments? If this kind of success is important, should those individuals be studied to determine their characteristics and children be sought who show these traits early in life? All these questions must be considered in implementing the *Triad* model, because Renzulli has designed the approach to be used with individuals who have the three interacting clusters of traits—creativity, task commitment, and high ability—not those who have only one or two of the clusters.

Selection of Students

As an integral part of the implementation of the *Triad* model, Renzulli (Renzulli, Reis, & Smith, 1981) has developed the Revolving Door Identification Model (RDIM). In this model, many students are identified as potential producers. These students become the "talent pool." Whenever these students have projects they would like to complete, they can "revolve in" to the special program and receive assistance in the development of their investigations. When the project is completed, if they have another idea, they can remain in the special program; if they do not have an investigation or project in mind, they "revolve out" of the program until they are ready for another Type III investigation. This approach to selection recognizes that there are many children who have the ability to be producers and that not all are sufficiently motivated to be high-level producers all the time. The RDIM is seen as an important adjunct to the curriculum framework of the *Triad* and is explained in more depth in Renzulli, Reis, and Smith (1981).

ELEMENTS/PARTS

Dimensions, Thinking Levels, or Steps

The *Enrichment Triad* has three types of enrichment: (1) Type I, General Exploratory Activities; (2) Type II, Group Training Activities; and (3) Type III, Individual and Small Group Investigations of Real Problems. The first two types of enrichment activities are considered appropriate for all learners; however, they are also important in the overall enrichment of gifted and talented students for two important reasons. First, they deal with strategies for expanding student interests and developing thinking and feeling processes, necessary elements in any enrichment program. Second, these two types represent logical input and support systems for Type III enrichment activity, which is the type appropriate for the gifted.

In Type I enrichment activities, the teacher plans experiences to put learners in contact with topics or areas of study in which they may have a sincere interest. In this type, children get a chance to explore a variety of content and thus get ideas about what might be a Type III enrichment activity appropriate for them. Type I enrichment also helps teachers decide what types of activities should be selected for Type II. Although much exploratory freedom is needed, students should be aware from the beginning that they are expected to have a purpose when exploring and that eventually they will be conducting further study in one of the areas of interest to them. An important point to remember in relation to Type I is that general exploratory activity is a cyclical and ongoing process, and even if students are involved in a specific project, they should be given continuous opportunities to keep generating new interests.

In Type II enrichment, the teacher uses methods, materials, and instructional techniques that are concerned mainly with the development of thinking and feeling processes. These are training exercises that will enable students to deal more effectively with content. Thinking and feeling processes have been the focus of many programs for the gifted in the past since research shows that certain thinking and feeling processes provide students with skills and abilities that are applicable or transferable to new learning situations and other content areas. These skills or processes are useful in the changing world, where knowledge is expanding continuously. Thus students are prepared to face new problem-solving situations.

Attention should be given to ensure that these processes are used only as necessary tools to facilitate investigations. If not used as tools, they will become ends, rather than means. Process should go hand-in-hand with the content, as both are important. Even if thinking and feeling processes cannot be defended as being exclusively appropriate for the gifted, they can be defended as an essential part of a total enrichment model for the following reasons: (a) they provide an opportunity for gifted students to reach the levels of thinking and feeling that their natural abilities allow; (b) they have the potential for introducing students to more advanced kinds of study and inquiry; and (c) they provide the gifted student, who is characterized by a wide range of interests, with the skills and abilities to solve problems in a variety of areas and new situations.

Type III enrichment, individual and small group investigations of real problems, is the major focus of this model, since it is the type of enrichment considered to be especially appropriate for gifted learners. According to Renzulli, approximately half the time that gifted students spend in enrichment activities should be in these types of experiences. Type III enrichment consists of activities in which the student becomes an actual investigator of a real problem or topic by using the kinds of methods scientists in the area use, even if not as sophisticated. The students must spend enough time in Types I and II to develop the independence skills necessary for conducting a real study before doing Type III activities. The main characteristics of Type III activities are as follows:

- The child takes an active part in formulating both the problem and the methods by which the problem will be attacked.
- There is no routine method of solution or recognized answer, although there may be appropriate investigative techniques upon which to draw and criteria by which a product can be judged.
- The area of investigation is of sincere interest to an individual or small group, rather than being a teacher-determined topic or activity.
- Students use *raw data* rather than the conclusions reached by others as their information in reaching conclusions and making generalizations.
- The student engages with a producer's rather than a consumer's attitude, and in so doing, takes the necessary steps to communicate results in a professionally appropriate manner.
- There should always be a tangible product that is presented to a real rather than contrived audience.

MODIFICATION OF THE CURRICULUM

In his model, Renzulli provides for some modifications in all aspects of the curriculum—content, process, environment, and product—to make it more appropriate for the gifted. The major modifications that are directly suggested by the model are in the areas of product and learning environment. It is important to note, however, that the model provides a framework for integrating a variety of content and process changes that are appropriate for the gifted. Renzulli even suggests that thinking and feeling processes be developed that will enable students to be effective problem solvers. However, he does not specify in the *Triad* model *which* thinking and feeling processes should be developed and *how* they should be developed.

Content Modifications

Content is modified in that the students learn not just facts about an area but the methods of inquiry within that discipline. The student is also exposed to a wide variety of topics within a discipline before selecting what to investigate. Content is modified also based on the student's interests. Students are encouraged and allowed to select topics of interest to them. Teachers assess student interests continually and attempt to provide experiences that will build on these student interests.

Process Modifications

In modifying the process, Renzulli emphasizes the role of process as a means, not an end. The teacher chooses different processes all the time, according to the students' interests, in order to equip them with the tools and skills to do an independent investigation.

The major process modification directly suggested by the *Triad* model is freedom of choice. In all the areas—content, process, product, and learning environment—students should be allowed the freedom to choose activities that are of individual interest. They should be able to select the topic or area of study, decide upon the method of investigation, and develop a product of interest that will be directed toward an audience they have chosen. Students should also be able to conduct the investigation in any appropriate environment. Freedom of choice is also encouraged in the three types of enrichment activities, although it is encouraged to different degrees. In Type I exploratory activities, the students often choose among options created by the teacher. (The students, of course, played a part in determining the original options since the teacher assessed their interests.) In Type II activities, the students perhaps have less choice, although the kind of investigations in which they are engaged will influence the Type II activities provided. With Type III investigations, students have complete freedom to choose topics, methods, products, and environments.

Higher level thinking is a process modification that is somewhat indirectly suggested by Renzulli's model. Although he does not specify how this should be done, he emphasizes the need for development of problem-solving skills in gifted students or of operations that help the student deal more effectively with content. These operations or processes include critical thinking, reflective thinking, inquiry, divergent thinking, and productive thinking. Renzulli specifically mentions the *Taxonomies of Educational Objectives* and Guilford's *Structure of Intellect* model as approaches that can be used in implementing this aspect of the *Triad*.

A second process modification somewhat indirectly suggested by the *Triad* approach is open-endedness. Renzulli emphasizes as a criterion for selecting Type II activities that these experiences have the power to elicit advanced levels of thinking from gifted students. Also, the divergent production section of Guilford's model can be a useful framework for developing and classifying creativity training exercises for use with gifted students. This model encourages open-endedness by expecting and encouraging a variety of responses for each question or activity.

Discovery learning is another process modification that is suggested by the *Triad* model. Although the *Triad* approach does not suggest or provide for the use of guided discovery, discovery learning is certainly an aspect of Type III investigations. Since students are expected to use the techniques of real inquirers in making their own investigations, they are practicing discovery learning in a real-world context. However, the *Triad* model does not provide teachers with strategies for developing activities that will facilitate discovery learning or the use of inductive reasoning, important components of this curricular modification.

A final process modification made by the *Enrichment Triad* is variety. Teachers are encouraged to use a wide range of methods, including field trips, observation of real professionals at work, simulation games, learning centers, lectures, and any other methods that can be devised. Another aspect of variety is that a wide range of thinking and feeling processes are developed through Type II activities. This necessitates the use of many different methods.

Product Modifications

Product modifications in all areas are made by the *Triad* model. Indeed, Renzulli has made more impact in this area than any other theorist or practitioner involved in education of the gifted. Renzulli goes so far as to suggest that no activity is a "true" Type III activity unless it results in a tangible product that is presented to a real audience, is designed to solve a real problem of interest to the student, has employed methods appropriate to the field of study, and uses raw data to generate unique conclusions. An important aspect of the process is that students are not acting as consumers of information, but as producers of it. The students are not just *emulating* professionals, they are actually *becoming* professionals.

To provide guidelines for the teacher in implementing Type III activities and thus making the product modifications appropriate for gifted students, Renzulli provides suggested strategies for identifying and focusing student interests (for example, interest development and identification, the Interest-A-Lyzer, and interest refinement and focusing), finding appropriate outlets for student products (that is, real audiences), providing students with methodological assistance, and developing a "laboratory environment." Suggestions include reference books and materials, along with methods and strategies.

Learning Environment Modifications

Renzulli also makes numerous suggestions for developing environments appropriate for gifted students. He advocates a student-centered atmosphere where independence is encouraged, few restrictions are present, complexity is essential, and high mobility is a *must*. In the learning environment appropriate for implementing the *Triad,* the teacher's major goal is to identify, focus, and facilitate student interests and ideas. In fact, student interests guide the selection of both content and process activities developed by the teacher.

In this atmosphere, the teacher cannot possibly be an information-giver, except when asked by the students. Although the teacher may direct certain activities, at least half will be completely determined by the students since half their time (according to the model) should be spent in Type III investigations. Students certainly must be permitted to be independent in other than academic settings since many of them will be involved in small group activities in which they are conducting studies. They should be allowed and encouraged to solve their own disputes when they arise, and they should assist the teacher in planning and implementing Type I and II activities that interest them.

The environment dimension of openness requires that few, if any, restrictions affect the students' participation. They should be encouraged to develop new ideas, produce different products, and use different investigative techniques. The physical environment must permit new people, exploratory discussions, and freedom to change directions when necessary. Complexity in the learning environment is encouraged by Renzulli in his suggestion that specialized equipment, varied reference materials, and sophisticated materials should be available. This includes both books and nonbook reference materials. To enable the teacher to develop a true "laboratory environment," a variety of types of work spaces must also be present. This includes tables, study carrels, soft areas for discussions, and easels for painting.

The *Triad* approach also requires an environment that permits high mobility. Students must be permitted to conduct their investigations in any environment that facilitates the process. Renzulli's ideas that are most related to this dimension of the environment are found under the heading "developing a laboratory environment." In a laboratory environment, students are actively engaged in gathering some form of relevant information that is to be used in the development of a particular product. Examples given by Renzulli are (a) a street corner and classroom where children recorded the number of automobiles that failed to stop, then analyzed the data for a presentation to the commissioner of public safety; and (b) the school cafeteria and science laboratory where students collected leftover food and unused napkins in an antiwaste campaign. In these cases, the students could not have conducted their investigations on their problem of concern if they had been confined to a classroom in a school. Thus, an environment permitting movement freely is an essential aspect of implementing Type II investigations.

Examples of Teaching Activities/Strategies

Type I Enrichment Activities

Three procedures the teacher can use to allow the student to explore a diversity of areas are interest centers, visitations or field trips, and resource persons or guest speakers. Interest centers should include a wide range of topics or areas of study. They should include not only material that is stimulating for further research, but also information related to methods of investigation in the field. A good example of provoking and stimulating material would be the completed investigations and products of other students. These should be included in interest centers.

Visitations should be to places where dynamic people are actively engaged in problem solving and the pursuit of knowledge. Instead of just looking at equipment and the environment, gifted learners should have an "escalated experience." This type of experience provides opportunities for looking into and becoming involved with what is on display, being presented, or being produced. For example, students should have opportunities to interact with artists, curators, engineers, and other professionals by seeing them at work and by actually taking part in some of their activities. Teachers must be selective when inviting a guest speaker. They must choose persons who are actively engaged in contributing to the advancement of art or knowledge in their respective fields or areas of endeavor. Some examples are local historians, poets, dancers, architects, photographers, and scientists.

The major role of the teacher in Type I enrichment is to develop interests and identify areas for further study; the teacher must also spend a large amount of time assisting students in analyzing their own interests. A planned strategy for helping students examine their present and potential interests could be based on an instrument called the Interest-A-Lyzer (Renzulli, 1977, pp. 75-82). This instrument consists of a series of hypothetical situations in which the student is asked to respond to open-ended questions. Looking at the responses, consistencies are analyzed and general patterns of interest are detected. Teachers using the instrument should make the children familiar with the content of the items, and they may modify the contents or add their own ideas, especially when dealing with young children or children who are culturally different.

Another aspect of the teacher's role is to expose students constantly to new areas for creative expression. For example, when recruiting community resource persons as guest speakers, teachers should choose persons who are involved in types of professions and activities that are different from those with which the students are familiar. A community survey would be good for this purpose as well as for identifying persons who might be willing to follow up an exposure activity and become involved with groups of students. A survey could even identify individuals who would be willing to become mentors. A sample form for surveying community resources is the Community Talent Miner (Renzulli, 1977, pp. 82-86).

Interest development centers, field trips, and resource persons are organized approaches to Type I. However, students should also be given informal opportunities to examine topics for possible study. For example, they should be allowed to browse in libraries or bookstores, encouraged to read simple "how to do it" books, and provided with unstructured group discussions.

Type II Enrichment Activities

Any model that provides valuable systems for organizing thinking and feeling processes and factors that are essential for human learning can be used effectively as a Type II activity. Some examples of these would be Bloom's *Taxonomy of Educational Objectives*, Krathwohl's *Taxonomy of Affective Behaviors*, Guilford's *Structure of Intellect*, Parnes's *Creative Problem Solving*, Hilda Taba's *Teaching Strategies*, and Kohlberg's *Discussion of Moral Dilemmas*. An important aspect of Type II is to select activities according to student interests whenever this is possible.

The development of thinking and feeling processes necessary for Type III investigations is the ultimate goal of Type II activities. Students must acquire the process skills and abilities that will enable them to solve problems in a variety of areas. The following are given by Renzulli (1977) as examples of process skills:

Brainstorming	Comparison	Elaboration
Observation	Categorization	Hypothesizing
Classification	Synthesis	Awareness
Interpretation	Fluency	Appreciation
Analysis	Flexibility	Value Clarification
Evaluation	Originality	Commitment (p. 25)

Type III Enrichment Activities

In Type III enrichment, the teacher's role is to be a manager in the learning process and to know when and how to enter into this process. The teacher thus has the following major responsibilities when managing Type III:

- identifying and focusing student interests
- finding appropriate outlets for student products
- providing students with methodological assistance
- developing a laboratory environment

Successful Type III enrichment activities depend on the interaction of these four basic responsibilities.

General interests must be refined and focused to enable students to identify a real and solvable problem. At this time, the teacher must make certain that students apply the proper investigative strategies so that they do not report instead of investigate. The teacher must also be careful not to rush students through the process or impose a problem on them; teachers should allow students to make their own decisions. Teachers must find appropriate outlets for student products, since one of the major characteristics of a real problem (as opposed to a training exercise or simulation) is that the producer is attempting to inform, entertain, or influence a relatively specific but real audience. This need to have an impact is one of the reasons why creative and productive persons are highly product-oriented; they always have an audience in mind. Since real-world audiences are frequently grouped together by topical interests, teachers can look for them as potential audiences for the creative work of their students. Some examples of audiences are historical societies, science clubs, dramatic groups, and persons interested in preserving a certain species of wildlife or promoting a particular social action cause. Another potential outlet consists of children's magazines that include the work of young people. Following are some specific examples of possible outlets and products in Type III:

- writing a journal article
- making a conference presentation
- issuing a statement to legislators
- producing a television arts company
- publishing a book
- writing a play
- developing a new theory
- developing a lattice
- writing a brochure

One final concern that must be mentioned is the quality of products. Teachers should make their students aware that the creative/productive process goes beyond just generating ideas and that they must work hard to refine each product before it is considered final. Students should avoid circulating or presenting products that have not been revised, edited, and polished.

The third responsibility of the teacher in Type III enrichment is providing students with the tools of inquiry, that is, the methodological techniques that are necessary to solve a problem. The teacher should provide students with books that offer step-by-step guidance in methodological activities in a specific area and provide instruction about advanced library skills, going beyond usual exercises that deal with the Dewey Decimal System and how to use the card catalog. Students must learn about the existence, nature, and function of different types of reference materials. These include reference books (for example, bibliographies, dictionaries, glossaries, indexes, atlases, reviews, abstracts, periodicals, surveys, almanacs, or anthologies) and nonbook reference materials (art prints, video-tapes, filmstrips, charts, maps, or slides). Teaching effectively about the use of reference materials involves developing a systematic plan so that students are continuously learning where and how information is stored. One important activity for the teacher is analyzing the difficulty level of the methodological reference according to the reading and conceptual levels of the student, and serving as a translator whenever a particular concept is beyond the student's level of comprehension.

Also important to the implementation of Type III enrichment is the development of a "laboratory environment" where the students inquire or investigate. A laboratory is not necessarily a physical place. It is the environment—the psychological one—the mood, atmosphere, and a series of investigative activities that can happen anywhere. What determines the presence of a laboratory environment is whether students gather, manipulate, and use raw data or existing information to produce something that is new and unique. Some examples of laboratories could be street corners, a grove of trees, an audiovisual viewing room, a town hall, and a public library.

A good strategy for teachers to use to get investigative activities started is a Management Plan (Renzulli, 1977, p. 71). This document, a somewhat simplified version of a proposal, provides a format for planning a project. It requires students to think ahead about the purpose of the investigation, the questions to be answered by it, the format of the product, where and to whom the product will be presented, the methodological resources to be used, and the criteria to be used in evaluating the product.

Learning Styles

Important to all three types of enrichment is respect for the individual learning style of each student, along with the general learning style preferences of gifted students. Stewart (1979) and others (Dempsey, 1975; Gallagher, Aschner, & Jenné, 1967; Hunt, 1975; Lundy, 1978; McLachlan & Hunt, 1973) have found that gifted students as a group differ from nongifted students in their preferences for certain types of learning activities. They rank independent study, simulations, and discussion higher than average students; they seem to be more field dependent than independent; and they prefer low structure over high structure classes. However, gifted students also differ widely in their preferences for certain types of experiences. To provide valuable information about individual preferences, teachers can ask children to respond to questionnaires such as (1) *The Learning Styles Inventory* (Renzulli & Smith, 1978), which assesses children's preferences for certain instructional techniques (for example, lecture, discussion, projects, independent study, programmed instruction, recitation and drill, peer teaching, simulated environments, and teaching games) and (2) *The Learning Style Inventory* (Dunn, Dunn, & Price, 1975), which classifies 18 elements of learning into the categories of environmental, emotional, sociological, and physical elements.

Using the Triad Model

As a concrete example of the *Triad* model in use, the following specific examples are given. The activities are all organized around the following abstract generalization: *Every society has had rules, written or unwritten, by which social control over the people's conduct is maintained.*

Possible Type I Activities

- Observe a city council meeting, and conduct interviews afterward with selected officers and members.

- Observe a legislative session.
- Schedule a lecture by a state or local legislator.
- Set up learning centers with copies of constitutions of various countries, books about constitutional issues, newspaper articles about constitutional and legal issues, and books about sociological analysis (that is, how to study societies and their means of social control).
- Schedule a lecture by a sociologist describing his or her work in investigating methods of social control.
- Have students read biographies of famous historians, sociologists, anthropologists, and statespersons.
- Show a film about Margaret Mead and her work.
- Schedule a lecture by a historian about the historical development of codes and how he or she has studied their development.
- Schedule a lecture by a cultural anthropologist about what kinds of things he or she does (for example, types of projects, how they are applied, and methods used).

Possible Type II Activities

- Have a Kohlberg discussion of a moral dilemma that involves an issue where someone must break a law to save a life.
- Have several Taba discussions using the interpretation of data strategy in examining stories about various societies and their laws.
- Have a Parnes creative problem-solving activity where the problem is in the area of how to study a society or how to settle a problem involving the breaking of a rule.
- Play the simulation game "Shipwreck" in which students create a society.
- Use Krathwohl's *Taxonomy* as a guide for making observations of students while engaged in this activity (that is, observe the level of development of their values related to social control).
- Devise a constitution for a hypothetical country.
- Have students lobby in the state legislature.
- Analyze the methods used by the different historians, anthropologists, and sociologists, including those eminent individuals studied and the individuals who have been guest lecturers or who have been observed.
- Study methods used by cultural anthropologists. (For example, show children how to use observation forms to decide who is in a position of authority based on how others react to this person.)

- Compare the characteristics of current state legislators and famous states-persons.
- Study the use of sociograms, that is, what information comes from them and how a person develops one.
- Develop a plan for creating and operating a school council that develops and enforces rules for the school population.
- Have the students present the plan to school officials, and get permission to establish the school council.
- Have students practice their forecasting ability by attempting to predict how different societies in certain periods of history reacted to the imposition of certain laws or codes of conduct. Afterward, read a history text or view a film to check the accuracy of their predictions.
- Using Williams's strategy number 18, Visualization, plan an activity in which the students examine certain laws and social codes from the following perspectives: (a) law enforcement officers; (b) lawmakers; (c) prisoners; and (d) the general public.
- Using Krathwohl's *Taxonomy* as a guide, plan a discussion of differing values of investigators and how these can influence their choice of strategies for conducting investigations.

Possible Type III Activities

- A group of students decided to investigate the law-making process in the city of Albuquerque. They interviewed the city council and made systematic naturalistic observations of the council in action. Their final report to the city council was of great interest to parents, teachers, and the council itself.
- One student decided she would like to compare the Mexican and American societies' processes of developing and implementing rules to govern society. The student proposed that she would read about the two societies. The teacher, however, encouraged the student to read, but also to design and send a questionnaire to Mexican and American lawmakers, and to compile the results of this survey. The report was then submitted to a professional journal.
- A group of students interested in school rules conducted a survey of all classrooms asking for opinions on (1) the rules most needed and (2) the rules most often broken. The survey resulted in the development of a proposed discipline policy for the school, which was presented to the principal of the school and the executive board of the Parent-Teachers' Association (PTA).
- In this project on school rules, the teacher was concerned at first about whether the students would be able to complete the project because many of

those in the group were new to the gifted program and had not had experience in directing their own investigations. In her observations of the working of the group, she used Treffinger's model to assess the levels of self-direction of the students. She was happy to discover that there were several students who possessed many skills at the highest levels. She worked on an individual basis with some of the students who were causing the group some problems in an attempt to develop some of the skills they were lacking.

- One student was interested in studying the penal systems in various societies, but she was having difficulty figuring out exactly what to study and how. The teacher suggested that the student use the CPS process to help in selecting a topic and developing her investigation.

- One student was having a great deal of difficulty developing criteria for evaluating his product, which was a research report to be submitted to a professional journal. He wanted to evaluate the paper himself, have it judged by several others, and revise it before submitting it for publication. The teacher suggested that he consider Bloom's *Taxonomy* and Guilford's product categories for the evaluation or that he use them to get ideas for criteria. (Students had previously learned these as classification systems.)

- One student decided to do a research project on the amount of eye contact between people in a shopping center as a way to investigate some of the unwritten rules governing actions. The paper was submitted to an anthropology journal.

It is important to note that only "possible" activities of each type are included. The teacher should survey the interests of the students and observe their participation in various activities to identify areas of interest and need. These interests and needs determine the learning experiences provided by the teacher or developed by the students. Interests can influence learning activities in a variety of ways. One way would be to use student interests to select the generalizations around which the activities are organized. Another would be to assess or determine student interests within the framework of a series of abstract, complex generalizations that are used as organizers. The first kind of influence might be most important in determining the Type I activities to be provided, while the second may be most appropriate for generating Type II experiences.

In the "possible" activities, various process models have been combined with the *Triad* to show how they can be used to generate Type II activities. There has also been an attempt to illustrate how other recommended curricular modifications could be incorporated into the basic framework.

Table 7-1 provides a summary of teacher and student activities and roles for each type of enrichment in the Triad model.

Table 7-1 Summary of Teacher and Student Activities and Roles in the Renzulli Enrichment Triad Model

Step, Type, or Level of Thinking	Student		Teacher	
	Role	Sample Activities	Role	Sample Activities
Type I: General Exploratory Activities	active participant; observer	Work in learning centers. Go on field trips. Explore new ideas. Interact with practicing professionals. Take an active part in activities of professionals.	Planner; Organizer; Interest-stimulator	Plan experiences to expose students to new fields of inquiry and the methods used in these fields. Plan continuous experiences to put learners in contact with topics or areas of study in which they may develop a sincere interest. Encourage students to visit the library. Develop interest centers. Arrange for visitations, field trips, and guest speakers. Choose as speakers active professionals. Allow and provide for informal opportunities for exploration.
Type II: Group Training Exercises	active participant; thinker	Play simulation games. Answer thought-provoking questions. Do thinking skill exercises. Identify interests and process needs. Discuss ideas and methods.	Trainer; Facilitator; Discussion leader	Plan group and individual exercises that will develop thinking and feeling processes that can be used in a variety of investigations. Plan process experiences to meet both individual and group needs. Develop higher-level thinking skills. Develop divergent as well as convergent thinking skills. Develop affective as well as cognitive skills

Table 7-1 continued

Step, Type, or Level of Thinking	Student		Teacher	
	Role	Sample Activities	Role	Sample Activities
Type III: Individual and Small Group Investigations of Real Problems	Problem-finder; data-gatherer; problem-solver; producer; inquirer	Develop a management plan Identify a problem of real concern. Conduct an investigation of a real problem. Work individually or in a small group. Identify a real audience for the product. Develop a product that is new and unique.	manager; resource	Assist students in developing a management plan. Assist students in identifying and focusing interests. Identify mentors. Identify appropriate outlets or audiences for student products. Provide students with methodological assistance. Assist in locating information. Develop a learning environment. Encourage going beyond the school environment. Wait for students to make their own decisions. Assist students in revising and "polishing" their work.

MODIFYING THE APPROACH

Renzulli's *Enrichment Triad* is in many ways a framework for providing curricular modifications in all areas that are appropriate for gifted students. All of the content and process modifications suggested by the author of this book can be easily incorporated into a program that uses the *Triad* as a framework. The model itself makes suggestions in all product areas and in all environment dimensions except one. The changes suggested are designed to illustrate how the *Triad* approach can be more effectively implemented to achieve the purposes of a comprehensive program for gifted students.

Content Changes

Renzulli's suggestions for content changes fall mainly into the areas of variety and methods of inquiry. He does not recommend abstractness, complexity, organization, economy, and the study of people in the sense that these have been recommended in this volume and in the initial book (Maker, 1982). However, as shown in the examples of activities these are easily incorporated. Type I and II activities have been organized around an abstract, complex generalization rather than some other framework, such as type of activity. Students were encouraged to explore a variety of concepts related to this idea. Many different types of experiences were provided. Each experience was carefully chosen to illustrate key concepts and to expose students to a variety of methods, a variety of disciplines, different "scientists" and different theories, and both present and past problems/ ideas related to the generalization.

In addition, the sample activities show how a person might integrate the study of eminent or famous people. Type I activities include exposure to biographies and autobiographies of famous individuals who made significant contributions in this area along with a film about Margaret Mead and her work. Type II activities include an analysis of the methods used by present investigators, comparing them with those employed by the eminent individuals studied and comparing the characteristics of present lawmakers with statespersons of the past.

Process Changes

The *Triad* model by itself does not directly suggest process changes in all the areas recommended for the gifted. However, the design of Type II enrichment encourages teachers to incorporate many process models into their teaching and suggests that the selection of such activities be based on the interests and needs of the students. Renzulli does suggest process modifications that should be made in the areas of higher levels of thinking, open-endedness, and discovery. Numerous guidelines are given for providing freedom of choice and for the use of a variety of methods.

In the sample activities, several process models have been used to design activities and to show how various process models often used in gifted programs can be combined with Renzulli's approach to provide a more comprehensive curriculum. With these additions, all the process modifications are made by the example.

Higher Levels of Thinking

Skills in the use rather than acquisition of information are developed through the following Type II activities: (a) the Kohlberg discussion of a moral dilemma involving breaking a law; (b) the Taba discussions of societies and their laws; (c) the Parnes activity involving how to solve a problem over the breaking of a law; (d) the Taylor activity in which students develop a plan for a student council government; (e) the Taylor activity in which students predict reactions to certain laws and then check the accuracy of their predictions; and (f) the Krathwohl-based discussion of values and their influence on methods used by those engaged in research.

Open-endedness

Many of the activities included as both Types I and II are designed to be open-ended and to stimulate the interests of the students in further pursuit of the problems or topics encountered. Some of the more interesting ones include observation and interviews with the city council, playing the Shipwreck simulation, and devising a constitution for a hypothetical country. By using the Taba *Strategies* for several discussions and the Kohlberg discussion, and by carefully designing questions, teachers can ensure that open-endedness in all its forms is a significant aspect of all Type II experiences.

Discovery

Discovery learning is a definite aspect of all Type III activities, as students are acting as real inquirers and are producing rather than consuming information. Guided discovery, supervised or practiced, in the inquiry process, has been incorporated through the use of Taba's *Interpretation of Data Strategy,* which leads students through a process of examining data, inferring causes or effects, developing supportable conclusions, and generalizing to new situations. If the Krathwohl discussion of values is conducted as recommended in Chapter 2 for use with the gifted, guided discovery would also be a part of that activity. The Taylor forecasting activity involving the students' predicting and then checking the accuracy of predictions would also involve discovery learning.

Evidence of Reasoning

This process modification can easily be incorporated into all discussions and activities without making major changes in the discussions. It would not be appropriate at certain steps or stages of steps in the Parnes process, however, as discussed in Chapter 6. Some models (the Taba strategy and the Kohlberg discussion) already include the asking of questions to elicit explanations of reasoning. Chapters on the various models describe how this process change can be accomplished with each of the approaches.

Group Interaction

Structured group interaction is accomplished through the simulation game, *Shipwreck*. Group participation can be observed by a small group of students, or the entire activity can be taped for later viewing by everyone. Analysis of group participation can include assessment of the roles assumed by individuals and their effectiveness in carrying out these roles. Analysis can also include attempting to identify individual values and the level of development of those values by using Krathwohl's *Taxonomy* as a guide for observation. The group may want to spend some time brainstorming procedures for more effective participation, or students may wish to discuss values and their effect on various interactions between people.

Pacing

Pacing, as a process modification, is particularly important during Type I and Type II activities when new material or ideas are presented to the students. Guest speakers should be reminded that these are gifted students and that they can absorb material quickly. They should also be prepared to answer in-depth questions from students about their work.

Learning Environment Changes

The only learning environment dimension not modified directly by the *Triad* model is acceptance versus judging. This dimension is important as a support for developing student products that truly belong to the students rather than to the teacher. The teacher must allow students to make mistakes and see the effects of their mistakes. An effective way to develop an environment that is appropriate for the gifted and for implementing Type III activities is to follow the suggestions made by Parnes in CPS. By keeping these in mind, the teacher will evaluate only at the appropriate times, encourage clarification and elaboration before evaluation, and encourage and implement evaluation techniques that address both the good and bad aspects of a product or an idea.

Although Renzulli does not address the group participation aspect of Type III activities, a few more suggestions about the independence dimension need to be made. Renzulli suggests that Type III investigations can be made by individuals or small groups of students. He does not address the question of how the teacher should handle difficulties that may arise during the course of these groups working together. To implement the learning environment modification that gifted students must develop—independence in both academic and nonacademic areas—students should be encouraged to develop their own group management procedures. They should also develop their own solutions to problems. If students have learned CPS, this is a natural process for them to use, both in developing a working plan and in solving problems.

Summary

The *Triad* model lends itself well to developing a program that is comprehensive in providing curricular modifications that are appropriate for the gifted. By integrating several process models and by organizing Type I and II activities around abstract, complex ideas, the content and process modifications not suggested by the *Triad* approach can be implemented.

DEVELOPMENT

Over a period of several years, Renzulli has been involved with programs for the gifted, both as a consultant in program development and as an evaluator. Based on these experiences and a growing concern for comprehensiveness and defensibility in gifted programs, he developed the *Triad* model. In developing the model, his approach was first to draw upon actual practices in enrichment programs and second to base the model on what is actually known about giftedness rather than the "romantic notions" that seem to abound in popular circles. His reviews of research on characteristics of individuals who are eminent and successful in their adult lives revealed the three well-defined clusters of characteristics: above average intelligence, creativity, and task commitment. Since these three clusters of traits must interact to manifest themselves, an individual must have some type of *real* problem to investigate. Renzulli incorporated the research of Ann Roe (1952) along with the ideas of Virgil Ward (1961) and Philip Phenix (1964) in the development of his model: (1) Ann Roe's classic study (1952) of 64 eminent scientists in which she concluded that the most important factor in the final decisions of these persons to become scientists was the sheer joy of discovery; (2) Ward's fundamental principles (1961) underlying differential education for the gifted, that superior students should become acquainted with the basic methods of inquiry within the various field of knowledge; and (3) Phenix's (1964) conclusion that learning methods of inquiry are valuable because they are modes of active investigation. Renzulli also adopts Jerome Bruner's (1960) conclusion that young children are able to engage in critical inquiry.

RESEARCH ON EFFECTIVENESS

Although much research was incorporated in the formulation of the *Enrichment Triad* model, no comparative studies of its effectiveness are available. Some program evaluations are available; however, since very little data are reported in these assessments, and the data consist mainly of teacher, student, and parent impressions rather than information on student growth, these evaluations are not summarized here. There have been studies showing that isolated aspects of Renzulli's model are effective. For example, a good Type II activity would be teaching students to use the Parnes CPS process. Several studies verify its validity. (See Chapter 6.) Another well-documented part of the *Triad* is the "independent study" aspect of its approach, which is present to a great degree in Type III activities. Studies show these procedures to be highly effective when used in programs for the gifted (Renzulli & Gable, 1976). What is needed, however, is research on the *Triad* as a *comprehensive approach*. Important questions to be addressed are the following: Do the parts fit well together? Does it work with young children? What is the best administrative structure to facilitate its success? Are there adequate measures of task commitment at early ages? Do those who show task commitment in school turn out to be task-committed adults? Do those who do *not* show task commitment in school turn out to be task-committed adults?

JUDGMENTS

Advantages

The most important advantage of the *Triad* is that it was designed specifically for use in gifted programs, and, as such, it is based on research about characteristics of the gifted who achieve. A related advantage is that it takes into account that gifted programs must be related to the regular curriculum, and they must build on or expand on the basic competencies taught to all children. With the *Triad,* the relationship between the gifted and regular programs must be considered. Because it was designed specifically for use with the gifted, the Triad model directly addresses the issue of and need for a qualitatively differentiated educational program for the gifted. Renzulli provides specific guidelines for making some modifications of all aspects of the curriculum—content, process, product, and learning environment—and he provides a framework for easily integrating others, thus making it more appropriate for the gifted. Other models may modify one or two aspects of the curriculum, but none provide as comprehensive an approach or framework as does Renzulli's.

Another advantage of the *Triad* is that it provides an overall program *framework*, including guidelines for program philosophy, definition of giftedness, identification of the gifted, teaching activities, and strategies for program evaluation. A number of program alternatives and curricular approaches shown to be effective with the gifted can easily be integrated into the *Triad* model, making a defensible and effective approach. Also, the *Triad* model is simple enough for parents, administrators, and students to understand without excessive educational rhetoric. Other advantages include the following: (1) it respects the interests and learning styles of gifted students; (2) it is based on and incorporated into a real-life environment; and (3) by providing a philosophy addressing which students should be served by a gifted program, it also provides guidelines for counseling out students who do not belong in the program.

Disadvantages

The most obvious disadvantage of the *Triad* model is its newness and the lack of research on its effectiveness as a total approach. Since it is the only framework designed specifically for use with gifted students, educators have jumped on the bandwagon without seriously considering the philosophical approach necessary for its implementation. Everyone has adopted the framework and incorporated existing curricula into it. Educators have made a few changes to make it all fit together, but they have not made the philosophical and programmatic commitments that will make it work. The philosophy is apparently hidden to some, but is clear to others. The *Triad* model emphasizes the selection of those children who show the most potential to succeed (according to society's definition of success) rather than, for example, children who (a) show an educational need for services based on their intellectual deviation from the average or (b) need a differentiated program because of their unique learning styles. This philosophy may be radically different from the school's, parent's, or teacher's beliefs. Seldom are these differences even recognized, and even less often are they reconciled.

Another disadvantage is that most of the research upon which the three-ring conception of giftedness is based was done with adults. It is impossible to determine whether these characteristics were the causes or results of success. This disadvantage has serious consequences, particularly in the selection of children from certain subgroups of the population. What about children from disadvantaged backgrounds who have never been exposed to an area of study or a task to which they can become committed? What do educators do about children from different cultural backgrounds whose cultural definition of success is not the same as a white, Anglo-Saxon, Protestant one? The gifted underachievers who are potential dropouts and who will most likely not demonstrate any task commitment may not be identified for a gifted program. If they are identified, they may be counseled out because they do not develop a Type III project soon enough. The motivation and persistence necessary to follow through on real-life activities may take years to develop, and indeed these characteristics may be the most important goals of education for these children. By developing continuing motivation while children are in school, educators may (a) prevent them from dropping out of school or (b) help them develop the skills that will enable them to become productive members of society.

Some of the more practical disadvantages of the *Triad* model include difficulty in assessing task commitment and creativity, the fact that teachers are not trained to implement a model such as this (that is, they are not scholars or methodologists in scholarly fields; they are trained to teach content rather than guide investigations), and the fact that the model is deceptively simple. At first glance, the philosophy seems clear and the implementation easy. However, many have realized after only a short time that the skills required are complex, and the practical problems are many and varied. Teachers must have a variety of resources available. They must know how to use these resources, and they must have time to locate them for children. Since the model is so new, few materials (for example, units, lesson plans, teaching strategies) are available to facilitate the implementation of the *Triad* approach.

CONCLUSION

Although the *Triad* model does have its drawbacks, with careful consideration of its philosophical base, along with its specific strategies and how these aspects fit into a unique situation, teachers can implement it appropriately. With the benefit of longitudinal studies of its effectiveness, educators may be able to develop qualitatively different programs for gifted children that are defensible to anyone who would question their existence.

RESOURCES

Background Information

Renzulli, J.S. *The enrichment triad model: A guide for developing defensible programs for the gifted and talented.* Wethersfield, Conn.: Creative Learning Press, 1977. The major theories of Renzulli's work on education for the gifted are presented in this well-written book. Renzulli states several purposes in the introductory chapter. First, he discusses education for the gifted and the many aspects of it that he considers indefensible. Second, he presents his "enrichment model," which is one he finds defensible and able to serve gifted students in a meaningful way. The *Enrichment Triad* model is discussed at length; the three aspects in detail that compose it are explained.

General exploratory activities, group training activities, and individual and small group investigations of real problems are the three components discussed. Finally, Renzulli offers practical suggestions for teaching gifted students. The book offers a thorough explanation of Renzulli's theory and practical application of his model.

Renzulli, J.S., Reis, S.M., and Smith, L.H. *The revolving door identification model*. Mansfield Center, Conn.: Creative Learning Press, 1981. The revolving door concept has created tremendous debate in the field of gifted education. This book explains in detail the assumptions, research, and practice behind the theory. The revolving door concept moves away from the traditional identification and concept of giftedness, and instead believes in a concept of gifted behavior. Students are not gifted, but demonstrate gifted behavior in specific areas or talents. The authors describe how to establish a program in a school where students "revolve" in and out of a gifted resource room, depending on their interests and abilities. Specific chapters include: "Research and Guidelines Underlying the Revolving Door Identification Model," "Major Components of the RDIM," "Forming the Talent Pool," "The Revolving In and Revolving Out Process," and "Modifying and Evaluating Revolving Door Programs." Comprehensive appendixes are included. The book presents an alternative concept of giftedness that is both provocative and potentially feasible.

Instructional Materials and Ideas

Ciabotti, P.A. *Gaming it up with Shakespeare: A combined study of drama and theatre*. Mansfield Center, Conn.: Creative Learning Press, Inc., 1980. The best storehouse of ideas and information for a teacher is other teachers, yet it is difficult to find published materials written by teachers for teachers. The *Creative Learning Press* has done exactly that: published a series of curriculum units based on Renzulli's *Triad* model. Each unit has been field tested by the authors in their classrooms. Drama and theatre is the subject of this book. The unit was used with sixth graders, but simple modifications would make it adaptable to any age group. There are three major sections, discussing Type I, II, and III activities. Procedures to follow and resources are given for each activity. A sample Type III project and a management plan are included. A well-organized book, *Gaming It Up* can serve as an entire unit or as a springboard for further ideas.

Dow, C. *Lunchroom waste: A study of "how much and how come."* Wethersfield, Conn.: Creative Learning Press, 1978. This is a classroom activity based on Renzulli's Triad model. All activities in this series have actually been used in the classroom. The authors are the individuals who both designed and applied the material. The activity is an in-depth investigation, which covered several months, of lunchroom waste and reasons for it at a middle school. The gifted students chose the topic, developed a research model, conducted interviews, and analyzed the statistics. The pamphlet describes the development and outcome, with objectives and accomplishments listed for each meeting. Appendixes include school library resources along with interview and poll questions and results. A completed management plan is included.

Dutton, N.C. *Civil defense: From town hall to the pentagon.* Mansfield Center, Conn.: Creative Learning Press, Inc., 1980. Using Renzulli's *Triad* model, two eleventh grade students chose to do an in-depth study of our civil defense system. This book is the journal of their teacher, which explains the activities of the students. The book is arranged chronologically, outlining the 23 weeks of the project which culminated in a report and several presentations. It is written in a narrative style by the author. As with the other books in the series, detailed resources and the management plan are included. Teachers will find every book in this series extremely informative and useful.

Heuer, J., Koprowicz, A., and Harris, R. *M.a.g.i.c. k.i.t.s.: Meaningful activities for the gifted in the classroom through knowledge, interest, training, and stimulation.* Mansfield Center, Conn.: Creative Learning Press, Inc., 1980. Teachers of the gifted continually search for stimulating, inexpensive, and meaningful activities which will encourage creative and higher level thinking skills. This book fits the bill. The "kits" are based on Type I and Type II activities of the Renzulli *Triad* model, with the possibility of Type III activities being self-initiated by interested students. Bloom's *Taxonomy* is also incorporated. A "magic kit" is, in effect, a way to create an instant learning center on a particular topic. The authors explain how to collect the necessary materials for a specific area of study (for example, dinosaurs, art, junk mail), and then they suggest activities using these materials. There are 21 topics. The activities are interdisciplinary, incorporating language arts, fine arts, the sciences, and social studies. Furthermore, a format is described for developing one's own kits and activities. The Creative Learning Press has consistently published well-written, useful teaching tools for educators; this book is no exception.

Mathews, F.N. Entomology: Investigative activities for could-be bug buffs. In L.M. Smith (Ed.), *Triad prototype series.* Wethersfield, Conn.: Creative Learning Press, 1978. This series of enrichment activities was designed to develop investigative skills in entomology. There are three categories of experiences in the packet, increasing in complexity and sophistication. General Exploratory Activities include films, discussions, field trips, and interest centers. The second category, Group Training Activities, includes collecting, mounting, classifying, dissecting, and tracking insects. The third enrichment activity, Individual and Small Group Investigations of Real Problems include specific, concentrated activities. Scientific experiments and the presentation of data in report form are key parts. Specific details for all activities and a management plan are included.

Page, B. *Cartoon art: An adventure in creativity*. Mansfield Center, Conn.: Creative Learning Press, Inc., 1980. This is another unit in the series written by teachers for teachers, published by Creative Learning Press. It traces the progress of a fifth grade student who discovered an interest in cartooning, after taking an Interest-A-Lyzer. Using Renzulli's *Triad* model, the student designed and published a comic book. The book has three sections, covering Type I, II, and III activities. One follows Eric from his initial exploring of cartooning with Type I activities to the actual production of his comic book, as his Type III project. A resource list, the management plan, and the comic book are included. This curriculum is consistent with Renzulli's theories, and is a very useful book for teachers. Also, it is reassuring to note the teacher had no knowledge of cartooning before beginning this project (with the exception of reading *Peanuts!*).

Chapter 8

Hilda Taba: Teaching Strategies Program

One of the most promising process models for use with gifted children is the generic teaching strategies program developed by Hilda Taba. Her series of four sequential questioning techniques resulted from almost 15 years of research on children's thinking and how it could be developed (Taba, 1964, 1966). Few of the approaches frequently used in this field can provide similar evidence of their effectiveness in producing growth in abstract reasoning. Yet, only scattered programs for the gifted employ the Taba *Strategies*. Perhaps this "spotty" use is due to the fugitive nature of much of the literature; perhaps it is due to difficulty in learning the strategies; or perhaps it results from the lack of an advocate who sees its potential and pushes for its acceptance. More important, perhaps Taba's insistence that *all* children can develop abstract reasoning skills if assimilation and accommodation activities are paced appropriately has led educators of the gifted to dismiss the teaching strategies as inappropriate.

Regardless of the reasons for only scattered use of the Taba *Strategies* in current programs, there is a more than adequate basis in theory and research to justify their use alone or in combination with other approaches in educating the gifted. A close associate of John Dewey, Taba incorporated many of his ideas along with the research and writing of Piaget, Bruner, and Vygotsky in developing her approaches to teaching and curriculum development. Although her strategies are of a generic nature and are appropriate for use in any content area, because of her social studies curriculum (Ellis & Durkin, 1972), Taba's methods are viewed by some as social studies techniques. However, as can be seen by examining the theoretical and empirical basis for the strategies, they are techniques for developing thinking skills, or, in Piaget's terms, methods for arranging the environment so that maximum cognitive growth can occur.

Briefly, the *Hilda Taba Teaching Strategies* are structured, generic methods in which the teacher leads students through a series of sequential intellectual tasks by asking them open-ended but focused questions. There are four strategies: (1) concept development; (b) interpretation of data; (c) application of generalizations; and (d) resolution of conflict (also called interpretation of feelings, attitudes, and values). The four strategies, although not designed to be hierarchical or sequential, can be used sequentially since they build on each other. Within each strategy, however, there is a definite sequence to the questions, with a theoretical and practical justification for the order.

On a personal note, my own involvement with the *Hilda Taba Teaching Strategies* has been interesting and rewarding. After the first series of training in their use, my reaction was similar to an "Aha!" experience. Another immediate reaction was that these strategies, particularly the second, interpretation of data, were close to what I had always attempted to do in my teaching, although my methods were always lacking in some way. Taba had perfected these methods and even had data to show they were effective! Further, the methods Taba developed for training teachers were the best I have encountered: demonstrations and modeling, analysis of the demonstration, step-by-step planning, team planning and team tryouts, and finally, classroom tryouts, taping, and self-analysis. Both the teaching strategies and the teacher-training process have had a profound, positive effect on my teaching.

ASSUMPTIONS UNDERLYING THE MODEL

In developing the teaching strategies, the following assumptions commonly made about children's thinking were rejected because they tend to retard progress in developing thinking skills:

- An individual must accumulate a great deal of factual knowledge before thinking about this knowledge.
- Thinking skills are only developed through "intellectually demanding" subjects (for example, physical sciences, math, and foreign languages).
- Abstract thinking is an ability that can only be developed in bright or gifted children.
- Manipulation of the environment will not improve or cause growth in thinking skills since cognitive growth is locked into a predetermined developmental time sequence.

These ideas were rejected and more positive alternatives proposed because of the results of Taba's three research projects (Taba, 1964; 1966; Wallen, Durkin, Fraenkel, McNaughton, & Sawin, 1969).

About Learning

Probably the most basic idea underlying the Taba *Strategies* is acceptance of Piaget's (1963) assumptions about cognitive development: the sequence, how it occurs, and the type of thinking exhibited at each developmental stage. Although it is impossible to discuss all of Piaget's ideas in this chapter, a few of the general principles will be briefly presented since they are necessary to understanding the teaching strategies.

First, there is an invariant sequence in which cognitive development occurs. Children begin at the sensorimotor stage and progress sequentially, without skipping any stages, through preoperational to concrete operations. Finally, they achieve formal operations at about age 11. Change, or cognitive growth, occurs through children's interaction with the environment and their attempts to construct their own reality or organize their world. As children interact with the environment and attempt to interpret it using increasingly sophisticated ways of thinking, the phenomenon of disequilibrium occurs; they experience discomfort because they begin to recognize previously unnoticed inconsistencies. When this happens, they attempt to consolidate and integrate various schemes for interpreting what is seen in order to achieve equilibrium (and be "comfortable") again.

Assimilation and Accommodation

The concepts of assimilation and accommodation are closely related to equilibrium and disequilibrium, and are crucial to understanding "pacing" in the Taba program. A somewhat simplistic but effective way of explaining the two ideas begins with the conception of a person's mind as a filing system with file folders representing categories (for example, dogs, furniture, books).* When new information comes in, it needs to be filed somewhere in the system. The individual doing the filing has essentially the following three choices: (1) fit the information as it is into one of the existing categories; (2) change the information in some way so that it fits into the existing system; or (3) change the system in some way so that it can handle the new information. This change can be a small one, such as adding a new category, or it can be more extensive through redefining a whole series of categories or even reorganizing the whole system.

In this example, filing the information as it is represents a form of *assimilation*. Changing the information is another form of assimilation, which occurs when the item does not fit, but there is no desire to change the system. *Accommodation* is represented by some change in the system, from limited (making a new category) to extensive (revising the entire structure). The changed system that results from an extensive revision is a more sophisticated one. Thus it is with cognitive growth. Individuals experience disequilibrium when they recognize inadequacies in their

---

*This idea, in its skeletal form, was first presented in a class taught by Dr. Herb Richards.

existing organization of reality, so they make changes that improve that organization. They now experience equilibrium again. Intellectual growth, then, can be seen as a progression of assimilation, attempted assimilations that will not work, necessary accommodations, and then new assimilations at a higher order.

Developmental Trends

As children progress through the stages of cognitive development, they become increasingly able to use more formal systems of logic and to rely on symbols of meaning. A second trend is away from egocentrism or an egoistic view of the world toward the ability to differentiate the self from the rest of the world. A third related trend in development is toward internalization and "interiorization." Actions become less overt and more internal. In this movement, individuals go through distinct stages. The thought processes of previous stages are incorporated into the thinking at higher levels, but at each higher level, the processes are qualitatively different from those at lower stages. As children mature, they develop cognitively at their own rate, with movement through the stages determined by the interaction of both internal and external factors.

Facilitating Cognitive Growth

The one aspect of Piaget's theory that is not accepted by Taba is in the area of environmental influences on cognitive growth. Although Piaget recognizes the importance of a child's interaction with the environment as the growth processes occur, he believes that deliberate manipulation of the environment to enhance development or to quicken its rate is a futile exercise. In other words, there is nothing educators can do to hasten or improve the quality of a child's cognitive development. They must simply wait for these natural changes to occur. Experiences that provide for horizontal elaboration (for example, enrichment within stages) can be helpful, according to Piaget, but vertical elaboration (for example, enrichment at different levels) is neither helpful nor desirable.

On this point Taba disagrees. Her basic assumption is that the environment is extremely important; it can, and should be manipulated so that maximum horizontal *and* vertical elaboration occurs. In other words, she agrees with the sequence identified by Piaget, but disagrees with his deterministic assumptions about how growth occurs.

One of the most important ideas underlying the Taba program is the following: "Thinking involves an *active* transaction between the individual and the data with which he [or she] is working" (Institute for Staff Development, 1971a, emphasis added). This idea has numerous implications for the learning process. It means, for one thing, that children do not develop their thinking skills by memorizing the products of adults' thinking. Children develop these skills by manipulating ideas, critically examining them, and trying to combine them in new ways. Data become meaningful only when individuals perform certain mental operations on those data. Even if children reach exactly the same conclusions an adult has after reviewing certain materials, the process of manipulating the information was necessary and valuable. This is not to say that children should not read the conclusions of others. They certainly should, but they should also be encouraged to reach their own conclusions and to examine the data of others critically to see if they would draw the same conclusions.

A second assumption relates content and process. Although Taba believes that thinking skills can be developed through any subject matter (that is, not just through the so-called intellectually demanding subjects), it is impossible to separate process from content. The "richness" and "significance" of the content with which children work will affect the quality of their thinking, as will the processes used and the initial assistance given in developing these processes. Because of this belief, every lesson has both a content and a process purpose that are interrelated and can be accomplished by the particular strategy. Selection of content that is rich and significant enough to be appropriate for developing thinking skills then becomes an important aspect of learning the teaching strategies, as does the organization of that content.

Another relationship between content and process centers around Taba's ideas about "thought systems" in each content area. Although the precise nature of the relationships between content areas and the processes used by scholars in those areas is unclear, Taba hypothesizes that there may be both generic processes of inquiry cutting across all types of content and certain specific processes of conceptualization in each area. For example, all areas deal with such processes as inferring cause-effect relationships. However, in the social sciences multiple causation and probabilistic reasoning are much more important than in the physical sciences, where phenomena are much more easily predicted. In short, the nature of the content and the "thought systems" in each content area will determine in part the most important thinking skills to be practiced by the students.

About Teaching

Unfortunately, not all teaching results in learning. Since teaching is a complicated process requiring an infinite number of decisions that must meet many criteria, each objective of teaching will require a different analysis and different teaching strategies.

The Importance of Specific Strategies

Productive teaching involves "developing strategies which are focused sharply on a specific target while at the same time integrating these specific strategies into an overall strategy that accommodates the generic requirements of multiple objectives'' (Taba, 1966, p. 42). In other words, there are many thinking skills that can be taught, and there are particular methods to use for developing different thinking skills. Before teachers can be successful in developing thinking skills, they must have a clear idea of how these thinking skills are manifested and what methods can be used to develop them. One specific effect of this idea on Taba's methods is that for each teaching strategy and for each step in each strategy there are particular "overt" and "covert" objectives. In other words, she has pinpointed the behavioral (overt) manifestations of the underlying (covert) thinking processes.

Related to the development of thinking skills and following from her agreement with Piaget's sequence of cognitive development is Taba's (1964) assumption about the sequencing of learning experiences. If educators assume there is a sequential order in the development of thought processes, there should also be a sequence in learning experiences so that each step develops skills that are prerequisites for the next step. This sequence would apply to the day-to-day learning experiences provided for children as well as to those experiences spanning one school year or a series of years.

Teacher Questions

A crucial factor in developing thinking skills and the sequencing of learning experiences is appropriate questioning by the teacher. Important aspects of teacher questions are *open-endedness,* allowing for and encouraging responses at different levels of abstraction, sophistication, and depth, and from different perspectives; *pacing,* which matches student capacity for mastering the skills at each step; and *sequencing and patterning.* Sequencing and patterning are particularly important in that the "impact of teaching does not lie only in the frequency of single acts" (Taba, 1966, p. 43), but also in the ways these single acts (questions) are combined into sequences and patterns.

Rotating Learning Experiences

Also following from an assumption about how development occurs is Taba's (1966) belief in the value of "rotating" learning experiences that require assimilation and accommodation. Putting this idea into practice suggests alternating experiences where children absorb information with those experiences that challenge their current mental schemes for organizing the information. Primitive or inadequate schemes can be challenged by having children consider examples or information that is "dissonant with their current schema" (p. 23) so that they are required to revise their present conceptualization. The teacher's task is not to correct the student or to point out these inconsistencies, but to present or otherwise arrange the situation so that students encounter the dissonant information with potential for causing change. Students must manipulate data themselves. To be successful, however, this process of rotating experiences must "offer a challenge that is sufficiently beyond the student's present schema to induce accommodation, and yet not so far removed that the student cannot make the leap" (p. 23). This underlying idea of rotation and challenge is closely related to Taba's concept of "pacing," which is discussed later.

Organization of Content

Since content is an important aspect of the learning process and sets limits on the kind of learning and on the teaching strategies that can be used, it must be organized to develop thinking skills. Suggested organizational schemes are those advocated by Bruner (1960), Ward (1961), and Taba (1962). Basic concepts and ideas provide the underlying system of organization rather than chronology or type of information.

About Characteristics and Teaching of the Gifted

Taba's (Institute for Staff Development, 1971a) assumption that "All school children are capable of thinking at abstract levels, although the quality of individual thinking differs markedly" (p. 148) resulted from her research showing that there was a low positive relationship between IQ and performance on the tests, and other measures of the effect of the teaching strategies. When growth was measured, results showed that students with low IQs gained as much as did those with high IQs. It is important to note here that, in the teaching strategies, pacing is important. With slow learners, new material is not presented as rapidly, and there are sufficient opportunities for concrete operations before transitions are made to abstract operations with symbolic content. With rapid learners, the pacing of these activities is matched to their needs. In short, the same basic intellectual tasks can be used with gifted and nongifted children, and can be effective in developing their abstract thinking capabilities. However, the pacing of assimilation and accommodation activities and the frequency of the rotation between them must be different.

No statements are made by Taba about the most effective grouping of students to achieve appropriate pacing for all students. Taba assumes that at least during some parts of the day, children need to be grouped according to learning rate. However, in many of the classrooms where the teaching strategies were tested, many discussions involved the whole class rather than small groups within it. Perhaps the reason there were few differences between gifted and other learners in Taba's research is that gifted children were always in groups with all ranges of ability. Thus, appropriate pacing for their needs was impossible.

Those who implement Taba's approach in programs for the gifted emphasize that although the strategies can be used with all children (and should be used part of the time with groups consisting of varied ability levels), having gifted children grouped with other gifted children part of the time is essential for maximum cognitive growth to occur. A theoretical justification for this idea comes from Piaget's (Piaget & Inhelder, 1969) statements about the importance of peer interaction in fostering cognitive growth. Since Taba accepts Piaget's assumptions about how cognitive development occurs and since the teaching strategies are designed to foster development along the lines suggested by Piaget, his ideas form an implicit assumption even though Taba did not make it explicit.

In discussing the importance of peer interaction, Piaget emphasizes that children learn from each other, they learn both content (for example, specific facts or pieces of information) and reasoning processes (for example, logic or ways of handling information). An important way in which cognitive growth occurs is through exposure to higher levels of reasoning. However, these higher levels must be only slightly higher than the child's present level of reasoning in order for the child to incorporate this reasoning into his or her repertoire. In addition, this "learning from others" is only beneficial when the child is "ready," which usually means when the child is in some transition stage in development. Extending this idea to the use of the Taba *Strategies* with gifted children, then, suggests that they need to be grouped with their gifted peers at least part of the time. One or two gifted children in a heterogeneous fourth-grade classroom will not learn as much from each other as will nine or ten gifted children drawn from all the fourth-grade classrooms in a school. A further extension of the idea suggests the value of multi-age grouping of gifted children.

Since Piaget's theory of cognitive development forms a theoretical basis for the Taba *Strategies*, it is important to consider his possible conception of giftedness. Although Piaget makes no direct references to giftedness, educators and psychologists have often interpreted his ideas without a full understanding of them. Most psychometric (measurement) conceptions of giftedness emphasize the importance of rate of development: a child who talks earlier, reads earlier, thinks abstractly at an early age, and does tasks normally accomplished only by older peers is considered more intelligent. Often, this same idea is carried over into interpretations of giftedness in Piaget's developmental scheme: those who progress through the stages more quickly will be (and are) more intelligent.

This perception of intellectual development ignores a concept important in Piaget's theory, the importance of horizontal elaboration. According to this idea, an individual who passes through all the periods of development more rapidly may not be as capable intellectually as a person who has passed through the periods more slowly. The individual who has moved more slowly will have more time to develop cognitive structures at each stage, and thus the individual will have a better base for the next higher stage because of the interaction with a greater variety of content. Although Taba does not directly address this Piagetian concept, it seems to be an underlying idea that influences her perception of giftedness.

Summary of Assumptions

The major ideas underlying the Taba *Strategies* can be summarized as relying heavily on Piaget's developmental theory, including the sequence of development, the major stages, and the importance of interaction with the environment. Her major disagreement with his theory, however, forms the basic rationale for the Taba *teaching strategies* program: thinking skills can be taught. If educators are familiar with the various thinking skills and their behavioral manifestations, and if they use precise teaching strategies designed to enhance these skills, they *can* arrange the environment so that maximum cognitive growth occurs.

ELEMENTS/PARTS

Four separate but related teaching strategies make up the Taba model: concept development, interpretation of data, application of generalizations, and resolution of conflict. Each has specific cognitive tasks and a rationale for their placement in the sequence.

Concept Development

This strategy deals with the organization and reorganization of information, and with the labeling of categories (Institute for Staff Development, 1971a). The name concept development indicates the end result, which is the development of concepts or broad categories of data that are related in some way. Students classify data and support their classifications. Concepts are formed, clarified, and extended as students respond to questions that require them to enumerate items, notice similarities and differences that form a basis for grouping items, label groups in different ways, regroup items in different ways, and give reasons for all groupings. In all cases, it is important that the students perform these operations for themselves; also, teachers must be able to ask the major focusing questions at the appropriate time and recognize when to employ other questions or tactics that will extend, clarify, refocus, or support a discussion intending to accomplish the objectives of concept development.

Rationale for the Concept Development Task

Concept development is considered the basic form of cognition on which all other processes depend. It is closely related to assimilation and accommodation, allowing each student to *clarify* (through verbalizing his or her own thoughts) and *extend* concepts (through building on others' ideas and having them build on his or hers). It enables students to participate at their own level, but also provides a model to which they can aspire. For example, one student may group items on the basis of their descriptive attributes (for example, color, shape), while another may make abstract groupings (for example, fruit, animals). Still another may be at an even higher level, adding or multiplying classes (for example, putting things together that are either wood or blue, or putting things together that are both wood and blue).

From a content standpoint, the task assists students and teacher by organizing data or information to be studied into units that are meaningful to the students and that can facilitate further investigation. When used in this way, the task also helps the teacher assess the breadth and depth of the students' concepts in order to plan individual and group experiences that will expand their concepts. In general, the strategy helps students develop (a) greater openness and flexibility in thinking, and (b) better processes for developing and organizing data.

Rationale for the Steps

Each step in the concept development strategy has a rationale for inclusion and a rationale for its placement in the sequence. The first step, *listing*, involves the process of differentiating relevant from irrelevant information, an important skill upon which all other skills will be built. Each student can make a useful contribution, and each can learn from the contributions of others.

At the second step, *grouping*, students become involved in the cognitive task of noticing common attributes and putting items together on the basis of these commonalities. They not only make their own groupings, but they also see the different ones made by other students. This promotes identification of multiple attributes and stimulates openness and flexibility in thinking (for example, seeing many sides of an issue). Making certain that the reasons for groupings are clear to all students is important for (a) helping students clarify their reasoning to themselves and others, and (b) enabling students to build on others' ideas by adding to a group made by someone else.

Labeling, the third step, is an abstracting or synthesizing process in that a student must find a word or a phrase to express the relationship or commonality among diverse items. The more accurate and inclusive a person's labels are, the more efficient that person is in handling a variety of information. When a teacher consistently asks for variety in labels, there are also positive effects on vocabulary development and creativity. When considering the appropriateness of labels, evaluation is taking place, so all children must understand why a label is appropriate or inappropriate.

The fourth step, *subsuming*, provides another opportunity to see different relationships and new attributes of the items. Perhaps more important, however, is that this step helps students see hierarchies in the relationships. In deciding what labels can fit under other labels, they begin to analyze the inclusiveness of each label.

At the fifth step, all the previous steps are *recycled*. This not only accomplishes the same purposes already mentioned, but also promotes openness and flexibility in thinking because it emphasizes that there are always fresh ways to look at the same data.

Interpretation of Data

As the name implies, this strategy deals with gathering information and making inferences about it (Institute for Staff Development, 1971b). Students form conclusions and generalizations about similar situations or events, based on the class discussions. In dealing with information and processing it, students then make inferences about cause/effect relationships and are asked to defend their statements. It is important that students have meanings or interpretations of data, and that they recognize the significance of this data as they relate to other events in the past, present, or future. Teachers must help students recognize the tentativeness and probabilistic nature of conclusions and generalizations, and they must help students reach these conclusions on their own. They also must be able to guide a discussion by using appropriate questioning techniques.

Rationale for the Interpretation of Data Strategy

This "discovery" or "inquiry" technique provides a sequential method for helping children use the observable data in their own experience as a starting point for developing their own conclusions and generalizations. In this strategy, students process the data in their own way and also have the opportunity to observe how others process the same information. Although it is appropriate for a variety of types of data (for example, scientific, literary, symbolic, or quantitative), the particular type of data will call for greater precision (for example, scientific and quantitative data) or more "reading between the lines" (for example, literary or symbolic data).

Rationale for the Steps

At the first step, *listing*, the same purposes are served as in the concept development task. Students have the benefit of their collective observations, and they must decide what is relevant and what is not. Sometimes the data may need to be transformed even at this initial step into similarities, trends, or sequences.

At the second step, *inferring causes and effects*, students apply their own reasoning, experience, and knowledge to the data to arrive at and give support for their inferences. By listening to different interpretations that are often equally justifiable, students learn to attend to and seek out the basis for differing ideas. Providing support for inferences helps students clarify their reasons and develops the habit of identifying the justification for their ideas.

The process of making inferences is carried further in the third step, *inferring prior causes and subsequent effects*. At this step, the fact that cause-effect relationships are usually complex and interrelated rather than simple and linear is emphasized. The third step also stresses the fact that many influences are far removed from the immediate data or situation. The development of new inferences based on supported inferences encourages students to probe deeply into the phenomena that influence their lives, rather than looking only at surface conditions.

The fourth step requires students to reach *conclusions* and emphasizes that, even though they may not have all the information they would like, they must make the soundest conclusion possible and support it.

Generalizing, the fifth step, is an efficiency-building technique similar to labeling. This task gives students practice in transferring knowledge gained in one situation to other situations where it might apply. In its most extreme form (for example, stereotyping), overgeneralization can be dangerous since an individual who does this is using knowledge about *too few* cases to infer about *too many* cases. Rarely do students practice this essential skill so that they can become more accurate and more tentative in their generalizing. At this step, students reach their own generalizations, justify them, have the opportunity to critically review the general statements developed by others, and also have their own generalizations critically examined.

Application of Generalizations

In this strategy the major objective is to help students apply previously learned generalizations and facts to other situations (Institute for Staff Development, 1971c). Students use these generalizations to explain unfamiliar events and to make predictions about what will happen in hypothetical or proposed situations. For example, if students are asked, ''What will happen if our country continues to pollute our streams and lakes?'' they must apply previous knowledge about the causes of pollution, the conditions present now in the water supply, and knowledge of the previous effects of pollution on lives and environments. This strategy develops in students the ability to make predictions about things that will happen in the future and enables them to apply what they have learned. The real test of a concept or generalization comes when it is applied in a real-life situation. As in all other strategies, students must support all predictions and inferences made. After discussing various predictions, reasons, and conditions, each student is asked to make judgments about the events that are most likely to happen based on the discussion and what they already knew. The teacher must use the appropriate questioning strategies, which will lead children through the intellectual tasks identified.

Rationale for the Application of Generalizations Strategy

In this strategy, students apply previously learned facts, principles, or processes in new situations to explain new phenomena or to predict consequences from known conditions. This process is an important vehicle for transfer of knowledge, enabling students to get more "mileage" out of their direct experiences. The application of generalizations strategy allows for and encourages divergent thinking in making predictions. However, it also requires students to establish both the parameters of logical relationships or data by which to judge the validity of predictions. These established parameters are also judged on their completeness; students must generate the chain of causal links that will connect the conditions and the predictions.

Rationale for the Steps

At step one, *predictions,* students are encouraged to use their creativity in brainstorming the possible results of some hypothetical situation. It requires the logical proposition of "If _____ , then _____ ." They are then asked to explain the reason(s) for making a particular prediction. Verbalizing the relationship they see between the situation and the prediction gives them practice in clarifying their own thinking and in hearing the thinking of others. This is also the part of the process from which the strategy gets its name. Students verbalize and explain the particular abstract principles, facts, or processes they are applying to the new situation.

The second step, *inferring conditions,* brings the discussion to a reality base by requiring that students build a logical, justifiable chain of relationships. This process strengthens and expands the basic idea of multiple causality as it becomes increasingly clear that no consequence directly follows from a given situation, but that many other factors must also be present.

The next step, *inferring consequences and conditions,* is essentially a recycling of the first two steps and, as such, serves the same purposes. However, it also serves additional purposes in that each time the processes are recycled, the predictions and conditions are further extended from the original situation and are therefore more complex and probabilistic in nature.

At the fourth step, *conclusions,* the same purposes are served as in step four in interpretation of data. Students are required to consider all the predictions, conditions, and reasons that were discussed and make a judgment on their own about which conditions they think are likely to prevail, which leads to a particular prediction coming true.

Examining a generalization, the fifth step, strengthens students' abilities to form their own general statements and to look critically at others' statements that may be too general, inaccurate, and unqualified.

Resolution of Conflict

This strategy, often called interpretation of feelings, attitudes, and values, leads students through a process helpful in resolving conflict situations (Institute for Staff Development, 1971d). It is an extension of all the other strategies, with human behavior as the data being interpreted. Its primary purpose is to help students deal more rationally and effectively with situations encountered in life by giving them practice in exploring the feelings, attitudes, and values behind people's behavior. Students are encouraged to take the viewpoints of all individuals involved in a conflict situation and discuss their possible motives, feelings, and reasons for feelings before talking about what each individual can do to resolve the conflict situation. They are asked to generate a variety of alternatives for action by each person and then to analyze these alternatives in relation to their general consequences and effects on all the other people involved in the situation. Based on the discussion, students evaluate the alternatives and make individual judgments about the most appropriate action that should be taken. After explaining their judgment and considering its possible long-range consequences, students are asked to consider a similar situation experienced by a member of their own group. The same process is followed with this situation, from exploration of reasons for behavior through evaluation of alternatives. Finally, on the basis of this discussion and prior experiences, students are asked to form a generalization about how people usually handle conflict situations of the type discussed. As in the other strategies, the teacher's role involves asking the appropriate questions that will elicit information, inferences, and conclusions from students.

Rationale for the Resolution of Conflict Strategy

This strategy, as an extension or combination of the previous two strategies, serves the same purposes as those tasks. However, the subject matter being interpreted and the principles being applied are particularly subjective: human behavior and emotions are the target areas. This strategy gives students practice in assuming the viewpoints of others, an ability which, according to Kohlberg (1971) and Selman (1971), is a necessary prerequisite for advanced moral reasoning to occur.

Rationale for the Steps

At the first step, *listing*, the same purposes are served as in the other strategies. Students learn to differentiate relevant from irrelevant data. It also builds the idea that a person must understand the facts and know what actually happened in a situation before taking any action.

In the second step, *inferring reasons and feelings*, the same purposes are served as in the inference steps of other strategies. Additionally, this is the major aspect of perspective taking. Students must learn to examine the possible motivations and feelings of all people involved in conflict situations before making judgments about their actions or suggesting alternatives.

Generating alternatives and examining their consequences is an important skill for everyone and is a skill that is seldom practiced. Usually people act now and think about it later, especially in emotionally charged conflict situations. Students need to realize that effective decision making requires careful consideration of all the factors and likely consequences of each alternative course of action.

At the next step, *evaluation*, students are asked to decide the most appropriate action. This involves much the same processes as at the conclusion step in the other strategies since students must think carefully about the discussion and interpret it in their own way.

In the next phase of the discussion, steps five through eight, students are asked to apply the same processes of *listing facts, inferring reasons and feelings, generating alternatives and consequences,* and *evaluating alternatives* in a situation in their own lives or in the life of one of their peers. This heightens the transfer effect and provides additional emphasis on the validity of these processes in handling the day-to-day situations these students may encounter.

At the last step, *generalizing*, students are asked to form an abstract statement about how people usually handle such situations. The same purposes are served as in the previous strategies.

Supporting Behaviors

Although the particular steps in each strategy are different, there are certain teacher behaviors that are necessary at all steps of a discussion. For example, teachers must always ask questions that are both open-ended and focused. Except for the listing step, they must always ask students to provide evidence or reasoning to support inferences unless they have provided that support when giving their answers. There are also certain kinds of supporting behaviors necessary for particular *types* of steps. For example, every strategy begins with a listing of information that is relevant to the focus of the discussion. When getting this information from the students, the teacher should encourage variety, ask questions that require students to clarify the meanings of words they use, and provide specific data or facts rather than giving inferences.

General Behaviors

At all steps of Taba discussions, the teacher must encourage participation by all students and ask open-ended questions that will permit and encourage a variety of answers. Teachers must follow the appropriate sequence of steps and must avoid negative acts, such as the following: (a) giving opinions or value judgments about student ideas; (b) rejecting, ignoring, or cutting off a student response; (c) doing the task students are supposed to do; and (c) editing or changing a student's idea.

Other general supporting behaviors are accomplished through the appropriate questioning techniques. In this regard, there are essentially four types of questions.

Questions Calling for Variety. These are questions that ask students to come up with completely different responses from those already given.

- What else might happen?
- What are some completely different ways these items can be put together?
- What are some other causes for that?
- What else could we call that group?
- What are some completely different things she could do?

Questions Calling for Clarification or Extension. These are questions that ask students to explain the meaning of statements or words, provide specific examples, or elaborate on an idea to extend its meaning.

- What do you mean by freedom?
- How is your idea different from Sally's?
- Please give me some examples of "transportation vehicles."
- Please explain more about that idea.
- What do you mean when you say _____ ?

Questions Calling for Reasons or Support for Ideas. These questions are used at all steps of discussions except when listing. They ask students to explain or cite reasons for the inferences, conclusions, or generalizations they have made. Since they are often threatening to students, care should be exercised in their use. They are used often, so the teacher must be able to vary the questions to avoid being repetitious.

- What are your reasons for grouping these items together?
- In what way are these items alike?
- Why do you think these items go together?
- How are these items alike?
- What is your basis for grouping these items together?
- What are you thinking that makes you say that?
- Tell us how you know that.
- What leads you to believe that?

- How do you know that _____ causes _____ ?
- How do you know that _____ results in _____ ?
- What makes you believe that _____ would be an effect of _____ ?
- What are your reasons for thinking that is true of all people?
- What from our discussion led you to that conclusion?

Focusing Questions. These are the initial questions that focus students on the task at a particular step. They need to be worded carefully so that they are both open-ended and clear in their focus. If students stray from the topic or focus, the initial question needs to be restated to bring them back on task. Focusing questions may also need to be reworded to avoid monotony. Following are some examples of different focusing questions for particular purposes:

Grouping

- Which items could you put together because they are alike in some way?
- Which things would you group together because they are alike?
- Which items go together because they are alike?
- Which items would you put together in groups?

Causes and Prior Causes

- What has promoted _____ ?
- What are some factors contributing to _____ ?
- What helped _____ to come about?
- What do you think prevented _____ ?
- How did _____ happen?

Effects and Subsequent Effects

- What has happened because _____ ?
- What resulted after _____ ?
- What were the results of _____ ?
- What have been some of the consequences of _____ ?
- What do you think happened as a result of _____ ?

Supporting Behaviors for Specific Steps or Types of Tasks

In describing the important behaviors for types of tasks and for summarizing the teacher and student roles and activities in the Taba model, similar types of tasks have been grouped together. The general types of tasks are the following: (a) getting the data (that is, the first step of all strategies except application of generalizations); (b) organizing data (that is, grouping, labeling, and subsuming in the concept development strategy); (c) making inferences (that is, causes, effects, prior causes, subsequent effects, predictions, conditions, and consequences); (d) generating alternatives (that is, alternatives for action in the resolution of conflict strategy); (e) making conclusions (that is, concluding about causes, effects, or predictions, and evaluating alternatives); and (f) making generalizations.

When getting the data, the teacher's main task, other than general support behaviors (for example, encouraging variety, clarification), is to make certain that students stick to the data rather than make inferences. If students begin to give inferences, the teacher should ask questions, such as: "What did you see (hear, read) that led you to believe that? Please give me an example of that from the story. What did her mother do that made you think that? In the concept development task, it is particularly important for the students to give specific examples rather than categories. Otherwise, there would be no items for grouping at the later steps.

Organizing data is a task that requires teachers to pay particular attention to their own organization in order to facilitate the discussion. One way to keep things moving (except with young children) and save time is to put numbers beside each of the items to indicate which group they are in rather than rewriting the items. If this is done at the labeling step, the number can be written on the board in a separate place with the labels beside them. For example:

3, 1	item	3	item	1 - LABEL	2 - LABEL
2	item	1	item	LABEL	LABEL
2	item	2	item	LABEL	3 - LABEL
3	item	1	item	2 - LABEL	LABEL

The first item is in two groups, 3 and 1. At the subsuming step, the task is easier since additional numbers are written beside the items when they are added to a group. With young children, however, this system would be confusing, so the items in each group and the labels must be kept close together. If groups are rewritten, space for writing labels above each group should be provided. Encouraging the whole group to participate is another important aspect of discussions that center around organization of data. For example, the teacher should encourage adding to the groups that have been formed based on the reasons the groups were initially made. Also, the whole group should be involved in recalling the reasons why groups were formed and in considering the appropriateness of labels. This should not be carried to the point of taking a vote, however.

The subsuming task is often difficult for young children to understand. They may need an example, and if so, the teacher should provide only one or two. If they have put items in two different groups at step two, this is a good example to point out. Sometimes young children will tend to combine groups or combine labels rather than subsume them. The teacher should respond to their combining by saying, ''Yes, these labels do go together, but which one goes under the other?'' or ''Yes, these groups are alike, but which items from one of the groups could go under one of the labels we already have?'' When items are moved at this step, they are not *removed* from the first group. They are added to other groups. Taking them out of the first group in order to put them in the second may reinforce the idea that they cannot belong in two places. This would be detrimental to the idea that things can be classified on the basis of multiple attributes.

The task of making conclusions is often difficult for students, and they may tend to summarize the discussion. Conclusions must show evidence of synthesis and personal reflection rather than be summaries that simply recount what was said. The statement should carry a personal conviction. To this end, the teacher should accept students' summaries, but push them for a conclusion (for example, ''Yes, that's what we said. Now, what do *you* think about what we said?'').

Generalizing is also a difficult task for children. It requires careful thought, so they should be given time to think and write down their ideas before sharing them orally. Often, telling students to write a complete sentence will help. More important, however, is the teacher's focusing question. The question must be narrow enough to give students an idea of what the teacher wants. For example, after an interpretation of data discussion about the effects of differences between two types of containers, if a teacher asks, ''What can you say generally about containers?'' anything they say is a shot in the dark. The question must relate to the focus of the discussion. In this example, since the students have been discussing effects (for example, what happens because there are differences between these containers), the generalization question must focus them on effects. A more appropriate question would be the following: ''What can you say generally about what happens when we use different kinds of containers?'' If the discussion were about causes, an appropriate question would be as follows: ''What general statement could you make about why we use different kinds of containers? Write a sentence about why you think there are differences in the types of containers we use to store things.''

The Importance of Planning

When implementing the Taba *Strategies*, detailed planning is extremely important if the objectives of each strategy are to be achieved. When learning the strategies and trying out a completely new approach or a complex idea, the teacher should develop a detailed plan that includes the following: (a) the content and process purposes of the strategy as a whole (including a sample generalization for all strategies except concept development); (b) the prediscussion procedures; (c) the behavioral objectives at each step that are specific to this lesson; (d) focusing questions for each step; (e) support procedures for each step; and (f) a ''cognitive map'' of possible student responses to the focusing questions at each step.

The sequence of the planning process is as follows:

- Identify the overall content and process purposes, developing a planning generalization when appropriate.
- Identify the prediscussion procedures and necessary materials.
- Develop the actual discussion plan for each step in a particular order. First, write the behavioral objective specific to that lesson by consulting the chart of general objectives, then write a focusing question for that step. Next, consider the focusing question, and write some possible student responses to the question on the cognitive map. Based on this tryout of the question, rewrite it to improve clarity if necessary, write the question asking for reasons or support, and write some support procedures that will be necessary for achieving the behavioral objective at that step.

By following this sequence in detail, the likelihood of a successful discussion is greatly increased.

After the strategies are learned and when a familiar topic is the focus, a shorter and simpler process is followed using a short form. With the short form, teachers only plan a focusing question for each step and develop a sample cognitive map.

Summary of Steps and Activities

Learning how to use the *Hilda Taba Teaching Strategies* program is not simple. The strategies are complicated, and differences between an inappropriate and an appropriate teacher question or behavior that can throw a whole discussion off track are often subtle. Although comprehensive, this description of the strategies would not enable a person to use them effectively. Demonstrations, practice with critiques from experienced leaders, classroom tryouts, and self-analysis are necessary components in the learning process. Many teachers feel that it has taken years of practice for them to perfect their techniques. However, they also attest to the effectiveness of the strategies when implemented appropriately. Table 8-1 presents a summary of student and teacher roles and activities in each type of task in the *Hilda Taba Teaching Strategies*.

MODIFICATION OF THE BASIC CURRICULUM

The Taba model suggests modifications of the regular curriculum that are appropriate for the gifted in process, content, product, and learning environment. Although it is primarily a process approach, because of Taba's (1962, 1964) comprehensive approach to curriculum development and implementation, the model provides for many changes that are important in gifted programs. Content

Table 8-1 Summary of Teacher and Student Roles and Activities in the Hilda Taba Teaching Strategies Program

Step, Type or Level of Thinking	Student		Teacher	
	Role	Sample Activities	Role	Sample Activities
Getting the data	observer active participant; listener	Notice what happened. Recall events or knowledge from past experience.	presenter questioner facilitator; active listener	Present a situation, provide an article to read, or provide some "intake" experience. Ask questions to get students to recall specifics or facts from past experience or the intake experience. Ask for clarification. Refocus. Get specifics and variety.
Organizing data	active participant; listener	Group like items together. Provide labels for groups. Subsume items under labels. Subsume labels under labels. Explain reasons for grouping, labeling, and subsuming. Listen to the ideas and reasons of others. Think of different ideas	questioner active listener facilitator	Ask questions that require students to group, label, subsume, and recycle. Ask for clarification. Refocus. Encourage student-to-student interaction. Ask for support or reasoning for all answers given. Ask for variety.

Table 8-1 continued

Step, Type or Level of Thinking	Student		Teacher	
	Role	Sample Activities	Role	Sample Activities
Making inferences	active partici- pant; listener	Make inferences about causes and prior causes of data. Make inferences about effects and subsequent effects of data. Make predictions about a hypo- thetical situation. Infer conditions necessary to make predictions come true. Infer consequences of predic- tions. Listen to the ideas and reasons of others. Think of different ideas. Explain reasoning behind inferences made.	questioner facilita- tor active listener	Ask questions that stimulate child- to make inferences (focus on the task). Ask for clarification. Refocus. Ask for support or reasoning for all answers given. Ask for variety.
Generating alternatives	active partici- pant; listener	Develop alternative courses of action for all individuals in- volved in a conflict situation. Think of new ideas. Listen to the ideas of others.	questioner facilita- tor active listener	Ask questions that focus children on the task. Divide class into small groups or pairs. Ask for variety. Ask for clarification.

Making conclusions	Think about the discussion and reach a conclusion about what will be most likely to happen. Evaluate alternatives for action. Explain reasons for conclusions. Reach a conclusion about important causes or effects. Listen to the ideas of others and react to them.	synthesizer listener active participant	questioner facilitator active listener	Ask questions which focus children on the task. Refocus when necessary. Ask for clarification. Accept summaries, but ask for interpretations and conclusions. Encourage student-to-student interaction.
Making generalizations	Make general, abstract statements about causes, effects, or human behavior. Examine the general atatements made by others and react to them. Explain reasons for general statements or evaluations of statements of others. Write complete sentences.	synthesizer generalizer active	questioner facilitator active listener	Ask questions which focus or refocus students on the task. Ask for clarification, extension, and elaboration when necessary. Encourage student-to-student interaction. Wait for students to think. Present a generalization for students to examine in the application of generalizations strategy.

modifications suggested by the approach are in abstractness, complexity, organization, economy, and methods of inquiry. Process changes are an emphasis on higher levels of thinking; open-endedness; use of discovery, requiring students to verbalize their reasoning or evidence; group interaction; and pacing. One product modification, transformation, is suggested. Four learning environment changes are suggested: student-centered, independence, openness, and accepting.

Content Modifications

A good example of the content changes suggested by Taba and Bruner is the social studies curriculum (Ellis & Durkin, 1972) developed and field-tested during the same time period as the teaching strategies. Since Taba assumed an interactive relationship between content organization and quality, and the processes taught, it seems natural that Taba would test these at the same time. The best way to explain how the Taba model suggests content changes is to provide examples from this curriculum. In the social studies curriculum, three levels of knowledge serve different organizational functions.

Key Concepts

The most abstract knowledge level is key concepts. These are words that represent highly generalized abstractions and were selected because of their power to synthesize and organize large numbers of specific facts and ideas. These words are developed in a more abstract and complex way at each higher grade level, and form threads running throughout the program. Some examples of key concepts are causality, conflict, cultural change, differences, institutions, interdependence, and modification. In an overview of the Taba program, generalizations pertaining to each key concept illustrate the meaning or use of that key concept. For example, the explanation of interdependence is the following:

All persons and groups of persons depend on other persons and groups in important ways. These effects on others are often indirect and not apparent.

The solution of important human problems requires human beings to engage in joint effort. The more complex the society is, the more cooperation is required.

Cooperation often requires compromise and postponement of immediate satisfactions. (pp. T4, T5)

Main, Organizing, and Contributing Ideas

The second level of knowledge consists first of main ideas, which serve as the answer to the question of what the students need to remember after forgetting specific facts. Each year's work centers around several main ideas, which may be treated as a hierarchy reappearing at several grade levels. The *main idea* expresses a relationship that applies both to the content being studied and to parallel examples of human behavior in other settings. Some examples of main ideas related to interdependence are the following:

> Main Idea 1:
> Interaction between people and their physical environment influences the way in which they meet their needs.
> Main Idea 3:
> The way people choose to live and the knowledge they have influence the use they make of their environment. (p. T31)

Main idea 1 is developed at grades three, six, and seven. In addition to the key concept of interdependence, this main idea also involves the concepts of modification, power, and tradition. Main idea 3 is developed at grades one, two, and three. It involves the key concepts of differences, modification, and tradition, in addition to the concept of interdependence.

The *organizing idea* is an example of the main idea as it pertains to the particular content being studied in each unit. It is stated in a way that enables students to understand and use it. *Contributing ideas* represent generalizations that illustrate further dimensions of the main idea. Examples of organizing and contributing ideas that relate to the main ideas listed earlier are the following:

> Main Idea 1:
> Interaction between people and their physical environment influences the way in which they meet their needs.
> Organizing Idea:
> The Bedouin modify their behavior and their environment in order to make a living. (p. T31)
> Contributing Ideas:
> Herders living in a desert area may be able to meet their needs by modifying their behavior. (p. T33)
> Herders in a desert area may be able to make a living by modifying their environment. (p. T34)
> The seasons influence the way in which herders of the desert meet their needs. (p. T34)
> Main Idea 3:
> The way people choose to live and the knowledge they have influence the use they make of their environment.
> Organizing Idea:
> The Yoruba people combined their skills as farmers and craftsmen.

Their organization allows them to live in a city and yet farm some distance from home. (p. T31)
Contributing Ideas:
The products of an agricultural group allow its producers to meet many of their needs. (p. T83)
A specialized society requires a means of exchange. (p. T83)
A specialized society fosters interdependence among its people. (p. T83)

Content Samples

The lowest level of knowledge, specific facts or content samples, provides the means for illustrating, explaining, and developing the main ideas as well as the organizing and contributing ideas. They are in the form of an in-depth study of human behavior and are selected because they demonstrate the main idea. They are sufficient in depth, richness, and breadth to provide the opportunity for students to develop their own generalizations, which approximate the main and organizing ideas. Some examples of specific content samples used to develop the main, organizing, and contributing ideas given earlier are the following:

Main Idea 1:
The Bedouin
    moves regularly in order to get food and water.
    herds animals adapted to the desert environment.
    uses animals for transportation.
The Bedouin
    plants some crops to feed their animals.
    gets water from wells.
    stores grain and food for winter use.
    uses animals to meet need for food, clothing, and shelter. (p. T34)
Main Idea 3:
The Yoruba farmer meets many of his needs
    by using mixed crop farming to feed his family.
    by using his cocoa crop to get cash to buy clothes, tools, etc.
The Yoruba uses the marketplace
    as a place for the exchange of goods.
    as a place for earning a living.
The Yoruba craftsmen exchange services.
    Blacksmith makes hoes for farmers.
    Leatherworker makes drum pieces for the drummer. (p. T83)

In these examples, the abstract key concepts and generalizations are used as the organizing framework for the content presented to students. These concepts and generalizations are also complex in that they include several traditional content areas and integrate methods of study or "thought systems" into the study of a particular discipline.

Process and Product Modifications

Process modifications appropriate for the gifted are integral parts of the Taba *Strategies*. Higher levels of thinking are developed through the sequential tasks (spurred by teacher questions) in each of the strategies and by each strategy as a whole. The four basic strategies are hierarchically arranged. Open-endedness is a necessary ingredient since all teacher questions are required to be open-ended and since the focusing and extending questions are also provocative. Having students verbalize their reasoning and support for inferences is also an integral, required aspect of the Taba *Strategies*. Taba also provides many suggestions for appropriate pacing in discussions, and she supplies specific techniques for facilitating interaction between students in a group.

The Taba model only makes direct product modifications in the area of transformation. When using the Taba model, emphasis is placed on student participation in analysis of content. Students are encouraged to organize, interpret, and evaluate the information they receive, and to develop their *own* conclusions and generalizations about it. Because of this active involvement, if the teacher is using the strategies appropriately, the products developed will be transformations. During this process, students also learn skills in appropriate evaluation of their own products and the products of others. They are encouraged to critique and react to others' logic and products.

Learning Environment Modifications

Correct and frequent implementation of the Taba *Strategies* ensures that the learning environment will be student-centered. Since the strategies are discussion techniques, if they are used frequently, the teacher will conduct few lectures. Also, since they place major focus on student ideas, the teacher does not become the central figure in discussions. Most of the general support behaviors discussed earlier would ensure a student-centered classroom, for example, asking open-ended questions, asking questions calling for variety, avoiding opinions or value judgments, encouraging student reaction/response to student ideas, and waiting for students.

Independence is fostered through the strategies by emphasis on student ideas. Students are encouraged to explain and justify their ideas, and teachers are discouraged from expressing their opinions of the ideas and from editing or changing the ideas when recording them. Specific skills involved in interpersonal independence are also taught through the fourth strategy, resolution of conflict. In this strategy, students generate alternatives, predict consequences, evaluate alternatives, and suggest ways of applying what they have learned to personal situations. Thus, this technique develops specific ways for students to manage their own playground and classroom behavior, an essential element in the development of independence.

An open environment is developed through appropriate implementation of the Taba *Strategies*. There are no restrictions on the types of answers that can be given, and the teacher does not suggest in any way that the students conform to an ideal. In fact, teachers encourage and push for divergent ideas through their methods of questioning. No restrictions are placed on the kind of generalization(s) that can be developed and stated as a result of a discussion.

Acceptance rather than judgment is another integral aspect of the Taba *Strategies*. Teachers are cautioned against providing an opinion or value judgment of a student idea. They are to accept all ideas and encourage the students to look at their own statements by asking questions of clarification, extension, and support. Student ideas are not even edited or changed when they are written on the blackboard. Teacher questions are designed to develop understanding of, clarification of, and support for student ideas rather than criticism of them. Such questions have the effect of encouraging thorough *examination* of ideas, which usually results in a consideration of both their positive and negative aspects, rather than only the negative.

EXAMPLES OF TEACHING ACTIVITIES

To provide a specific example of the teaching strategies and to illustrate the relationship between process and content, a series of four lessons will be described. They would be used to develop the key concepts and main ideas given as examples in the previous section.

Concept Development

The first lesson, concept development, is designed to clarify and extend the key concept of interdependence. It could be used at the beginning of the year or at the beginning of a unit where the concept is introduced. It could also be used at the end of the year as a way to get students to integrate all their knowledge related to the concept. They would be drawing from the specific content of several units (for example, from information about both the Bedouin of the Negev and the Yoruba of Ife). When used at the beginning of the year, it serves a diagnostic function for teachers, and when used at the end, it can serve as an evaluative one. Following are the focusing question(s) for each step in the lesson:

Step 1. Listing—What are some specific ways the people we have studied depend on each other or on other people or tribes?

Step 2. Grouping—(a) Which of these ways of depending on each other would you group together because they are alike? (b) Why would you group those together?

Step 3. Labeling—(a) Based on the reasons why we put these ways of depending together, what would be a good label for this group? (b) Why is _____ a good label?

Step 4. Subsuming—(a) Which of these ways of depending that is already under one label could also go under another label? (b) What are your reasons for putting _____ under _____ ?

Step 5. Recycling—(a) Now, look back at our original list of ways people depend on each other. Which of these ways could be put together in *completely different* groups? (b) What are your reasons for putting those together? (c-f) Ask the initial focusing questions for steps three and four about these new groupings.

Interpretation of Data

The second lesson, interpretation of data, involves students in analyzing specific data related to the lives of the Bedouin. The planning generalization is main idea 1. (See Table 8-2.) Since this main idea is also developed in the unit about the Yoruba, a similar lesson could be used with that specific data. At step five in the lesson, students are expected to state a generalization that goes beyond their specific knowledge of either of the groups studied. This generalization may be similar to the main idea developed.

In this lesson, the focus is on *causes* for the Bedouins' lifestyle. A similar lesson could be planned focusing on *effects* relating either to the Bedouin or Yoruba. In this detailed plan, the lesson has both a content and process purpose, and behavioral objectives, focusing questions, and support procedures are developed for each step in the discussion. A major part of this planning process is the development of the cognitive map, which is a listing of the possible responses students might make to the focusing questions. This helps teachers see where the discussion *could* go and helps them develop support procedures necessary to keep the discussion moving. This cognitive map includes the possible data (step one), possible causes (steps two and three), possible conclusions (step four), and possible generalizations (step five). When conducting the lesson, however, teachers must always remember that the cognitive map is developed *only for planning purposes,* and they should not attempt to elicit answers from students that are written on the cognitive map.

Table 8-2 Sample Discussion Plan for Interpretation of Data Lesson

DISCUSSION PURPOSES

Content: To draw warranted conclusions about the following relationships:

People and their physical environment → the ways people meet their needs

Process: To make and support cause and effect inferences, to draw warranted conclusions, and to generalize from specific instances to other such instances.

TOPIC The Bedouin of the Negev

LEVEL Intermediate

PREDISCUSSION PROCEDURES

Arrange students in a semi-circle.

Have chalkboard/chalk available.

MATERIALS

Pages 9-61, "The Bedouin of the Negev," People in Communities, Menlo Part, CA: Addison Wesley, 1972.

Behavioral Objectives	Focusing Questions	Support Procedures
Step One – Data Students will enumerate what they know or have read about the ways the Bedouin people meet their basic needs for survival.	What are some things you know about the Bedouin people? What are some things you have learned about the ways Bedouin people meet their basic needs for food and shelter?	Encourage students to list data about their lifestyle, food, shelter, and habits. –Seek a variety of observations. –Focus on facts rather than inferences.

Step Two: Causes

a. Students will state inferences about the causes for the ways Bedouins meet their basic needs.

   a. What do you think are some causes for, e.g., the Bedouins moving from place to place except in the winter?

   Choose data to follow up that will provide the most promise of eliciting causes relating to environment and people.

   b. Why would, e.g., the dry climate cause them to move around?

   Ask for a variety of causes for each piece of data.

b. Students will cite evidence or reasoning to support their inferences.

   a. What causes, e.g., children to need to learn mainly from their parents?

   Ask for support for inferences immediately after inferences are given. When asking for support for inferences, the basic question is "Why does (cause) cause (data) ?

   b. Why would, e.g., moving around cause them to need to learn from their parents?

Step Three: Prior Causes

a. Students will state inferences about the prior causes of the causes given at Step Two.

   a. What are some of the reasons why, e.g., the pastures are picked over by summer?

   Step Three can be repeated many times. One can even ask for prior causes of the prior causes.

Table 8-2 continued

Behavioral Objectives	Focusing Questions	Support Procedures
b. Students will cite evidence or reasoning to support their inferences.	b. Why do you think, e.g., winter rains would cause pastures to be picked over by spring?	Choose causes and prior causes that will elicit answers relating to the environment and people.
	a. What are some of the causes, e.g., each man having several wives?	Ask for a variety of prior causes for each cause.
	b. Why would, e.g., needing a large family cause men to have several wives?	When asking for support for inferences, the basic question is "Why does _(prior cause)_ cause _(cause)_ ?
Step Four: Conclusions		
a. Students will state conclusions about the causes for the Bedouin lifestyle.	a. Thinking back over our discussion, what would you say are the most important causes for the Bedouins' meeting their basic needs in the way they do?	Encourage each child to reach his or her own conclusions. Encourage a variety of conclusions.
b. Students will cite evidence or reasons for their conclusions.		Ask for clarification of ideas, if needed.

| | b. Why do you think, e.g., the climate is an important cause for the Bedouin lifestyle? | Encourage synthesis rather than just summaries. Conclude about <u>causes</u>. |

Step Five: Generalizations

a. Students will generalize about the causes for the ways most people meet their basic needs.	a. What would you say generally about the causes for all people everywhere living the way they do?	Allow time to jot down some ideas before responding. Ask students to write a sentence or statement.
b. Students will cite support for their statements.	b. Why do you think, e.g., the characteristics of people and their environment determines the way people meet their needs?	Encourage each student to make a statement. Ask for clarification when needed. Encourage students to bring in information about other people they have studied.

Note: The phrase following "e.g." in some focusing questions is one example of a question that should be asked. All appropriate student ideas are extended through such questioning.

Table 8-2 continued

COGNITIVE MAP

Planning Generalization: Interaction between people and their physical environment influences the way they meet their needs

Possible Prior Causes and Causes		Possible Data
	They must continually move to find grass.	
	The climate is usually mild.	The Bedouins live in tents.
	There is little rain.	Barley crops are planted in the fall.
Winters are cold.	The desert is dry and doesn't support much grass.	
There are no rains in spring.	Pastures are picked over by summer.	The Bedouins move from place to place except in the winter.
Most have large herds.	Winters are cold and rainy.	
Rains come in winter.		Baby animals are born in the winter.
They store their heavy tents in the winter.	They live in heavy tents in the winter.	The whole family helps with the harvest.
They stay in one place in the	Most of the year they are moving.	
	They seldom see each other except	Winter is a social time.

winter.

A large family is needed to
care for animals

Some social life is needed.

Each man has several wives.

The land supports very few
people.

They must constantly look for
food and water.

The country is not technologi-
cally advanced.

in winter.

Often, the religious month comes
in winter time.

Families live together.

Children are needed to help with crops
and animals.

Families move around.

There are very few towns and cities.

Meeting basic needs takes most of their
time.

They very seldom go to the
marketplace to buy goods.

Children learn mainly from their
parents.

Money is made from selling
animals.

Table 8-2 continued

Possible Conclusions	Possible Generalizations
The climate of the desert causes the people to live the way they do.	People everywhere develop ways to meet their needs for survival that depend on the environment in which they live.
The Bedouins have to live in tents and move around because they have to follow the grass for their herds.	The people (their habits, inherited traits, religion) and the environment in which they live (temperature, amount of rain, patterns of rain, the terrain) determine the way in which food, shelter, and clothing are obtained and the type of food, shelter, and clothing needed.
The Bedouins live together in tents because they are in a lonely desert and must have some time and chance to socialize.	
The major reasons for the Bedouin lifestyle being the way it is are the climate, the terrain, and the traditions of the people.	

To develop the concept of interdependence further, interpretation of data discussions could be held that focus on the ways the Bedouin and Yoruba depend on their own people and on others. For example, within each extended family, each person has duties that contribute to the whole group, the Bedouin travel to the market to purchase imported goods, and in hard times, the Bedouin graze their herds on Israeli lands. These examples of interdependence are listed as data, and the discussion can focus on either causes of this dependence or effects of it. Several discussions of different people can take place.

Application of Generalizations

The next discussion, application of generalizations, follows interpretation of data by asking students to predict what kind of lifestyle might be developed by a group of people in some futuristic society. In presenting a hypothetical situation, the teacher describes the physical environment of another planet and provides a description of the habits, traditions, and values of the people who have landed on the planet. The students are asked to predict what will happen to the people. Following are sample discussion questions at each step of application of generalizations:

Step 1. Predictions

a. What do you think these people will be like after 30 years?
b. Why would you predict that they will, e.g., develop highly industrialized cities?

Step 2. Conditions

a. What other things will have to happen or be true in order for, e.g., these people to develop highly industrialized cities?
b. What are your reasons for believing that, e.g., technology on the rest of the planet would have to be very advanced?

Step 3. Consequences and Conditions (Recycle 1 and 2)

a. Suppose that all you said was necessary and the people did, e.g., develop highly industrialized cities. What would happen as a result of that?
b. Why do you think, e.g., that these people would become the rulers of the planet?
c. Under what conditions, e.g., would these people become rulers or take control of the planet?
d. Why would it be necessary, e.g., for the other people to be living in scattered small cities?

This step can be continued or recycled as many times as necessary to focus students on a *variety* of possible, opposite predictions.

Step 4. Conclusions

  a. From all we've said, what would you conclude is likely to be the lifestyle of these people in 30 years?
  b. Why have you decided, e.g., they will become an industrialized nation?

Step 5. Generalizations

  a. Considering our discussion of what might happen to these people, what changes or additions, if any, would you make in the following statement: "All persons and groups of persons depend on other persons and groups in important ways?"
  b. Why would you, e.g., change it to read "depend on other persons, groups, and the environment?"

In this discussion, the two main ideas presented earlier are used as the planning subgeneralizations that students are expected to apply in making their predictions. At step five, they are asked to go beyond these subgeneralizations and examine an even bigger or more abstract idea, a "description" of the key concept of interdependence.

Resolution of Conflict

After the interpretation of data and application of generalizations discussions or at any other point in a unit, the discussions can focus on the people, their feelings, their attitudes, and their values. One way to do this is through a resolution of conflict lesson involving conflict between new and old ways of life. For example, students read a story about a Bedouin son who is a member of a large family of uncles, aunts, and cousins. His father is considered the head of the family. The son wants to use his money earned from selling cattle to buy a jeep, and eventually he wants to go to school in town. The son tries to convince his father of the usefulness of a jeep to their family and tribe, but his father does not want to listen. Following are the focusing questions that would be asked in such a discussion.

Step 1. Listing

  • What happened in the story?
  • What did the son do/say?
  • What did the father do/say?

Step 2. Reasons and Feelings

    a. Why do you think, e.g., the son wanted to buy the jeep?
    b. How did the boy's father feel about, e.g., the son wanting to buy the jeep?
    c. Why do you think the father felt, e.g., threatened?

Step 3. Alternatives and Consequences

    a. What are some things the son *could* do to resolve the conflict?
    b. If the son, e.g., goes ahead and buys the jeep even though his father disapproves, what do you think will be the consequences?
    c. Why do you think, e.g., the father will disown the boy?

Step 4. Solutions and Long-Range Consequences

    a. Looking over the possible solutions we have listed, what do you think is the best thing the boy can do?
    b. Why would, e.g., saving his money be the best thing for the boy to do?
    c. What do you think would be some of the long-term effects of, e.g., the boy saving his money?
    d. What leads you to believe that, e.g., the father will eventually allow the son to go to college if he saves the money now rather than spending it on the jeep?

Step 5. Listing–Similar Situation

    • Thinking about this story, what are some similar situations you have experienced or know about in which there was a conflict over new and old ways of life?
    • What happened?
    • What were the new and old ways?
    • What did you (or the other person) do?

Step 6. Feelings

    a. How did you feel about, e.g., your parents wanting you to go to a private school?
    b. Why do you think you felt, e.g., upset?
    a. How do you think your parents felt about, e.g., you wanting to go to an integrated public school when they offered to pay private tuition?
    b. Why do you think they felt, e.g., hurt?

Step 7. Evaluation

a. What were your reasons for choosing, e.g., the public school?
b. Thinking back on the situation, how would you evaluate your decision?
c. Why do you think, e.g., you did the right thing?

Step 8. Alternatives and Consequences

a. In what ways might you have handled the situation differently?
b. What do you think would have been the consequences of, e.g., dropping out of school completely?
c. Why do you think, e.g., your parents would have realized that you were right?

Step 9. Generalizations

a. Thinking back over the situations we have discussed in which there is a conflict between old and new ways of life, what could you say generally about the way people handle situations like that?
b. What did we say or what do you know that would lead you to believe that young people usually choose new ways?

A lesson similar to this could also be planned in which the conflict is between two Bedouin tribes, or between the Bedouin and people living in Beersheba or one of the other market places. Other lessons could involve a conflict between the Bedouin and the Yoruba, two groups that had been studied recently. These lessons integrate knowledge from several content units and can be used before, during, and/or after the units. If used before, they may enhance interest in the upcoming units of study and serve a diagnostic function. When used during a unit, they could serve as another way to apply the information learned. When used after a unit they could serve as a vehicle for integrating knowledge gained from the two content units.

MODIFYING THE STRATEGIES

Content Changes

Although the Taba model makes many of the content, process, and learning environment changes recommended for the gifted, the approach will be more appropriate for use with gifted children if certain additions are made. For example, the two content changes not made by the model are variety and the study of people. The study of people can easily be integrated by using the Taba *Strategies* as methods to study the lives of productive, eminent people. Interpretation of data can be used to make inferences about the causes for the characteristics of people or to make inferences about the effects these characteristics had on their products or their careers. Application of generalizations could be used to predict what would have happened to a famous or eminent individual if that person lived today or in a different period of time. Resolution of conflict can be used to examine conflicts in the lives of the individuals, either inner, personal conflicts or conflicts between individuals. The students can then discuss similar situations in their own lives.

A second content change, variety, can be accomplished in a way that is similar to the modification of Bruner's approach described in Chapter 3. Using this worksheet, the teacher can write the key concept at the top. The main idea becomes the "generalization." Instead of listing the concepts involved in the generalization, the contributing ideas can be listed. Organizing ideas and content samples that pertain to the main idea are then listed as data, either data taught in the regular curriculum or data needing to be taught in the special program. Exhibit 8-1 provides an example using the ideas presented earlier in this section.

In this example, in the regular curriculum, students learn about farmers and herders in this country. To further develop the concept of interdependence in the special program, they would learn about the Bedouin and the Yoruba as other examples of how people must depend on each other and how the environment influences their lives. By analyzing the content taught in the regular program according to key concepts and ideas, the organization is retained, and what is taught in the special curriculum is different from the regular curriculum.

Process Changes

Only two process modifications need to be incorporated into the Taba model: freedom of choice and variety. To ensure freedom of choice of topics, one teacher of the gifted (Maker, 1982) allows the students to choose general topic areas for discussion several weeks in advance. She then selects the planning generalizations and reading materials, and plans a Taba discussion on the topics chosen. Other ways of integrating freedom of choice would be the following: (a) in the application of generalizations strategy, students could choose one or more of the predictions given at the first step and develop reasons, conditions, and consequences for it; (b) in the resolution of conflict strategy, students could choose conflict situations to discuss, they could select alternatives to develop, and they could write about similar situations of their own choice; (c) in the concept development strategy, they could choose either the concepts to be discussed or the data to be used at the listing step; and (d) interpretation of data could involve interpreting (discussing) the data chosen by students.

Another way to incorporate freedom of choice would be to allow students to choose areas of study, investigate them independently, and then organize discussions so that all students "pool" their knowledge and findings. For example, in the

Exhibit 8-1 Sample Worksheet for Overall Curriculum Design
(Worksheet #6b: Building Content Plans upon the Regular
Curriculum)

Key Concept: Interdependence

Main Idea # 1 :   Interaction between people and their physical

environment influences the way in which they meet their needs.

Contributing Ideas:

a. Herders living in a desert area may be able to meet their needs

by modifying their behavior.

b. Herders in a desert area may be able to make a living by

modifying their environment.

c. The seasons influence the way in which herders of the desert

meet their needs.

d. The products of an agricultural group allow its producers

to meet many of their needs.

e. A specialized society requires a means of exchange.

f. A specialized society fosters interdependence among its people.

Organizing Ideas and Content Samples in the Regular Program	Organizing Ideas and Content Samples in the Special Program
Farmers in the western United States modify their environment and their behavior to meet their needs (CI #b)	The Bedouin modify their behavior and their environment in order to make a living (CI #b).
Farmers	The Bedouin
–irrigate their crops	–move regularly to get food
–build very few fences	and water

Exhibit 8-1 continued

-use large ranches rather than small farms	-use animals for transportation
	-herd animals adapted to the desert environment
-organize cooperative groups to supply water to all	
	-plant some crops to feed animals
	-store grain and good for winter
Farmers of the United States sell their crops to provide money for needed goods and services (CI #f)	-use animals to meet need for food, clothing, and shelter
	The Yoruba craftsmen exchange services (CI #f)
Farmers buy	The blacksmith makes hoes for farmers.
-specialized equipment for harvesting	
	The leatherworker makes drum pieces for the drummer.
-materials for building homes	
-veterinary services	
-repair services for equipment	

social studies example, each student or group of students could select the people of interest to them. Using the basic plans for the lessons presented as examples, each student or group would list data at step one that pertained to the group of people they were studying. After the first step, all students should be encouraged to make inferences about all data, not just the information they reported. In this way, students not only have freedom to study topics of interest to them, but they also learn a variety of information from other students.

Variety in methods is integrated through alternating different methods with the basic discussion strategy. The first step, getting the information, is a part of each strategy. Students can get the information they need to participate in a discussion in many different ways such as the following: playing a simulation game; reading an article; listening to a tape; participating in a role-playing incident; listening to a lecture; watching a film; watching a television program; and making observations. The author once conducted a lesson on prejudice in which the students' task was to observe and record evidence of prejudice through taking pictures, taping conversations, or making notes on things they had heard or seen. These observations were then used as a basis for concept development, interpretation of data, and resolution of conflict discussions.

Other variations can be made by having the same intellectual tasks done by the children, but in small-group or individual settings. One example is making the concept development task into a game. The students are given a variety of cards with either pictures or words pertaining to a certain concept. They are to make as many different groupings as possible, provide at least three labels for each group, and indicate which items go under different labels. The teacher can discuss the groupings with students individually and ask their reasons for groups, labels, and subsuming, or the teacher can have a small group of the students share their groups, labels, subsuming, reasons, and regroupings. Another easy way to vary any of the strategies is to alternate small- and large-group activities and to integrate individual activities. With the application of generalizations strategy, for instance, students can work in small groups to develop their predictions. The groups then share these predictions and discuss reasons. Resolution of conflict lends itself to small-group or individual work when the task is to generate alternatives. Students could also develop a "similar situation" in this strategy through a writing assignment.

The easiest way to vary the Taba *Strategies* is to alternate between small and large groups, or to vary the groupings. Since interaction with at least a small group is important, any individual work would need to be shared in a discussion setting.

Product Changes

Since the Taba model only makes direct changes in one area (transformation), the Taba *Strategies* need to be used differently to provide product modifications. One of the most important ways to use the strategies would be to teach students the steps involved in each strategy. This can be done easily by having "debriefing" sessions after the discussions to show students the steps (intellectual tasks) and questions asked by the teacher at each step. After participating in several discussions, the students will learn the processes and will be able to use them in their individual investigations and product development.

As an important aspect of this process, the teacher should show students how the different strategies can be helpful to them in their product development. The concept development strategy is useful at the beginning of a project to organize questions about a topic. The author has often used this with graduate students as a way to help them develop thesis or dissertation topics. The graduate students first list or brainstorm all the questions they have about a topic, then they group, label, subsume, and regroup these questions. Often this exercise assists them in clarifying what they want to investigate and in selecting the major questions and minor subquestions.

Concept development is also useful as a process for organizing a final product. When writing articles, chapters, and even longer pieces, the process can be used in the following way: (1) list all the important information that needs to be included, as specifically as possible; (2) group the similar items together; (3) develop titles for the groups; (4) subsume items; (5) examine each category to see whether all the essential information has been included; and (6) try another regrouping of all the information to see if there is a better organization. The titles for the groups become subheadings, and the items within each category are then combined and explained to form the text.

The concept development strategy can also be used in research to analyze the content of responses to open-ended questions. All of the responses to a particular question can be listed, preferably one response to a note card. These cards can then be sorted by one person into piles containing similar items. After the groups have been completed, titles can be given, then the subsuming task is attempted. A second person can then take the titles of the groups along with a description of the groups and attempt to classify the items into the groupings established by the first individual. The degree to which they classify items into the same groups is the index of agreement. If the index of agreement is high, the groupings remain the same, perhaps with minor changes, but if their agreement is low, completely new groupings may need to be made.

The interpretation of data strategy is useful as a technique for developing discussions and conclusions after an experiment has been conducted. The data collected in the experiment comprise the information used at step one. The investigator or writer then follows through the process by developing inferences about either causes or effects of the data, or both causes and effects. Prior causes and subsequent effects are also listed, as are conclusions and generalizations. These inferences, conclusions, and generalizations are then used as the basis of discussion of and conclusions about the research. Use of this strategy before actually beginning the task of writing can make the writing easier and can ensure that many different aspects of the experiment will be considered rather than just the most obvious.

Application of generalizations is a useful process for developing products that involve making predictions or forecasting future events. As such, it is an extremely useful tool in developing hypotheses to guide experimental research. In addition to the development of hypotheses, the strategy can be used to predict how audiences might react to a certain product. Each individual could use the process when developing a product, or the teacher could lead group discussions to assist each student in the development of products acceptable to different audiences.

When students are involved in group investigations or development of products, conflicts are bound to arise. The resolution of conflict strategy is an excellent process for solving these problems. It can also be used to develop fictional stories involving some kind of conflict between people.

In summary, the Taba *Strategies* can provide useful processes for students and teachers in the development of products that address real problems, are directed toward real audiences, and are evaluated realistically.

Learning Environment Changes

The only two learning environment modifications not made by the Taba strategies are complexity and high mobility. These changes are certainly necessary if students are to develop professional products of the calibre expected of the gifted. Students need a variety of complex references and equipment for their use, or they need access to these items. Movement in and out of the classroom is necessary for access to supplies and environments not in the classroom, and allows flexible grouping arrangements so that interaction with gifted peers can occur during discussions.

Summary

Although the Taba *Strategies* make many of the content, process, and learning environment changes recommended for the gifted, certain modifications and additions still need to be made if Taba's approach is to be used as a comprehensive curriculum for the gifted. It can easily be combined with Renzulli's model, with Bruner's approach, and with Treffinger's model for self-directed learning.

DEVELOPMENT

Two aspects of Taba's approach discussed in this chapter—the specific teaching strategies and the social studies curriculum—were developed along separate, but related lines. The *Hilda Taba Teaching Strategies* program (Institute for Staff Development, 1971) resulted from the refinement of the teaching strategies and teacher training program used in three studies of the effectiveness of teaching strategies in the development of children's thinking (Taba, 1964, 1966; Wallen et al., 1969). The Taba *Program in Social Science* (Ellis & Durkin, 1972) was developed concurrently but was more complete before the studies of children's thinking than were the strategies. In the research projects, as in Taba's theoretical orientation, content and process were somewhat separate entities, but played complementary roles. For instance, in the research projects, Taba's (1964) overall objective was "to examine the development of thought under the optimum training conditions" (p. 27). These optimum conditions included the following: (a) a curriculum designed to develop thinking skills; (b) teaching strategies focused specifically on the mastery of certain thinking skills; and (c) an adequate time span for a developmental sequence in training.

Development of the social studies curriculum that was ultimately published by Addison-Wesley (Ellis & Durkin, 1972) was actually begun much earlier, with Taba's involvement in the development of a social studies curriculum for Contra Costa County, California. Development of the teaching strategies program began with the first research project in 1964. Hilda Taba's untimely death in 1967 left much of her work incomplete. Several of her associates completed the different projects: Norman Wallen and his associates at San Francisco State college completed the research project in 1969; Lyle and Sydelle Ehrenberg, with the help of other associates of Taba, completed the teacher training and teaching strategies program, and founded the Institute for Staff Development to provide this training nationwide; and Kim Ellis and Mary Durkin were primarily responsible for the completion of the curriculum in social science.

In the research projects, which provided the setting for development of the strategies and refinement of the curriculum, emphasis was on how thought could best be developed in elementary school children. The first study (Taba, 1964) was exploratory, serving as a setting for the development of the methodological tools (for example, methods of categorizing thought processes, methods of coding classroom interaction, and criterion measures [tests] necessary for studying the development of thought). During the course of this study, teaching strategies became the most important variable being studied. Thus, throughout the first study and subsequent ones, the following three dimensions of classroom interaction were studied: (1) behavior of the teachers; (2) behavior of the students; and (3) the content or product of the interaction. While the first study only concentrated on the effects of strategies of trained teachers (in 20 classrooms from grades two through six), the second study (Taba, 1966) compared the classrooms of trained teachers with classrooms of untrained teachers. The final study involved the training of leaders around the country who in turn provided training for teachers. Thus, the strategies were revised and refined through a long process of trial and error, assessment of effectiveness, and input from numerous classroom teachers with different teaching styles and skills.

RESEARCH ON EFFECTIVENESS

To assess the effectiveness of the teaching strategies (Taba, 1964), two kinds of instruments were devised and used in conjunction with the *Sequential Tests of Educational Progress* (STEP) social studies achievement test. The first was an objective test, *The Social Studies Inference Test* (Taba, 1964), in which students are presented with a series of stories followed by a list of statements (inferences) about the story. Students read the story and the statements, and decide whether each statement is probably true, probably false, or whether a person cannot tell from the story if the statements are true or false. Scores are provided on the dimensions of *inference* (that is, the students select correct inferences), *caution* (that is, students are overly cautious and select the "cannot tell" alternative much more often than necessary), *overgeneralization* (that is, students make inferences that are not warranted by selecting an inference when they should choose the "cannot tell" alternative), and *discrimination* (that is, students can discriminate between the items given in the test problem).

The second measure developed for assessing the effectiveness of the teaching strategies was a system for coding and analyzing classroom interaction using tapes of discussions held during the year. The system of coding included scoring each "thought unit" (that is, remark or series of remarks expressing a complete idea) by three different sets of codings. The first coding was a *designation* of the sources, whether it came from the teacher or student, and whether the person was seeking or giving information. The second coding was *function* and included two large groups, managerial or content-free (for example, agreement, approval, disagreement, disapproval, management, reiteration), and content-related (for example, focusing, refocusing, change of focus, deviation from focus, controlling thought, extending thought on the same level, and lifting thought to a higher level). The third type of coding identified the *level of thought*. The same system was used for both teacher and student behavior, and a different system was developed for each cognitive strategy: grouping and labeling, interpreting and making inferences, and predicting consequences. Within each strategy, the specific tasks were ordered from low to high levels whenever possible. A procedure was also developed for relating the levels of thought across cognitive tasks.

To analyze interaction patterns, several measures were obtained for each child, each classroom, and each grade level, and across all classrooms and grade levels, including the following: amount of participation; interaction between teaching strategies and thought levels; frequency of success of extending and lifting functions; amount and effect of other teacher functions; and amount of thinking at three levels across the three types of strategies. Children were also classified as high or low participators. Finally, these aspects of children's participation in the discussions were compared with their performance on the *Social Studies Inference Test* and with the other variables assessed (that is, IQ scores, mental age, social studies achievement, reading achievement, and socioeconomic status of the family).

Effectiveness with All Children

Taba's research was conducted in classrooms of heterogeneously grouped children of wide ranges of ability. Some of the general conclusions of the studies that have implications for the teaching of all children, briefly listed, are the following:

- Formal operational thinking appears much earlier than Piaget assumes, but follows the sequence he identifies. There is a steady growth of formal thinking from grades two through six, with this type of thinking occurring in about one-sixth of all thought units in grade six (Taba, 1964).

- The most marked influence on cognitive performance of the children was the teaching strategies. Of these strategies, two variables were of particular importance: teacher questions and the sequencing or patterning of teacher acts. Teachers got what they requested most of the time. If they asked for thinking at a low level, the children generally responded on a low level. When teachers asked for thinking at a high level, the children generally responded at that level. However, the level of thinking of students was affected not only by the single teacher question preceding it, but also by the whole pattern of teacher behavior prior to the student's response (Taba, 1964).

- The teacher function of reiteration (for example, the habit of restating or repeating what children have said), is used abundantly by teachers and constitutes almost half of all teacher functions (46 percent), but *has little impact* on the course of discussion (Taba, 1964).

- The students in experimental groups performed better on the tests and in discussions than did students in the control groups (Taba, 1966).

- The trained teachers had a greater success rate in getting students to respond at the higher levels than did the untrained teachers, even though the trained teachers sought more high level thinking (Taba, 1966).

- Teacher training is more effective when directed toward specific strategies rather than overall improvement in teaching (Taba, 1964).

Effectiveness with Gifted

One of the most surprising findings of the first study (1964) was the generally low relationship between the level of thinking and traditional variables that influence thought (that is, IQ, achievement, reading comprehension, and economic status). When growth was measured, the relationships were almost nonexistent. To explain this phenomenon and justify the use of the strategies with *homogeneous* groups of gifted children at least part of the time, it is necessary to explain further the results of the research relating to the patterns of teacher functions—particularly extending and lifting—and the pacing of these functions in the total discussion. An important aspect of the use of the Taba *Strategies* is to pace the discussion and rotate assimilation and accommodation activities so that all children can participate. For this reason, the discussion must remain at the lowest level until there is an adequate basis for moving as a group to the next highest level. This is where the teacher functions of extending and lifting are significant. A discussion begins at the lowest level with a process such as listing. Teachers then must keep the discussion at this level by extending (that is, asking for additional ideas, examples, new ideas, or explanations of ideas given). When they feel the group has an adequate basis at this level, they ask a question that ''lifts'' the level of thought required (for example, moving from listing to grouping in the concept development strategy or moving from listing to inferences about causes or effects in the interpretation of data strategy). If teachers remain too long at a low level, the discussion may never reach the higher levels. On the other hand, if they attempt to move students too quickly from the lower to higher levels, often the children are unable to make the leap requested, so they return to the lower level. To illustrate these points, the four class discussion patterns presented by Taba (1964, p. 129) are shown in Figure 8-1.

In pattern A, the teacher attempts to raise the level of thinking early in the discussion and continues to attempt to lift it without providing an adequate basis at the lower levels. The children are unable to maintain these levels and keep returning to the lowest level. Pattern B represents an effective discussion in which the teacher remains at the lower levels long enough to accumulate a large amount of information before moving the children to higher levels. The teacher is generally effective in keeping the discussion moving upward. In pattern C, the teacher constantly attempts to move the discussion too high and too quickly without much basis at the lower levels or any steps in between. The result is that the children repeatedly return to the information level. Pattern D represents still another ineffective strategy. The teacher is constantly changing the focus of the discussion, which results in the children being unable to accumulate enough information about any focus to be able to move to higher levels and remain there.

These results indicate that when gifted children are grouped with other gifted children, discussions can be paced much more rapidly. Not as much time must be concentrated on the lower levels before moving upward. Perhaps interaction pattern B could be modified in this way (Taba, 1964):

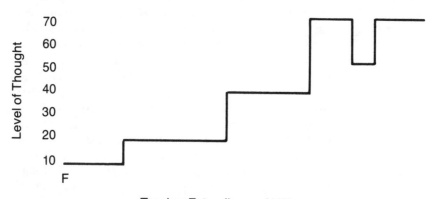

Teacher Extending and Lifting

Figure 8-1 Class Discussion Patterns

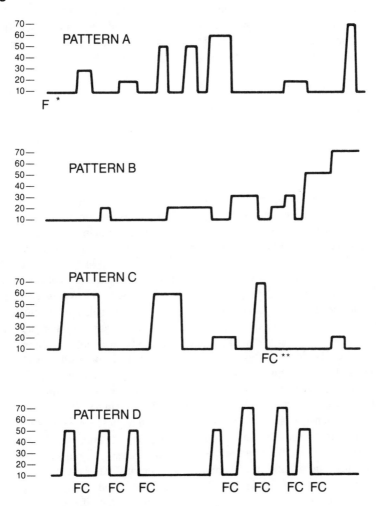

* F—Focus
** FC—Change of focus

Source: H. Taba. *Thinking in elementary school children* (USOE Cooperative Research Project No. 1574). San Francisco, Cal.: San Francisco State College, 1964. (ERIC Document Reproduction Service No. 003285.)

The author's and other teachers' experiences verify the validity of this idea. Perhaps the most significant reason for the fact that low IQ children's growth in cognitive skills was as great as that of high IQ children was that most discussions had to be paced so that *all* children could move upward together. This increases the boredom and decreases the challenge of the tasks for gifted children.

JUDGMENTS

Advantages

The *Hilda Taba Teaching Strategies* program has many advantages recommending its use in programs for the gifted. Perhaps the most obvious is its strong research base, which shows the effectiveness of the strategies in developing higher levels of thinking in children. This research not only provides general information about its effectiveness, but has resulted in the development of specific strategies and clear methods for applying them to achieve the desired objectives. An excellent teacher training program and specific procedures for teacher self-evaluation, for analysis of classroom interaction, and for student evaluation have also been developed during the course of the research. A curriculum organized to facilitate the development of thinking and designed for use with the strategies is also available. These supporting programs or procedures can be combined into a total approach that is comprehensive and based on research showing its validity.

Another advantage of the teaching strategies is their generalizability or transferability. Once learned, many aspects of the strategies can be incorporated into a total approach that goes beyond the use of specific strategies. For example, asking open-ended but focused questions is a skill that is extremely important for use with gifted children, as are the appropriate pacing of discussions and the asking of questions that require children to verbalize their reasons. After learning the Taba *Strategies*, teachers find that these skills become internalized. Also, this approach can easily be combined with others used in programs for the gifted. Since Taba's ideas about the organization of content are almost identical to Bruner's, the combination of Bruner-based curricula with the Taba *Strategies* is an easy one. This combination can enhance the effectiveness of both approaches since there is only one curriculum (in social science) built around Taba's approach, but there are numerous ones based on Bruner's ideas. Also, the Taba *Strategies* fill a definite "process" need not addressed in depth by Bruner. The strategies can also be combined with Kohlberg's model as seen in Chapter 5. Furthermore, they provide a nice addition to Renzulli's *Enrichment Triad* and Treffinger's model for *Self-Directed Learning*.

A final advantage is the comprehensiveness of the approach if both the curriculum and teaching strategies are used. An approach such as this would provide almost all of the content, process, and psychological learning environment modifications advocated for gifted children. It provides one of the product changes and sets the stage for others to be made. The relationships of content and process are made explicitly clear when combined in the Taba model.

Disadvantages

Since the Taba *Strategies* are complicated and require the learning of subtle teacher behaviors, they are difficult for many teachers to learn. They require for some a complete change in style and, as such, take a long time to internalize. In the author's teacher training program, for example, at least one three-hour semester course is necessary for teaching the strategies. During this semester, to learn the strategies adequately, teachers must practice them, tape their discussions, analyze their own performance, and then receive evaluations of their performance. Some even feel a need for extended practice in a supervised practicum setting where discussions are videotaped and later analyzed, or the discussion is observed and then discussed.

One problem with the training and later use of the Taba *Strategies* is that the training manuals (one for each of the four strategies), which in the past could be purchased by trained leaders for use in teaching teachers, are now out of print. To get copies, a person must be granted permission, pay a copyright fee, and reproduce the manuals. This can be an expensive and time-consuming process. As with the manuals, other information regarding the strategies and their use is extremely difficult to find. The research reports are out of print, and only one is available through an information service. For these reasons, the research is difficult to replicate and the information difficult to disseminate.

Although the personal experience of many teachers indicates that the Taba *Strategies* can be even more effective with homogeneous groups of gifted children than with the gifted who are in heterogeneous classrooms, there is no research to support this belief. The gifted children did show growth in cognitive skills when the strategies were used. However, this growth was not any greater than in those with lower ability, which raises the question of whether their superior capacity was being challenged by the particular ways the strategies were being used in classrooms involved in the research. Some comparative studies need to be conducted.

CONCLUSIONS

The advantages of Taba's approach far outweigh its disadvantages if the training is available. It is hoped that providing at least this overview of the strategies and research on their use, will cause readers to be interested enough to search for the literature and/or a trained Taba leader who can help in learning the strategies. Perhaps some readers will also be stimulated to pursue the replication of Taba's research and extend it further to determine the specific effectiveness with gifted children.

RESOURCES

Background Information

Institute for Staff Development. *Hilda Taba teaching strategies program*: Unit I. Miami, Fla.: Institute for Staff Development, 1971: Institute for Staff Development. *Hilda Taba teaching strategies program*: Unit II. Miami, Fla.: Institute for Staff Development, 1971; Institute for Staff Development. *Hilda Taba teaching strategies program*: Unit III. Miami, Fla.: Institute for Staff Development, 1971; Institute for Staff Development. *Hilda Taba teaching strategies program*: Unit IV. Miami, Fla.: Institute for Staff Development, 1971. The *Hilda Taba Teaching Strategies* program, based on Taba's work in the 1960s, has been developed for classroom teachers who are interested in utilizing her approaches to education. There are a total of eight volumes, four each for the secondary and elementary levels. The Taba program has four major strategies; therefore, for each of the two grade levels, there is a volume for each strategy. The four strategies have been detailed in this chapter. The individual volumes contain objectives, planning materials, tryout plans and ideas, and skill refinement activities centered on the particular strategy. Also included are more theoretical materials for the teacher, such as self-evaluation forms for discussion leading and background reading material. There is a reference list and glossary. Finally, an individual is able to evaluate the effectiveness of the unit. The lack of a clear and detailed introduction describing the basic philosophy of the *Hilda Taba Teaching Strategies* is the one major oversight in the materials.

Ellis K., and Durkin, M.C. *Teacher's guide for people in communities* (The Taba program in social studies). Menlo Park, Calif.: Addison-Wesley Publishing Co., 1972. A social studies curriculum has been developed based on the theories of Hilda Taba. *Teacher's Guide to People in Communities* is one book in the series. This particular text is for use in elementary schools. It is well illustrated, and the subject matter is interesting and unusual. The book is divided into two parts: an extensive teacher's edition and the actual text used by students. The teacher's guide discusses the objectives, content, learning activities, and teaching strategies of the program. The chapters in the text are then analyzed for these components to aid the teacher in instruction.

Units in the text center around different cultures in the world. Each chapter in a unit has a central "main idea," similar to an objective, which is used to emphasize the key concepts of the Taba philosophy. These main ideas are continually reintroduced throughout the series. The curriculum is spiraling in content and encompasses both the affective and cognitive domains.

Chapter 9

Calvin Taylor: Multiple Talent Approach

Perhaps the most controversial of the teaching-learning models presented in this volume is the approach of Calvin W. Taylor, an early researcher in the area of creativity development. The approach is controversial in the field of education of the gifted and talented for two related reasons: (1) Taylor writes many articles about the talent potential of all children, and (2) educators seem to read a few articles or their titles and fail to read further or explore the underlying ideas. Such articles as "Nearly all students are talented: Let's reach them" (Note 14) triggered slogans such as "Potentially All Kids Are Gifted," which threatened to undermine years of work in some states. The slogan was dangerous because special educators had been struggling for some time to get categorical funding for gifted children by developing the idea that they are a definable group of children who need special educational services because of their unique characteristics and needs, which is still the rationale for including gifted programs as a part of special education. If, as the slogan suggested, most children are gifted, there is no justification for considering them a special group with special needs.

The problem with this slogan was that it expressed only part of Taylor's ideas. To understand his ideas behind the title "Nearly all students are talented . . . ," a reader had to examine the article carefully and consider Taylor's definitions of "gifted" and "talented."* The usual distinction made between the terms gifted and talented is that, while gifted refers to intellectual abilities, talented refers to the so-called nonintellectual or less general abilities, such as creativity, superior capabilities in the visual and performing arts, leadership abilities, and mechanical or psychomotor skills. Taylor's distinction, however, is in terms of *degree*. He refers to the gifted as those who are at the very top in any identified talent area and the talented as those who are between average and gifted in any talent area. Thus,

---

*Presentation to the Illinois Creative Problem Solving Institute (CPSI), Buffalo, New York, July 1971.

in the article, he was suggesting that if schools would recognize and develop a wide range of abilities rather than concentrating so fully on academic talent, a much greater percentage of children would be considered talented in *at least one talent area*. Statistically, he figured that:

> If we limit ourselves merely to one talent, only 50% of the students will have a chance to be above average (the median). However, if we consider two talents, the percent above average in at least one of the two talents will be in the high 60's; for three talents, in the 70's; for four talents in the low 80's, etc. Across several talents, nearly 90% will be above average in at least one talent area; and almost all others will be nearly average in at least one of the talent areas. Therefore, almost all students are above average. From the same evidence, about one-third of the students will be highly gifted in at least one of the multiple-talent areas (Taylor, Note 14, p. 2).

In this article, Taylor is not suggesting that educators reform only methods for identifying and teaching gifted children, but that the entire educational system be reformed so that a variety of talents, such as creativity, communication, planning, forecasting, and decision making, and academic abilities are a focus of all classrooms. Taylor's approach has validity both as a philosophical basis for the education of all children and as a basis for curriculum planning within a program for the gifted so that these gifted programs assume a broad approach to the development of talents and abilities. It is for this reason that the model was included in this book. The use of the model is the focus of this chapter.

ASSUMPTIONS UNDERLYING THE MODEL

About Giftedness and Talent

The most central and perhaps most controversial assumptions Taylor makes are related to the nature of giftedness and talent. In addition to his definition of the two terms, he stresses the importance of recognizing and developing many different areas of talent in schools, rather than the narrow range of academic abilities that are usually the focus of education (Taylor, 1968a). According to Taylor (1968a), individuals, especially children of school age, have far more talents than they use. Educators are wasting much of this talent by allowing it to lie dormant for so many years while children are in school. By recognizing and developing these varied talents, the following positive benefits will occur: many more people will be able to excel in at least one area, thus making more people feel good about themselves;

people will become more self-directed as they experience and display their unique talent profiles (Taylor, 1968b); schools will not "lose" as many students through dropouts (Taylor, 1968b); and, conversely, some individuals who are always at the top in academics will experience the feeling of being closer to the bottom in some talent area, thus gaining a more realistic picture of themselves in relation to other people (Taylor, 1968b). Often this "realistic picture" only becomes clear after people are out of school and in the world of work.

Taylor supports many of his ideas by citing the research of J.P. Guilford (1967) in his development of the *Structure of Intellect* or, as Taylor describes it, Guilford's "periodic table of the mind." In this model, Guilford (1967) has identified as many as 120 separate human abilities that are considered aspects of intelligence. Taylor (1968a) suggests that a model such as Guilford's, even though accurate, may be impossible to use as a model for classroom practice since it contains so many separate elements. His suggested alternative is to group together some of these abilities into six or seven world-of-work areas: academic, communication, creative, planning, decision making, and forecasting. Thus, Taylor's model is practical for classroom teachers to use and a way to make education more relevant by concentrating on real-world talents and abilities.

An implicit and sometimes stated assumption is that the people who excel in different talent areas will be different people (Taylor, Note 15). As quoted earlier, Taylor believes that as more talents become the focus of educators' efforts, they will identify a larger percentage of children and will finally be able to say that 90 percent are above average in some area and a third are highly gifted in some area.

To illustrate this point, Taylor uses the now well-known "Talent Totem Poles," which show the placement of seven hypothetical children on six talent totem poles. (See Figure 9-1.) As can be seen from examining these totem poles, the children are at different places. No one child is consistently at the top or consistently at the bottom. In real life, however, this is not always the case. Often, the same children excel in almost everything they do. In fact, a real totem pole developed at the Bella Vista School in Salt Lake City, the experimental school that has implemented most of Taylor's ideas, shows that certain children (Ann, Randy, and Kathy) are consistently at the top or close, while certain other children (Linda and Steve) are consistently at the bottom. (See Figure 9-2.) The overwhelming research on relationships between human abilities (Cattell, 1971; Cattell & Butcher, 1968) shows a high correlation. Certainly it is not a one-to-one correspondence, but there is a high degree of relationship. Support for these ideas of Taylor's comes mainly from Guilford's (1967) research showing a low or nonexistent relationship between the abilities identified in his *Structure of Intellect* model. However, the factor analytic methods used to identify abilities in Guilford's model assume factors to be at right angles to each other, that they are not related. In fact, the orthogonal rotation of factors does not allow factors to be correlated. (See Chapter 4 for a more complete discussion of this idea.)

Figure 9-1 Taylor Talent Totem Poles

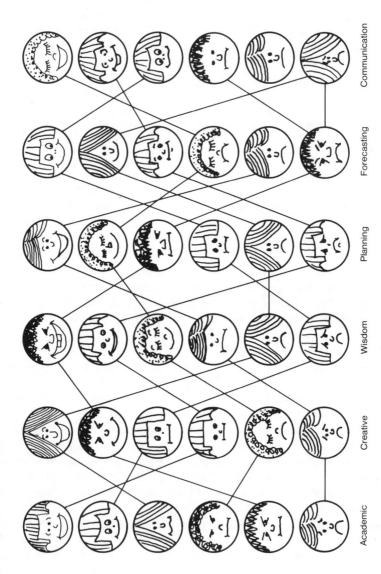

Source:

Figure 9-2 The Taylor Talent Totem Poles*

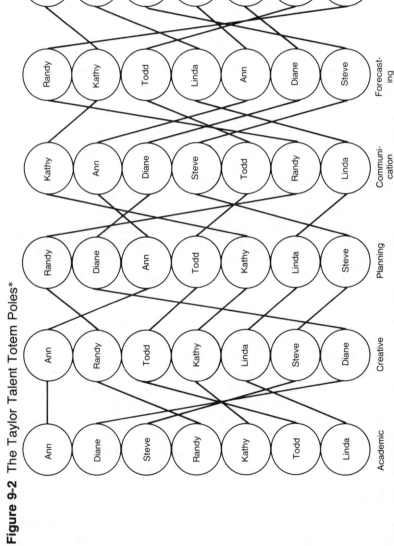

*The Taylor Talent Totem Poles were designed by Darrel Allington and Vern Bullough, Bella Vista School, Salt Lake City.

Source:

The intent of this discussion is not to suggest that Taylor is incorrect in assuming that more people would be considered gifted or above average if the focus were on a wide range of talents. The questionable parts of his statements are the actual percentages. He seems absolutely certain they are accurate, but he provides no real evidence of their derivation from research or actual classroom practice.

About Teaching

If teachers and other educators accept these assumptions about the nature of talent and its presence in different individuals, certain changes will, and indeed must, occur. Most important, talent searches and talent development should occur in the regular classroom while children are acquiring knowledge (Taylor, Note 14). Teachers can develop open-ended activities that will allow the expression and development of several different talents, or they can deliberately plan activities that will develop each of the different types of talent (Taylor, 1968a). In other words, certain kinds of activities, especially in the self-expression area, are open-ended enough that children can use a wide variety of talents to achieve the same purpose. Other activities require different approaches for each type of talent. Some teachers may be better at developing a particular type of talent; therefore, they should be allowed to specialize (Taylor, 1968b). However, all children should experience each type of talent or each type of learning and thinking process (Taylor, Note 14). Finally, to make this *Multiple Talent Approach* successful, there should be a focus on what the children are learning (that is, how and how well they are expressing a particular talent) rather than on what kind of information the teacher is imparting (Taylor, Note 15).

An interesting statement Taylor (Stevenson, Seghini, Timothy, Brown, Lloyd, Zimmerman, Maxfield, & Buchanan, 1971) makes is that "too many school activities are not relevant and too many relevant activities are not in school programs" (p. 9). Reflecting back upon my own educational experiences after a year or so in the "real world," I decided that every skill learned, indeed everything used except the knowledge I was attempting to impart to my sixth graders, came from my extracurricular activities. In out-of-school settings such as after-school clubs, athletics, and music, individuals learn how to plan events, how to handle difficult people, and valuable leadership skills. Why could these activities not be a regular part of the educational program? What happens to the students whose parents are unable or unwilling to take them to a meeting or allow them to stay after school, or to those who are not elected to offices in clubs? Even today they may have no opportunity while in school to gain some valuable skills.

About Learning

The most significant assumption Taylor (Note 15) makes about learning is that children will learn more or grow more in knowledge if his *Multiple Talent*

Approach is used. This assumption is supported by two related ideas. First, children will acquire more knowledge because they will be using more than one way to acquire it. Second, since the major focus is on talent development rather than on the knowledge being gained (for example, knowledge is the byproduct or means to the end rather than the end itself), students will learn more. An underlying assumption is that turning the focus away from knowledge itself enhances learning.

A second assumption is that the adult potential of many students is greatly enhanced because their base of experience is broadened while they are children (Taylor, 1968a). Students have begun to use some talents early that might have gone unused or underdeveloped until adulthood. By using activities that are related to the world of work or everyday world, teachers increase the transfer effect of school learning to real-life situations (Taylor, Note 14). To support these assumptions, Taylor (Stevenson et al., 1971) calls attention to the "tightly closed, circular system" created by some methods. Educators base many of their predictions of children's success along with their expectations for classroom success on a child's performance on an IQ test. Although intelligence tests measure only a small number of the identified human abilities, they were built to correlate with grades in school, and they do so well. However, educators try to make the correlation higher by giving special attention to those who achieve lower or higher than their IQ scores would predict. Special attention or privileges are often given to those who get high grades in academics. However, most of the research shows that grades in school are of little or no value in predicting success in a career. Taylor suggests avoiding a tremendous talent loss by recognizing and developing as early as possible a wide variety of abilities that are necessary for success in the real world.

ELEMENTS/PARTS

Talent Areas

At various times in the development of his approach, Taylor has included different talent areas. However, his final grouping seems to be the following: academic, creative, decision making, planning, forecasting, and communication (Stevenson et al., 1971).* There are definitions along with guidelines for recognizing and developing talents in each of these areas. Since academic talent is already being developed well in schools, guidelines for its development are not usually included in his publications.

---

*All references to Taylor's ideas in this section are to this basic publication.

Creative Talent

Creative talent is defined as the ability to go beyond, to put together pieces of information or new ideas that seem unrelated and come up with new solutions or new ways of expression. It includes the following three subtalents or components: fluency, flexibility, and originality. *Fluency* is the ability to produce many different ideas or solutions. Quantity is the byword rather than quality. Numbers count. *Flexibility* is the ability to generate many different types of ideas or solutions. A person who is flexible will consider a problem from many points of view and will give answers or responses in a variety of categories. *Originality* is the ability to generate unique ideas and solutions or to consider the problem from an unusual point of view. An individual who is original consistently connects ideas not considered together before and solves problems in new or unusual ways. Creative talent is best developed by activities that encourage the generation of ideas without specifically looking for a solution. The teaching process often follows the following basic pattern of eight steps:

1. Present a problem or something to consider.
2. Allow students time to think, and list ideas.
3. Provide a setting for sharing, revising, and refining ideas.
4. Set aside a period of time to allow incubation.
5. Share additional ideas.
6. Have students select their best solution.
7. Have students select their most original solution.
8. Carry out the solution or decision.

Eberle (1974) provides the following guidelines for identifying creative talent:

The Talented Creator . . .

1. Produces a large number of ideas for a given situation.
2. Has a tolerance for disorder.
3. Often starts more than he [or she] can finish.
4. [His or her] thinking and ideas may run contrary or opposite to others in class.
5. Produces ideas or products that are novel and unique.
6. At times, his [or her] work contains great detail, tends to be a "production."
7. Considers contrasting ways of approaching a task or solving a problem, in producing a variety of ideas he [or she] is usually slow to effect closure.
8. Adds his [or her] own ideas and notions to the work of others to produce a different, more complete and interesting idea or product.

9. His [or her] thinking and expression is often spontaneous, unrestrained, unorthodox, and at times seemingly lacking in practical value.
10. Curious, can be challenged, a risk-taker (p. 19).

For an additional listing of characteristics, Chapter 7 contains those considered important by Renzulli and his colleagues (Renzulli et al., 1976).

Decision-Making Talent

Decision-making talent is the ability to evaluate data carefully before making judgments, and involves experimental evaluation, logical evaluation, and judgment. *Experimental evaluation* involves considering the possible solutions from a variety of points of view, examining all possible conditions that would limit or enhance the success of a solution, and looking at the relationship of personal needs to the decision to be made. In *logical evaluation,* the possible solutions or decisions are examined according to their value. Each decision is considered in relation to established logical criteria with ratings assigned on that basis. In logical evaluation, the individual also considers goals, what sequence to follow in implementing the decision, and what the end result might be. *Judgment* is the actual decision making or reaching a conclusion about the best thing to do and defending that decision. In developing talent in decision making, teachers need to assist students in learning the following components of the process:

- Consider carefully and thoroughly all aspects of the situation. Discuss this in a group.
- Examine each possible decision, and the arguments for and against that decision.
- Assign a weight or rating to each argument.
- Reach a conclusion by considering the arguments and their ratings.
- Defend or support the decision made as the best based on their evaluation and logic.

Eberle (1974) provides a list of characteristics of talented decision-makers:

The Talented Decision-Maker . . .

1. Remains emotionally apart from the problem.
2. Weighs consequences, withholds early judgment.
3. Considers more than one course of action.
4. Poses many influential questions and seeks out the answers.
5. Engages in experimental evaluation; asks, "What if?"

6. Has data to support his [or her] decision.
7. Applies evaluative criteria in making choices.
8. Is willing, not afraid, to make a decision.
9. Willingly defends his [or her] decision.
10. Sticks with his [or her] decision and acts accordingly (p. 22).

Additionally, Shartzer (Note 16) lists the following traits of an effective decision maker:

1. Considers thoughts, feelings, reactions of other people who will be involved in the final decision.
2. Relates own needs and willingness to accept decisions to the final judgment.
3. Considers goals and objectives as they relate to the decision-making process.
4. [Has] wisdom or common sense.
5. [Is] willing to discuss situations with various people and accept their advice.
6. Evaluates decisions and changes when needs arise—does not "stay in a rut." (p. 4).

Planning Talent

The ability to plan effectively involves skills in the following three areas: (1) elaboration; (2) sensitivity to problems; and (3) organizing. *Elaboration* is the ability to develop detailed sequences explaining what is to be done. It involves being able to identify the purpose, the process, and the end product. *Sensitivity to problems* is the ability to understand how outside or personal factors may affect how something is done. Included is the ability to identify conditions that can or cannot be changed and the possible consequences of one's acts. *Organization* includes the ability to secure materials and human resources and to arrange for the time, space, and money necessary to accomplish a task. A person with good organizational skills also considers economy and efficiency along with the most effective use of individual competencies and interests. Planning ability, according to Taylor (1971), is developmental. Before students can be expected to make complex plans, they must have experience in making and executing simple plans. To teach or develop this ability, students should be involved in alternate planning, replanning, diversified planning, unplanning, and flexible planning. Eberle (1974) provides a series of cues for the teacher who wishes to develop this ability. Included in those cues are the following: "*Arrange* your *work* in an *organized plan* so that . . . ;" *Design* a *systematic way* to . . ." (p. 12).

To help the teacher identify individuals who are talented planners, Renzulli et al. (1976) provide the following list of characteristics:

1. Determines what information or resources are necessary for accomplishing a task.
2. Grasps the relationship of individual steps to the whole process.
3. Allows time to execute all steps involved in a process.
4. Foresees consequences or effects of actions.
5. Organizes his or her work well.
6. Takes into account the details necessary to accomplish a goal.
7. Is good at games of strategy where it is necessary to anticipate several moves ahead.
8. Recognizes the various alternative methods for accomplishing a goal.
9. Can pinpoint where areas of difficulty might arise in a procedure or activity.
10. Arrange steps of a project in a sensible order or time sequence.
11. Is good at breaking down an activity into step-by-step procedures.
12. Establishes priorities when organizing activities.
13. Shows awareness of limitations relating to time, space, materials, and abilities when working on group or individual projects.
14. Can provide details that contribute to the development of a plan or procedure.
15. Sees alternative ways to distribute work or assign people to accomplish a task.

Other characteristics include the following:

- "Capitalizes on individual competencies" (Shartzer, Note 16, p. 3);
- "Clearly identifies the objective, goal, or outcome he [or she] hopes to achieve" (Eberle, 1974, p. 13);
- "Checks his [or her] plan with others, seeks criticism and suggestions for improvement" (Eberle, 1974, p. 13);
- "Uses symbols, drawings and notation to clarify and elaborate" (Eberle, 1974, p. 13).

Forecasting Talent

Forecasting is the ability to predict future events, that is, to evaluate cause and effect sequences and decide what is most likely to happen based on this evaluation. It includes conceptual foresight, penetration, and social awareness. The subskill of conceptual foresight is the ability to foresee patterns or chains of events and their causes and effects. Penetration is the ability to see clearly the details of all aspects of a situation, that is, to predict how situations or conditions might change and to understand how these changes might affect a prediction. Social awareness is skill in predicting how other people will react and how their reactions will affect future events. It includes the ability to foresee whether change will impose unpleasant or unacceptable conditions upon others and whether change will cause a positive or negative effect on people.

To develop forecasting talent, teachers should encourage children to keep an open mind and to explore all of the possible conditions affecting the result before making their predictions. Another useful exercise would be to follow the process outlined in Taba's *Application of Generalizations Strategy* (see Chapter 8):

- Present a hypothetical situation.
- Ask students to make predictions about what *might* happen if this situation occurs.
- Ask for reasons to support these predictions.
- Ask what conditions would be necessary to make each prediction come true, and tell why these conditions are necessary.
- Reach a conclusion about the *most likely* result, and support this conclusion.

Eberle (1974) also provides guidelines for identifying students with forecasting talent:

The Talented Forecaster . . .

1. Anticipates effects and outcomes.
2. Evaluates past knowledge and experiences.
3. Reorganizes past knowledge and experiences.
4. Views situations objectively.
5. Takes into consideration and displays empathy for human reactions.
6. Is attuned to his [or her] feelings and hunches.
7. Is not overly concerned about being right in his [or her] predictions.
8. Is socially aware, knows what is going on around him [or her].
9. Is sensitive to actions that would effect the situation and others.
10. Clearly perceives situations of cause and effect (p. 16).

In addition, Shartzer (Note 16) presents the following characteristics:

1. Remembers past events and their causes and effects.
2. Recognizes what details are known as well as what details must be known before acting.
3. Anticipates how situations and conditions will change (p. 4).

Communication Talent

The ability to communicate effectively is the ability to send a verbal or non-verbal message that is understood by the recipient. Developmental facets in the ability to communicate are expressional fluency (that is, skill in expressing thoughts, ideas, and needs; skill in understanding these expressions made by others); associational fluency (that is, understanding the interrelationships between ideas; seeing what relation there might be between personal thoughts, ideas, and experiences and those of other people); and word fluency (that is, using words to give precise meaning; to add color, beauty, and depth; and to convey emotions). A teacher who wishes to develop communication talent should assist students in understanding the complexity of human interaction, including the many barriers that can inhibit communication (for example, varied cultural backgrounds, differing values, individual goals) and how these barriers can be overcome.

Renzulli et al. (1976) divide communication talent into two areas: expressiveness and precision. They provide the following characteristics of talented communicators:

Communication Characteristics—Expressiveness

1. Uses voice expressively to convey or enhance meaning.
2. Conveys information non-verbally through gestures, facial expressions, and "body language."
3. Is an interesting storyteller.
4. Uses colorful and imaginative figures of speech such as puns and analogies.

Communication Characteristics—Precision

1. Speaks and writes directly and to the point.
2. Modifies and adjusts expression of ideas for maximum reception.
3. Is able to revise and edit in a way which is concise, yet retains essential ideas.
4. Explains things precisely and clearly.
5. Uses descriptive words to add color, emotion, and beauty.
6. Expresses thoughts and needs clearly and concisely.
7. Can find various ways of expressing ideas so others will understand.
8. Can describe things in a few very appropriate words.
9. Is able to express fine shades of meaning by use of a large stock of synonyms.

10. Is able to express ideas in a variety of alternate ways.
11. Knows and can use many words closely related in meaning.

Shartzer (Note 16) gives the following two additional characteristics:

1. Recognizes commonalities between his [or her] and others' experiences.
2. Relates own thoughts and ideas to others' experiences (p. 3).

Thinking Abilities

One final aspect of Taylor's approach is the addition of guidelines and activities that he calls "productive thinking skills." These include divergent, convergent, and evaluative thinking. Divergent thinking is generating information with emphasis on variety, while convergent thinking is generating information with emphasis on unique or best outcomes. Evaluative thinking is the process of judging information in terms of certain standards.

Although he does not clearly explain the relationship of these productive thinking abilities to the talent areas, in some sections of the activity guide (Stevenson et al., 1971), it seems that he is saying that these three types of thinking abilities can be observed and also developed in many of the activities for different talent areas. In other words, these thinking abilities cut across several talent areas. For example, evaluative thinking is necessary for both decision making (for example, choosing and applying criteria to an idea or proposed solution) and planning (for example, judging the appropriateness of a course of action). Evaluative thinking might be needed, although to a lesser degree, in forecasting (for example, evaluating the possible predictions and concluding about what would be the most likely consequences) and communication (for example, judging what form of communication would be best to use with a particular person). Divergent thinking, a significant part of creativity, is also necessary for effective planning (for example, developing many alternatives) and forecasting (for example, generating several possible predictions). Convergent thinking would be involved in communication (for example, choosing the best or most conventional way to convey a message), planning (for example, deciding on the best or most effective sequence of steps to accomplish a goal), and decision making (for example, implementing a decision), and in the other talent areas. Since these three aspects of productive thinking were identified by Guilford (1967), along with the additional aspect of memory as categories of "operations," an aspect of intelligence, and since they are discussed in depth in Chapter 4, they will not be described here. They are, essentially, component abilities that can and should be developed through several talent areas, since they are skills contributing to the successful expression of many types of talent.

Implementing the Approach

The purpose for including Taylor's model in this volume is to suggest that it be used *within* a program for the gifted as a way to develop these varied talents in the identified gifted children. Even though the model was developed as a total educational approach and certainly has merit (and humanistic appeal), the focus of this section is on its use only within a special program. Many of the factors involved in its implementation would be the same regardless of the scope of its influence.

When implementing a *Multiple Talent Approach,* an appropriate beginning is to design learning experiences in each area of talent, get all the students involved in each type of experience, and then observe their participation, looking for areas of strength and weakness. As more experiences are provided, teachers can begin to find their own strengths and weaknesses as talent developers, and they can team with others to provide a total talent approach if necessary. As the program progresses, children can be allowed or encouraged to choose from activities in talent areas. However, they should, according to the model, participate in activities designed to develop all talent areas, therefore early or complete specialization would not be appropriate.

The characteristics listed earlier in each category can be used both as indicators of talent and as guides for developing a particular talent. When students are observed, their patterns of strength and weakness within each talent area can be developed into an individual profile and used to plan a talent development program. To design further activities in these talent areas, two publications provide guidelines and sample learning activities: Stevenson et al. (1971) and Eberle (1974). The reader is referred to the resources section at the end of this chapter for a description of these publications.

MODIFICATIONS OF THE BASIC CURRICULUM

The major curricular modifications suggested by Taylor's model are in process, that is, stressing the use rather than acquisition of information. However, the model does suggest certain content and product modifications depending on the talent areas being developed. By concentrating on ideas and skills not usually learned in school, the Taylor model introduces variety into the curriculum. It teaches some of the methods of inquiry, or at least some generic aspects of methodology, through its concentration on world-of-work abilities. Most scientists, for example, must be able to plan their experiments or studies carefully to avoid wasting valuable time or resources. They must be able to make valid predictions (hypotheses) based on past experience, and they must be able to communicate their results effectively. Even greater skills in planning and decision making are necessary if a person is directing or coordinating a large research project. Indeed, the most appropriate use of Taylor's model in a gifted program would be in combination with the development of skills of inquiry. As students learn the more scholarly aspects of methodology, they could also be learning the more practical side.

The Taylor model strongly suggests the use rather than acquisition of information through all talent areas. The entire philosophy of the model centers around having students who are active rather than passive, who *do* rather than listen. The talent area of planning, for example, involves students in making plans for their own activities and for hypothetical ones. Communication talent involves developing ways to express ideas so that others can understand them. Other talents also develop ways of more effectively using information.

In addition to stressing the use rather than acquisition of information, this *Multiple Talent Approach* suggests open-endedness, a form of discovery learning, some freedom of choice, and variety. Open-endedness and freedom of choice are somewhat related in this instance; in certain types of activities, students are encouraged to accomplish a particular purpose through whatever means or whatever talent area the student chooses. There are also many "right" answers since students select and apply criteria for evaluation, develop and implement their own plans, and communicate in their own way. There are usually numerous "right" or effective ways of handling day-to-day situations.

Taylor's model also suggests the use of forms of discovery learning in certain talent areas. In most of the activities, students develop a plan, make predictions, or develop some procedure. The teacher then asks questions that require students to perform some step or process. Different answers or reactions are then discussed in a group situation. In effect, the teacher is leading them through a process of discovering effective ways of personally doing something successfully.

Product modifications would occur in most instances. Since activities are designed as practical, relevant, world-of-work experiences, the problems would be real and the evaluation appropriate. In most cases, the audience would be real or simulated, and the final product would be a transformation rather than summary of existing information. However, these last two product modifications are not explicitly stated by or generated from the model. They would be present most, but not all, of the time.

Taylor also suggests the following learning environment modifications recommended for the gifted: student-centeredness; independence; openness; and acceptance. Some of these ideas are not fully developed in his model, but the basic ideas are present. With regard to student-centeredness, the philosophy of the model requires that emphasis be placed on student ideas, questions, and problems. Because learning activities must be realistic, with an orientation toward the world of work, students are not required to listen to teachers lecture or talk, but are expected to produce ideas and products. There is no specific indication of the type of interaction pattern Taylor would encourage in discussions, but since the activities are open-ended and divergence is encouraged, the pattern would probably be student-centered.

Encouraging student independence in nonacademic activities is an important aspect of Taylor's approach, particularly in the talent areas of planning, decision making, and forecasting. With regard to planning, having students plan their own group and individual activities in the class is emphasized. They should develop plans for parties, field trips, management functions, and academic activities. Decision making involves examining their own decisions to determine their effectiveness, while forecasting involves attempting to predict how others would react to something. These predictions and decisions relate to day-to-day interaction with other students as well as to more theoretical or academic content.

Openness (divergence) and acceptance are also significant aspects of Taylor's approach, particularly in developing creative talent. Taylor suggests developing an environment similar to that recommended by Parnes, with emphasis on quantity rather than quality in the idea production stage, with deferred judgment, and which considers the potential of all ideas. Both students and teachers are encouraged to generate ideas without specifically looking for a solution. Divergence is encouraged in behavior and ideas through the recognition and development of a variety of talents.

EXAMPLES OF TEACHING ACTIVITIES

The following sample activities will be two types suggested by Taylor. The first is a series of separate learning experiences in each talent area. Although they are built around a theme to enhance the learning of methods of inquiry, they are separate and should involve all children. In other words, all students should participate in every activity to gain experience in each talent area. The second is a series of learning activities that are open-ended enough to allow students to choose their areas of self-expression.

The following series of activities is designed to develop this methodological generalization: *The growth of knowledge in science occurs through questioning, observation, experimentation, manipulation of materials, observation of results, and revision of original theories.*

Creative Talent

In Step 1, students are asked to consider the following problem: "You are a scientist who has been curious about the long- and short-range effects of volcanic ash on the health of residents of the area surrounding a volcano that periodically erupts. What are all the ways you can find out the answer(s) to this dilemma?" In Step 2, in small groups, the students discuss the problem and list some ideas. After working in a small group for a while, they report these ideas to the large group and list as many additional ideas as possible. In Step 3, the students select one or two of the wildest ideas and figure out ways to make them practical. These revised or refined ideas are discussed with the small group. In Step 4, students put these ideas in the back of their minds for a while and return to them again the next day. In Step 5, in a large group, the students see how many new ideas can be added to the list. In Steps 6 and 7, back in the small groups, they select their group's most original and best solutions. The most original may not be the best. Finally, in Step 8, the small groups begin working on a way to carry out their best solution.

Decision-Making Talent

From the previous activity, the students discuss in the same small group how they decided on the best solution. What criteria did they use? What different criteria or standards were used by each person in the group? How did the group make the final decision? Without looking back at the solutions, they discuss what criteria should be used to evaluate each possible solution in order to select the best. Out of all these criteria, those that are most important and those that do not overlap are chosen. In the large group, the whole list of alternative solutions are discussed and ten of the best alternatives chosen. In small groups or individually, the students apply the selected criteria to each of the ten alternatives, and assign a rating of 1 to 3 for each alternative on each criterion. This will yield a total score for each solution.

After this small group and individual work, students reconvene for a large-group discussion. In this discussion, the teacher's purpose is to stimulate their thinking in new ways about each of the alternatives. The teacher then takes each solution the students have chosen and some from the original list that show promise but were not selected, and asks the students the following series of questions about *each* alternative:

- What would be some of the consequences of this alternative being implemented?
- How would it affect people?
- How would it help in answering the first question?
- What are some of its limitations?

Based on this discussion and without reviewing the initial ratings, each student decides on the best solution and defends that solution. Now, individuals compare their new conclusion with the total scores derived from the systematic rating of each solution.

The teacher then asks the following questions:

- How do your selections compare?
- Why do you think they are similar or different?
- Of the two methods of evaluation or decision making, which do you prefer?
- Why?
- What are the advantages and disadvantages of each method?

Planning Talent

Since students have carefully considered several alternatives and have tentatively decided upon a solution, they can now develop this idea into a definite plan of action. Each student has selected a "best" solution. Individually or in small groups according to the solution they have selected, students plan an actual experiment to find out the answer to their question. The only limitation is that it must be something they can actually carry out; it must be realistic. Students are free to work on their own to develop these plans, and they bring them to class in two or three days.

When the plans are developed, the teacher works with students in groups of 10 to 15 individuals. Each small group is asked to share its plan. After hearing each proposed plan, the teacher asks the following series of questions:

- What are the elements of a good plan for a scientific experiment?
- List the specific kinds of details that must be included in a good plan.
- Which of these elements would you group together because they are alike?
- Why would you group them together?
- What would be some good labels for the groups?
- Why would that be a good label?
- Which items already in one group could also go into another?

After this, the items are again regrouped and labeled. Students think about this discussion and their plans, and develop, individually or in small groups, an outline for developing plans for scientific experiments. The following day these outlines are shared. The teacher looks at each outline carefully to see that all necessary elements are included. If so, the best outlines are made available for future use by the class. If important elements are left out, the teacher asks questions to stimulate their thinking about what would happen if certain types of plans were left out.

Each individual or small group can then examine its plan based on the discussions and make any needed revisions or additions. After this, the teacher works with the individuals or groups on each plan. He or she considers each one carefully and asks the following series of questions if appropriate:

- What are some problems that could occur?
- How will each of these problems be handled?
- What are some outside forces that might affect the plan?
- How will the plan be modified if _____ happens?
- What is your sequence of steps?
- How can this plan be made more efficient?
- What is each person's responsibility?

The students are now ready to refine the plans one last time and carry them out. The teacher helps secure materials, facilities, and access to equipment. When each individual or group has completed its experiment, the teacher again discusses with them the effectiveness of their plans and how they could be improved the next time. The teacher can ask such questions as the following:

- What was good about your plan?
- What would you do differently next time?
- What were some unanticipated problems or situations?
- How did you handle them?
- How could you have solved these problems through more effective planning?
- How could the process have been made more effective or efficient?

Communication Talent

Now that the students have completed experiments to answer a scientific question, they are ready to consider how to communicate in the best way their results to other interested individuals. As a large group, students consider *what* they would like to communicate. Questions to stimulate their thinking include the following:

- What were some interesting results?
- What were some surprising results?
- What results had theoretical significance?
- What results had practical significance?

Next, they are asked to think about *with whom* they would like to share these results. Some questions would be the following:

- What individuals or groups would profit from knowing what you found?
- What groups or individuals are investigating similar questions?

- Whose job would be made easier by knowing the results of your experiment?
- Who would be curious about your results?

After considering what and to whom, they are now ready to think about *how* these results should be communicated to each identified audience. Each small group or individual is asked to name one person or group with whom they wish to share their results. The large group then considers each of these audiences (one audience at a time) and answers the following questions:

- What results would you share with this audience?
- What are all the ways you could communicate these results? (Brainstorm and list all the possible ways.)
- How do you think this audience would judge your presentation of results (that is, what would they be looking for)?
- With this in mind, which of the ways you have listed would you choose for sharing your results?

The various small groups then work together and decide with whom to share their results, and they develop a way to do so. If they decide on a multimedia presentation, they develop this. If a paper seems to be the best method, a paper is written. During this time, the teacher works with individuals and groups. When each is ready, they try out the ''communication'' on the large group of classmates. This group acts as a simulated audience and points out areas needing clarification or elaboration. The whole group then brainstorms possible ways of improving the communication. It is then revised if necessary and presented to the real audience. Students should ask for an evaluation if it is not automatically provided. The teacher should discuss these evaluations with the students and help them develop better means of communication for the next time. Follow-up activities could include discussing how scientific communication differs from other communication and what the elements of a good scientific report are. Individual words could be chosen and a list of synonyms developed as alternative ways of saying the same thing (word fluency).

Forecasting Talent

In the next activity, students are asked to extend their thinking about the present activity and to predict what might happen in a new situation based on what happened in the previous experiment: ''Suppose that the volcano continues to erupt at least twice a month with about the same force as in the past. What do you think the health of the local residents will be like in five years?'' After allowing the students to think for a few minutes, the teacher should ask the following questions in the order listed:

Step 1. What do you think might happen to the local residents? (List all predictions, only stopping the flow to seek clarification of unclear ideas.)

Step 2. Why do you think this might happen (that is, what were some of the results of your experiment that led you to believe that might happen)? (Ask for reasons for all predictions.)

Step 3. What other conditions would be necessary, both before and during this time, to make this prediction come true? Why would that be necessary? (Ask for conditions and reasons for as many of the predictions as possible.)

Step 4. Suppose all the conditions you listed as necessary did happen and this prediction (select a few medium-range predictions from the list) did come true. What would happen then? Follow the same procedures as in number three with each of the new predictions.

Step 5. Based on this discussion and what you already know, what would you conclude would be most likely to happen to the health of the local residents in five years? How did you reach this conclusion? Why did you conclude that would be the most likely result?

During this discussion, the teacher should be an active listener, noticing the types of conditions and consequences listed by students. He or she should make certain the students consider the human element (social awareness), patterns or chains of cause-effect relationships (conceptual foresight), and possible changes that might occur that would affect the predictions (penetration).

MODIFYING THE APPROACH

Content Changes

Taylor's model directly suggests only two content modifications appropriate for the gifted. For this reason, the teaching examples presented incorporate content changes not recommended by a ''pure'' use of the approach.

In the previous example there is a high degree of coordination between activities to develop each talent. In fact, they even have a logical sequence. According to Taylor's model, this sequencing and coordination is not necessary. However, to achieve the element of economy, such organization is highly desirable. A second element not included by Taylor is having a complex generalization serve as an organizer and as a more abstract idea to provide a long-range focus, thus making the approach more appropriate for use with gifted students. In this case, the generalization used is a methodological one, concerned with the scientific method. It is abstract and complex, containing a variety of concepts and being appropriate for many disciplines or fields of study. This example illustrates how the practical side of research can be integrated with the theoretical one.

Another content modification that can easily be integrated was not illustrated by the example, that is, the study of eminent or famous people. To continue with the same example, the study of people can be developed through each talent area by studying the life of a famous individual who has conducted research related to volcanic eruptions. This study could include those persons who have looked at sociological effects, effects on health, or geological aspects of volcanic action. Students could examine the person's research methods, methods for making decisions, research plans and implementation, communication of results, and accuracy of hypotheses or predictions. They could compare these methods with their own and discuss the differences and similarities along with the possible reasons for these likenesses and differences.

Process Changes

Although Taylor's approach uses many elements of a discovery method, the example has a stronger emphasis on discovery than is recommended by Taylor. Every talent is developed through a process using elements of discovery. For example, in the planning activity, a didactic (or deductive) approach would have been to discuss the elements of a good plan and even give the students a sample plan *before* having them make any plans of their own. Children would carry out their own plans and then develop ideas for more effective planning as a result of discovering their own mistakes.

Other aspects of the examples are developed from Taylor's model with some elements of Taba's approach added to enhance or make the questioning of students more systematic. (See Chapter 8.) In the first example, Taylor's suggested eight-step process is followed closely as students list ideas, discuss and refine, incubate, list additional ideas, select the most original idea, select the best idea, and begin to work on the implementation of an idea. The decision-making example follows nicely from the previous activity since the students were involved in some decision making. In this example, students use two means of making decisions; one is a structured, logical approach (that is, logical evaluation), and the other is a less structured, more open-ended approach (that is, experimental evaluation). They then make their final decisions based on both kinds of evaluation. These two kinds of processes are discussed by Taylor. However, it is also necessary to have students compare the two processes and discuss their strengths and weaknesses, which is not a part of Taylor's guidelines.

The planning talent example also follows easily from the decision-making activity. Once a decision is made, it is usually necessary to develop some sort of plan (either brief or detailed) for implementing the decision. In this example, the subskills listed by Taylor are included, as is the Taba *Concept Development*

Strategy. The students are asked to develop detailed plans and to refine these plans (elaboration); to anticipate possible problems and plan ways to handle them (sensitivity to problems); to include their strategies for overall organization and to include sequential steps (organization); and to develop, through a discussion of the elements of a good plan, an outline for planning future experiments (Taba concept development). The skills of alternate planning, replanning, diversified planning, unplanning, and flexible planning are developed as the students develop, revise, discuss, refine, carry out, and then evaluate their own plans. They also discuss how planning differs depending on the situation.

The communication example also follows directly from the previous activity. Although this example concentrates on verbal communication rather than nonverbal, it includes development of expressional fluency (for example, deciding what results to communicate, practicing, receiving criticism); associational fluency (for example, deciding how to communicate with various audiences, practicing for simulated audiences, role-playing audiences); and word fluency (for example, developing lists of synonyms). Other aspects include the elements of real audiences and appropriate evaluation, and product modifications necessary for gifted students.

From this to the forecasting example, there is also a logical flow. Students use previous experience to predict what might happen in a new situation. The Taba strategy, application of generalizations, provides an appropriate sequence of questions. The teacher needs to be alert to what students are saying so that they consider all types of influences in making their predictions.

The addition of elements of Taba's *Strategies* not only provides sequence and structure to the Taylor model, but also develops the process modification of having students express their reasoning or provide support for their ideas. This combination of strategies also ensures that group interaction will occur and provides guidelines for the teacher that can assist in appropriate pacing for different groups of students.

The process modification, freedom of choice, is suggested by Taylor in his recommendation that open-ended activities be developed that will allow for the expression of a variety of talents. Students are encouraged to choose their method of expression. This idea could be carried further. The teacher could encourage the students to choose from a variety of activities or from a variety of content areas. Treffinger's model could also be used in conjunction with this approach as a way to structure the process and assist the teacher and students in moving from teacher-directed activities to entirely student-directed ones.

Following are activities that are open-ended enough to allow the expression of a variety of talents:

- *Activity 1:* Develop, design, or figure out a way to express your appreciation to your mother for everything she has done for you. This can be done individually or in a small group. *Talents:* creativity, planning, decision making, communication

- *Activity 2:* Develop an image of the future, and share it with an individual or a group. It can be as elaborate or simple as you wish it to be. *Talents:* planning, creativity, decision making, communication, forecasting

- *Activity 3:* Create your ideal environment, and share it with someone who can help to make your actual environment more ideal. Design it as a way to convince the person to make some needed changes. *Talents:* creativity, planning, forecasting, decision making, communication

Table 9-1 provides additional activities.

A final process change that must be made is structured group interaction in which students practice and analyze their own performance as leaders and/or participants in group activities. This change is easily integrated by having the group activities videotaped or audiotaped, and then by viewing or listening to the tapes. The previous activities that would easily lend themselves to taping would be the creativity exercise, decision making, planning, and forecasting. The lists of characteristics of individuals with each type of talent can be used as observation tools or as a structure for tape analysis. Other behaviors related to group participation or leadership could also be used for the observations.

Product and Environment Changes

Although the teaching example presented earlier incorporates all the product modifications recommended for the gifted, Taylor does not suggest all these changes. He does recommend that problems and questions be relevant, which would imply that the problems are real. However, the students do not necessarily select the problem they will investigate. No suggestions are made pertaining to "real" audiences, but consideration of the audience is a definite aspect of communication talent. Evaluation and transformation are definite aspects of Taylor's approach.

In the example, students are actively engaged in developing products that address problems real to them, that are directed toward real audiences, that involve appropriate audiences, and that are transformations rather than summaries of existing information. Within the problem area of erupting volcanoes, students may choose a topic or an aspect of the investigation. During activities related to communication talent, they consider audiences who would be interested in their product and develop ways of more effectively communicating with those audiences. Decision-making talent activities develop in students the skills involved in more effectively evaluating their own products. The thinking skill, evaluative

Table 9-1 Summary of Teacher and Student Roles and Activities in Calvin Taylor's Multiple Talent Approach

Step, Type, or Level of Thinking	Student		Teacher	
	Role	Sample Activities	Role	Sample Activities
Creative Talent	creater; problem solver	Invent a game. Create new uses for familiar objects. Create an object of art that expresses some emotion. Create a useful object by recycling junk. Invent a machine that is energy efficient.	stimulator; questioner	Ask questions that lead students through the process of listing, refining, incubating, choosing, and implementing. Develop provocative or interesting situations that can be presented to students for creative activity.
Decision Making Talent	decision maker	Decide what will happen at the end of an unfinished story. Decide what to take on a two-week trip when you are allowed only one small suitcase. Decide what your ideal person would be like. Decide where to live if given unlimited choices. Decide what to do about an unjust law. Decide on a list of people to be included in a peace conference.	stimulator; questioner	Develop situations or pose situations for students to make decisions about. Pose questions that encourage (or require) students to consider a variety of alternatives, relate their decisions to their goals, consider the effects or results of their decisions, and develop both their logic and their intuition to enhance their effectiveness. Assist students in defending their decisions.

| Planning Talent | planner; executer | Plan all activities for a day; at the end of the day, evaluate the plan. Plan a party, have it, and then evaluate its success; plan another and learn from past mistakes. Plan a class field trip. Plan a reenactment of some event from the past—either real or fantasy. Draw a blueprint for a school. | questioner; stimulator | Develop situations for planning. Create situations for students to develop and carry out their own plans. Ask questions that require students to elaborate on their plans, become more sensitive to problems, design alternatives for solving possible problems, design effective and efficient organizational plans, develop step-by-step procedures, and use resources wisely. |
| Forecasting Talent | fore-caster | Predict effects from causes and causes from effects. Predict what would happen if there were no gravity. Predict what will happen in the world 20 or 50 years from now; explain why these things may happen. Predict what your family will be like in 5 years. Predict what will happen in a science experiment. | stimulator; questioner | Develop hypothetical situations for students to make predictions about. Assist students in establishing cause-effect relationships. Ask questions that will stimulate students to use their past experiences to predict future events, notice how conditions change and how these conditions affect predictions, notice how people effect and are affected by events, notice how their own behavior affects others. |

Table 9-1 continued

Step, Type, or Level of Thinking	Student		Teacher	
	Role	Sample Activities	Role	Sample Activities
Communication Talent	communicator	Describe an object based on only the sense of touch. Give directions to a blind person. Develop a set of universal symbols that can be used in all countries. Try to send a message to a person without using words or gestures. Try to send a message to one person that is not understood by everyone else. Choose a feeling—figure out several ways to express it both verbally and nonverbally. Make a report of an event from the point of view of a participant, a close observer, and a distant observer. Make a report of an event that only contains facts; make another report (of the same event) that only contains impressions.	stimulator; questioner	Develop situations for students to practice communicating with real or simulated audiences. Create situations for analyzing the effectiveness of communication. Ask questions that encourage students to see how actions and words are related, relate their experiences to the experiences of others, select words with clear meanings, seek alternative ways of expressing each idea, develop a large vocabulary. Provide situations for students to practice both verbal and nonverbal communication.

thinking, which is involved in many of Taylor's talent areas, helps develop the ability to assess effectively individual products.

The learning environment changes of complexity and high mobility, although not addressed by Taylor, are essential if a person is to use it in the ways suggested by the example. To develop these high-level products and conduct research, students need access to sophisticated materials and equipment, and they must have the freedom of movement that will allow them access to a variety of learning environments.

Summary

The Taylor model can provide a useful structure for a gifted program when modified in certain ways or combined with other models. The teaching example presented in this chapter has shown how it could be combined with the Taba *Strategies*. It could also be used effectively in conjunction with Bruner's approach or combined with Renzulli's *Triad*. It could also be used effectively with Treffinger's model for *Self-Directed Learning*.

DEVELOPMENT

Initial ideas in the evolution of the multiple talent approach seem to have been stimulated in Taylor by the research of J.P. Guilford in developing the *Structure of Intellect* model of human intelligence. However, this theoretical model may only serve as a complement to Taylor's ideas or as a research base to support them.*
Some of the stimulation and the research base comes from the work of Taylor, Ellison, and others through the Institute for Behavioral Research in Creativity. This institute has been involved in both basic and applied research in creativity, the relationship of behavioral characteristics and biographical information to creative productive performance, and career development.

Many of the initial practical aspects of the approach have been developed by teachers at the Bella Vista Elementary School in Salt Lake City. The school faculty, later supported by a federal grant (called Project Implode and directed by G.M. Stevenson), collected and/or produced teaching materials and activities that could be made available to other practitioners wishing to implement the approach. The report of that project, *Igniting Creative Potential* (Stevenson et al., 1971), is a gold mine of teaching activities for developing the various talents. All have been used successfully by regular classroom teachers in a variety of situations. Since

---

*It is difficult to put together a clear picture of the development of Taylor's model since his writing is often sketchy in the area of methodology. His writing preferences lean toward being provocative rather than definitive in presenting his research.

that project ended, the approach has been replicated in several schools and is now a nationally validated project.*

JUDGMENTS

Advantages

The most important advantage of Taylor's model is its relevance to real-world activities through a practical grouping of talents and abilities. It can provide a much-needed dimension to programs for the gifted by its new ways of looking at students. By using the model, the intellectually gifted students in a program will be viewed not only in terms of their academic strengths and weaknesses, but also in terms of their nonacademic abilities. These more practical skills can then be included in school experiences and in extracurricular activities. It is hoped that a wider range of learning would occur, thus developing more well-rounded students.

A multidimensional view of giftedness has humanistic appeal to most people and can aid in gaining initial public support for a program for the gifted. Often a narrow definition of giftedness as academic ability promotes the feeling that gifted programs are elitist and that educators are taking the best students to make them better. A different view of giftedness that emphasizes nonacademic abilities and allows more children to be considered talented does not stimulate as much public resistance. Educators could develop a definition of giftedness and a program plan that states that the top one or two percent of children in each of five or six talent areas would be served in a program for the gifted. Specific provisions for each of the talent areas could be developed gradually (that is, a talent area could be added every year or every other year) to avoid a massive initial program that may be unmanageable. Of course this is not really the way Taylor intends his model to be used. He emphasizes that talent development should be a part of the total educational approach and not solely the responsibility of a special program. However, the two approaches—a special program for the top children and regular classroom programs emphasizing multiple talents—are not incompatible. In fact, they could complement each other well.

As a total educational approach, the *Multiple Talent* model has numerous advantages. It provides a positive way of looking at children, a practical approach to education, and a promising way to reach all children. In special education programs for the handicapped, for example, the *Multiple Talent Approach* provides a much-needed positive side. Indeed, it is an approach that has been advocated by this author (Maker, 1979). Since programs for handicapped students are designed to provide remediation for weak areas and special educators are so well-trained in identifying and developing weaknesses, they often overlook a

---

*Personal communication with Calvin W. Taylor, November 1978.

child's talents or strengths. These strong areas, in addition to having potential as career areas, can serve as avenues for developing strengths. There is growing evidence from research that emphasis on the development of certain kinds of strengths can improve weak areas (Maker, 1979).

In a practical sense Taylor's model is easy to implement in a classroom since the talents are skill areas that adults (teachers) must use frequently. There are classroom-tested idea books available. Expensive materials are not necessary; most of the activities can be implemented with the materials usually present in a classroom. They just need to be used with a slightly different focus.

As a way to make curricular modifications appropriate for the gifted, Taylor's model is helpful in the content, process, and product areas. In addition to the changes directly suggested by the model (for example, different content, methods of inquiry, and use rather than acquisition of information), several other changes are easily incorporated into the model (for example, discovery learning, real audiences, and real problems).

Disadvantages

On the negative side, using all of Taylor's ideas as the basis for a categorically funded special education program could jeopardize the funding for such a program. It is simply not possible to justify a special education program that could potentially serve 30 to 50 percent of the students in a school. Since Taylor suggests that one-third of the students will be "highly gifted" in some area and 90 percent will be above average, if a program served only the highly gifted and the gifted, and if Taylor is correct in his percentages, it would probably serve at least 50 percent of the students.

A second disadvantage is the apparent lack of research supporting or testing the ideas. In his articles, Taylor often makes the statement "Our research shows . . . ," but he does not report the actual data to support the statement. What type of research exists, or does it exist? It is certainly impossible to replicate the results if no information about the initial studies is made available to readers.

Although the talent areas do reflect a different emphasis, they are not mutually exclusive or well defined. For example, the proposed step-by-step sequence for development of talent in creativity includes two steps that relate to decision making (for example, choosing the best solution or the most original solution) and one step that relates to planning (for example, implementing the solution). Even though "choosing the best solution" is the whole act of decision making, it is not suggested that appropriate decision-making activities be incorporated when developing creativity talent. This encourages an unrealistic situation: using an appropriate process for making decisions when decision-making talent is the instructional focus, but using an inappropriate one when creativity is the instructional focus. In this case, the step-by-step procedure (that is, the talent development guideline) does not go well with the definition and subskills of fluency, flexibility, and originality. Choosing the best solution and implementing the solution are not steps in developing these three skills. There are several other similar examples of category overlap.

In addition, certain subskills within talent areas overlap or are ill-defined. For example, in the talent area of decision making, two subskills, experimental evaluation and logical evaluation, would be almost the same if a person used only the definition given instead of developing individual ideas about the two types. Both types involve carefully considering a variety of alternatives and then choosing the best of these. The only difference is that in logical evaluation a person goes through the process more systematically by writing down each alternative, evaluating each, and then choosing the best from the list. With so much overlap between talent areas, it is difficult for teachers to develop learning activities ''pure'' enough to develop a particular talent or observations to identify talented children. Additionally, with so much overlap between categories, it is even more difficult to believe that Taylor's percentages of talented people are accurate.

CONCLUSION

Although Calvin Taylor's *Multiple Talent Approach* in its *entirety* may not be appropriate for categorically funded programs for the gifted because of its philosophy that most children are talented in some way, adaptations of the model can enhance a program. It provides a new way of looking at students and can serve as a model for making education more relevant to the real-life needs of adults. Gifted students, who may be skilled academically, may need help in developing some of the practical skills addressed by this model. Taylor's approach encourages the development of thinking skills and the acquisition of knowledge at the same time as the development of these practical talent areas.

RESOURCES

Instructional Materials and Ideas

Eberle, B. *Classroom cue cards for cultivating multiple talent: A tool for teachers having application at all grade levels and in all content areas.* Buffalo, N.Y.: D.O.K. Publishers, 1974. Based on Taylor's *Multiple Talent Approach,* Eberle has developed a practical list of suggested *cues* or questions to assist the teacher in developing the six talents. Although the bulk of the book is devoted to teaching strategies, it also includes lists of identifying characteristics for each category: academic-learning, communication, planning-organizing, forecasting-predicting, creative-productive, and evaluation-decision making.

Stevenson, G., Seghini, J.B., Timothy, K., Brown, K., Lloyd, B.C., Zimmerman, M.A., Maxfield, S., & Buchanan, J. *Project implode*. Salt Lake City: Bella Vista-IBRIC, 1971. Project Implode is based on the research findings of C.W. Taylor, J.P. Guilford, Paul Torrance, and Frank Williams. The book was written by teachers for teachers. Participants in the project believe individuals are capable of thinking in more creative, productive ways than they normally do, i.e., they do not use all their creative capacities. The basic goal of the book is to gather and create materials and strategies which can be used by teachers to develop productive thinking and the six multiple talent areas. These are creativity, planning, communication, forecasting, decision making, and academic categories. The book is divided into separate chapters based on these categories. There are three more chapters which focus on the components in creative thinking: divergent production, convergent production, and evaluation. Each chapter outlines six to eight activities to develop the creative ability discussed in the particular chapter.

Chapter 10

Donald J. Treffinger:
Self-Directed Learning

One of the important priorities expressed by educators of the gifted is a need to develop self-directedness or independent learning skills in students so that they can continue their learning without constant supervision or assistance from an adult. Often these educators, along with the parents of gifted children, assume that because their children are gifted, they automatically are—or will become if "turned loose"—self-directed learners. Indeed, gifted children are more independent than other children. However, not all gifted children are independent learners, and, even if they are more independent than other children, they probably do not possess the skills that will enable them to direct their own learning completely or conduct their own research, unless they have had some practice in being self-directed. Children who have been told what to learn, how to learn it, and when and where to learn it, and who have always had their learning and products evaluated by someone else cannot be suddenly expected to take over these responsibilities and handle them well.

When independent study programs began to be popular and were implemented in many open or alternative schools, a frequent cause of their demise was that the students were unable to manage their own learning, that is, they "goofed off," played around, and wasted (in the eyes of their parents and the school authorities) both the time and money spent on them. The biggest problem was that the students needed some training and practice in certain prerequisite skills before being set free to learn on their own. Donald J. Treffinger's model provides exactly the structure needed to develop *gradually* in students the skills necessary to become self-directed learners. In fact, it is a model for moving both teacher and student toward a setting in which self-directed learning can occur. Its primary goal is the sequential development of skills in managing individual learning, which builds on the strengths of gifted children, enhances their involvement in their own learning, and increases their motivation by allowing them to study in areas of interest to them.

ASSUMPTIONS UNDERLYING THE MODEL

Before discussing the assumptions made by Treffinger (1975), it would be helpful to first review the assumptions or "myths" he rejects in the development of his model. First, self-directed learning is "neither random nor disorganized" (p. 48). It involves and requires a great deal of organization and planning on the part of both teacher and student. Although movement and activity on the part of students is necessary, it is purposeful activity, activity directed toward the attainment of specific goals. Second, "self-directed learning is not 'unstructured' " (p. 48); its concern is not for eliminating structure, but for creating a structure that works for the benefit of students rather than inhibiting or restricting them. A third conception of self-directed learning that is rejected is that independent learning ignores the development of social skills. Children involved in directing their own learning should (and do) have many opportunities for working with other children and for working alone.

Another common misunderstanding about self-directed learning and other individualized approaches is that merely changing the rate or pace of learning is the most important aspect of the approach. Although students are given opportunities to pace their own learning, other aspects, such as the content and outcomes of learning, are also student-determined as they become better managers of their own learning.

Finally, "evaluation is not absent in self-directed learning" (p. 50). In Treffinger's model, evaluation is not eliminated; its focus is changed. Rather than having a teacher pass judgment on a student's work and label it as adequate or inadequate, both the teacher and learner look critically at the progress of the learner and attempt to identify areas of concern, evidence of progress, and successful/unsuccessful accomplishments as a step toward identifying new goals and objectives for the next learning sequence. Other myths and rejected assumptions (Treffinger, 1975) are the following:

- "Self-directed learning is not 'selfish' in an unconstructive sense" (p. 49).
- "Self-directed learning does not 'just happen,' but involves skills which are acquired through planned instructional experiences" (p. 50).
- "Fostering self-directed learning is not accomplished merely by providing 'activities for the student to do' " (p. 51).

About Teaching

A central idea underlying the model is that teaching involves the following four basic factors that can be used to analyze any instructional event or sequence: (1)

identification of goals and objectives; (2) assessment of entering behavior; (3) identification and implementation of instructional procedures; and (4) assessment of performance. In most classrooms, all these factors are completely under the direction and control of the teacher. The teacher decides what will be learned by the class as a whole and what will be learned by individual children. He or she then assesses the present level of competence, presents the content, arranges practice, provides exercises and activities, and finally, evaluates performance and assigns grades. To foster self-directed learning, the teacher can provide systematic experiences that involve varying degrees of self-direction in each of these four areas. For example, in identifying goals and objectives under a teacher-directed model, the teacher decides what will be learned. In the first step toward self-direction, the teacher provides choices or options for the students. In the second step, the teacher involves the students in creating the options. At the third step, or *Self-Directed Learning,* the learner controls the choices, and the teacher simply provides the resources and materials.

Movement toward self-directed learning must involve all four aspects of the instructional process, that is, identification of goals and objectives, assessment of entering behavior, identification and implementation of instructional procedures, and assessment of performance. If students have determined their own areas of study, the teacher should not be the only source of assessment of entering behavior (or existing level of development or knowledge). Also, if students have determined their own methods of study, practice time, and activities, the teacher should not completely control the evaluation and subsequent assignment of grades. Students also need to be moved sequentially through the different levels of self-direction in each of the areas, essentially from teacher direction to teacher options with student choice, then to options created by both student and teacher, and finally to options and choices determined by students. The teacher's role undergoes a dramatic change, from the person who makes the decisions to the one who advises, assists, and provides resources for the learning options selected by students.

About Learning

Treffinger makes two assumptions about learning. First, children will learn better if involved in their own learning. Second, they will be more motivated to learn if they are directing their learning in areas of their own choice. These assumptions are closely related to Bruner's (1960) and Kagan's (1965) ideas about discovery learning. When children are active rather than passive participants in the learning process, they learn more, remember it longer, and develop more self-confidence in their ability to figure things out on their own. This contributes to greater motivation for *learning* rather than doing what they are told by an adult.

About Characteristics and Teaching of the Gifted

Although the model was not developed exclusively for use with gifted children, Treffinger (1975) sees it as a priority for use with these students. This idea is based on the assumption that the model builds on certain unique characteristics of gifted students, particularly their independence of thought and judgment, their self-starting nature, and their perseverance. The model also builds on other characteristics, such as being curious about many problems and issues, capable of abstraction and generalization, and "motivated by the unknown and the puzzling" (p. 49). Because of these traits, self-directed learning for gifted children is not selfish or trivial. By using the natural desires of gifted students to learn about or investigate "adult" problems and important issues, teachers can make certain that students are involved in studying content areas that are important in their overall development.

A related reason for considering self-directed learning as a priority in the education of gifted students is that it enables educators to accomplish other goals that are often discussed but seldom accomplished, such as applying what is learned in school to other day-to-day challenges. In addition, the skills involved in directing individual learning in school are similar to (if not exactly the same as) the skills involved in lifelong learning and scholarly inquiry. How many scholars only learned to manage their own time effectively and direct their own studies after completing a dissertation and getting out of school?

ELEMENTS/PARTS

Levels

Within each of the four instructional areas (identifying goals and objectives, assessing entering behavior, implementing instruction, and evaluating performance), Treffinger identifies four levels. These levels are examples of the movement from teacher direction to self-direction and involve essentially two intermediate steps. In the first step toward self-direction, the teacher creates options from which the students choose. In the second step, the students are involved in creating the choices. Table 10-1 contains specific descriptions of each of the levels within the four areas of instruction.

Implementing the Approach

In implementing Treffinger's model and moving students toward self-direction in learning, teachers must first assess their own performance with respect to how much self-direction they have been encouraging or allowing each student. Are all

Table 10-1 Treffinger's Model for Self-Directed Learning

Decisions To Be Made	Teacher Directed	Levels of Self-Direction		
		Self-Directed – 1	Self-Directed – 2	Self-Directed – 3
Goals and Objectives	Teacher prescribes for class or for pupils	Teacher provides choices or options for pupils	Teacher involves pupil in creating options	Learner controls choices, teacher provides resources and materials
Assess Entering Behavior	Teacher tests and makes specific prescription	Teacher diagnoses, provides several options	Teacher and learner use diagnostic conference, tests employed individually if needed	Learner controls diagnosis, consults teacher for assistance when unclear about needs
Instructional Procedures	Teacher presents content, provides exercises and activities, arranges and supervises practice	Teacher provides options for learners to employ independently, with learner's own pace	Teacher provides resources and options, uses student contracts which involve learner in scope, sequence, and pace decision	Learner defines projects, activities, etc.
Assess Performance	Teacher implements evaluation and gives grades	Teacher relates evaluation to objectives, gives student opportunity to react or respond	Peer-partners used in providing feedback; teacher-student conferences for evaluation	Student self-evaluation

Source: Adapted by permission from D. J. Treffinger. Teaching for self-directed learning: A priority for the gifted and talented. *The Gifted Child Quarterly*, 1975, 19, 46-49.

plans being made by the teacher? Are children now being allowed to suggest areas of study? Are children's choices being limited to rate and pace rather than involving the more important choices of areas of content and sequence of activities? Who conducts the evaluation? Are peers involved at all? How much freedom is the teacher willing to allow?

After looking at themselves, teachers must take a serious look at each of their students to determine their levels of self-direction in each of the four areas. With most students, it may be safe to assume that all are still at the teacher-directed level, but with gifted students, such an assumption would be a definite mistake. Even young gifted children are often capable of identifying options or areas of study to add to those developed by the teacher. This would place the child at level two of self-direction in identifying goals and objectives. On the other hand, few children have had much practice in evaluating their own performance, so the same child may still be unable to identify appropriate standards for judging success. In short, each student's level of self-direction in each area should be roughly determined, and they should be allowed to function at their highest level in all possible activities. If a student is already a self-directed learner, he or she should be assisted at that level and not required to progress through the lower levels with other students (or with the teacher).

To assess a student's level of self-direction, the teacher can employ a variety of methods ranging from informal observation to collecting ratings from other adults and from children themselves. The teacher can also use more formal assessment procedures, such as tests of research and study skills. The most common form of assessment is a self-report, in which students are asked to rate themselves on a series of characteristics necessary for self-directed learning. Self-reports are usually in the form of a questionnaire concentrating on these characteristics. One example is the *Self-Directed Learning Readiness Scale* (Guglielmino, 1977; Mourad, 1979; Torrance & Mourad, 1978), which asks students to respond to statements about themselves, indicating that they strongly agree, agree, are uncertain, disagree, or strongly disagree. Items such as the following are included:

- "I love to learn new things."
- "I like for my teacher to tell me exactly what to do."
- "If there is something I want to find out, I can figure a way to do it."

Other instruments, such as learning style inventories, also assess student preferences in areas relating to independent learning. For example, the *Learning Style Inventory* (Dunn, Dunn, & Price, 1975) contains items that are related to student emotional characteristics, such as motivation, persistence, responsibility, and the need for either structure or flexibility. Another instrument, the *Learning Styles Inventory* (Renzulli & Smith, 1974) assesses (among other areas) student preferences that are related to projects (for example, working on a project with other students with little help from the teacher or working with other students on a project the teacher suggests) and independent study (for example, planning a project individuals will work on by themselves or working individually to collect information on a topic chosen by the student).

Although self-reports are valuable sources of information about students' perceptions of their own abilities and preferences, additional procedures are necessary to supplement this information. Students can be placed in simulated situations where characteristics related to self-direction are observed by the teacher; peer evaluations can be utilized; and teacher or parent ratings can be obtained.

To facilitate the assessment of student self-directedness as it relates to each of the dimensions of instruction identified by Treffinger, a checklist similar to the one shown in Exhibit 10-1 could be devised. In this checklist, items have been adapted from various instruments and from reports of research on the characteristics of self-directed learning. They have been categorized according to the areas and levels of Treffinger's model. The same checklist used for assessing the entering level of each child could also be used for designing activities to give children practice in developing skills and for evaluating their progress toward becoming self-directed learners. Several sources, including the student, previous teachers, parents, and the present teacher, should provide information related to each characteristic, thereby developing a composite picture of each student.

In addition to the assessment of each child's independence skills with respect to Treffinger's levels, the teacher can identify certain characteristics of successful, independent learners; assess a child's level of development on each of them, and use them as independent learning goals. A useful list of competencies is given by Atwood (1974):

II. Investigation and organization
    A. Investigation
        1. Recognize and understand a variety of investigatory techniques and why they are used
            a) Conduct observations
            b) Conduct surveys
            c) Conduct multi-media research
            d) Conduct interviews
            e) Conduct experiments
            f) Participate in simulations
        2. Know what sources are available and appropriate for investigation
            a) Recognize and use a variety of media as sources of data and ideas
            b) Give examples of specific sources for a variety of data

Exhibit 10-1 Sample Checklist for Rating the Independent Learning Characteristics of Students

Level	Area	Characteristics/Skills
1	Identification of Goals and Objectives	a) When given several choices of topics or areas to study, can choose a topic of interest b) Likes to choose learning activities from a small number of choices c) Asks questions about topics being studied d) Establishes priorities when given a small number of choices e) Is good at games of strategy when it is necessary to anticipate only one move ahead f) When some consequences or effects are listed, can predict additional ones
2		a) When given a general subject area and examples of topic areas within the general topic, can identify additional questions or topics to study b) When given a general subject area, can identify several topic areas to study or several interest areas c) Sometimes asks questions about new topics d) Establishes priorities when provided with choices e) Is good at games of strategy when it is necessary to anticipate a few moves ahead f) Sometimes foresees consequences or effects of actions

Exhibit 10-1 continued

Level	Area	Characteristics/Skills
3	Identification of Goals Objectives	a) Without being given a subject or topic area, can identify a variety of topics or problems of interest b) Likes to develop own learning options c) Constantly asking questions about new topics d) Develops own priorities from unlimited or undefined choices e) Is good at games of strategy when it is necessary to anticipate many moves ahead f) Always foresees consequences or effects of actions
1	Assessment of Entering Behavior	a) When given options of several areas of need, can select areas of greatest need b) When given a list of prerequisite skills necessary for accomplishing a goal, can understand why these are necessary c) Can accept and understand the teacher's assessment of skill development in identified areas d) When given a list of details that may be necessary for accomplishing a goal, can select those that are important

Exhibit 10-1 continued

Level	Area	Characteristics/Skills
2	Assessment of Entering Behavior	a) When given several examples of areas of need, can suggest additional ones to be assessed b) Can identify, with the help of a teacher, the prerequisite skills necessary for accomplishing a certain task or project c) Can contribute to a discussion of own level of skill development in identified areas d) Can take into account most of the details necessary to accomplish a task
3		a) Can identify prerequisite skills necessary for accomplishing a task or project b) Can match own assessment of entering skills with assessment on standardized or teacher-designed instruments c) Can identify areas of personal need not already identified by the teacher d) Can take into account all the details necessary to accomplish a goal

Exhibit 10-1 continued

Level	Area	Characteristics/Skills
1	Identification and Implementation of Instructional Procedures	a) Chooses learning center activities with sequential task cards b) Can stick with a self-identified topic or project for a week without losing interest c) Can stick with a self-identified topic or project for two weeks without losing interest d) Can stick with a self-identified topic or project if the teacher gives continual reinforcement and reminders e) When given several examples of sources of information, can select the most appropriate f) When given options for information or resources, can determine which ones are necessary and/or desirable for accomplishing a task g) When given a set of steps that may be necessary for accomplishing a task, can select those which are necessary and can develop a realistic sequence h) When given alternatives that may be methods for accomplishing a task, can select the most important, most effective, or most interesting i) Allows time to execute steps only if constantly reminded or has deadlines for intermediate steps

Exhibit 10-1 continued

Level	Area	Characteristics/Skills
2	Identification and Implementation of Instructional Procedures	a) Chooses learning center activities with many suggested activities b) Chooses learning centers with openended activities c) Can stick with a self-identified topic or project for a month without losing interest d) Can stick with a self-identified topic if a contract has established the procedures, due date, and objectives e) Can identify several sources of information on a certain topic f) When given some options for information or resources can generate additional ones which are necessary and/or desirable for accomplishing a task g) Can break down an activity into general component steps, but needs assistance in identifying smaller components and in sequencing steps h) When given examples of alternative methods for accomplishing a task, can generate additional ones i) Allows time to execute most steps in a process effectively, but must do some things hurriedly at the end

Exhibit 10-1 continued

Level	Area	Characteristics/Skills
3	Identification and Implementation of Instructional Procedures	a) Chooses learning centers with materials but no specific suggested activities b) Develops own learning centers c) Can stick with a self-identified topic or project (for an indefinite period of time) until it is completed without losing interest d) Can utilize the card catalog and other means to identify all possible sources of information on a given topic e) Can select the most effective and efficient sources of information on a given topic f) Can determine, without assistance, what information or resources are necessary for accomplishing a task g) Can break down an activity into sensible sequential steps h) Can identify various alternative methods for accomplishing a goal i) Allows time to execute all steps in a process effectively

Exhibit 10-1 continued

Level	Area	Characteristics/Skills
1	Assessment of Performance	a) Needs daily feedback from teacher on progress toward goals on teacher-identified criteria b) Can react or respond to teacher evaluation of progress (agree or disagree) c) Can realistically react (or respond) to teacher-determined areas of strength and weakness in own products d) When given criteria which would be used by different audiences in evaluating products, can understand why these criteria would be important
2		a) Needs intermittent feedback from teacher or progress toward goals b) Can suggest additional criteria for evaluation of performance when given examples from the teacher c) Can discuss progress toward goals with teacher d) Can pinpoint some general areas of strength and weakness in own products e) When given a list of possible criteria for evaluation of a product by various audiences, can select those which are important

Exhibit 10-1 continued

Level	Area	Characteristics/Skills
3	Assessment of Performance	a) Can determine criteria for evaluation of progress with only teacher advice when asked b) Can closely match self-evaluation with the evaluations made by others c) Can pinpoint general and specific areas of strength and weakness in own products d) Can determine criteria which would be used by various audiences in evaluating a product

3. Know why and how sources are organized
    a) Understand why sources are organized
    b) Recognize and understand the parallel between media and the places media (sources) are stored
    c) Recognize and understand various patterns of organization
    d) Understand the concept of cross-referencing
B. Organization
    1. Understand why data is organized
        a) Recognize organization techniques that facilitate understanding (of data)
        b) Recognize organization techniques that facilitate future reference
        c) Recognize organization techniques that communicate data and ideas
    2. Know how to select data for organization
        a) Identify relevant and irrelevant material
        b) Identify topics and themes
        c) Identify sequences
        d) Identify main ideas and details

    3. Organize data in a variety of ways
      a) Use classification patterns and techniques
      b) Use sequential patterns and techniques
      c) Use symbolic patterns and techniques

III. Analysis and evaluation

  A. Analysis
    1. Understand why and how to pull data apart
      a) Distinguish between main idea and supportive details
      b) Distinguish between fact, fiction and opinion
      c) Recognize cause and effect relationships
      d) Recognize trends and patterns
    2. Know how to interpret individual findings
      a) Make comparisons and analogies
      b) Draw conclusions
      c) Make inferences
      d) Weigh possibilities
      e) Make predictions

  B. Evaluation
    1. Understand how to assess data from a variety of viewpoints
      a) Verify data
      b) Recognize forms of bias
      c) Determine adequacy of data
    2. Understand how to assess a variety of interpretations of the same data
      a) Compare interpretations with previous knowledge
      b) Compare interpretations with other data (Atwood, 1974)

Examples

After identifying each student's present level of self-direction, the next step is to design activities that will further develop skills at the present level and move students gradually to the higher ones. The following examples present three children from the same classroom who are at differing levels of self-direction. For the sake of simplicity, each child is characterized as being at the same level in all four areas of instruction. However, in a real situation, one child might be at a different level in each of the areas.

Self-Directed, Level 1

Amy, the first child, is a newly identified gifted nine-year-old, who has been in traditional classrooms where little, if any, self-directedness is allowed. However, as a somewhat typical gifted student, she has shown signs of an independent nature and prefers to work on her own to a certain extent.

During her first few weeks in the program, Mr. Jenkins, her special teacher, observed her closely during free choice time. He noticed that she enjoyed having a small number of learning center activities from which to choose, but that she preferred centers that provided sequential task cards to follow. She was unable to develop her own learning activities at the open-ended centers and would frequently request that Mr. Jenkins suggest some things for her to do. After these observations, he decided to start working with Amy to increase her skills in independent learning. The first challenge was to assist her in making choices from a wide variety of activities and to see if she could be encouraged to begin identifying some new learning center activities. He also decided, at the same time, to try having Amy work for longer periods of time on activities they identified together for her to do. They first developed a two-day plan for learning center time in which Amy was given a list of six possible experiments that could be done at a learning center of her choice (science). She was to complete four of the experiments and write her observations. At the end of the two days, Amy and Mr. Jenkins were to have a conference to discuss the experiments, Amy's progress, and any problems she might have had.

After the first day, it was clear that Amy was having trouble with the task. She kept coming back to the teacher to ask where to get materials, to ask about specific steps in her experiments, and to ask for advice about which experiment she should try next. Mr. Jenkins thought he should help her plan more carefully at the beginning so she would know in advance what to do. He then sat down with Amy and developed a two-day "contract." (See Exhibit 10-2.) Together they reviewed the choices and decided which experiments and activities Amy would do. They decided on a time to meet again, and both signed the contract. At the end of the two days, Amy came proudly back to talk with Mr. Jenkins about her successful experience. She was happy to have been able to work on her own. They discussed the results of her activities and any problems in working on her own. Together they identified some possible solutions to the problems and decided to develop a contract for a longer period of time.

Self-Directed, Level 2

Tom, an 11-year-old, also a newly identified gifted student, has recently moved to the school from a nontraditional setting where he has been encouraged during the past year to assume more responsibility for his own learning. He is now able to

Exhibit 10-2 Amy's Learning Contract

I, Amy L____, agree to do the following experiments or activities at the science learning center. I will work on my own as much as possible until I am finished. I will find my own materials and will work hard.

___X___   Look at an onion skin under the microscope. Draw a picture of how it looks.

___X___   Mix a solution of iodine and water and put it on an onion skin. Look at the onion skin under the microscope and draw a picture of how it looks.

_____   Do the taste test on all mystery powders and write what happened.

_____   Do the smell test on all mystery powders and write what happened.

___X___   Make a clay boat that will float. Draw a picture of it and write how long it floated.

___X___   Make a clay boat that will float and carry at least 5 marbles without sinking. Draw a picture of the boat and write how long it floated and how many marbles it held.

I will finish this contract on Tuesday and will talk about my experiments or activities with my Teacher.

Signed,

_____

student

_____

teacher

identify problems to investigate within a topic area and to develop with his teacher alternative ways for solving the problems.

As Mr. Jenkins and Tom began to talk about possible learning activities for Tom, it became clear that Tom had never researched a topic and written a review using more than a couple of standard references. After he asked Tom a few questions about the card catalog, Mr. Jenkins suggested that before Tom began to look for references on his topic, he should learn how to use the card catalog to locate sources in the school and public libraries. Tom agreed and suggested further that he learn about other reference sources since his topic, "Terrorism," had been the subject of recent newspaper and magazine articles. Tom thought this new information would be valuable. Based on this need that Tom identified, Mr. Jenkins decided to give Tom and a few other students a short test to see how much they already knew about references. Mr. Jenkins then planned a short minicourse to teach what they did not know.

During the minicourse, Tom did some preliminary checking on possible sources of information about terrorism, so he felt ready to discuss his investigation and develop a plan for it. He and Mr. Jenkins then scheduled a long conference to develop a learning contract. The contract they developed was somewhat more open-ended than Amy's but had the structure and clarity Tom needed in order to continue on his own. (See Exhibit 10-3.) While they were discussing the research and how Tom would use different references, Mr. Jenkins was pleased with the detail and sequencing of Tom's plans. Tom had even made telephone calls to a local university requesting suggestions for individuals who might be interviewed on the topic. A tentative plan was developed, along with an estimated time schedule for completion. They both agreed that in a few weeks they would get together again, and by that time they would be able to set a more definite date of completion.

The only problem Tom seemed to have was in figuring out what criteria to use in evaluating his project. His work had always been graded by someone else, so he had assumed this would still be true. When Mr. Jenkins asked, "What standards shall we use in judging the quality of your work?" Tom just looked blank and asked, "What standards shall *we* use?" "Yes," said Mr. Jenkins. "It is important that these standards be decided upon ahead of time so you will know what to work toward." It was clear from this conversation that Tom needed some help in developing this part of his contract. Mr. Jenkins then suggested that Tom look through some research reports done by other students and write what he thought was good about them, what he thought was bad about them, and what things he thought would separate the good ones from the bad ones. After this process and after thinking seriously about his own project, Tom talked again with Mr. Jenkins about the criteria and methods for evaluation. Two days later, they met again, discussed the other research reports, and together decided how Tom's project would be evaluated.

Exhibit 10-3 Tom's Learning Contract

Title and Description of Project: *I plan to research the topic of terrorism and present my findings to the class. At the same time that I am learning about the topic, I will also learn how to use a lot of different references.*

Proposed Areas of Exploration:

1) *History of terrorism*

2) *Countries where terrorists have been or are now active*

3) *Possible causes*

4) *Possible effects*

Sources of Information for Each Area

Area   Source(s)

1   *newspaper and magazine articles, books*

2   *newspaper and magazine articles, books, T-V news*

3   *articles, books, interview, T-V news*

4   *articles, books, interview, T-V news*

Steps to be Accomplished (in order of completion):

1) Use card catalogue in school library to locate books.

2) Use other reference sources (e.g., Reader's Guide) in school library to identify articles.

3) Review sources from school to determine whether additional ones are needed.

4) Locate additional sources (if any) suggested by these resources.

Exhibit 10-3 continued

5) If necessary, use card catalogue and other references to locate resources in other libraries (public and University).

6) Locate someone to interview--make calls to University, local historical society, etc., to attempt to find a subject.

7) Develop questions for interview based on readings.

8) Check questions with Mr. Jenkins and discuss interview procedures.

9) Organize information and make outline. Go over outline with Mr. Jenkins.

Description of Product:

The product will be a written research report that has seven sections. They are (1) What is terrorism? (2) History, (3) Facts about Terrorism, (4) Some Causes and Effects, (5) One person's encounter with Terrorism, (6) Some solutions, and (7) A list of references.

Evaluation of Product:

Method	Person	Criteria
checklist	self	completeness, accuracy, interest, use of references, organization
checklist	Mr. J	same as above
checklist	Marcy	same as above

Exhibit 10-3 continued

```
Conferences

Day    Date    Time    Comment

Tues   4/18    8:30    _____

Thurs  4/20    9:00    _____

Tues   4/25    8:30    _____

___    ___     ___     _____


Expected Date of Completion:    _____


                        Signatures:

                                    _____

                                              Student


                                    _____

                                              Teacher


Notes:

_____

_____

_____
```

Self-Directed, Level 3

Marcy, the third student, is a 13-year-old who has been in Mr. Jenkins program for three years and other gifted programs since she was 7. She has always been an independent person, but has also developed skills in managing her own time, which allows her to work for several months on a project with only minimal involvement of her teacher. Since she has been working with Mr. Jenkins for three years, she understands how much self-directedness is allowed and encouraged in his program. Marcy is a curious girl and always has ideas for a million projects or investigations. Her biggest problem is being able to narrow down a topic so that it is manageable in a reasonable length of time. Since Marcy recognizes this as a problem, she always comes to Mr. Jenkins for help when beginning a new project. They usually spend several days discussing a general topic area, with Mr. Jenkins asking questions about Marcy's interests until they can identify a reasonable project or investigation. Since she is a realistic planner, Marcy realizes she cannot do everything related to a topic and wants to concentrate on the most important or most interesting aspects.

This time, Marcy became interested in color theory (Lüscher, 1969) or the relatively new area of psychology that is concerned with the prediction of personality characteristics based on people's preferences for certain colors. As a result of their first conversation, Mr. Jenkins found out that she wanted to know how the color tests are done, something about the underlying theory, how this theory differs from other personality theories, and what psychologists think about the validity of this popularized idea. She also wanted to try out the tests on some people so that predictions made as a result of the test could be compared to her knowledge of the individual's personality characteristics.

To help Marcy choose what to study and to help her develop some skills in narrowing a topic, Mr. Jenkins decided to use some *Creative Problem Solving* strategies in the problem-finding step. (See Chapter 6.) After explaining to her what he'd like to try and getting her enthusiastic approval for the idea, Mr. Jenkins asked Marcy to begin at the fact-finding step. She would develop a brief chart of things that she already knew, things that needed to be found out, and the sources for unknown information. The purpose of this activity was to find out more about the topic so that she would have a better idea of its magnitude. She might also identify some areas of particular interest at the same time.

The next activity Mr. Jenkins asked Marcy to do was to brainstorm or list as many open-ended, creative questions (problem-finding) as she could about color theory. Over a period of a few days, she wrote on note cards all the questions she might possibly ask about the topic. Armed with her half-inch stack of cards, Marcy came back to Mr. Jenkins for her next conference. Together they spread out the cards and read through the questions. Mr. Jenkins asked Marcy to begin grouping together (Taba's concept development strategy) the questions that seemed similar. They worked on the task for quite a while, grouping and regrouping the questions until they were satisfied with the categories.

The categories they developed were the following: (a) *theoretical development* (What other theories led to this one? From what "branch" or "school" of psychology was it generated? When did it begin?); (b) *theoretical validity* (What do practicing psychologists and university professors think of the theory? What research has been done to test the accuracy of predictions? What would happen if it were given to friends whose personality is known?); and (c) *the test itself* (Exactly how does a person conduct the color test? Why is it done that way? How are predictions made from it? How long does it take?). Mr. Jenkins then asked Marcy which she thought would be most interesting or most beneficial: selecting the one most important question out of each category (resulting in an overview of the theory) or selecting one category and asking the questions within only that category (resulting in an in-depth study of some aspect of the theory). After much talk and several days of thinking, Marcy decided that her main interest was in the validity of the theory, but that she would need to answer a few of the questions from other categories, and she would certainly need to learn how to do the test so she could try it on some known individuals.

Marcy now had to design her investigation and get started on the project. Using the major questions as a guide, she developed a brief outline of the steps she would take. (See Exhibit 10-4.) The whole project would be completed by the end of the semester and presented to the class.

Later, Marcy might decide to present her project elsewhere, but at the moment she is planning only a class presentation. Since she is a good planner, Marcy is only expected to ask for assistance when needed and to tell Mr. Jenkins when she needs resources or materials. Her outline of steps is filed in her folder, where she also keeps brief notes about her progress. Mr. Jenkins may check the folder periodically, as he does with all students as a way to keep up with her progress if they do not have a chance to talk about it.

All Levels

As a way to keep in touch with his students and to provide a setting for them to learn from each other's successes and mistakes, Mr. Jenkins holds Monday morning meetings that are a modification of the "Process Seminars" (Bodine, Note 17) developed to support students involved in long-term independent study programs.

These seminars serve a dual function. One purpose is to provide a setting where students can discuss the subject matter of their investigations and projects, getting assistance from other students and learning about several content areas. A second, perhaps more important, purpose is to provide a structured time for students to discuss the processes they are using, the problems they are having, and the solutions they are finding. They can discuss their progress toward becoming self-directed learners, and they can learn from each other's progress. An interesting thing that Mr. Jenkins has learned as a result of these seminars is that his students seem to learn more about becoming independent from each other in these group settings than they learn directly from him. Perhaps this happens because they can observe others who are at different stages or levels in their ability to direct their own learning.

Exhibit 10-4 Marcy's Tentative Outline

Name   *Marcy G*

Topic   *Color Theory*

Questions

What are the important parts of the theory?

How was it developed?

What do psychologists think of it?

What research has been done on it?

How does one do the test?

What would happen if it were given to friends?

Sources

Lüscher's book, psychology department teachers at university and high school

Materials Needed

construction paper, paint

Possible Evaluation

Interest to class, interest to psychologists, a reasonable number of sources

Progress Notes:

In the seminars, students must talk about something every week; they must give a progress report, bring up a problem needing a solution, or tell about a particularly successful or interesting experience related to their investigation. In addition to free discussions, seminars often have special topics that relate to the development of self-directed learning. Some of the more recent topics discussed by Mr. Jenkins's class are the following:

- "What is self-direction? What have you done that you consider self-directive behavior?" (Bodine, Note 17, p. 3)
- How do you know when you have learned something? What role do grades play in the process? What role does the teacher or your peers play in deciding how much progress you have made?
- What things do you want to learn about? How do you decide what is most important to learn? What part should your teacher or your parents play in deciding what you should learn?
- What is the role of the teacher in the whole process of developing self-directedness in students? What things does your teacher do well? What else would you like him to do that he does not already do? What does he do poorly?
- "What is motivation? What motivates you?" (Bodine, Note 17, p. 4) What things decrease your motivation? What part do other people play in your motivation?

Expanding the Model

As can be seen from these three examples, the most extensive of the four aspects of the instructional process is that of implementing instruction. This involves making decisions about types of activities, sequencing, pace, where the learning will take place, and the final result or product of learning. To assist students in moving through the levels of self-directed learning and to assist teachers in their task, Treffinger's (1977) model must be expanded in this one aspect so that the steps or stages can be broken into smaller units. (See Table 10-2.) In this expanded version, implementing instruction has been divided into the three areas of process, product, and learning environment, since all these are decisions that must be made about every learning activity. To show how the expanded model might work and to provide a summary of the previous example, the three students—Amy, Tom, and Marcy—and their topics are used to illustrate the levels.

Instructional Styles

In a later article, Treffinger and Barton (1979) further assist the teacher by identifying and describing five instructional styles that teachers can use in moving students and themselves from a teacher-directed approach to a learner-directed

Table 10-2 An Expanded Model for Self-Directed Learning

Decisions to be Made	Levels of Self-Direction		
	Self-Directed 1	Self-Directed 2	Self-Directed 3
Content	Amy chooses learning centers from a small number of choices. She sometimes asks Mr. Jenkins to help her decide what to do.	Tom and Mr. Jenkins discuss several possible topics. They both make several suggestions.	Marcy knows she would like to learn about color theory and how to do the Luscher test, as well as try it out on friends
Assessment of Entering Skills & Need	Mr. Jenkins Observed Amy and gave her several options for things to work on.	Mr. Jenkins asks Tom several questions about use of the card catalog and discovers that Tom needs to work on his skills in use of this resource. Tom then points out that he will also need to learn how to use other reference sources. Tom takes a pre-test on referencing followed by a mini-course.	Marcy recognizes her own difficulty in narrowing a topic and asks her teacher for assistance. Mr. Jenkins usually asks several questions to help Marcy clarify her interests. This time, they decide to try two of the CPS steps for that purpose. It was Marcy's decision to do an in-depth study rather than an overview of all aspects of color theory.
Process	Learning centers chosen by Amy have sequential	A learning contract is developed co-operatively which	Marcy develops by herself a tentative outline of steps to

Table 10-2 continued

Decisions to be Made	Levels of Self-Direction		
	Self-Directed 1	Self-Directed 2	Self-Directed 3
	task cards to follow. Mr. Jenkins begins a new plan in which he developed with Any a list of experiments to be done.	specifies the sequence of steps Tom will follow, including a review of litera- ture and interviews with experts. It does not specify the date of com- pletion yet, but will provide a schedule after Tom begins to get a better idea of the magnitude of his tasks.	follow in the study.
Product	The task cards in learning centers specify the pro- ducts. Later, the cooperatively developed contract provides the pro- duct.	The learning contract specifies the pro- duct. Several options were sug- gested by both Tom and his teacher. The final decision was made by Tom with the advice of Mr. Jenkins.	Marcy decided to present her results to the class in an audio-visual presentation. Later, if she is satisfied with the quality of the results, the report will be written and/or presented to an audience other than her class.

Table 10-2 continued

Decisions to be Made	Levels of Self-Direction		
	Self-Directed 1	Self-Directed 2	Self-Directed 3
Learning Environment	Amy chooses structured learning centers in the classroom. She works on her experiments mainly at the science learning center, but can gather needed materials from other places.	Again, a cooperative decision was made by Tom and his teacher. Some references will be found in the school library, but others must be located through the public library or the University library. Since interviews will also be conducted if subjects are identified, the environment will be determined by who is to be interviewed.	Where to conduct her research and the testing is entirely determined by Marcy.
Evaluation	Mr. Jenkins and Amy discuss the results of her experiments and develop solutions to problems. Amy reacts to the evaluation and gives her	Since Tom had had no experience in evaluating his own work, a bit more direction was needed here. Mr. Jenkins suggested that he review other research reports and write down some	Marcy will decide whether to share her results with others, and has developed her own evaluation procedures and criteria, including a rating scale to be completed by both

Table 10-2 continued

Decisions to be Made	Levels of Self-Direction		
	Self-Directed 1	Self-Directed 2	Self-Directed 3
	additional thoughts.	possible criteria for determining quality. Mr. Jenkins also	her peers and her teacher after her presentation.
Evaluation (continued)		made several additional suggestions. Both teacher and student provided options, and the final evaluation was a cooperative one.	

one. Theirs is a modification of Mosston's (1972) teaching styles and includes (from the most teacher-directed to the most learner-directed) the command style, the task style, the peer partner style, the pupil-teacher contract style, and the self-directed style. In the command style, the teacher controls almost all of the decisions, and children simply do what they are told. In the task style, the teacher begins to provide choices for the children, usually through learning centers or stations from which some choices can be made. In the peer partner style, the teacher identifies pairs of students who can work together on certain skills. One member of the pair needs assistance, and the other is strong in that area. These partners are matched and rematched depending on the skill area. Initially, the teacher works with the teaching partner to plan learning experiences, and later the students plan mostly on their own. In the next style, the pupil-teacher contract style, the student and teacher cooperatively plan individual learning contracts or learning agreements. In the self-directed style, of course, the students begin to initiate their own learning plans, conduct studies, and evaluate their own products.

Although this description of instructional styles may be helpful to teachers as a general process to follow, it is not as systematic or gradual as the model presented earlier (Treffinger, 1975). There is a huge step between the peer partner style and the learning contract style, and between the learning contract style and the self-directed style. To plan learning experiences that will facilitate the transition between styles, an individual must go back to the earlier model for more extensive guidelines.

MODIFICATION OF THE BASIC CURRICULUM

Content and Process

The major modifications made by Treffinger's model are in process. However, it provides for the content modification of variety since students are allowed to make their own choices at higher levels about the content to be studied. In the lower levels, for example, students are encouraged to choose from options and add to the options; at the highest level, they are encouraged to choose their own content areas. Since gifted students are interested in big ideas, real problems, and adult topics, they will often choose content that is different from the subjects usually taught. The model also helps develop methods of inquiry by providing the structure for students to develop methods and plans for conducting their own learning activities. Thus, they not only learn how to *use* the methods of scholars in a particular field, but they also learn how to *develop* these methods and carry them out on their own.

In the process area, as students move toward self-direction, the modifications of open-endedness, discovery, freedom of choice, and variety in methods become more pronounced. As students begin to assume more of the responsibility for their own learning, for example, the learning becomes more open-ended because the project is entirely under the control of the student. The teacher, at this level, serves only as an advisor. When students are encouraged to draw their own conclusions from information they have collected, the element of discovery is added. At the higher levels, students are also given more freedom to choose their methods, topics, products, and evaluation.

Product and Learning Environment

As with process, products and learning environments become more appropriate for gifted students as the teacher and student move toward self-direction. Students choose the form of their products when at the highest levels of self-direction. Thus, they are free to decide whether to address real problems and whether to direct their products toward real audiences. They are also free to decide how and by whom the product will be evaluated. Since the form and substance is their own choice, students can decide to develop only a summary of existing information rather than a transformation. The teacher's responsibility is not to require that students develop a particular type of product but rather to encourage them to go further with their ideas and produce a "professional-type" product. Certainly, every product cannot be a professional one. An additional responsibility of the teacher is developing in students a belief in the importance of original, sophisticated products.

When gifted students participate (or learn) at the highest levels of self-direction, all of the learning environment modifications necessary for the gifted must be present. Treffinger's model addresses all these dimensions of the environment with the possible exception of complexity. Complexity is definitely necessary if students are to develop sophisticated products, but Treffinger does not make specific suggestions related to this dimension. The entire model provides a structure and specific suggestions for the teacher to assist in developing an environment where self-directed learning can and will occur.

Certainly, the environment will be student-centered rather than teacher-centered if students choose what to study, how to do their investigations, the products to develop, and the methods for evaluating learning. Since Treffinger's model is a comprehensive one, students are involved in all aspects of the instructional process, including the usual areas of involvement (choice of topic and methods) and some aspects of instruction in which students are usually not involved (setting goals and objectives, assessing entering behavior, and assessing performance). For this reason, the environment encourages independence to a greater degree and includes nonacademic along with academic areas. The environment is open since the students choose what to learn, where and how. The environment must permit and encourage a high degree of movement, as students are allowed to choose where and how they will study. To be completely free to choose in the instructional area, students must be allowed ready access to the school library, media services, and other learning options. This requires freedom of movement in and out of the classroom.

MODIFYING THE APPROACH

Treffinger's model for *Self-Directed Learning* was developed for a specific purpose: to provide a structure for moving students and teachers from a teacher-directed setting to an environment where self-direction and independence can occur. It was not intended as a total approach to curriculum development for the gifted and is not advocated as such by its author. The *Self-Directed Learning* model meets a need not adequately met by any other approach advocated for use in gifted programs, and it should be combined with other approaches when appropriate. It is easily integrated with any basic model chosen as the basis for curriculum development. The model is also compatible with a comprehensive curriculum for the gifted that does not use a particular teaching-learning model as a base.

Content Changes

The major content modifications would involve developing or selecting abstract, complex generalizations around which the content is organized. To incorporate the other modifications, these generalizations should include those pertaining to creative, productive people and to the methods of inquiry within different fields of study. At the teacher-directed level, the teacher would select the generalizations and key concepts, and the specific data used to reach the generalizations. At the second level, the teacher could provide options for the students in either or both of the following ways: (a) present the possible abstract ideas that could be studied and allow the students to choose; (b) select the generalizations and concepts as organizers, but allow students to choose the specific data or area they will study. In the second option, the generalizations are used as the organizing scheme for creating the options. When students and teachers are at the third level, both students and teachers can identify optional areas of study within a planning generalization, or the students could be allowed to create options that do not relate at all to the abstract idea(s) used by the teacher for planning purposes. The teacher's role at the highest level of self-direction can be that of a stimulator or a person who encourages students to pursue "big ideas" and abstract concepts rather than the collection of data or specific facts. The learner is in control, but the teacher is a guide and facilitator.

Process Changes

The *Self-Directed Learning* model can easily be integrated with any of the process models to structure the options offered to students. If combined with

Bloom, for example, at the teacher-directed level, the teacher would develop all learning activities and present them to the students. At the next level the teacher could create optional learning activities at each level of Bloom's *Taxonomy* and allow the students to choose from activities at each level. If the students have learned the taxonomy, they can create optional activities when at the third level of self-direction. When students are at the highest level of self-direction, the teacher should not place any requirements on students related to the taxonomy, but certainly should encourage students to work at the highest levels whenever possible. Treffinger's approach could be used in a similar manner with the other process models.

Another way to integrate this approach with others is to suggest that students use a particular process or model when choosing or developing options. Two examples of this idea are included in the sample activity described earlier. To assist Marcy in her study, Mr. Jenkins suggested that she use *Creative Problem Solving* in the initial stages. She also used Taba's *Concept Development Strategy* as a way to organize her questions for the investigation.

The process modification of requiring students to express their reasoning can be integrated in a variety of ways. One way would be to ask students to explain why they have selected a particular option for goals, instructional procedures, or evaluation. Another would be to have them explain their self-evaluations. Of course, when teachers question students about what they have learned, concentration on reasoning would also be important.

When planning group interaction experiences at the teacher-directed level, the teacher should choose. At the later levels of self-direction, however, the students could choose from several optional activities and could also choose from several optional ways of observing the group's interaction. At the highest levels, the students should be encouraged to develop their own learning experiences that would facilitate group interaction and the development of leadership abilities. They could set their own goals, assess their own skills, and then develop ways to learn and to evaluate their success.

Pacing of instruction and the presentation of new information are the responsibilities of the teacher at the teacher-directed level, but become a shared responsibility at the second two levels. When students are self-directed, they are responsible for pacing their own activities.

Summary

Treffinger's model for *Self-Directed Learning* provides a structured way for teachers to develop experiences that will move their students and themselves toward student-directed learning. Rather than assuming that gifted students already possess the self-management skills that will enable them to be independent learners, the model provides a way to develop these skills gradually. In this process, both teacher and student roles change drastically as students assume more responsibility. (See Table 10-3.) The teacher moves from director to a provider of options, and then to a resource person or facilitator when needed by the student. On the other hand, the student moves from passive learner to a developer and chooser of options, and then to diagnostician, director of learning, and self-evaluator.

DEVELOPMENT

The model is a logical one and was developed by Treffinger as a way to facilitate the movement of students toward self-directed learning. It is considered a tentative plan or a set of hypotheses rather than a set of conclusions based on research. The plan was developed from research on the characteristics of students and from studies of programs designed to foster divergent thinking and creative problem solving. According to Treffinger (1975) many of the educational programs designed to stimulate creativity and develop positive attitudes are necessary, but are not sufficient for establishing an appropriate learning environment for gifted students. By adding the elements suggested in his model, Treffinger feels that educators can effectively meet the learning needs of gifted children; they can make learning more joyful, more applicable to the day-to-day world, and more flexible for meeting children's unique needs.

RESEARCH ON EFFECTIVENESS

Although research on the characteristics of students and on effective programs for developing creativity and problem solving was incorporated into the development of this model, there is currently only one study available that assesses its validity (Barton, 1976). In this study, Barton found that elementary students and their teachers in heterogeneous classrooms were able to move from a command style to one in which they assumed responsibility for carrying out much of their own learning. In addition, the students still learned as much academically as did a control class. All students, not just the gifted, increased in self-direction and independence. A frequent component of programs for the gifted is independent study. Independent study or completely self-directed learning is highly successful with gifted students (Renzulli & Gable, 1976). Gifted students who have participated in these programs feel that independent study has a positive influence on the following: (a) their motivation and career (increases their excitement about learning, helps them make decisions about future careers, and allows them to choose content areas and depth of content); (b) their study habits and thinking processes (increases critical thinking, and helps in organizing and focusing indi-

Table 10-3 Summary of Teacher and Student Roles and Activities in the Treffinger Self-Directed Learning Model

Step, Type or Level of Thinking	Student		Teacher	
	Role	Sample Activities	Role	Sample Activities
Teacher Directed	passive	Learn what the teacher identifies as important. Participate in pre-tests of specific skills. Complete learning activities as identified by the teacher. Receive evaluation or assessment of progress.	director	Decide on goals and objectives for the class and for individual students. Test and make specific prescriptions for each child. Present content, provide exercises and activities, arrange for practice of skills. Implement evaluation procedures, develop criteria for success, assign grades.

Self-Directed, Level 1	chooser	provider
	Choose goals or areas of study from those identified by the teacher.	Develop optional goals or areas of study.
	Choose areas of strength or weakness (as identified by the teacher) to work on.	Develop diagnostic procedures, share with students, provide optional areas to be worked on.
	Choose learning activities.	Provide learning activities to be done independently by students.
	Do learning activities independently and at own pace.	Evaluate students in relation to objectives, share evaluation with students, provide an opportunity for students to respond or react.
	React to and discuss teacher evaluation of progress.	

Table 10-3 continued

Step, Type, or Level of Thinking	Student		Teacher	
	Role	Sample Activities	Role	Sample Activities
Self-Directed, Level 2	developer of options	Assist teacher in creating options or identifying areas of study. Discuss with teacher one's own areas of need as well as interests, strengths, and weaknesses. Take tests identified with the teacher as necessary or desirable. Assist teacher in indentifying learning options,	developer of options	Involve students in creating options or identifying areas of study. Have individual conferences with each child to cooperatively identify areas of need, strength, weaknesses, and interests. Employ individual tests if necessary and if cooperatively identified by student and teacher. Provide resources, develop options with students, and assist in setting up learning contract.

Involve students in decisions regarding the scope of activities, their sequence and the rate of learning.

Involve students in developing methods and criteria for evaluation.

Develop student-teacher conferences for student evaluation.

Utilize peer-partners and other sources of student evaluation.

Develop a learning contract by choosing from options cooperatively developed with the teacher.

Implement learning contract as developed with the teacher.

Assist in identifying and developing methods and criteria for evaluation.

Participate in student-teacher conferences for evaluation of progress.

Table 10-3 continued

Step, Type, or Level of Thinking	Student		Teacher	
	Role	Sample Activities	Role	Sample Activities
Self-Directed, Level 2 (continued)		Suggest new areas of study based on results of evaluation.		
Self-Directed, Level 3	director of learning; diagnostician; evaluator of learning	Set own goals and objectives. Determine needs and areas of strength, weakness, and interest. Develop and determine projects, learning activities, places to study, pace of learning. Consult the teacher	resource person; advisor; facilitator	Assist student in identifying goals and objectives. Provide resources and materials. Assist students in assessing own levels of performance or needs. Assist students in developing learning activities when consulted. Assist students in self-evaluation or in using the results of self-evaluation to plan new learning activities.

Self-Directed, Level 3
(continued)

when advice is
needed

Evaluate performance —
decide on criteria,
methods, who is
responsible.

Use evaluation results
to plan new goals
and objectives or
new learning
activities.

viduals' thoughts); and (c) the degree of challenge and opportunity for self-expression in school (allows freedom to express their own ideas and develops more positive interactions with teachers) (Bodine, Note 18). In many cases, parents also are pleased with their children's progress in an independent learning program, and the parents list many of the same positive influences as do their children.

However, more research is needed to test the effectiveness of the levels in Treffinger's structured, developmental approach. Do students who begin at the lower levels actually develop skills needed for directing their own learning? Are the four levels in the appropriate sequence? Are they gradual enough, or are there intermediate steps? All these questions need to be answered before the model can be considered a successful approach. To enable teachers to apply the model more effectively, answers to questions about student characteristics and how they interact with the model are needed. For example, at what ages should educators begin to encourage self-direction in gifted children? What developmental differences are there at different ages? All these questions await further study.

JUDGMENTS

Advantages

The Treffinger model takes into account the unique present and probable future characteristics of gifted students, and is designed to enhance their strengths. With a teacher who is excited about the approach and a learning environment flexible enough to allow the model to work, this approach should be successful.

Another advantage of this model is its potential for enhancing the success of some other approaches used in education of the gifted by complementing their weak areas. For example, a frequent difficulty noted by teachers attempting to use the Renzulli *Enrichment Triad* is that their students do not possess the skills in self-management and self-direction that will enable them to do Type III investigations. Treffinger's model provides a way to develop these skills.

In general, this approach is different from many of the other models used in education of the gifted because it concentrates on some of the more "practical" skills of inquiry (management of time, sequencing of activities, and identification of resources) rather than on "thinking" or information processing abilities. It also provides for some of the process modifications of curricula that are not specifically addressed by any of the other models, such as freedom of choice.

Finally, there is some preliminary, short-term research showing that students can move toward more self-directed learning. In this process, they also continue to achieve academically at the level expected based on comparisons with a control group.

Disadvantages

The biggest disadvantage of this model is the lack of research on its effectiveness when used over a period of time. If given a choice, will gifted students actually study subjects or areas that will build a foundation for later learning? Except for one study, educators can only speculate about the model's effectiveness as a total approach. Even though it is clear that the model can provide a helpful and effective complement to other approaches, it is doubtful that a self-directed learning program could stand alone as a total approach to education of the gifted. There are too many unanswered questions and too many needed curricular modifications that are not addressed by the model.

A final disadvantage is that the model requires a particular kind of teacher, that is, a person who is willing and able to move from a directive role to a facilitating role as the students become effective directors of their learning. Not all teachers are willing to make these changes, and not all parents are willing to see teachers give up the major responsibility for their children's learning. Parental pressure can create an additional negative factor for teachers who were not quite certain of their willingness to change roles. It is difficult to maintain a teacher-directed program for some children and attempt to move others toward more independence, so a teacher's response to parental concern may well be to abandon the attempt.

CONCLUSIONS

Although developed for a somewhat narrow purpose, the model fills a need not met by other approaches discussed in this book. It can (and should) be combined and integrated with other models to provide a comprehensive structure for curriculum development for the gifted. At the highest, ultimate levels of self-direction, the teacher becomes a guide or facilitator who encourages the students to pursue abstract, complex ideas, to choose learning experiences that develop higher levels of thinking, and to develop products that are at a level of sophistication equal to their abilities.

Treffinger's model for *Self-Directed Learning* can provide a valuable complement to other approaches used in programs for gifted children. It is a developmental practical approach that builds on some of the more salient (and often troublesome) characteristics of gifted children, such as the following: their stubbornness when told what to do; their curiosity about a wide range of topics; their constant questions; their nonconforming nature; and their tendency to direct the activities in which they are engaged. The model is not difficult to learn or understand, but it may be hard to implement.

RESOURCES

Background Information

Della-Dora, D., & Blanchard, L.J. *Moving toward self-directed learning: Highlights of relevant research and of promising practices*. Alexandria, Va.: Association for Supervision and Curriculum Development, 1979. This publication is intended to be a reference source for people interested in fostering self-directed learning. The book attempts to present the highlights of relevant research and programs in the past 50 years so that more application can take place in the classroom. Chapters include "Promising Practices and Relevant Research," "Needed Research," "Social-Cultural Forces Affecting Self-Directed Learning," and "Developing Self-Directed Learning Programs." The chapter on social-cultural forces has some interesting insights into the impact of race and sex on classroom dynamics. The book is a fairly scholarly piece of work, not light reading.

Instructional Materials and Ideas

Atwood, B.S. *Building independent learning skills*. Palo Alto, Calif.: Education Today, 1974. The purpose of this book is to help students become independent thinkers or to be able to reason by themselves. The main components of an independent thinker are communication, investigation and organization, analysis and evaluation, and transformation. The introductory chapter outlines each component in detail. Next, there is a chapter describing each component. In the chapters are numerous suggestions to encourage the development of each specific component discussed. Ideas include projects, field trips, and explorations. There is a resource list for teachers. No age group is specified. The layout is attractive, and the book reads well.

Chapter 11

Frank E. Williams: Teaching Strategies for Thinking and Feeling

One of the most commonly used approaches in programs for the gifted is Frank E. Williams's model for developing thinking and feeling processes. Not only is there an inexpensive idea book available (Williams, 1970), but also a total kit (Williams, 1972) that includes books, tapes, inservice training materials, and many practical materials for implementing the approach. Since the approach is a simple and practical one, many school districts "bought" the program and have based their entire gifted program's curriculum on this approach.

The Williams model (Williams, 1972, 1980) was not developed specifically for use with gifted children. In fact, its major purpose is to provide a model for enhancing the cognitive and affective processes involved in creativity and productivity in all children. The thinking processes of fluency, flexibility, originality, and elaboration, along with the feeling processes of curiosity, risk taking, complexity, and imagination, are developed through the traditional subject matter content. The teacher uses a series of 18 strategies or modes of teaching. Williams's model assumes that for optimum learning to occur, there must be a proper mix or interaction between three basic elements: (1) what children are or can become (pupil behaviors); (2) the curriculum (subject matter content); and (3) what teachers can do with both the curriculum and the students (teacher behaviors). In any teaching situation, all three elements act upon each other. Because of this interaction, the design of any learning experience for any child should consider all three elements.

From this basic philosophy, Williams (1970) developed a morphological model with the following three dimensions: (1) the curriculum; (2) teaching strategies; and (3) student behaviors. As with other morphological frameworks, this model depicts the components as interrelated parts of a whole. There is no hierarchy of strategies or behaviors either implied or intended. The framework can be used as a structure for curriculum planning, instruction, and teacher training. In short, it provides a vehicle for intersecting a given subject area with any teaching strategy to produce student behavior that is creative.

ASSUMPTIONS UNDERLYING THE MODEL

About Learning and Thinking

According to Williams (1972), learning requires three things: "a purpose or goal, a subject to think and feel about, and a guided plan to which the learner responds in his [or her] own individual way" (p. 91). This process cannot be depicted adequately by the currently used hierarchical models, which essentially look at pupil outcomes and teaching processes as occupying one dimension and being ordered from simple to complex. Williams's criticism of such approaches stems from what he feels are two basic limitations of these models in representing children's creative growth and development. First, the mental processes contributing to creativity, such as ability to hypothesize, synthesize, and transform, are always located at the top or higher levels of the taxonomies. According to Williams, this placement implies that "creative thinking consists of higher mental processes which may not appear much before middle childhood" (1970, p. 58). If hierarchical models are accurate representations of children's actual behavior, then the development of creativity and imagination must wait until a child is more sophisticated. Of course, anyone who has worked with young children realizes how imaginative, flexible, curious, and open youngsters can be, and these individuals are concerned about preserving qualities that are important in creativity.

The second limitation of hierarchical models discussed by Williams is similar. Since a hierarchical model implies that later operations are built on earlier ones and that a person must master the earlier processes before moving to the later ones, creativity may be developed best by first concentrating on some of the more convergent behaviors, such as knowledge and comprehension. Williams (1970) believes, as other creativity experts do, that early and too great an emphasis on convergent learning actually inhibits the development of creativity.

Williams may be correct in his belief that educators interpret hierarchical models as implying that children cannot accomplish the higher mental processes until they are older. However, at least two of the models—Bloom's *Cognitive Taxonomy* and Krathwohl's *Affective Taxonomy*—suggest that all ages and ability levels of students are capable of higher levels of thinking. Incorporating Piaget's ideas into the schema suggests that young children are creative in a concrete rather than abstract or symbolic sense, which certainly fits with reality. Types of creativity are no doubt different at different age levels.

With regard to the second limitation, Williams (1970) may be more accurate. There is at least more agreement among professionals (Parnes, 1966; Torrance, 1979) that excessive emphasis on the acquisition of knowledge as opposed to the production of ideas limits the development of creativity. The key words, however, are excessive emphasis. Parnes (1966) certainly points out the value of knowledge in the production of creative ideas.

Regardless of the appropriateness of Williams's criticisms of taxonomic models, his morphological model was developed as a more accurate representation of children's thinking and feeling processes and their development. In this kind of structure, one or more parts or dimensions are combined to form a new arrangement. Thus, Williams presents his model as one showing the integration of student behaviors, content, and teaching strategies.

Three other assumptions made by Williams (1972) relate to the nature of effective learning and to the relationships between cognitive and affective processes. First, learning is more effective when children are active producers rather than passive recipients and when they are learning in a way that builds on their unique learning styles and abilities rather than assuming all children are the same. Positive self-concepts, mental and emotional health, and willingness to learn are all benefits that result from active, fun, individualized learning. A second assumption is that more effective learning of subject matter can occur if the development of thinking and feeling processes occurs simultaneously with the learning of subject matter. His third assumption is that thinking is not isolated from feeling (Williams, 1971a). Every time individuals think about something, they also have an associated feeling. For example, at the lowest levels of Bloom's (1956) and Krathwohl's (1964) hierarchical *Taxonomies,* individuals do not gain *knowledge* they do not want to *receive.* At the highest levels, individuals *internalize* certain ideas and values through *evaluating* how they fit into their particular way of life. (See Chapter 2 for other explanations of the relationships between the *Cognitive* and *Affective Taxonomies*.)

About Teaching

Williams (1972) also makes several assumptions about the roles of education and teachers. He suggests that the major goal of education should be to help each child realize his or her full potential. To accomplish this goal, teaching practices must be related to and built on what is known about the individual learning modes and abilities of children. Teaching practices and school experiences must also make sense to children and fit into their personal lives. Another prerequisite to children's realizing their full potential is the development of a variety of thinking and feeling processes that are not currently a part of every classroom. An implicit assumption behind this idea, though not specifically stated, is that the most important neglected processes are those related to creativity and divergent thinking. The most effective way for a teacher to develop a variety of thinking and feeling processes is by using multiple teaching strategies. Such strategies are designed to bring out children's hidden strengths instead of compensating for their neglected weaknesses.

Williams suggests that developing creative thinking and feeling processes should occur in a heterogeneous classroom or at least in a classroom with a wide range of creative abilities. He states that all children will benefit—gifted and talented, underachievers, slow learners, average students—as well as the teacher. In a situation where the children have different strengths and weaknesses, Williams believes that they will learn from each other and from the teacher.

Finally, teachers do not have to be creative themselves to develop creativity in children. Williams (1972) believes, however, that teachers must be innovative, since he considers the development of creativity an innovative concept. Because his ideas are different, for teachers to put them into practice effectively, they must thoroughly understand the theory behind the model and be completely committed to its goals. In addition to a thorough understanding of the theory, he believes that teachers also need to have extensive inservice training in its application to the classroom. Teachers need training mainly because in the past creativity, if even a part of the classroom, has been only a peripheral aspect of the curriculum rather than an integral one. Incorporating creativity development into the subject matter curriculum is an absolute necessity and requires a trained teacher.

About Characteristics of the Gifted

Williams's (1970) definition of giftedness focuses mainly on creativity, although he points out that there is a relationship between creativity and intelligence or achievement. However, rather than looking at a child and deciding "yes, this child is creative" or "no, this child is not creative," Williams suggests that children be viewed in terms of their unique pattern of creative strengths and weaknesses. Developing a complete picture of the child's unique pattern includes assessing and observing the thinking behaviors of fluency, flexibility, originality, and elaboration, along with the feeling behaviors of curiosity, imagination, complexity, and risk taking since these are the clusters of characteristics always found in creative, productive individuals. At one point, Williams discusses the "ablest, more highly talented" (1972, p. 149) who are strong in all of the thinking-feeling areas. He sees these children as being high risk takers and high in fluency, flexibility, and originality. They are also "strongly independent and self-sufficient" (Williams, 1972, p. 151) and more intelligent, and they have a higher degree of self-confidence. In other words, he seems to be suggesting that talents in the thinking and feeling processes included in his model are associated with intelligence, self-direction, and self-confidence. Although gifted students *on the average* (Gowan & Demos, 1964; Makovic, 1953; Torrance, 1965) are more independent and self-directed than children who are not gifted, there is certainly no basis for assuming that all gifted students are self-directed. Every child is different. Some who are high in the creative thinking and feeling behaviors identified by Williams may not be self-directed or have high self-esteem.

About Teaching the Gifted

Williams (1970) states that the purpose of the model is "not to make more children creative but to release and recognize more creativity in all children" (p. 108). To release this creativity, an individualized approach based on the children's talents and skills is best. However, he does suggest that "the very ablest, more highly talented in all of the thinking-feeling areas should be encouraged to go off on their own . . ." (p. 149) to work on things of interest to them while ". . . the less talented children, or those you have observed as needing special help, should be provided this opportunity to work more closely with you or some qualified teaching assistant . . ." (p. 149).

The first recommendation results from his assumption that because students are gifted or talented, they possess skills of self-direction and independence that will allow them to work successfully on their own. The second recommendation results from the more questionable assumption that children who are less talented need to work more closely with the teacher, while those who are talented can make it on their own. Although Williams does not seem opposed to special education provisions for gifted children, such statements as these tend to perpetuate the myth that gifted children can best be served by being simply "turned loose," while special assistance is only needed for children who are having problems.

ELEMENTS/PARTS

The Williams model (1972) is a morphological one somewhat similar to the *Structure of Intellect* model of human intelligence developed by Guilford (1967). (See Figure 11-1.) (See Chapter 14.) It has three dimensions that interact in any teaching-learning situation.

Dimensions

The Curriculum

This facet includes the traditional subject matter content areas in schools, that is, art, music, science, social studies, arithmetic, and language. The author suggests substituting the content areas used in a particular setting if they are not the same as Williams's areas. In a gifted program, Williams notes, the teacher could substitute areas such as "ecology, marine life studies, man and population growth, psychology, and career development" (Williams, 1972, p. 87).

Teaching Strategies

Included in this dimension are the "situations, techniques, or methods" (Williams, 1972, p. 87) teachers can use in their classrooms in all of the subject matter

Figure 11-1 A Model for Implementing Cognitive-Affective Behaviors in the Classroom

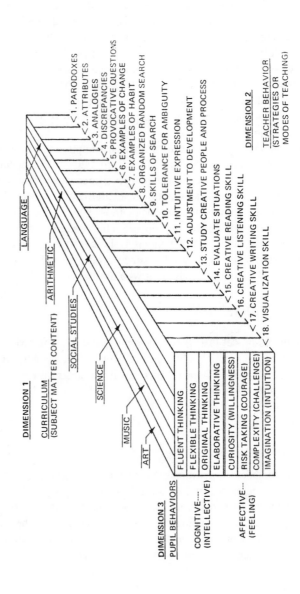

$$D1 \rightleftharpoons D2 \rightarrow D3$$

DIMENSION 1

<u>CURRICULUM</u>
(SUBJECT MATTER CONTENT)

- LANGUAGE
- ARITHMETIC
- SOCIAL STUDIES
- SCIENCE
- MUSIC
- ART

DIMENSION 2

TEACHER BEHAVIOR
(STRATEGIES OR
MODES OF TEACHING)

- 1. PARODOXES
- 2. ATTRIBUTES
- 3. ANALOGIES
- 4. DISCREPANCIES
- 5. PROVOCATIVE QUESTIONS
- 6. EXAMPLES OF CHANGE
- 7. EXAMPLES OF HABIT
- 8. ORGANIZED RANDOM SEARCH
- 9. SKILLS OF SEARCH
- 10. TOLERANCE FOR AMBIGUITY
- 11. INTUITIVE EXPRESSION
- 12. ADJUSTMENT TO DEVELOPMENT
- 13. STUDY CREATIVE PEOPLE AND PROCESS
- 14. EVALUATE SITUATIONS
- 15. CREATIVE READING SKILL
- 16. CREATIVE LISTENING SKILL
- 17. CREATIVE WRITING SKILL
- 18. VISUALIZATION SKILL

DIMENSION 3
PUPIL BEHAVIORS

COGNITIVE----
(INTELLECTIVE)

- FLUENT THINKING
- FLEXIBLE THINKING
- ORIGINAL THINKING
- ELABORATIVE THINKING

AFFECTIVE----
(FEELING)

- CURIOSITY (WILLINGNESS)
- RISK TAKING (COURAGE)
- COMPLEXITY (CHALLENGE)
- IMAGINATION (INTUITION)

Source: Reprinted with permission from F.E. Williams, *Classroom ideas for encouraging thinking and feeling* (Buffalo, N.Y. 14214: D.O.K. Publishers, 1970), p. ii.

areas. The 18 methods or processes have a minimum of overlap when used as they are defined by the author. Following is a list of strategies along with a definition and some examples of each:

- Teach about *paradoxes*. A paradox is a true situation opposed to common sense, a statement or observation that contradicts itself. Although true in fact, it does not seem to be so. The strategy develops a sensitivity to differences between facts and popular notions.

  Examples: In social studies, pose the situation that explorers discovered they could arrive in the West by traveling east. Ask students to think of as many geographical contradictions as possible and try to explain them. In language arts, have students list all the superstitions they can. Have them make a story about one of the superstitions.

- Ask students to look at *attributes*. Attributes are characteristics of things, that is, inherent properties, conventional symbols, or qualities of items.

  Examples: In science, after playing around with magnets, ask students to list all the attributes or qualities of things that are attracted to magnets. Have them list all the qualities of things that are not attracted to magnets. In language arts, have the children list as many adjectives as they can to describe an object the teacher is holding.

- Use *analogies*. Analogies emphasize similarities between things that otherwise may seem unlike. They make comparisons between these things or between the things and the circumstances surrounding them.

  Examples: First, have children brainstorm about the traffic signs. Then have them make comparisons between these traffic signs and punctuation marks used in writing (language arts). In social studies, have students make a list of all the fads that existed when their parents were their age and a list of current fads. Ask them to make comparisons between past and present fads to see if there are common reasons for them.

- Point out *discrepancies*. Discrepancies include gaps in knowledge, unknown information, or "missing links."

  Examples: Ask children to think of all the things they do not know about people from another country. Have them list all the ways this information could be found. Have children think about what it might be like to live in a glass house. Ask them to make a list of all the ways their lives might be different if they lived in a glass rather than a regular house.

- Ask *provocative* questions. These are questions intended to get children excited about inquiry, to explore, and to discover new knowledge.

  Examples: After a science lesson on water and its different forms, ask children whether they would rather be a raindrop or a cloud, and why they feel that way. During a unit on living things, ask students to tell all the things they could learn about a tree by looking at its leaves. Then have them answer the question, "What would the world be like if all the trees were destroyed by human carelessness?" (Williams, 1970, p. 41).

- Cite examples of *change*. Demonstrate to children how dynamic the world is or can be. Provide situations for making substitutions or modifications.

  Examples: Discuss the ways people preserve things (for example, freezing fish or bronzing baby shoes). Ask students to think of a list of things that are preserved, kept, or sustained. Then have them think about how and why these things are preserved. Have children develop a list of words by changing only the initial consonant. What is the longest list that can be made?

- Use examples of *habit*. This strategy develops a sensitivity to avoiding rigid or habit-bound thinking through discussing or showing the effects of thinking bound by habits.

  Examples: Discuss the habitual use of a base ten numbering system. After using other bases, have children think of situations where other bases would be more appropriate. During a unit on transportation, point out the effects of tradition and habit-bound thinking on innovations. Pose questions such as why engines are usually placed at the front of a car, propellers are usually placed on the front of engines, and drive wheels are usually placed on the rear of a car. Then discuss some results of breaking out of these patterns of thinking.

- Allow for an *organized random search*. Develop a structure, and use it to lead randomly to another structure. Set ground rules, and allow children to explore within these boundaries.

  Examples: Teach children a form such as cinquains. Give a few examples, and then ask them to develop some of their own. The form is the following:

> line 1—one noun
> line 2—two adjectives describing the noun in line 1
> line 3—three words expressing an action
> line 4—four words expressing a feeling
> line 5—one noun that is a synonym of the single noun of line 1

When working with number facts, have students think of all the possible ways to make a certain number.

- Teach the *skills of search*. This strategy teaches several different ways of searching for information including historical search or looking for ways something has been done before; trial and error search and then describing how it was done; and experimental search or controlling experimental conditions and reporting the results.

Examples: Have children imagine they are stranded on a desert island. Ask what are all the ways a person could get off the island? After listing all ideas, ask them how they can find more. After talking about seeds and which seeds grow, have students do experiments with different kinds of seeds to see which ones grow.

- Build a *tolerance for ambiguity*. Provide situations that are challenging and intriguing. Present open-ended situations that do not encourage or force closure.

  Examples: Read a story, and stop at an interesting part. Have the students tell what they think the ending might be or write an ending. Emphasize that there can be many endings, and there is no "right" way to end a story. Ask students to think about what might happen if certain natural cycles changed (for example, seasons following each other in a different order or ocean tides changing every week).

- Allow for *intuitive expression*. This strategy encourages the skills of expressing emotions, making guesses based on "hunches," and noticing things through all the senses.

  Examples: Show pictures of people expressing different emotions. Have children guess why the person might be feeling that way. Show a film about a natural phenomenon. Have half the students write about it from the point of view of a meteorologist and half of them write about it from the point of view of an artist.

- Teach not for *adjustment* but for *development*. Look at how failures or accidents have been positive, how to learn from mistakes, and how to develop or change rather than simply adjusting to things.

  Examples: After studying how the government functions and making field trips to government offices, have students design an ideal government. Ask them to decide what qualities ideal governments should have and how these qualities can be achieved. After studying about how scarce and costly paper is in Japan, ask children to imagine that their family is so poor they cannot buy paper, and list all the writing surfaces they can that could be used in place of paper.

- Have students *study creative people and creative processes*. In this strategy look at the people who have been recognized for their creativity and examine the processes they used that led to their creativity.

  Examples: Have students look at the life of an inventor and an artist. Ask them to consider how these people are similar and how they are different. After considering what they are like as individuals, have them look at the similarities and differences in how the people developed their products. Have the children make a list of all the characteristics they can that relate to an eminent individual, such as Ben Franklin. Ask them to list their own attributes and then compare their characteristics to those of the eminent individual.

- Encourage students to *evaluate situations,* choose solutions by careful consideration of consequences and implications, and predict from the results of ideas and actions.

  Examples: Beginning with a random collection of items, have students predict which ones will sink or float. Have them tell why the prediction was made, and then try out items to see whether their prediction was accurate. In social studies, after a unit on exploration showing that movement is always from east to west, have students consider the possible causes and effects of westward movement.

- Develop skills in *creative reading.* In this strategy, students learn to generate ideas through reading and to read "not what it says, but where it takes you" (Williams, 1970, p. 99).

  Examples: During the year, ask students to keep a list of the many expressions used by writers, especially colloquial ones such as "It was raining cats and dogs!" After becoming aware of paradoxes, when students read newspapers, watch TV, or read magazines, have them look for paradoxical situations and keep a list.

- Develop skills in *creative listening.* This strategy emphasizes idea generation through listening. Students are encouraged to listen for information that leads them from one thing to another.

  Examples: After each student has created an imaginary animal, have students make up stories about the animals. Have students compose stories in a group setting. The student who created an animal starts a story, then other students add a sentence until each has added one sentence to the story. Have students listen to an audiotape or the teacher's reading of a story. As they listen, they should make two lists. In one list, have them write what information they acquired, and, in the other, list what guesses or inferences they can make from what they heard.

- Develop skills in *creative writing.* In this strategy, students are taught to write their ideas clearly and to express their feelings and emotions through writing.

  Examples: In the old activity of writing autobiographies, discuss how a student's life story can be made more interesting. Ask students to generate new ways of *organizing* the information (that is, use a method different from chronological) and *presenting* the information (that is, changing the format). As a follow up to the activity in which students discussed how various items could be preserved or saved, have them write a story about something they would like to preserve and tell why.

- Develop skills in *visualization.* Give students practice in describing objects or situations from unusual viewpoints or looking at things from an unusual or different perspective. Encourage the expression of ideas in three-dimensional form.

Examples: Discuss dreams and some ideas about why people dream. Also talk about artists and how they make their dreams into pictures, and how poets make their dreams into poems. Have children describe five or more of their own dreams by drawing pictures of them. Brainstorm colors that express emotions. After discussing these ideas, while listening to a story or a piece of music, put the emotions expressed by the story or music into an abstract "mood" painting.

Although all of the strategies would certainly be useful at some point in working with creative children, Williams (1970) states that the most effective strategies to use with the more able, highly talented children would be the following: (a) exploring discrepant events; (b) asking and seeking answers to provocative questions; (c) exploring examples of change and habit; (d) developing skills of search; (e) learning how to tolerate ambiguity; (f) teaching for development rather than adjustment; and (g) learning to evaluate situations.

Pupil Behaviors

Student behaviors developed by the strategies through the curriculum are divided into cognitive (intellect) and affective (feeling). Based on research on the behaviors involved in creativity, Williams (1972) has identified eight clusters of behaviors. Following are his descriptions and examples of these behaviors.

List of Thinking Behaviors:
1. Is *fluent* in thinking. Usually comes up with the *most* ideas, responses, solutions, or questions. Produces a *quantity* of ways or suggestions for doing things. Always thinks of *more than one* answer. A count of these determines how fluent a child is.
   Examples:
   - The child who has a flow of answers when a question is asked.
   - The child who draws several pictures when asked to draw one.
   - The child who usually has several ideas about something while others struggle for one idea.
   - The child who asks many questions.
   - The child who uses a large number of words when expressing himself [or herself].
   - The child who always produces more than others in the class.
   - The fastest worker in the class, who does more than just the assignment.

2. Is *flexible* in thinking. Usually is able to produce a *variety* of ideas, responses, questions, or solutions. Seeks many *different* directions or alternatives. Has the ability to *shift* approaches or *change direction* in thinking about things. A count of the *number of changes* or *categories* within which thinking occurs determines how flexible a child is. Fluent children are not flexible if all their ideas are of one kind. Flexible thinkers need not necessarily be fluent, but each idea will be of a different variety.

Examples:

- The child who thinks of various ways to use an object other than its common use.

- The child who has different interpretations of a picture, story or problem other than the one being discussed.

- The child who can apply a principle or concept in subjects other than the one in which it was introduced.

- The child who shifts and takes another point of view or considers situations differently from others in the class.

- The child who, when discussing a situation, will always take a different position from the rest of the class.

- The child who, when given a problem, usually thinks of a number of different possibilities for solving it.

3. Is *original* in thinking. Usually able to think of *novel, unique* expressions. Has *clever* ideas rather than common or obvious ones. His [or her] thinking is *unusual* and he [or she] chooses to figure things out and express them in *new* ways. A count of the number of *uncommon* responses or productions away from the usual determines how original a child is. This may be the child who is neither fluent nor flexible, but after listening to others will think of a new approach that is rarely thought of by the rest of the class. An original thinker has the capacity to *combine* pieces of the usual into a new and *unusual* whole.

Examples:

- The child who likes objects in the room placed off side or prefers asymmetry in drawings and designs.

- The child who is dissatisfied with a stereotyped answer and instead seeks a fresh approach.

- The nonconformist who cannot help being different and always has a new twist in thinking or behaving.

- The child who enjoys the unusual and will rebel against doing things the way everyone else does them.

- The child who deviates from others to do things his [or her] own way.
- The child who, after reading or listening to a problem solution, will go to work on inventing his [or her] own new solution.
- The child who not only questions the old way but will always try to figure out a new way.

4. Is an *elaborative* thinker. Usually wants to *add to* or *elaborate upon* ideas or productions. Loves to *stretch* or *expand* upon things. Seeks to *embellish* materials or solutions by making them more elegant and interesting. The elaborator may not be an originator, but once he [or she] gets hold of a new idea, he [or she] can *modify* or *expand* upon it. A count of the number of times he [or she] senses something lacking and *adds on details* to improve it determines how elaborative a child is.

Examples:

- The child who will add lines, colors, and details to his [or her] own or another child's drawing.
- The child who senses a deeper meaning to an answer or solution by producing more detailed steps.
- The child who takes off with someone else's idea and modifies it.
- The child who will accept an idea or someone else's work but will always want to "jazz it up."
- The child who is uninterested in things that are barren or plain and always attempts to add detail to make them more beautiful (pp. 35-39).

List of Feeling Behaviors:

1. Is keenly *observant* and *inquisitive* by nature. Always *curious* about people, objects and situations. Likes to *wonder, explore, ask questions,* and *puzzle over* things.

Examples:

- The child who questions everything and everyone.
- The child who loves to explore mechanical things.
- The child constantly searching for "why."
- The child who is more prone to question why things are not done differently than the usually accepted way.
- The child who constantly searches books, maps, pictures, etc., looking for new ideas.
- The child who needs no real push to explore something unfamiliar.
- The child who uses all of his [or her] senses to make sense out of things.

- The child sensitive to problems.
- The child alert to details that produce meaning.

2. Has a very strong *imagination*. Can *visualize* and *dream about* things that have never happened to him [or her]. Can deal with *fantasy* but knows the difference between that and reality.
Examples:
   - The child who can tell a story about a place he [or she] has never visited.
   - The child who can feel intuitively something that has not yet happened.
   - The child who can predict what someone else has said or done without ever knowing that person.
   - The child who can go somewhere in his [or her] dreams without ever leaving the room.
   - The child who likes to build images of things he [or she] has never seen.
   - The child who can see things in a picture or drawing that no one else has seen.
   - The child who can wonder about something that has never happened.
   - The child who can make inanimate objects come to life.

3. Is *challenged* by *complexity*. Thrives on *complicated* situations. Likes to tackle *difficult problems*. Has a preference for *"digging in"* to intricate solutions and things.
Examples:
   - The child who appreciates complex ideas or problems.
   - The child who becomes intrigued with messy situations.
   - The child who likes to delve into the most complicated task.
   - The child who will choose a more difficult way out.
   - The child who wants to figure things out for himself [or herself], without help.
   - The child who enjoys something harder to do than other children.
   - The child who thrives on trying again and again in order to gain success.
   - The child who will not give up easily.
   - The child who needs harder problems because of the challenge.
   - The child who seeks more difficult answers rather than accepting an easy one.

4. Is a *courageous risk-taker* willing to *make guesses*. Usually *not afraid of failure* or *criticism*. Plays on hunches just to see where they will take him [or her]. Is not bothered by uncertainty, the unconventional, or lack of structure.

   Examples:
   - The child who will defend his [or her] ideas regardless of what others think.
   - The child who will set high goals of accomplishment and not be afraid of trying to reach them.
   - The child who will admit to a mistake.
   - The child who is willing to try the difficult task.
   - The child who really wants to try something new and hard.
   - The child who is not concerned by disapproval from classmates or teachers.
   - The child who is not easily influenced by friends or teachers.
   - The child who prefers to take a chance or a dare (pp. 70-73).

Implementing the Approach

The Williams model can be used as a structure for curriculum planning, instruction, and teacher training. All three, of course, are highly related. The model provides a structure for looking at short- and long-term objectives (that is, pupil behaviors as outcomes) and how these objectives can be met (that is, teaching strategies as methods) through certain content areas. This makes it an effective model for curriculum planning. Teaching strategies can be selected from existing materials and classified according to the model. To assist in classifying materials and strategies according to the model, Williams (1972) provides a checklist that can be completed for each material and then filed for easy access, or teaching strategies can be generated using the model as a structure for giving ideas and putting them into a standard format. Regardless of whether selecting materials or strategies and classifying them, or generating new strategies, the following questions are asked:

- What is it that you want children to do? (lesson activity)
- Where does this activity lead each child? (pupil behavior)
- What do you do to cause such behaviors? (teacher strategy)
- Within what subject should this occur? What kind of data is needed? Where does the activity fit into the curriculum? (Williams, 1972, p. 145)

When using the Williams model for inservice training, teachers are taught this model and how it can be used for curriculum planning and instruction. Two related purposes are served by its use: the teachers design activities to develop pupil behaviors not usually addressed in classrooms, and they are taught a way to expand their repertoire of teaching strategies by using some methods they may not have tried.

Using the model for instruction seems to be the most important of the three uses. To make this explanation more concrete, an example of the use of Frank Williams's model with a group of ten sixth graders is given and described.

Ms. Burnley is a teacher of the gifted with a resource room program. She has ten identified intellectually gifted students from the sixth grade, and she would like to implement the Williams model with this group as a way to increase their creative behavior.

To use the Williams model for instruction, a logical individualized approach is followed. The first step is to determine the characteristic thinking and feeling behaviors of each child, identifying his or her unique pattern of strengths and weaknesses. To form the most accurate picture of each child, a variety of procedures should be used, including both observation by the teacher and standardized tests. Each child should be observed by the teacher in a variety of situations and over a long period of time. To begin her observations, Ms. Burnley decided to combine two observation forms discussed in the creativity kit (Williams, 1972). (See Figure 11-2.) She wanted one sheet that could be used for observing both the thinking and feeling behaviors exhibited by each student. She listed each child's name in the left column and all the behaviors at the top. She then duplicated the form so that she could use a new one for each separate observation. As observations were made, she placed a tally mark (/) in the column indicating which behavior was observed.

To make her observations go more smoothly and quickly, she decided to "team up" with the learning disabilities resource teacher. She offered to assist Mr. Ottoman in his observations of his students' on-task behavior in return for his assistance with her observations. (After a few days of observing her children, he decided to also observe his students' creative behavior so he could identify their strengths.) They developed a system of observing two children at a time for five minutes. At the end of five minutes, two new children became the focus of their attention until the whole group had been observed. These observations were made over a two-week period in a variety of activities that were open-ended enough to allow creative expression. Figure 11-2 shows the tallies for one observation period. A total of ten observations was made on each child. Observational data were also collected by carefully observing each child during the day and recording an overall rating for each child at the end of the day.

To supplement their observations, the two teachers asked their students to give their perceptions of the creative behaviors of their peers. As discussed by Maker

Figure 11-2 Ms. Burnley's Observational Checklist of Creative Behaviors

Date __August 21, 1980__   Observation # __2__   Activity __Creative Problem Solving__

Students	Fluency	Flexi-bility	Origin-ality	Elabor-ation	Total Thinking	Curi-osity	Risk-Taking	Complex-ity	Imagin-ation	Total Feeling	Total Crea-tivity
Brad G.	//	/	/	//	6		//	/		3	9
Dolores G.	/				1	/			/	2	3
Jim D.			/	/	2	/		/	/	2	4
Juan G.	//	/	/		4	/		/	/	3	7
Luis R.	/	/	/	//	4		/		/	2	6
Manuel P.	///	//	///	//	10	//	//		//	7	17
Monica L.		/	//	//	5	/	/	/	/	4	9
Sally S.	/				1	/				1	2
Susan B.	/		//	/	2		/	/		2	4
Tom W.		/	//	//	5		/		/	1	6

Comments

Source: Adapted from F.E. Williams, *A total creativity program for individualizing and humanizing the learning process* (Englewood Cliffs, N.J.: Educational Technology Publications, 1972).

(1982), an important aspect in the success of peer referral is the design of *specific* questions appropriate for this age child. Following are the questions Ms. Burnley and Mr. Ottoman designed for each behavior:

- Who in this group usually comes up with the most ideas? (fluency)
- Who in this group usually thinks of the most different kinds of ideas? (flexibility)
- Who in this group usually thinks of completely new ideas? (originality)
- Who in this group usually comes up with many details and descriptions of his or her ideas? (elaboration)
- Who in this group asks the most questions and seems the most curious about everything? (curiosity)
- Who in this group is always the first to try something new even though it may be difficult? (risk taking)
- Who in this group likes to tackle difficult or complicated problems? (complexity)
- Who in this group tells the best imaginary stories or dreams up the most fantastic pictures? (imagination)

Each child in the group was told to write the names of one or two children whom they thought most fit the description in the question. The two teachers then made a chart listing the nominations received by each child. (See Table 11-1.) As seen in Table 11-1, two students, Brad and Manuel, were nominated the greatest number of times in all areas. They were also the students who were observed by the teachers as exhibiting the most creative behaviors. Other children perceived by their peers as creative were Monica L. (15), Susan B. (10), and Juan G. (8).

In addition to the observational and peer referral data she had obtained, Ms. Burnley needed standardized test data to complete her profiles on each student. She first consulted the cumulative folder for each student to see what information was already available. To her dismay, Ms. Burnley found that no child had been given the same battery of tests. All had been given individual intelligence tests and a self-concept inventory, and all had achievement test scores. However, several different measures of creativity had been given. Some of the children had been given the figural form of the *Torrance Tests of Creative Thinking* (TTCT), while others had been given the verbal form. Some children had been given one or two of the *Guilford Creativity Tests for Children*. Others had taken one or both instruments included in the *Creative Perception Inventory, What Kind of Person Are You?* (WKOPAY) or *Something About Myself* (SAM). A few students had taken Williams's *How Do You Really Feel About Yourself* inventory. To get a realistic picture of the kind of data she had, Ms. Burnley then analyzed these and several

Table 11-1 Summary of Peer Nominations for Ms. Burnley's Sixth-Grade Gifted Students

Date _____

Name	Flu	Flx	Or	El	Total Thinking	CU	RT	CO	Im	Total Feeling	Total Creativity
Brad G.	7	7	9	3	26	4	7	5	1	17	43
Dolores G.	0	0	0	1	1	1	0	0	0	1	1
Jim D.	1	0	0	1	2	0	0	1	1	4	4
Juan G.	1	1	0	2	4	2	1	0	1	4	8
Luis R.	1	0	0	0	1	0	0	0	1	1	2
Manuel P.	5	6	10	8	29	5	8	3	6	22	51
Monica L.	2	3	0	1	6	4	3	4	4	15	21
Sally S.	0	0	0	1	1	0	0	1	1	2	3
Susan B.	1	1	0	1	3	0	1	4	2	5	10
Tom W.	2	0	0	2	4	0	0	1	1	2	6
Total # of Nominations	20	18	19	20	77	16	20	19	18	73	149

other tests to see which of the creative behaviors in the Williams model were assessed by each test. Her analysis of the tests can be found in Table 11-2.

Of course, there were more instruments available for assessing the thinking behaviors than the feeling behaviors. After checking this list of tests against the tests in children's folders, Ms. Burnley decided to make a complete profile on each child that would consist of four measures of each creative behavior. She selected the instruments that had been given to some of the children since these tests, when combined, would give a complete profile for each child. She then administered whatever tests a particular child had not been given.

Table 11-2 Instruments for Assessing Thinking and Feeling Behaviors

Instrument	Thinking				Feeling			
	Flu	Flx	Or	El	CU	RT	CO	Im
Torrance Tests of Creative Thinking (TTCT) - Verbal	X	X	X					
Torrance Tests of Creative Thinking (TTCT) - Figural	X		X	X				
Guilford Creativity Tests for Children	X	X	X	X				
Something About Myself (SAM)					X_2	X_1	X_2	X_2
What Kind of Person Are You? (WKOPAY)					X			X
Purdue Creativity Test	X	X	X					
How Do You Really Feel About Yourself?					X	X	X	X
Thinking Creatively With Sounds and Words	X	X	X	X				
Thinking Creatively Through Action and Movement	X	X	X	X				

[1]This behavior is assessed by the Self-Strength subscale.

[2]This behavior is assessed by the Intellectuality subscale.

After this testing, the next step was to compile all the testing and observational data on each child. If all data could be compiled on one form, interpretations could be made and instructional plans formulated without shuffling through hundreds of papers. Ms. Burnley examined each of the forms in the Williams (1972) kit. Most of these forms used the format of a bar graph based on percentile ranking or on the number of times a certain behavior was observed. However, if she chose to use these forms, Ms. Burnley would have two profiles for each child, one with observational data and one with standardized test data.

To facilitate her development of profiles, Ms. Burnley decided to use a modification of the *Baldwin Identification Matrix* (Baldwin & Wooster, 1977). (See Maker (1982), Chapter 8 for a more detailed description of the modified matrix.) As described in Maker (1982), the basic process to follow in using a matrix such as this is to develop first a system for weighting the scores for a class or group of children. These weights can be developed from national norms based on averages and standard deviations, or can be developed from class, school, or grade level averages. Weighted scores are somewhat similar to standard scores and give a rather crude way of comparing scores across several instruments.

In developing the matrix for her class, Ms. Burnley decided to use national norms for the standardized test data and class norms for the observational and peer referral data. (See Table 11-3.) She examined each test and the test manuals to determine the best way to develop a weighting system. If there were averages and standard deviations or percentile rankings, these were used as a basis for the weights. For example, the achievement test scores of her children were reported in percentiles. She used a ten-point range for each weighted score. For intelligence tests, the average of 100 and a standard deviation of 16 were used as the basis for weighting. With the observational data, she used the number of times observations were made (ten) multiplied by the greatest number of times a certain behavior had been observed in a child (four for thinking behaviors and two for feeling behaviors) to establish the ranges of possible scores. Weights were assigned based on these ranges. For example, the total number of observations multiplied by the maximum number of observations of flexibility ($10 \times 4 = 40$) gives a range of 0 to 40 for that behavior. Thus, each weighted score has a range of approximately four points. (See Table 11-3.) For the feeling behaviors, the range was 0 to 20. For the peer referral data, since there were ten students, the weighting system was simple. It was based entirely on the number of referrals each child received on each behavior. Table 11-3 gives the weighted scores and ranges for each of the tests Ms. Burnley used.

Next, the raw scores and weighted scores for each child were recorded on a bar-graph matrix. Figure 11-3 shows a profile for one child in the class, Brad G. On this profile, the different measures of behaviors are clustered together so that they can be analyzed for interpretation. There is also one bar that is an average score for that characteristic. In compiling the profiles, a person simply records the

Table 11-3 Ranges and Weights of Creativity Scores for Ms. Burnley's Class

Instrument and Behavior	Scores/Ranges/Weights									
	1	2	3	4	5	6	7	8	9	10
TTCT - Figural	21-36	37-52	53-68	69-84	85-100	101-116	117-132	133-148	149-164	165-180
Fluency	21-36	37-52	53-68	69-84	85-100	101-116	117-132	133-148	149-164	165-180
Originality	21-36	37-52	53-68	69-84	85-100	101-116	117-132	133-148	149-164	165-180
Elaboration	21-36	37-52	53-68	69-84	85-100	101-116	117-132	133-148	149-164	165-180
TTCT - Verbal	21-36	37-52	53-68	69-84	85-100	101-116	117-132	133-148	149-164	165-180
Fluency	21-36	37-52	53-68	69-84	85-100	101-116	117-132	133-148	149-164	165-180
Flexibility	21-36	37-52	53-68	69-84	85-100	101-116	117-132	133-148	149-164	165-180
Originality	21-36	37-52	53-68	69-84	85-100	101-116	117-132	133-148	149-164	165-180
How Do You Really...	0- 4	5- 9	10-14	15-19	20- 24	25- 29	30- 34	35- 39	40- 44	45- 50
Curiosity	0- 1	1.1-1.2	2.2-3.2	3.3-4.3	4.4-5.4	5.5-6.5	6.6-7.6	7.7-8.7	8.8-9.8	9.9- 11
Risk-Taking	0-1.2	1.3-2.5	2.6-3.8	3.9-5.1	5.2-6.4	6.5-8.9	7.8-9.0	9.1-10.3	10.4-11.6	11.7-13
Complexity	0-1.2	1.3-2.5	2.6-3.8	3.9-5.1	5.2-6.4	6.5-8.9	7.8-9.0	9.1-10.3	10.4-11.6	11.7-13
Imagination	0-1.1	1.2-2.3	2.4-3.5	3.6-4.7	4.8-5.9	6.0-7.1	7.2-8.3	8.4-9.5	9.6-10.7	10.8-12
SAM	0- 4	5- 9	10-14	15-19	20-24	25-29	30-34	35-39	40-44	45-50
Curiosity	0	1	2	3	4	5	6	7	8	9
Risk-Taking	1	2	3	4	5	6	7	8	9	10

Instrument and Behavior	Raw Scores with Ranges and Weights									
	1	2	3	4	5	6	7	8	9	10
Originality	1	2	3	4	5	6	7	8	9	10
Elaboration	1	2	3	4	5	6	7	8	9	10
Curiosity	1	2	3	4	5	6	7	8	9	10
Risk-Taking	1	2	3	4	5	6	7	8	9	10
Complexity	1	2	3	4	5	6	7	8	9	10
Imagination	1	2	3	4	5	6	7	8	9	10
Independence (Observation)	1-6	7-13	14-20	21-27	28-34	35-41	42-48	49-55	56-62	63-70
Intelligence	21-36	37-52	53-68	69-84	85-100	101-116	117-132	133-148	149-164	165-180
Achievement	0-9%	10%-19%	20%-29%	30%-39%	40%-49%	50%-59%	60%-69%	70%-79%	80%-89%	90%-100%
Science	0-9%	10%-19%	20%-29%	30%-39%	40%-49%	50%-59%	60%-69%	70%-79%	80%-89%	90%-100%
Reading	0-9%	10%-19%	20%-29%	30%-39%	40%-49%	50%-59%	60%-69%	70%-79%	80%-89%	90%-100%
Math	0-9%	10%-19%	20%-29%	30%-39%	40%-49%	50%-59%	60%-69%	70%-79%	80%-89%	90%-100%
Social Studies	0-9%	10%-19%	20%-29%	30%-39%	40%-49%	50%-59%	60%-69%	70%-79%	80%-89%	90%-100%
Self-Concept (Piers-Harris)	0-9%	10%-19%	20%-29%	30%-39%	40%-49%	50%-59%	60%-69%	70%-79%	80%-89%	90%-100%

Table 11-3 continued

Instrument and Behavior	Scores/Ranges/Weights									
	1	2	3	4	5	6	7	8	9	10
Complexity	0	1	2	3	4	5	6	7	8	9
Imagination	0	1	2	3	4	5	6	7	8	9
Observation										
Fluency	0-7	8-15	16-23	24-31	32-39	40-47	48-55	56-63	64-71	72-80
Flexibility	0-7	8-15	16-23	24-31	32-39	40-47	48-55	56-63	64-71	72-80
Originality	0-7	8-15	16-23	24-31	32-39	40-48	48-55	56-63	64-71	72-80
Elaboration	0-7	8-15	16-23	24-31	32-39	40-48	48-55	56-63	64-71	72-80
Curiosity	0-3	4- 9	8-11	12-15	16-19	20-23	24-27	28-31	32-35	36-40
Risk-Taking	0-3	4- 9	8-11	12-15	16-19	20-23	24-27	28-31	32-35	36-40
Complexity	0-3	4- 9	8-11	12-15	16-19	20-23	24-27	28-31	32-35	36-40
Imagination	0-3	4- 9	8-11	12-15	16-19	20-23	24-27	28-31	32-35	36-40

Instrument and Behavior	Raw Scores with Ranges and Weights									
	1	2	3	4	5	6	7	8	9	10
Peer Referral										
Fluency	1	2	3	4	5	6	7	8	9	10
Flexibility	1	2	3	4	5	6	7	8	9	10

Figure 11-3 Talent/Ability Profile Based on Williams's Model

Name   Brad G.   Date September 2, 1980   Age 12½

Thinking Behaviors

Ability/Procedure	Standard or Raw Score	Weighted Score									
		1	2	3	4	5	6	7	8	9	10
Fluency	6.75										
TTCT Figural	116										
TTCT Verbal	163										
Observation	33										
Peer Referral	7										
Flexibility	7.6										
TTCT Verbal	180										
Observation	47										
Peer Referral	7										
Originality	7.5										
TTCT Figural	130										
TTCT Verbal	150										
Observation	35										
Peer Referral	9										
Elaboration	3.6										
TTCT Figural	84										
Observation	26										
Peer Referral	3										

Ability/Procedure	Standard or Raw Score	Weighted Score									
		1	2	3	4	5	6	7	8	9	10
Curiosity	4										
SAM	2										
How Do You...	4										

Figure 11-3 continued

Feeling Behaviors

Ability/Procedure	Raw Score	Weighted Score
Observation	7	
Peer Referral	4	
Risk-Taking	7.8	
SAM	7	
How Do You...	10	
Observation	33	
Peer Referral	7	
Complexity	5.5	
SAM	4	
How Do You...	3	
Observation	8	
Peer Referral	1	
Imagination	3.2	
SAM	4	
How Do You...	3	
Observation	8	
Peer Referral	1	
Independence/Self-Direction	50	
Intelligence	150	

Thinking Behaviors

Ability/Procedure	Standard or Raw Score	Weighted Score 1	2	3	4	5	6	7	8	9	10
Achievement	9										
Science	98%ile										
Reading	88%ile										
Math	99%ile										
Social Studies	68%ile										
Self-Concept	88%ile										
Overall Average											

raw score from each measure, checks the table to find a weighted score for that raw score, and then records the weighted score by shading in all the boxes up to the end of that score.

When all assessment data had been compiled on her group, Ms. Burnley was ready to interpret the profiles and design educational programs for her children. She first looked at Brad G.'s profile.

Brad G.'s strong areas are in the thinking behaviors, particularly in verbal ability. He is a high risk-taker, but is rather low in imagination and curiosity. He is highly intelligent, has a high self-concept, and is independent and self-directed. Since Ms. Burnley's philosophy is to build on both the strengths and weaknesses of her children and to use their strong areas to build on the weaker areas, she needed to design a unique plan for each individual. She needed to encourage the development of Brad's imagination and curiosity through his verbal thinking behaviors while allowing and encouraging his independence.

Since Brad G. fits the profile of a "highly able" child as discussed by Williams (1972), Ms. Burnley began with Williams's suggestions. She started with the strategy of "exploring discrepant events" and attempted to interest Brad in a self-directed investigation of some event. This would allow him to use his independence and risk taking by working on his own, and would hopefully stimulate his curiosity through exploration of "discrepant" events.

She then consulted the idea book (Williams, 1970) for some ideas. The table at the beginning of the book provides a listing of ideas classified according to the thinking or feeling processes developed in the lesson, the content area, and the strategy used. Since Brad's major interests were in the science and math areas, she checked the listing for curiosity, discrepancies, and science. She found many ideas listed, but first chose Idea 171 (p. 98) because it combined several recommended strategies, was designed for middle grades, and would be of interest to Brad. She decided to try Ideas 272, 300, and 308 later if he did not become interested in questions posed in the first strategy.

The initial questions were posed to the entire group. Ms. Burnley asked the children to wonder and make guesses about what might happen if the following took place:

- the cycle of ocean tides would change every week.
- the cycle of seasons would not follow each other as we know them now; i.e., winter, summer, spring, fall, etc.
- the cycle of sunrise in the morning would reverse and instead rise at dusk.
- months on the calendar would switch around annually so December might occur in June and September in February, etc.
- birds would fly south in the spring instead of fall. (p. 98)

After they had spent some time speculating about what might happen in each of these situations, the teacher asked students to think of as many cycles as they could that affect people's lives, to speculate about some possible consequences of changes in these cycles, and to think about what effect such changes might have on people's lives. The following day, they discussed the ideas each student had listed. All were given the opportunity to study further about some topic of interest to them.

When Ms. Burnley talked with Brad individually, he said that he was not particularly interested in cycles in nature, but that he was interested in cycles in people, particularly biorhythmic cycles. He wanted to know if he could begin a study of biorhythms. This was fine with his teacher. She suggested that he first spend some time thinking about the topic and what he wanted to know. He was to do some reading, talk to people, and develop a list of as many questions as he could (curiosity and fluency) about the topic.

Ms. Burnley allowed Brad to work completely on his own, released from the class to use the library when necessary. Several days later, Brad said that he would like to show her his list of questions. He had developed several pages of questions that were interesting to him. To assist Brad with his project and to develop further his skills of search, Ms. Burnley helped him develop a chart listing his questions and some possible sources for answers. He could work further on the list on his own. She would then need to assist Brad in developing a plan for a realistic study. Since she was familiar with Brad and others like him, she knew that he would develop a complicated and involved project. Her hardest task would be to help him design a manageable, realistic project that would still be of interest to him.

About a week later, Brad came back with his list of questions and sources. He was excited about his success so far, and he was determined to answer *every single question*. First, Mrs. Burnley tried to encourage Brad to select only one or two questions to answer. When he insisted that it was important to answer them all, she then suggested that he at least decide upon an order for answering them. He should look at the list to determine which questions needed to be answered before he could even attempt the next one. This seemed like a good idea to Brad, so he went off on his quest for answers. The first step for him was to use all the library resources at school since these were the easiest to get. After reading all of these, he then went back to Ms. Burnley for help.

At this point, Ms. Burnley knew that Brad had developed genuine interest in his topic and that soon she would not be able to help him herself, so she began to look for someone interested in the topic who might be willing to spend some time with Brad. She first checked with the other teachers, then looked at the interest survey she had conducted of the parents of her children. One parent had listed biorhythms as a hobby, so she contacted the parent and made arrangements for Brad to work with him. This setup worked well for a while, but soon the parent came to Ms. Burnley and suggested that she find someone with a more scientific interest since

Brad apparently wanted to do some experiments. Together they located a biologist who was doing some research on biorhythms and was willing to assist Brad in doing some of his research in return for Brad's assisting him with his study. This was exciting to Brad because he would be working with a real scientist in a real lab.

During the time that Brad was working with the scientist, Ms. Burnley arranged occasional conferences so that she could assist when necessary and provide guidance if needed. When Brad completed his research, she suggested that he write a report for submission to a journal. This seemed like a great idea to Brad who was always willing to try something new. He also wanted to present his research to some other students, so Ms. Burnley thought this might be a good opportunity to encourage his imagination. She agreed to arrange for a presentation if he would accept a challenge: to write a science fiction story incorporating some of the information he had gained about biorhythms. Brad accepted the challenge and was again off on his own to work.

In this example, the teacher has followed a step-by-step process leading to the implementation of an individualized plan for developing creative behaviors in her students. The process she followed and the tasks at each step are summarized in Table 11-4. Since the student's role is the same throughout, the student roles are not listed in this table as in other chapters. It is important to point out in this example that the teacher should be careful when guiding the independent work of her students. Most importantly, teachers should be aware of students' skills in self-direction and give guidance whenever it is needed. In giving this guidance, however, they must make suggestions, not commands. Children must realize their own limitations, and then must be allowed to make their own decisions. The teacher can encourage the development of realistic or creative products, and can encourage a realistic study. However, if students insist on a project the teacher feels will be too complicated, they should be allowed to attempt it whether they succeed or fail.

MODIFICATION OF BASIC CURRICULUM

Process Modifications

The Williams model suggests some modifications of the curriculum to make it more appropriate for gifted students. The major changes are in the area of process, that is, open-endedness, the use of a discovery approach, freedom of choice, and use of a variety of methods. Perhaps the most important modification is open-endedness. More than any other model, except perhaps Taba's, Williams's approach incorporates open-ended, provocative questions and learning experiences. Several of the teaching strategies, (for example, paradoxes, discrepancies, provocative questions, and tolerance for ambiguity) directly address this aspect of teaching

Table 11-4 Summary of Steps and Teacher Roles in Implementing Williams's Teaching Strategies for Thinking and Feeling

Steps	Teacher Role	Activities
1. Determine the characteristic behavior of each child.	observer; tester	Make observations of each child over a period of time in a variety of settings. Develop procedures for compiling observational data. Supplement observational data with tests and other procedures such as sociometric (peer referral) data.
2. Develop a profile of creative behavior for each child.	record-keeper	Develop or locate a system useful for recording a variety of data on each child. Develop a table of weighted scores for the group. Develop a matrix of talents and abilities. Compare each child to herself as well as to the group.
3. Interpret each profile and develop a generalized ap-	test interpreter	Look carefully at the various measures to determine whether there are definite strengths and weaknesses or whether the child's abilities are somewhat even.

		Determine areas of content interest that could be used to develop creative strengths or weaknesses. Determine the level of self-direction for each child through observation or trial and error. Develop an approach that develops weaknesses through strengths and interests using strategies appropriate for highly able children.
proach for each child.		
4. Select or create teaching strategies to use with the group as well as with individual children.	developer; selector; facilitator	Find ideas from the idea book that can be used as they are or modified. Develop new ideas using the lesson mapping procedure.

methods for the gifted. These strategies require that teachers develop and pose open-ended, stimulating, and challenging questions that could easily interest a gifted student.

Although not addressed quite as directly as the concept of open-endedness, a discovery approach is present in most of the teaching strategies in the model. Most of the ideas included place the teacher in the role of a questioner and the student in the role of the discoverer. The biggest difference between this and traditional discovery approaches is that in the Williams strategies the teacher usually encourages students to "discover" as many ideas (or solutions or principles) as possible rather than discovering a particular idea or principle. Williams also suggests freedom of choice, particularly for the highly able students, by allowing students to choose an area of study and to develop an original product based on that study. The final process modification is suggesting a great variety of methods. Since there are 18 different strategies to be used in any content area to encourage eight different behaviors (resulting in a slightly different "twist" to each activity), the result is a great deal of variety in teaching strategies. This should help decrease the possibility that gifted students will become bored.

Content and Product Modifications

In the areas of content and products, the model suggests three modifications. Two of the strategies, organized random search and the skills of search, concentrate on methods used by professionals. In the first strategy, students are taught to use a particular method or structure, and to apply it to a different situation, thereby creating something new. In the second, skills of search, students learn various methods that are used by professionals and learn how to apply them. A third strategy is also appropriate and important to use with gifted students—the study of creative people and creative processes. This aspect of creativity, the study of real people and how they were creative, is important to show students the more personal side of creativity. Since they are likely to be the creators of the future, the study of other eminent individuals may facilitate their success or at least help them adjust to it.

The one product modification suggested by the model is not quite as clear-cut as the content modifications. In one section of the program, Williams suggests that highly able children be allowed to "go off on their own" to develop their creative products. He recommends that the teacher make certain that the final project as a product of independent study "goes further" than a report that is turned in for a grade. The examples of acceptable products (for example, a child's book, an art piece, a research report for a journal, or a film) all seem to be transformations rather than summaries. Although he does not address the aspects of audiences and problems, the products recommended are sophisticated.

Learning Environment Modifications

With respect to the learning environment, Williams suggests aspects of all the changes recommended for the gifted. He suggests the development of a student-centered, independent, open, accepting learning environment by providing a list of ways teachers can both directly and indirectly develop children's creativity. The indirect ways constitute most of those related to the environment, but some of the direct ones can be considered dimensions of the environment. The following recommendations are listed under the environmental dimensions to which they seem to relate most directly.

Student-Centered

- Maintain an attitude of learning with the children. Do not profess to know all the answers, and be willing to explore student ideas.
- Treat the questions and ideas of children with a great deal of respect, and keep the emphasis on "rightness" or "correctness" to a minimum.

Independence

- Allow children opportunities to help plan projects that involve their environment, such as decorating the room and improving the playground.
- Provide a period of time each day for working with a small group of children, and encourage them to plan the use of the time.
- Have a suggestion box for students to tell how they would like the classroom improved.
- Encourage (and even demand) achievement and accomplishment, but only in areas chosen by the student.
- Respect the children, and show that you are confident they will act appropriately and responsibly.
- Avoid allowing overdependency or appearing to reject the child.
- Allow each child to progress at his or her own pace without showing anxious concern about the development of skills and abilities.
- Provide a safe psychological environment that is available to the child when needed, but allow and encourage the child to venture away from it.

Openness

- Be playful, and encourage fantasy and imagination rather than always "bringing them back to reality," even if the task was serious.
- Allow children a free period of time each day to use as they please.

- Show that you believe each child is unique and capable of becoming or being a creative individual.
- Allow noise and messiness in the classroom. Quiet and orderly classrooms do not ensure that learning and creativity are taking place.

Accepting

- When children have new ideas, talk and listen to them in a sensitive manner, sometimes encouraging them to go further with their ideas.
- Listen carefully to children, and attempt to "see things through their eyes."
- Give children honest approval when they produce a product or develop an idea.
- Challenge students by discussing reality, but stimulate them with fantasy.
- Recognize that each child's creative production may be new to him or her even though you may have seen it millions of times.

The environmental dimensions of complexity and high mobility are discussed by Williams mainly in conjunction with his recommendations for the handling of gifted children who are developing independent projects. With regard to complexity, for example, he has compiled a glossary of curriculum materials for use by both students and teachers. This *Media Resource Book* is a part of the *Total Creativity Program* (Williams, 1972), and contains lists of films, filmstrips, audio- and videotapes, and other multimedia devices that can serve as aids to students involved in individualized study.

To assist students in independent study, Williams also recommends that the learning environment be as flexible as possible to allow movement within the classroom and outside. This includes releasing students to work with children from other classrooms and releasing them for certain periods of time each week to work on their own in the library, resource room, or with an expert from outside the school. Children should also be allowed to search for and use media that will assist them in developing their products.

MODIFYING THE APPROACH

Content Changes

To make Williams's model a more comprehensive approach for use with the gifted, content, product, and process changes need to be incorporated or added by combining this model with others. The areas of greatest weakness are content and product. With the exception of variety, content changes needed by the Williams model could be accomplished by combining his approach with that of Bruner.

Bruner's ideas about the use of abstract, complex generalizations to organize content could be used since Williams suggests use of traditional content areas, but does not provide guidelines for structuring them. This kind of organization would be most appropriate when designing group activities in which all or some of the children would participate. Individuals could then investigate topics related to the group activity or choose those that are completely unrelated. Complete freedom in individual study would be necessary, but the teacher should provide some group activities.

In the example presented earlier, the group activity involving the posing of "what if" questions from science could be used to develop the following abstract, complex generalization: *Many phenomena in nature, as well as those created by humans, follow a rhythmic cycle that is repeated in predictable time periods. If this cycle is disrupted, the organism or phenomenon may not function adequately.* This generalization integrates content from the traditional disciplines of biology, physics, psychology, medicine, sociology, and anthropology. Many of Williams's teaching strategies can be used to develop this idea and to stimulate creativity at the same time. For example, using strategy nine, skills of search, students could list all the ways they could find out about cycles in the different disciplines. Using strategy twelve, teaching for adjustment rather than development, students could think of ways they could change their lives to meet a situation where the pattern of seasons is different from the accustomed one (for example, moving to a country south of the equator, living on the equator, or living in the Southwest rather than the Northeast). They could also discuss how living organisms have changed their natural cycles in order to survive. Many other similar activities could be developed with this abstract idea as the organizer.

To ensure that the content presented in the gifted program is different from that learned in the regular program, an analysis of the curriculum should be conducted. Using key concepts and generalizations as the organizers, a process such as that described in Chapters 2 and 8 can be followed.

Process Changes

Even though the Williams model makes many of the process changes appropriate for the gifted, the modifications of proof/reasoning, group interaction, and pacing are not provided directly by the model. Asking students to provide support for their ideas or explanations of their reasoning could easily be incorporated into most of the strategies. It is important, however, that, in asking these "why" questions, the teacher does not inhibit the children's creativity. To avoid this, the strategy recommended for Taba's *Application of Generalizations Strategy* could be used. In this strategy, students list their predictions using a brainstorming format so that a variety of ideas can be expressed. After all of the ideas have been listed, the teacher asks for reasons why the predictions were made. Such a procedure would be appropriate for Williams's strategies of attributes, analogies, discrepancies, habit, tolerance for ambiguity, the study of creative people, and evaluating situations. All these strategies involve reasoning and also have an emphasis on a quantity of ideas. In certain other strategies (for example, para-doxes, provocative questions, change), "why" questions have already been included. In others (for example, visualization, creative writing, creative reading, creative listening, intuitive expression), asking for reasons would be inappropriate in many cases. In other strategies, depending on the activity, asking for reasons might also be inappropriate.

Activities in which gifted students interact with each other and then discuss their participation is another process change that needs to be made when using the strategies for thinking and feeling with the gifted. Some strategies that could easily lend themselves to this kind of activity are the following: attributes; examples of habit; and intuitive expression. Using the attributes strategy, students can list the attributes of good leaders, good group members, good followers, or any other role that can be assumed in a group. These attributes can then form the basis of observations of group activity. An interesting activity using the examples of habit strategy could be to have the students watch for evidence of habit-bound thinking and observe its effect on group interaction. The methods used in the strategy of intuitive expression suggest observing groups to detect their emotions and record different ways of expressing certain emotions. Students can also observe the effect of these emotions on the group's interaction.

The element of pacing is perhaps less important with this model than with some others because of the nature of the strategies. Since there is seldom any "presenta-tion of new information" but rather questions and provocative activities, teachers do not have to be concerned with how rapidly new information is presented to students. However, they do need to be aware of how quickly group activities must move. Many of the strategies recommended for use with the gifted involve individual investigations, so the teacher must allow students to pace themselves.

Product Changes

Three of the product modifications appropriate for the gifted are not suggested by Williams, but were incorporated into the example presented earlier in this chapter. In the example, the teacher began by presenting students with several provocative questions designed to stimulate their interest in the topic area of cycles. When one student expressed interest in biorhythms, the teacher encour-aged this interest and assisted the student in identifying areas of interest within this general area. She suggested that the student gather information and then make a list of questions he would like to have answered about the topic. Various other strategies were used, including finding an expert who was willing to work with the student in the area of interest. When the student had progressed far enough to begin thinking about a product, the teacher suggested both a journal article and a science fiction story. These are products that would be directed toward real audiences. To extend the activity further and also incorporate realistic evaluation, the teacher could have had the student develop criteria for evaluating each product. The products could then have been assessed by several individuals: the student, a panel of peers acting as a particular audience, and finally, the real audience itself. After each evaluation, the student should have been encouraged to revise his product to make it more effective.

Summary

The Williams *Teaching Strategies for Thinking and Feeling* make many of the process and all of the learning environment modifications presented as appropriate for the gifted. To use the model as a comprehensive curriculum development plan for the gifted, however, requires certain changes or combining the model with another complementary one. Williams's model could easily be combined with Bruner's approach, with the Renzulli *Triad* (Williams, 1979), or with the Taba *Strategies*.

DEVELOPMENT

Because he does not believe that hierarchical models of human development are accurate representations of intelligence and its development, Williams (1971a) designed a morphological model that shows child behavior, teaching strategies, and content as interrelated parts of a whole. Strongly influenced by Guilford, Williams adapted this model of human intelligence to make it more appropriate for use in classrooms. Since Guilford's model was not intended for use in curriculum planning and since it did not include affective factors, a new model was needed. Combining his knowledge of the research on creativity and studies of teaching with his experience with children and the structure of Guilford's model, Williams developed his model. The first version included 23 strategies, but after field testing, the number of strategies was reduced to 18 to avoid overlap and repetition. This field testing occurred as an aspect of the National Schools Project (Williams, 1972). Based on this project, the *Total Creativity Program* (1972) was developed.

RESEARCH ON EFFECTIVENESS

Most of the research reported (Williams, 1972) deals mainly with the practicality of the approach. Williams reports that teachers can and do use the strategies, and that they can effectively design learning activities using the model as a structure for generating them. Teachers trained in the use of the strategies can recognize situations in which the strategies are used more accurately than those who have not received training (Williams, 1971b). Based on the results of the National Schools Project, Williams (1972) also lists the following components of effective inservice training for schools wishing to implement the *Total Creativity Program:*

- Administrators and teachers should be involved together as a team.
- The total staff should be involved in the training process.
- Training must not be conducted at the end of a school day.
- A competent trainer who is familiar with the rationale and theory of the model and with the demands of teaching is a must. If a local individual can conduct at least some of the training in between visits from an outside consultant, the effectiveness of the training is enhanced.
- Training must be conducted over a reasonable period of time (for example, one to two years) in order to be effective.
- There must be some evaluation of the effectiveness of the training.

During the field testing of the Williams model, an analysis was made of the types of strategies designed and used by teachers. The greatest numbers of lesson ideas (out of a total of 251) were designed to develop curiosity (51), original thinking (48), and flexible thinking (43). Fewer were designed to develop imagination (36), elaborative thinking (24), and fluent thinking (23). The smallest numbers were designed to develop complexity (14) and risk taking (12).

The types of strategies used most frequently were also analyzed by grade levels (primary, middle, and upper). It is interesting to compare this analysis of the five most-used teaching strategies to a listing of the strategies recommended most for use with highly able children. Only one of the seven strategies recommended for highly able children (provocative questions) appeared in the top five used by primary teachers. Two (evaluating situations and skills of search) were included in the top five used in the middle grades, and three recommended strategies (discrepancies, evaluating situations, and skills of search) were included in the top five used by upper-grade teachers. Three of the recommended strategies (examples of change, tolerating ambiguity, and development rather than adjustment) were neither included in the top five used by many of the teachers nor were they included in the top ten used by primary teachers. It seems that even the teachers who participate in training programs such as these need practice in designing and using activities that will be challenging to the gifted students in their classrooms.

In a correlational study (Williams, 1979a), students chosen from gifted programs in four large schools were classified into four groups based on their scores on identification instruments and checklists, and then they were given additional instruments to assess the four affective and four cognitive behaviors in the

Williams model. The four initial groups were the following: (1) *cognitive-convergent* (those who scored highest on measures such as IQ and achievement tests); (2) *cognitive-divergent* (those who scored highest on measures of learning and creativity characteristics; (3) *affective-convergent* (those who scored highest on tests of self-concept), and (4) *affective-divergent* (those who scored highest on motivational characteristics). The following three instruments were administered to these students: (1) the *Drawing Test of Creative Thinking* (Williams, 1979b); (2) the *How Do You Really Feel About Yourself Inventory* (HDYRFAY) (Williams, 1979b); and (3) the *Williams Scale* (Williams, 1979b). Correlations of the scores showed what might be expected. Children selected for their high scores on the cognitive- or affective-*divergent* measures generally performed better on the tests of behaviors included in the Williams model. The greatest differences between groups two and four divergent, and one and three convergent were in the better performance of groups two and four on flexible and original thinking as well as curiosity and imagination.

This research indicates what should already be clear to most individuals who are selecting children for gifted programs: those who are highly intelligent will not necessarily be high in creativity characteristics, particularly flexibility, originality, curiosity, and imagination. A second conclusion is equally self-evident: tests of divergent thinking test the ability to think or act divergently better than convergent tests. Even though these results seem self-evident, many programs have been found in which students are selected for a creativity program based on IQ and achievement. An important finding of the research, however, that certainly merits further study is that the affective-divergent groups also scored higher on most of the cognitive measures than the cognitive- and affective-convergent groups. Since educators seldom use affective measures, these data indicate that more frequent use would be justified.

JUDGMENTS

Advantages

The Williams (1972) *Total Creativity Program* has several advantages. The first and perhaps most important is its unique combination of thinking and feeling behaviors. No other approach discussed in this book, with the possible exception of Renzulli's, recognizes in its procedures the major role the affective domain plays in learning, producing, and thinking. This is the only approach that includes the development of affective characteristics involved in creativity. A second related advantage is that the model concentrates on a specific and well-defined set of behaviors. These are observable, measurable behaviors derived from research on the characteristics of creative productive adults.

Another strength of this model is its emphasis on open-endedness of learning experiences and teacher questions. As discussed earlier, several of the strategies directly address this concept through both open-endedness and provocativeness. None of the other approaches discussed in this section provides such helpful guidelines in the development of learning experiences that satisfy this requirement.

The Williams model also advocates an individualized approach, including assessment and observation of thinking and feeling behaviors, compilation of information, interpretation of profiles, and design of both individual and group learning experiences based on the needs of the children. Not only does the program advocate an individualized approach, but it also provides teachers with aids and practical tools. Tests and observational procedures have been developed and are readily available for pre- and postassessment of creative behaviors. A variety of practical materials are available for implementing the approach, including an idea book and an inservice kit for self-study or group study. (See the resource list at the end of this chapter for descriptions of these materials.)

Disadvantages

There are also several disadvantages to the Williams model. First of all, even though the strategies and the total approach have been field-tested in a variety of classrooms, no research is reported on the effectiveness of the strategies. In effect, there is no research to indicate that if teachers do all 18 strategies and attempt to develop the eight behaviors in their students they will actually increase the students' creative behaviors. Data on the effectiveness of the strategies should have been relatively easy to collect during the field testing, but the only data available are on the elements necessary for effective inservice and the frequency of use of the strategies. Data on student gains are conspicuously absent.

A second disadvantage of the model is its lack of empirical or logical "power." The model itself was not derived from a particular theoretical position or set of theoretical principles. Even though it is stated that the Williams model was derived from Guilford's *Structure of Intellect* model of human intelligence, the only resemblance it bears to this theoretical base is that it is morphological or integrated rather than hierarchical. The thinking behaviors of fluency, flexibility, originality, and elaboration are concepts first developed by Guilford (1967) as part of his definition of divergent thinking, but are not a major part of his model of intelligence. It could be argued that the subject matter in Williams's model is comparable to the content of Guilford's, the teaching strategies compare to the processes, and the pupil behaviors parallel the products. However, the individual items included in these facets do not appear to be related to those in Guilford's at all.

Another weakness of the approach is its lack of comprehensiveness as a total approach. It was not developed for use in gifted programs, but as a way to develop creativity in all children. Indeed, Williams advocates using his and other models popular in gifted programs to improve education for all children (Williams, 1980). Even though its emphasis on specific behaviors is an advantage, its concentration on a limited range of behaviors is a disadvantage. The development of divergent thinking and feeling is not enough. Educators must develop a whole range of thinking and feeling behaviors in their gifted children, including divergent ones. For this reason and the fact that only two of the content modifications and one of the product modifications appropriate for the gifted are addressed by the approach, the Williams model must be combined with other models to form a comprehensive program for gifted students.

CONCLUSIONS

Just as the other approaches discussed in this book, Frank Williams's model does not provide a comprehensive program for curriculum development for gifted students. However, it offers certain unique features that highly recommend its use in programs for the gifted. The process modifications, individualization, and concentration on the cognitive and affective behaviors necessary for creativity development would be ample justification for its use as a component in a program for the gifted.

If readers decide to implement this approach, however, they are urged to develop procedures for assessing the effectiveness of the strategies, since such data are not available. Use of the needs assessment instruments for evaluation of progress is strongly advised, as is comparison of this method with others to determine the most effective strategies for use with gifted children.

RESOURCES

Background Information

Williams, F.E. *A total creativity program for individualizing and humanizing the learning process: Identifying and measuring creative potential* (Vol. I). Englewood Cliffs, NJ: Educational Technology Publications, 1972; Williams, F.E. *A total creativity program for individualizing and humanizing the learning process: Identifying and measuring creative potential* (Vol. II). Englewood Cliffs, NJ: Educational Technology Publications, 1972. The main purpose of the *Total Creativity Program* developed by Frank Williams is to give teachers useful, concrete activities for encouraging and developing creativity through the basic disciplines. The kit does not require expensive materials or major alterations in the classroom, but can be easily adapted to everyday classroom use. It is a multimedia approach using posters, worksheets, cassettes, and two books. There is an instructor's manual. The program can be utilized in three separate ways: (1) by a trainer of teachers, (2) by participants in a training program; or (3) by a teacher in the classroom. The two books included in the kit, which discuss the identification and development of creative potential, are primarily for the first two purposes. The total program also includes the idea book described in the following section along with a booklet of media resources for developing creativity.

Instructional Materials and Ideas

Williams, F.E. *Classroom ideas for encouraging thinking and feeling* (2nd ed.). Buffalo, NY; D.O.K. Publishers, 1970. Too often in the classroom, the processes of inquiry, discovery, and creative problem solving are discouraged or ignored. Frank Williams has included in this book more than 380 ideas to encourage those skills that are so often neglected. The model on which the activities are based is presented in the introduction. It develops eight behaviors in both the cognitive and affective domains, the major curriculum areas, and 18 classroom teaching strategies. Each idea has a specific skill as an objective, which is stated at the beginning of the activity. Also included is the subject matter that the idea employs. The teaching strategies are listed and then followed with a brief description of the activity. Two indexes are given for locating specific activities, one by processes delineated in the model and the other by curriculum subject. There are primary and upper-grade sections.

Chapter 12

Developing a Comprehensive Approach

The previous chapters have presented a thorough review of each of 11 teaching-learning models currently used in and appropriate for use in developing a curriculum for gifted students. No one model by itself provides a comprehensive approach, and no model by itself should be *expected* to be a comprehensive approach. The majority of the models reviewed were not developed for use in gifted programs. Most were developed for some specific, well-defined purpose, but educators have used them in a variety of different ways, some appropriate and many inappropriate. The biggest problem seems to be that educators assume that by using one particular teaching-learning model as the basis for a curriculum, all the needs of the gifted students in that program will be met.

Bloom's *Taxonomy,* for example, was developed for the narrow purpose of *classifying educational objectives,* according to their complexity, as a way to facilitate communication among professionals about the objectives of instruction. It was never intended as a framework for developing a sequence of questions to guide a discussion, and it certainly was not intended to form the basis of curriculum development for the gifted. Yet, it has been used in too many instances as the *only* curricular modification provided for gifted students. The same is true of Williams's and Guilford's models. Although the Williams strategies were developed as ways to stimulate a narrow range of human behaviors (for example, the thinking and feeling behaviors involved in creativity) and Guilford's model was developed as a theory to explain human intelligence, both of these approaches are used by educators as their *only* curriculum development models for programs for the gifted.

Thus it is important that readers and the authors of the models interpret the comments in this section that involve the assessment of the comprehensiveness of models as an honest attempt to show how a comprehensive curriculum can be developed. Rather than recommending that educators ''start all over again'' with new models or new approaches, beginning with what exists and moving forward from that point is more effective. For instance, if a program has used Bloom's *Taxonomy* as a basis for curriculum development, then, rather than throwing it out and learning a different approach, a better approach would be to build on the previous program, adding a complementary model or adding components to Bloom's approach.

Any criticism perceived is criticism of the large-scale adoption of certain approaches by educators rather than criticism of the authors of the models (unless, of course, they have advocated the use of their model as a sole approach to education of the gifted). Authors have generally been clear about the goals of their models and the reasons for their development, but educators have often ignored the underlying assumptions made by the developers and have used the models for many purposes not included in the intent.

Certainly, not every teacher or program developer will wish to develop a curriculum in which *all* the modifications recommended in this and the companion volume (Maker, 1982) are incorporated. The number and range of curricular modifications needed in a program will depend on the characteristics of the students. All the recommended curricular changes were designed to *build on and extend the present and potential future characteristics of gifted students.* Thus, if the students in a particular program do not possess the characteristics that the curricular change was designed to enhance, this particular curricular modification would not be necessary unless it is seen as a way to *develop* a particular characteristic that is not present but is desirable. In addition, other curricular modifications not discussed in this volume may be necessary or desirable because of different characteristics of the gifted students in the program.

CURRICULUM DEVELOPMENT

In developing a curriculum for the gifted, Maker (1982) suggests a multifaceted process including the following: (a) involvement of the key individuals who assess the situation in assisting in development of goals and in program development; (b) development of a definition of giftedness; (c) assessment of the needs of the students; (d) development of a philosophy; (e) development of program goals; (f) choice of teaching-learning models; (g) development of objectives and strategies; (h) development of evaluation procedures; and (i) development of a plan for implementing the curriculum. Space does not permit an explanation of this process since it has been adequately described elsewhere. This discussion will assume that program goals have been developed that include the provision of curricular modifications in all the aspects of content, process, product, and learning environment recommended by Maker (1982) and briefly outlined in Chapter 1 of this volume.

When choosing the teaching-learning models that will form the basis of a curriculum for the gifted, the first step is to assess the appropriateness of the existing models for the particular situation. A checklist and questions for this purpose have been presented in Chapter 1. (See Figure 1-1.) Each individual familiar with the situation and the models should evaluate the models and compare their ratings to determine those which would be potentially appropriate for the program. A second assessment should then be made to determine the model's comprehensiveness for providing needed modifications of the curriculum. A worksheet designed for this purpose was also presented in Chapter 1. (See Figure 1-2.)

ASSESSING THE MODELS

To assist the reader in assessing the comprehensiveness of the teaching-learning models presented in this volume, the worksheet presented in Figure 1-2 has been completed. (See Figure 12-1.) This assessment provides a summary of material presented in the "Modifications of the Basic Curriculum" section in each chapter describing a model. Those who do not understand why a particular assessment was made should review this section in the appropriate chapter. All evaluations are based on whether the model makes direct, specific suggestions regarding how to implement a particular curricular adaptation. Some models indirectly address an idea, but do not include specific suggestions. In these cases the model is not listed as making that particular curriculum change.

The column totals in Figure 12-1 provide a summary of the comprehensiveness of the models by giving the total number of modifications provided. As can be seen, the most comprehensive overall are Parnes, Renzulli, Taba, Taylor, Williams, and Treffinger. However, no model makes more than 17 out of the 25 total modifications. The pattern of checkmarks should also be examined to determine the areas of strength and weakness for each approach. Bruner's approach, for instance, although not one of the most comprehensive in overall ratings, provides most of the content changes needed. Taba's model, although not the most comprehensive overall, provides more of the process changes than any other approach. This information is useful in helping decide which models can be combined or used together.

A third source of information in the worksheet is the row totals. These totals indicate the number of available models that provide a particular curricular modification. Fewer models provide for content changes, while all except one provide for the process modification of emphasis on higher levels of thinking. Two of the modifications are made by only one model. This information can be helpful in suggesting the range of options available for making a certain curricular adaptation.

Figure 12-1 Sample Worksheet for Overall Curriculum Design (Worksheet #5b: Evaluation of Models)

Rate each model on each criterion by placing a √ in the column if the modification is made by the model. If not, leave space blank.

Curricular Modifications		Bruner	Bloom	Krathwohl	Parnes	Renzulli	Taba	Kohlberg	Taylor	Williams	Guilford	Treffinger	TOTALS	Comments
Content Modification	1. Abstractness	√	√				√	√			√		5	
	2. Complexity	√	√				√	√			√		5	
	3. Variety		√	√			√	√	√	√	√	√	8	
	4. Organization							√			√		2	
	5. Economy							√			√		2	
	6. Study of People							√					1	
	7. Methods	√	√	√	√	√	√	√			√		8	
Process Modification	8. Higher Levels of Thinking	√	√	√	√	√	√	√	√	√	√	√	10	
	9. Open-Endedness	√	√	√	√	√		√	√	√	√	√	9	
	10. Discovery	√		√	√	√		√	√	√		√	6	
	11. Proof/Reasoning	√						√					2	
	12. Freedom of Choice			√		√	√	√				√	5	
	13. Group Interaction						√	√					2	
	14. Pacing										√		1	
	15. Variety			√		√		√	√	√	√	√	7	

Curricular Modifications

		Bruner	Bloom	Krathwohl	Parnes	Renzulli	Taba	Kohlberg	Taylor	Williams	Guilford	Treffinger	TOTALS	Comments
Product Modifications	16. Real Problems	✓			✓	✓			✓			✓	5	
	17. Real Audiences				✓	✓						✓	2	
	18. Realistic Evaluation		✓		✓	✓			✓		✓	✓	5	
	19. Transformation	✓			✓	✓	✓	✓	✓	✓	✓	✓	9	
Learning Environment Modifications	20. Student-Centered				✓	✓	✓	✓	✓	✓		✓	7	
	21. Independence				✓	✓	✓	✓	✓	✓		✓	7	
	22. Open				✓	✓	✓	✓	✓	✓		✓	7	
	23. Accepting				✓	✓	✓	✓	✓			✓	6	
	24. Complex									✓		✓	2	
	25. High Mobility					✓				✓		✓	3	
	TOTALS	10	6	2	14	17	12	16	14	14	8	14		

CHOOSING MODELS

After the appropriateness and comprehensiveness of the different models have been assessed, the individual must decide whether to adopt one approach as the basis for curriculum development and modify it so that it is comprehensive, to adopt two or more approaches that are complementary, or to adapt *and* adopt. Certainly any one of these three options would be appropriate, depending on the situation. If, for example, an earlier assessment showed that only one approach was evaluated highly by those involved (based on its appropriateness, flexibility/adaptability, practicality, and validity), this approach should form the basis of the program. Modifications could then be made to improve its comprehensiveness. In most cases, however, several models would be acceptable, allowing a range of options for different purposes. Combining several models also ensures that variety will be an important aspect of the curriculum and that curricular modifications will be made in more ways than one.

Perhaps the most effective strategy would be to employ a combination of options, that is, adopt complementary models and adapt each of them to form a comprehensive approach. With this strategy equal emphasis would be placed on each curricular modification, and the possibility that a well-integrated program will result is increased.

To assist the reader in this task, tables have been developed that summarize for each model the curricular modifications that need to be added, the suggested changes, and the other models that could be combined with it to provide a particular change. In the column providing a list of other models that can be used with the approach it is not suggested that *all* these models be used, but that they are all possibilities. In each separate section describing modifications of the model, particular models have been recommended as the most effective complementary ones.

The information presented in each of these tables is a summary of the "Modifying the Approach" section of Chapters 2 through 11. Not all suggestions from each chapter have been listed. Only a representative listing has been made. Learning environment modifications have not been listed since they are essentially the same in most cases and their presentation would have been repetitious. The tables are only to assist the reader by providing a quick summary. When actually implementing the approaches, the individual chapters should be reviewed.

Bloom

Bloom's *Taxonomy* was not developed as a structure for curriculum development for the gifted. It was intended as a system for classifying educational objectives to facilitate communication among educators. To use Bloom's *Taxonomy* as a comprehensive approach to curriculum development, a variety of adaptations in content, process, and product dimensions of the curriculum must be made. (See Table 12-1.) None of the learning environment changes have been addressed by the approach, so combination with other models or adaptation is also necessary in this dimension. The major changes are teaching the taxonomy to students and beginning activities at the application level. The taxonomy can be combined or used in conjunction with most of the other models reviewed. For further information, see Chapter 2.

Bruner

Although Bruner's approach was not designed specifically for use with the gifted, it was intended as a model for curriculum design. As such, it makes adaptations in many areas that are recommended for the gifted. The major modifications needed to make Bruner's a more comprehensive approach for use with the gifted are in the areas of process, product, and learning environment. (See Table 12-2.) Although an environment like that recommended for the gifted would be necessary for implementing his approach, Bruner does not make specific recommendations for developing such a climate. His approach to content is highly appropriate for the gifted. Bruner's model is compatible with most other models, but best for use with Taba and Renzulli. For further information, see Chapter 3.

Guilford

Guilford's model was not constructed for curriculum development. It was created to explain human intelligence. However, it has been and can be used for curriculum development for the gifted if combined with other models and adapted in certain ways. (See Table 12-3.) The *Structure of Intellect* (SI) theory and SOI applications of the theory make some modifications in the content, process, and product areas, but none in learning environment. Guilford's model can be used in conjunction with several other approaches, but is best combined with Bruner or Taba, Renzulli, Parnes, and Treffinger. For a further explanation of these ideas, see Chapter 4.

Kohlberg

Kohlberg's theory of moral development and his strategies for *Discussions of Moral Dilemmas* were developed to explain moral/ethical development and to provide a structure for raising levels of ethical development. However, because of its concentration on high levels of behavior and on reasoning, it makes many curricular modifications appropriate for the gifted in all areas except products. To provide a comprehensive model, however, it needs to be used in conjunction with other approaches. (See Table 12-4.) Product adaptations are easily included by encouraging students to develop further products related to moral issues identified

Table 12-1 Modifying and Complementing Bloom's Taxonomy

Program Goals	Suggested Adaptation of Model	Complementary Models
Organize content around basic concepts and abstract generalizations	Organize activities at all levels of the taxonomy around abstract, complex content	Bruner Taba
Strive for economy in learning experiences	Organize activites as described above. Begin activities at the application level.	Bruner Taba
Provide opportunities for students to study creative people and creative processes.	Use the taxonomy as a structure to design activities for the study of eminent, creative/productive people	Williams
Cover content areas that are different from the regular curriculum	Teach the taxonomy to students and encourage them to use it as a way to structure their investigations	Bruner Taba Parnes Taylor Renzulli Treffinger Williams

Provide open-ended activities and ask open-ended questions	Ask open-ended provocative questions. Design activities at all levels of the taxonomy that are open-ended	Bruner Kohlberg Parnes Renzulli	Taba Taylor Treffinger Williams
Provide experiences using a discovery approach	Begin activities and discussions at the application level.	Bruner Renzulli Taba	Taylor Treffinger Williams
In all cases where appropriate, ask students to explain their reasoning or provide support for their answers	Ask "why" questions when appropriate at all levels after first	Kohlberg Taba	
Provide opportunities for students to choose topics and methods of studying topics	Use the taxonomy to design activities of a variety of types from which students can choose. Provide a variety of activites at each level of the taxonomy and allow students to choose.	Parnes Renzulli Treffinger Williams	

Table 12-1 continued

Program Goals	Suggested Adaptation of Model	Complementary Models
Provide structured simulation and group interaction activities in which students can develop leadership and group participation skills	Use the taxonomy as a tool for observing group interaction. Use the taxonomy to develop activities for group interaction/involvement.	Taba
Pace the presentation of new material rapidly	Move through activities and questions at the two lowest levels quickly	Taba
Use a variety of methods	Design a variety of types of activities at each level of the taxonomy	Guilford Taylor Kohlberg Treffinger Parnes Williams Renzulli
Provide situations allowing students to address real problems	Use activities at the analysis level to help students identify real problems to investigate	Bruner Taylor Parnes Treffinger

Provide situations in which students can direct their products toward real audiences	Teach the taxonomy to students for use in providing audiences a way to evaluate their products. Encourage students to elaborate upon and share the products of synthesis with real audiences.	Parnes Renzulli
Provide situations in which student products can be evaluated appropriately, and provide for the development of skills in self-evaluation	Teach the taxonomy to students as a method for evaluating their own products.	Guilford Taylor Parnes Treffinger Renzulli

Table 12-2 Modifying and Complementing Bruner's Approach

Program Goals	Suggested Adaptation of Model	Complementary Models
Provide situations in which students can direct their products toward real audiences	Extend children's work by asking "what would the anthropologist (or other professional) do with her work?" Encourage students to share the results of their studies with real audiences.	Parnex Renzulli
Provide situations in which student products can be evaluated appropriately, and provide for the development of skills in self-evaluation	Extend children's thinking and work by asking "How are an anthropologist's (or any other professional's) products judged?"	Guilford Taylor Parnes Treffinger Renzulli
Provide opportunities for students to choose topics and methods of studying topics	Allow students to select areas of study within a particular content (i.e., related to the concept being developed).	Parnes Treffinger Renzulli Williams Taylor

Provide structured simulation and group interaction activities in which students can develop leadership and group participation skills	Use simulation games and structured interaction activities in addition to the basic methods suggested by Bruner. An example is <u>Dig</u>. Use the methods of sociologists, anthropologists, and others who study the behavior of leaders to study group interaction.	Kohlberg Taba
Pace the presentation of new materials rapidly	Provide fewer examples of the key concepts being developed than would be provided for all students.	Taba
Use a variety of methods	Encourage the use of a variety of investigative techniques. Make field trips to observe scientists, poets, or other professionals at work.	Guilford Taylor Kohlberg Treffinger Parnes Williams Renzulli
Cover content areas that are different from the regular curriculum	Analyze data taught in regular program according to each key concept and generalization. Teach only that information not already taught.	Bloom Parnes Guilford Renzulli Kohlberg Taylor Krathwohl Treffinger

Table 12-2 continued

Program Goals	Suggested Adaptation of Model	Complementary Models
Provide opportunities for students to study creative people and creative processes	Study significant people related to each basic concept studied – people who contributed significantly to our understanding of that concept.	Williams
In all cases where appropriate, ask students to explain their reasoning or provide support for their answers	Ask students to explain their reasons or give support when they have "discovered" a certain conclusion.	Kohlberg Taba

Table 12-3 Modifying and Complementing Guilford's Structure of Intellect Model

Program Goals	Suggested Adaptation of Model	Complementary Models
Organize content around basic concepts and abstract generalizations	None listed. Use in conjunction with Bruner or Taba. Use product dimension categories or transformations and implications to judge the abstractness and complexity of generalizations developed.	Bruner Taba
Strive for economy in learning experiences	Organize learning experiences around abstract generalizations in addition to organizing around SI abilities to be developed.	Bruner Taba
Provide opportunities for students to study creative people and creative processes	Use in conjunction with Williams. Teach students the SI theory, dimensions, and categories. Have students use SI categories in all dimensions to examine people, processes, and methods.	Williams
Cover content areas that are different from the regular curriculum	Use in conjunction with other models. Teach SI theory as a method for analyzing human abilities.	Bloom Taba Bruner Taylor Parnes Treffinger Renzulli Williams

Table 12-3 continued

Program Goals	Suggested Adaptation of Model	Complementary Models	
Provide experiences using a discovery approach	Use in conjunction with other models. When students have completed an activity, have them identify the SI abilities involved. Exercise SI abilities involved in discovery learning (e.g., convergent production; figural, symbolic or semantic content; relations, systems, transformations, implications.	Bruner Renzulli Taba	Taylor Treffinger Williams
In all cases where appropriate, ask students to explain their reasoning or provide support for their answers	When doing activities involving convergent production or evaluation, when appropriate, have students explain how they arrived at their answers.	Kohlberg Taba	
Provide opportunities for students to choose topics and methods of studying topics	Allow students to choose from a variety of activities which have been developed to exercise different abilities. Allow students to participate in designing their own educational programs.	Parnes Renzulli Taylor	Treffinger Williams

Provide structured simulation and group interaction activities in which students can develop leadership and group participation skills	Use categories in the behavioral dimension to structure observations of the group. Use behavioral dimension categories as pre and post measures of effectiveness of group interaction procedures.	Kohlberg	
		Taba	
Pace the presentation of new material rapidly.	Students pace themselves as they work individually on activities. After group activities, ask for feedback on your pacing of the lesson	Taba	
Use a variety of methods	Avoid tendency to use only SOI workbooks as teaching strategy. Analyze games and learning activities according to SI abilities involved.	Kohlberg	Taylor
		Parnes	Treffinger
		Renzulli	Williams
Provide situations allowing students to address real problems. Provide situations in which students can direct their products toward real audiences.	As a general strategy for product development, after a student's products have been evaluated by audiences, by the teacher, or by the student, identify the SI abilities involved in the development of the product. Work on these underlying strengths or weaknesses as a way to improve future products.	Bruner	Taylor
		Parnes	Treffinger
		Renzulli	

Table 12-4 Modifying and Complementing Kohlberg's Discussions of Moral Dilemmas

Program Goals	Suggested Adaptation of Model	Complementary Models
Provide content in all areas that is abstract	Present dilemmas that involve abstract ideas.	Bloom Guilford Bruner Taba
Provide content with complex ideas in all content areas	Present dilemmas that involve complex ideas. Present dilemmas that involve issues from several different content areas or disciplines.	Bloom Guilford Bruner Taba
Organize content around basic concepts and abstract generalizations	Present dilemmas which illustrate the moral/ethical side of key concepts and generalizations that are being developed.	Bruner Taba
Strive for economy in learning experiences	Select only dilemmas that are the best illustration of the issues to be developed.	Bruner Taba
Provide opportunities for students to study creative people and creative processes	Present moral/ethical dilemmas faced by famous individuals. Compare student resolution of the conflict to that made by the person studied.	Williams

		Authors
Cover content areas that are different from the regular curriculum	Present moral/ethical dilemmas faced by investigators.	Bloom, Bruner, Parnes, Renzulli, Taba, Taylor, Treffinger, Williams
Provide experiences using a discovery approach	Present dilemmas faced by others. Compare student resolution of the conflict to the resolution by other people.	Bruner, Renzulli, Taba, Taylor, Treffinger, Williams
In all cases where appropriate, ask students to explain their reasoning or provide support for their answers	Ask "why" whener appropriate after Step 2.	Taba
Provide opportunities for students to choose topics and methods of studying topics	Give students freedom to choose moral issues or dilemmas they would like to discuss.	Parnes, Renzulli, Taylor, Treffinger, Williams

Table 12-4 continued

Program Goals	Suggested Adaptation of Model	Complementary Models
Pace the presentation of new material rapidly	Spend more time at steps after #2.	Taba
Provide situations allowing students to address real problems	Encourage students to develop products resulting from discussions of moral dilemmas that address a problem or issue of interest to them.	Bruner Taylor Parnes Treffinger Renzulli
Provide situations in which students can direct their products toward real audiences	Encourage students to direct these products toward real audiences.	Parnes Renzulli
Provide situations in which student products can be evaluated appropriately and provide for the development of skills in self-evaluation	Encourage students to evaluate their products themselves and have them evaluated by peers and/or the audience.	Guilford Taylor Parnes Treffinger Renzulli

	Bloom	Taba
Encourage students to develop products resulting from discussions of moral dilemmas that are similar to the following: original essays about issues, result from original research such as a survey of attitudes toward an ethical issue.	Bruner	Taylor
	Guilford	Treffinger
	Parnes	Williams
	Renzulli	

Encourage students to develop products that are transformations rather than summaries of existing information during discussions. Kohlberg's approach is compatible with most models, but can benefit most from being combined with Taba, Renzulli, Treffinger, or Parnes. For further information, see Chapter 5.

Krathwohl

Like Bloom's, Krathwohl's *Taxonomy* was not created for curriculum development and certainly not for the gifted. It is a system designed for classifying objectives in the affective domain, and it was developed to facilitate communication between professionals. Of all the models reviewed, Krathwohl's *Taxonomy* makes the least number of curricular modifications for the gifted. However, it can be used in conjunction with other models or adapted to provide a framework for curriculum development in the affective area. (See Table 12-5.) No other model provides this addition. Krathwohl's *Taxonomy* is easily combined with Bloom's *Taxonomy,* with Bruner and Taba, with Renzulli and Parnes, or with Treffinger, Williams, or Taba. For more information, the reader is referred to Chapter 2.

Parnes

Like most of the models reviewed, Parnes's *Creative Problem Solving* (CPS) process was not developed as a curriculum for gifted students. It was designed as a process for developing creative solutions to problems. Because of its emphasis on creativity and the use of creativity in a problem-solving setting, however, CPS provides an important dimension needed in a program for the gifted. Without adaptations, the model provides for most product and learning environment modifications appropriate for the gifted and for some of the content and process changes. When combined or used in conjunction with models like Taba or Bruner, it provides a comprehensive approach. (See Table 12-6.) For more information, refer to Chapter 6.

Renzulli

Renzulli's *Enrichment Triad* was designed as a comprehensive framework for program and curriculum development for gifted students. As a framework, it was not intended to provide specific guidelines for curriculum development in all areas. Renzulli, for example, recommends that certain process models be used to develop his Type II activities. Depending on which process models were used, the facilitator would make different process modifications. As recommended by Renzulli, the *Triad* can be used with process models such as Bloom, Parnes, Krathwohl, Guilford, Williams, Taylor, Taba, or Kohlberg. (See Table 12-7.) It can also be used with a content model such as Bruner's or with Treffinger's as a way to assist students in developing their Type III investigations. For more information, review Chapter 7.

Table 12-5 Modifying and Complementing Krathwohl's Taxonomy

Program Goals	Suggested Adaptation of Model	Complementary Models	
Provide content in all areas that is abstract	Develop abstract generalizations that relate to affective behavior and values	Bloom Bruner Guilford	Kohlberg Taba
Provide content with complex ideas in all content areas	Develop complex generalizations that relate to affective behavior and values.	Bloom Bruner Guilford	Kohlberg Taba
Organize content around basic concepts and abstract generalizations	Organize content and activities around abstract generalizations and concepts.	Bruner Taba	
Strive for economy in learning experiences	Begin activities at the valuing level.	Bruner Taba	
Provide opportunities for students to study creative people and creative processes	Study the affective development of eminent creative/productive people. Teach the taxonomy to students to use as a structure for examining the lives of these people.	Williams	

Table 12-5 continued

Program Goals	Suggested Adaptation of Model	Complementary Models	
Cover content areas that are different from the regular curriculum	Teach the taxonomy to students to use as a way to conduct investigations. Teach the taxonomy as an educational classification system.	Bloom Bruner Parnes Renzulli	Taba Taylor Treffinger Williams
Provide open-ended activities and ask open-ended questions	Ask open-ended questions at all levels of the taxonomy. Design open-ended provocative activities at all levels.	Bruner Guilford Kohlberg Parnes Renzulli	Taba Taylor Treffinger Williams
Provide experiences using a discovery approach	Begin activities at the valuing level. Teach to students as a way to structure their own inquiry.	Bruner Renzulli Taba	Taylor Treffinger Williams
In all cases where appropriate, ask students to explain their reasoning	Ask "why" questions when appropriate at all levels except the first.	Kohlberg Taba	

or provide support for their answers		
Provide opportunities for students to choose topics and methods of studying topics	Provide a variety of learning activities at each level of the taxonomy and allow students to choose.	Parnes Treffinger Renzulli Williams Taylor
Provide structured simulation and group interaction activities in which students can develop leadership and group participation skills	Use the taxonomy to design group interaction activities. Use the taxonomy as a structure for observing the interaction of a group.	Kohlberg Taba
Pace the presentation of new materials rapidly	Move through the lower levels rapidly.	Taba
Use a variety of methods	Design a variety of types of activities at each level of the taxonomy	Guilford Taylor Kohlberg Treffinger Parnes Williams Renzulli

Table 12-5 continued

Program Goals	Suggested Adaptation of Model	Complementary Models
Provide situations allowing students to address real problems	Teach the taxonomy as a way to identify problems to investigate – as a way to analyze underlying ideas.	Bruner Taylor Parnes Treffinger Renzulli
Provide situations in which students can direct their products toward real audiences	Teach the taxonomy to students as a model they can give to real audiences as a way to evaluate their products. Encourage students to share the products of their activities at the characterization level with real audiences.	Parnes Renzulli
Provide situations in which student products can be evaluated appropriately and provide for the development of skills in self-evaluation	Teach the taxonomy to students as a way to evaluate their own products	Guilford Taylor Parnes Treffinger Renzulli
Encourage students to develop products that are transformation rather than summaries of existing information	Encourage students to develop products that show evidence of the characterization level, or at least the organization level.	Bloom Taba Bruner Taylor Guilford Treffinger Parnes Williams Renzulli

Table 12-6 Modifying and Complementing Parnes's Creative Problem Solving Process

Program Goals	Suggested Adaptation of Model	Complementary Models
Provide content in all areas that is abstract	Problem situations presented should involve abstract concepts and ideas.	Bloom Kohlberg Bruner Taba Guilford
Provide content with complex ideas in all content areas	Problem situations should involve complex concepts and ideas. Fact-finding should involve several content areas or disciplines.	Bloom Kohlberg Bruner Taba Guilford
Organize content around basic concepts and abstract generalizations	Organize content around abstract, complex ideas and select problem situations that relate to these ideas. Organize content around problem situations and use fact-finding as a way to gather information	Bruner Taba
Strive for economy in learning experiences	Choose only problem situations that do not overlap with content already presented/developed in other ways	Bruner Taba
Provide opportunities for students to study creative people and creative processes	Identify problems faced by creative/productive people and use CPS to develop solutions. Compare own solutions to actual solution by the person studied.	Williams

Table 12-6 continued

Program Goals	Suggested Adaptation of Model	Complementary Models
Provide experiences using a discovery approach	Teach the CPS process to students so they can use it to structure their own inquiry or discovery learning.	Bruner Taylor Renzulli Treffinger Taba Williams
In all cases where appropriate, ask students to explain their reasoning or provide support for their answers	Ask questions calling for support only when appropriate (e.g., selection of problem statements, selection of criteria for evaluation, development of action plans).	Kohlberg Taba
Provide structured simulation and group interaction activities in which students can develop leadership and group participation skills	Tape the use of CPS in a group setting and analyze the group's interaction. Use CPS as a method for developing solutions to group interaction problems.	Kohlberg Taba
Pace the presentation of new material rapidly	None listed.	Taba

Table 12-7 Modifying and Complementing Renzulli's Enrichment Triad

Program Goals	Suggested Adaptation of Model	Complementary Models	
Provide content in all areas that is abstract	Develop abstract generalizations for each content area to be explored.	Bloom Bruner Guilford	Kohlberg Taba
Provide content with complex ideas in all content areas	Develop complex generalizations for each content area to be explored.	Bloom Bruner Guilford	Kohlberg Taba
Organize content around basic concepts and abstract generalizations	Organize Type I and Type II activities around these abstract, complex generalizations.	Bruner Taba	
Strive for economy in learning experiences	Choose all Type I and Type II experiences very carefully so that they illustrate key concepts and ideas and expose students to a variety of key ideas in the different disciplines.	Bruner Taba	

Table 12-7 continued

Program Goals	Suggested Adaptation of Model	Complementary Models	
Provide opportunities for students to study creative people and creative processes	Include as Type I activities exposure to biographies and autobiographies of famous individuals who have contributed to the key concepts being studied. Compare methods of inquiry used by these people with current methods in different fields of study.	Williams	
Provide for structured development of higher levels of thinking	None listed. Combine with other process models to meet this objective. These will be Type II activities.	Bloom Bruner Guilford Kohlberg Krathwohl	Parnes Taba Taylor Williams
Provide open-ended activities and ask open-ended questions	None listed. Combine with other process models to meet this objective. These will be Type II activities.	Bruner Guilford Kohlberg Parnes	Taba Taylor Treffinger Williams
Provide experiences using a discovery approach	None listed. Combine with other process models to meet this objective. These will be Type II activities.	Bruner Taba Taylor	Treffinger Williams

In all cases where appropriate, ask students to explain their reasoning or provide support for their answers	Incorporate "why" questions into all Type II activities when appropriate	Kohlberg Taba
Provide structured simulation and group interaction activities in which students can develop leadership and group participation skills	As Type II activities, include those requiring group interaction. Tape the activity or have "live" observations.	Kohlberg Taba
Pace the presentation of new material rapidly	Remind guest speakers (during Type I activities) to pace their presentation of material rapidly. During discussions and other Type II activities, pace those requiring "lower levels of thinking" rapidly.	Taba

Taba

Hilda Taba's *Teaching Strategies* and curriculum development theory were constructed as models for use with all children. However, since the purposes included a major focus on the development of abstract thinking, the Taba model is highly appropriate for use in gifted programs. It makes many of the content, process, and learning environment changes recommended for the gifted, but does not provide suggestions for products. These changes can easily be integrated by adapting the model, particularly by using the strategies for different purposes in the development of products. (See Table 12-8.) The Taba *Strategies* can also be used with Renzulli's *Triad* or with Parnes to make these changes. Additional information is contained in Chapter 8.

Taylor

Taylor's *Multiple Talent Approach* was developed as a total school model for developing and emphasizing the enhancement of a variety of talents and abilities in all children. The approach can also be used within a categorically funded program for the gifted as a model for the development of a variety of talents in gifted students. As a model for talent development, the approach makes major modifications in the process and learning environment areas of the curriculum. It can be adapted or supplemented by other approaches to provide a comprehensive model. (See Table 12-9.) It is compatible with all other models. The reader should refer to Chapter 9 for more information.

Treffinger

Treffinger's *Self-Directed Learning* model was not developed as a total approach to curriculum development (or implementation for the gifted). It was designed to provide guidelines for teachers to use in developing an environment where self-directed learning can occur. Since self-direction is a goal of many gifted programs and since independence is a salient characteristic of most gifted students, Treffinger's model is appropriate for use in programs for the gifted. It can be combined with a content model such as Bruner's or Taba's and with several process models that systematically develop higher levels of thinking. (See Table 12-10.) For further information, the reader should consult Chapter 10.

Williams

Frank Williams's *Teaching Strategies for Thinking and Feeling* were developed as strategies for enhancing the cognitive and affective behaviors involved in creativity and are a part of a model for individualizing and humanizing education

Table 12-8 Modifying and Complementing Taba's Teaching Strategies

Program Goals	Suggested Adaptation of Model	Complementary Models
Cover content areas that are different from the regular curriculum	Using worksheet suggested for Bruner (Chapter 3), analyze regular curriculum to determine what specific information is being taught and what else needs to be taught.	Bloom Parnes Guilford Renzulli Kohlberg Taylor Krathwohl Treffinger
Provide opportunities for students to study creative people and creative processes	Use interpretation of data strategy to discuss characteristics of creative/productive people and the causes and/or effects of these characteristics.	Williams
Provide opportunities for students to choose topics and methods of studying topics	Allow students to choose general topic areas for discussion and plan lessons around these topics. In the resolution of conflict discussion, have children select conflict situations they would like to discuss.	Parnes Treffinger Renzulli Williams Taylor
Use a variety of methods	Alternate different methods with the basic discussion strategy (e.g., a concept development game). Use a variety of ways for the first step, getting the information (e.g., simulation games, field trips, slides, films).	Guilford Taylor Kohlberg Treffinger Parnes Williams Renzulli

Table 12-8 continued

Program Goals	Suggested Adaptation of Model	Complementary Models
Provide situations allowing students to address real problems	Teach students to use the concept development strategy for organizing and reorganizing data to select a problem or topic area to investigate. Use concept development as a study for writing results of a study or investigation.	Bruner Taylor Parnes Treffinger Renzulli
Provide situations in which students can direct their products toward real audiences	Use the application of generalizations strategy to predict how different audiences might react to a certain product. Use the interpretation of data strategy to form conclusions about the causes and effects of results of experiments (use with audiences).	Parnes Renzulli
Provide situations in which student products can be evaluated appropriately, and provide for the development of skills in self-evaluation	Use the strategies (e.g., all except resolution of conflict) to develop criteria and processes for evaluation of products.	Guilford Taylor Parnes Treffinger Renzulli

Table 12-9 Modifying and Complementing Taylor's Multiple Talents Approach

Program Goals	Suggested Adaptation of Model	Complementary Models	
Provide content in all areas that is abstract	Develop abstract generalizations for each content area to be studied.	Bloom Bruner Guilford	Kohlberg Taba
Provide content with complex ideas in all content areas	Develop complex generalizations that integrate several content areas or disciplines to be studied.	Bloom Bruner Guilford	Kohlberg Taba
Organize content around basic concepts and abstract generalizations	Organize talent development activities around abstract, complex generalizations.	Bruner Taba	
Strive for economy in learning experiences	Select talent development activities carefully to illustrate abstract, complex ideas and develop talent at the same time.	Bruner Taba	
Provide opportunities for students to study creative people and creative processes	Compare own plans made with plans made by eminent, productive individuals. Use forecasting activities to predict what would happen to the eminent individual if the person lived today or at a different time.	Williams	

Table 12-9 continued

Program Goals	Suggested Adaptation of Model	Complementary Models
In all cases where appropriate, ask students to explain their reasoning or provide support for their answers.	Combine forecasting talent activities with Taba's application of generalizations strategy. When developing decision making and forecasting talent and evaluative thinking ability, ask "why" questions when appropriate.	Kohlberg Taba
Provide structured simulation and group interaction activities in which students can develop leadership and group participation skills	Have group activities videotaped and then analyze the tapes. Certain talent areas would lend themselves easily to this kind of activity: creativity, decision making, planning, and forecasting. Use guidelines for communication talent as a structure for observing group interaction or participation.	Kohlberg Taba
Pace the presentation of new material rapidly	None listed. Combining with Taba's discussion techniques will give guidelines for pacing.	Taba
Provide situations in which students can direct their products toward real audiences	Encourage students to present their products developed through all talent areas to real audiences.	Parnes Renzulli

Table 12-10 Modifying and Complementing Treffinger's Model for Self-Directed Learning

Program Goals	Suggested Adaptation of Model	Complementary Models	
Provide content in all areas that is abstract	At teacher-directed level, select and/or develop abstract generalizations as the focus of learning activities. At higher levels, have students assist in their development and/or selection.	Bloom Bruner Guilford	Kohlberg Taba
Provide content with complex ideas in all content areas	At teacher-directed level, develop complex generalizations to serve as the focus of learning activities.	Bloom Bruner Guilford	Kohlberg Taba
Organize content around basic concepts and abstract generalizations	Organize content (data) around abstract, complex ideas. Present activities at the teacher-directed level, but allow students to choose data or ideas to study at later levels.	Bruner Taba	
Strive for economy in learning experiences	Encourage students to select learning experiences that will be the best for reaching a big idea (at later levels). Select learning experiences for economy at teacher-directed level.	Bruner Taba	

Table 12-10 continued

Program Goals	Suggested Adaptation of Model	Complementary Models
Provide opportunities for students to study creative people and creative processes	Provide as an option the study of creative/productive people whose work pertains to a big idea being developed.	Williams
Provide open-ended activities and ask open-ended questions	Combine with a process model for structured development of higher levels of thinking. Offer options at all levels or of all types of thinking. Encourage students to choose a variety or choose those they need to develop.	All other models
In all cases where appropriate, ask students to explain their reasoning or provide support for their answers	Ask students to explain why they have chosen a particular option or why they have assessed their needs in a particular way.	Kohlberg Taba

Provide structured simulation and group interaction activities in which students can develop leadership and group participation skills	Encourage students to develop their own methods for observing group interaction. Develop "process seminars" for students to share independent learning experiences.	Kohlberg Taba
Pace the presentation of new material rapidly	At self-directed levels, students will pace themselves. At teacher-directed levels, use suggestions from Taba, and ask students for feedback on pacing.	Taba
Provide situations in which students can direct their products toward real audiences	Encourage students to develop their products for presentation to real audiences.	Parnes Renzulli

by concentrating on creativity development. Because of their focus on creativity, the strategies can be highly appropriate for use in gifted programs. Many modifications appropriate for the gifted are made by the model in the areas of learning environment and process, but it needs to be supplemented or adapted to provide necessary content and product modifications. (See Table 12-11.) Williams's strategies can be used effectively with any of the models reviewed. The reader should refer to Chapter 11 for further information.

INTEGRATED APPROACHES

After models have been reviewed, chosen, and adaptations made or listed, the student objectives and learning activities must be developed. This process involves reviewing the student needs assessment, program goals, and purposes/provisions of the models.

Each curriculum that is finally designed will be different, even if the same models form the basis, because each developer and each situation will be different. Maker (1982) has presented four sample curricula that have integrated a variety of models in the development of comprehensive programs to meet the needs of gifted students. It is impossible to summarize each of these, but to give a brief example of an integrated approach, a summary of child needs, units and activities, models, and academic areas is presented in Table 12-12.

This curriculum was designed for an elementary resource room program in a middle-class school. The emphasis was on development of the following strengths of the gifted students in the program: curiosity; critical thinking; leadership; independence; affective skills; self-expression; and creative thinkng. The general approach was a combination of units, special projects, and sharing activities. A range of school subjects was integrated, with units developed to build on rather than duplicate the regular program. Evaluation results showed the curriculum to be highly effective in accomplishing its purposes.

CONCLUSION

In this volume a wide range of teaching-learning models have been presented that can be helpful in developing a comprehensive curriculum for gifted students. All were designed for different purposes and have different strengths and weaknesses when considered as comprehensive approaches. All also have different advantages and disadvantages in a practical sense. Few have been validated through research as effective programs, and even fewer as effective models for use with the gifted. No comparative research indicates which models may be more appropriate than others, but many practitioners are sold on one or more of the approaches. In this collection, I hope that all of you will find *at least one* that works for you and your children!

Table 12-11 Modifying and Complementing Williams's Strategies for Thinking and Feeling

Program Goals	Suggested Adaptation of Model	Complementary Models	
Provode content in all areas that is abstract	Develop abstract generalizations in each discipline to be studied.	Bloom Bruner Guilford	Kohlberg Taba
Provide content with complex ideas in all content areas	Develop complex generalizations that integrate content from several disciplines to be studied.	Bloom Bruner Guilford	Kohlberg Taba
Cover content areas that are different from the regular curriculum	Analyze regular curriculum according to each generalization and key concept. Teach in the special program only that information not taught in the regular curriculum. See Worksheet in Chapter 3 for this purpose.	Bloom Guilford Kohlberg Krathwohl	Parnes Renzulli Taylor Treffinger
Organize content around basic concepts and abstract generalizations	Organize strategies and development of creative behaviors around abstract, complex generalizations rather than just around the "general" discipline	Bruner Taba	

Table 12-11 continued

Program Goals	Suggested Adaptation of Model	Complementary Models
Strive for economy in learning experiences	Select activities carefully because they are the best possible strategies and they illustrate the big ideas being developed.	Bruner Taba
In all cases where appropriate, ask students to explain their reasoning or provide support for their answers	Incorporate "why" questions into the discussions whenever appropriate. Use strategy recommended by Taba's application of generalizations so creativity will not be inhibited (make predictions, then go back and ask for reasons).	Kohlberg Taba
Provide structured simulation and group interaction activities in which students can develop leadership and group participation skills	Use attributes, examples of habit, and intuitive expression as ways to observe and discuss group interaction.	Kohlberg Taba

Pace the presentation of new material rapidly	Since many activites will be individual rather than group, allow students to pace themselves. In group discussions, follow the suggestions made by Taba.	Taba	
Provide situations allowing students to address real problems	When students express interest in a topic, encourage them to pursue it further and make an ivnestigation of a real problem.	Bruner Parnes Renzulli	Taylor Treffinger
Provide situations in which students can direct their products toward real audiences	When students have studies an area, developed a product, or conducted an experiment, encourage them to refine it and present it to a real audience.	Parnes Renzulli	Treffinger
Provide situations in which student products can be evaluated appropriately, and provide for the development of skills in self-evaluation	Have students to develop criteria and procedures for evaluation of their own products. Using criteria developed by students as well as that provided by audiences, have all student products evaluated by the student, peers, audiences, and the teacher.	Guilford Parnes Renzulli	Taylor Treffinger

Table 12-12 Summary of Child Characteristics, Activities, Models, and Content Areas

Child Needs	Learning Activities	Models	Academic Areas
Cultivation of Natural Curiosity	Units – Introduction to the following topics through units: Culture, Archaeology, Anthropology, Drama, Photography, Drama, Photography, Architecture, Painting, The Human Body, Chemistry, Electricity, Energy Forms, Astronomy, Career Opportunities	Bruner, Renzulli, Taba	Social Studies, Science, Art, Math, Reading
Development of Critical Thinking Skills	Units – Each unit requires higher levels of thinking. Activities – Deductive thinking skills series (Mindbenders), Inductive Thinking skills series, Aha!, Thinklab, Two-minute mysteries, Conceptual Blockbusting Discussions	Bloom, Ennis, Parnes, Taba	Math, Reading, Language, Development

Development of Leadership Skills	Unit – Leadership Skill Techniques Activities – Role Playing, Body Language, Creative Problem Solving, Brainstorming, Assuming Leadership Roles in Each Unit, Teach a Lesson	Kohlberg Parnes Simon Taba	Language Development
Development of Independence Skills	Units – Goal Setting Research Skills, Library skills-SEARCH, Community Resource Investigation Skills (children are then required to use these skills in all subsequent units), Scientific Method of Research Experimentation Activities – Setting Goals, Flowcharting, Evaluation of own products, using the Readers Guide, Individual Interest Research, Research Projects, Brainstorming, Learning Proper Letter Formats	Parnes Renzulli Taba	Library Skills Research Skills Writing Language Development

Table 12-12 continued

Child Needs	Learning Activities	Models	Academic Areas
Development of Affective Skills	Activities – Transactional Analysis, Values Clarification, Discussion of Moral Dilemmas, Sharing Time, Counselor-led Activities	Simon Taba	Language Development
Development of Self-Expression	Units – Self-Expression Methods, Careers Activities – Drama, Mime, Creative Writing, Poetry, Photography, Art, Sign Language, Body Language	Renzulli Taba	Art Writing
Development of Creative Thinking	Units – Each unit requires creative thinking Activities – Aha! Making it Strange, Brainstorming Creative Problem Solving, Scamper, Imagination Express, Guided Fantasy, Experiences in Visual Thinking, 52/62 Ways to Have Fun with Your Mind	Bloom Ennis Parnes Taba	Math Art Language Development

Source: J. Maker. Curriculum development for the gifted. Rockville, Md.: Aspen Systems Corporation, 1982.

References

REFERENCE NOTES

1. Ayers, J.D. *Justification of Bloom's taxonomy by factor analysis*. Paper presented at the Annual American Educational Research Association Convention, Chicago, February, 1966.

2. Milholland, J.E. *An empirical examination of the categories of The Taxonomy of Educational Objectives*. Paper presented at the Annual American Educational Research Association Convention, Chicago, February 1966.

3. Zinn, K.L. *The use of the taxonomy and computer assistance in assembling sets of objectives, test items, and diagnostic test sequences*. Paper presented at the Annual American Educational Research Association Convention, Chicago, February 1966.

4. Dapra, R.A., & Felker, D.B. *Effects of comprehension and verbatim adjunct questions in problem-solving ability from prose material: Extension of mathemagenic hypothesis*. Paper presented at the annual convention of the American Psychological Association, New Orleans, 1974.

5. Andre, T. *The role of paraphrased and verbatim adjunct questions in facilitating learning by reading*. Paper presented at the annual meeting of the Midwestern Educational Research Association, Bloomington, Indiana, 1978.

6. Limburg, J.B. *The taxonomy of educational objectives of the cognitive domain*. Unpublished paper, 1979. (Available from Dr. C.J. Maker, Department of Special Education, University of Arizona, Tucson, Arizona).

7. Maker, C.J. *Intelligence test construction–A comparison of methods*. Unpublished paper, 1974. (Available from Dr. C.J. Maker, Department of Special Education, University of Arizona, Tucson, Arizona).

8. Torrance, E.P. Personal communication, April 13, 1979.

9. Hess, J. *Final Report, ESEA, Title III*. Glendora Public Schools, Glendora, California, 1972.

10. Hoepfner, R. Evaluation of the third year of the East Whittier City School District Title III project. In M. Meeker (Ed.), *A book of collected readings on application of the Guilford S. I. to educational practice*. El Segundo, Calif.: SOI Institute, undated.

11. Keisel, S. *The creative problem solving model*. Unpublished paper, 1979. (Available from Dr. C.J. Maker, Department of Special Education, University of Arizona, Tucson, Arizona.)

12. James, J. *Sidney Parnes: Creative problem-solving model*. Unpublished paper, 1978. (Available from Dr. C.J. Maker, Department of Special Education, University of Arizona, Tucson, Arizona).

13. Bodnar, J. *Creative problem-solving model.* Unpublished paper, 1974. (Available from Dr. C.J. Maker, Department of Special Education, University of Arizona, Tucson, Arizona).

14. Taylor, C.W. Nearly all students are talented: Let's reach them. *Utah Parent Teacher*, February, 1968.

15. Taylor, C.W. Creative and other talents. *Utah Educational Review*, March-April, 1967.

16. Shartzer, C.J. *Identifying talented children.* Unpublished paper, 1972. Springfield, Ill.: Illinois Department of Education, 1972. (Available from Dr. C.J. Maker, Department of Special Education, University of Arizona, Tucson, Arizona).

17. Bodine, R.J. *The 'process' seminar–A vehicle for understanding.* Unpublished paper, undated. (Available from S and D Center, Lakeview High School, 1001 Brush College Road, Decatur, Illinois).

18. Bodine, R.J. Personal communication, November, 1976.

REFERENCES

Atwood, B.S. *Building independent learning skills.* Palo Alto, Calif.: Education Today Co., 1974.

Baldwin, A., & Wooster, J. *Baldwin identification matrix inservice kit for the identification of gifted and talented students.* Buffalo, N.Y.: D.O.K. Publishers, 1977.

Barton, B. *Toward the development of a self-directed learner: A pilot study.* Unpublished Masters thesis, University of Kansas, 1976.

Begle, E., & Wilson, J. Evaluation of mathematics program. In The National Society for the Study of Education (Eds.), *Sixty-ninth yearbook* (Part I). Chicago: University of Chicago Press, 1970.

Blatt, M. *Studies of the effects of classroom discussion upon children's moral development.* Unpublished doctoral dissertation, University of Chicago, 1969.

Bloom. B.S. *Taxonomy of educational objectives: The classification of educational goals. Handbook I: Cognitive domain.* New York, N.Y.: Longmans, Green & Co., 1956.

Briggs, K.C., & Myers, I.B. *Myers-Briggs type indicator.* Atlanta, Ga.: Educational Testing Service, 1971.

Bruner, J.S. *The process of education.* Cambridge, Mass.: Harvard University Press, 1960.

Callahan, C.M., & Renzulli, J.S. The effectiveness of a creativity training program in the language arts. *The Gifted Child Quarterly, 1977, 21,* 538-545.

Cattell, R.B. *Abilities: Their structure, growth and action.* Boston: Houghton Mifflin, 1971.

Cattell, R.B., & Butcher, H.J. *The prediction of achievement and creativity.* New York, N.Y.: The Bobbs-Merrill Co., 1968.

Chausow, H.M. *The organization of learning experiences to achieve more effectively the objectives of critical thinking in the general social science course at the junior college level.* Unpublished doctoral dissertation, University of Chicago, 1955.

Dempsey, R.D. Cognitive style differences between gifted and average students (Doctoral dissertation, United States International University, 1975). *Dissertation Abstracts International, 1975, 36,* 2998B-2999B. (University Microfilms No. 75-29, 379).

Dressel, P.L., & Mayhew, L.B. *General education: Explorations in evaluation.* Washington, D.C.: American Council on Education, 1954.

Dressel, P.L., & Nelson, C.H. *Questions and problems in science.* Princeton, N.J.: Educational Testing Service, 1956.

Dunn, R., Dunn, K., & Price, G.E. *Learning style inventory.* Lawrence, Kan.: Price Systems, 1975.

Eberle, B. *Classroom cue cards for cultivating multiple talent.* Buffalo, N.Y.: D.O.K. Publishers, 1974.

Eberle, B., & Stanish, B. *CPS for kids: A resource book for teaching creative problem-solving to children.* Buffalo, N.Y.: D.O.K. Publishers, 1980.

Education Development Center. *Man: A course of study* (MACOS). Washington, D.C.: Curriculum Development Associates, 1970.

Ellis, K., & Durkin, M.C. *Teacher's guide for people in communities* (The Taba program in social studies). Menlo Park, Calif.: Addison-Wesley Publishing Co., 1972.

Ennis, R.H. A definition of critical thinking. *The Reading Teacher,* 1964, *18,* 599-612.

Feldman, B. *Deficit skills of children who do not learn to read.* Unpublished doctoral dissertation, University of Southern California, 1971.

Felker, D.P., & Dapra, R.A. Effects of question type and question placement on problem-solving ability from prose material. *Journal of Educational Psychology,* 1975, *67,* 380-384.

Frick, J.W., Guilford, J.P., Christensen, P.R., & Merrifield, P.R. A factor analytic study of flexibility in thinking. *Educational and Psychological Measurement,* 1959, *19,* 469-496.

Gallagher, J.J. *Research summary on gifted child education.* Springfield, Ill.: Office of the Superintendent of Public Instruction, 1966.

Gallagher, J.J. *Teaching the gifted child* (2nd ed.). Boston: Allyn & Bacon, Inc., 1975.

Gallagher, J.J., Aschner, M.J., & Jenné, W. *Productive thinking in classroom interaction.* Reston, Va.: Council for Exceptional Children, 1967.

George, W.C. Accelerating mathematics instruction. *Gifted Child Quarterly,* 1976, *20,* 246-261.

Getzels, J.W. Problem-finding and the inventiveness of solutions. *Journal of Creative Behavior,* 1975, *9,* 12-18.

Getzels, J.W., & Jackson, P.W. *Creativity and intelligence: Exploration with gifted students.* New York, N.Y.: John Wiley & Sons, Inc., 1962.

Gibbs, J. Kohlberg's stages of moral judgment: A constructive critique. *Harvard Educational Review,* 1975, *45,* 127-134.

Gowan, J.C., & Demos, G.D. *The education and guidance of the ablest.* Springfield, Ill.: Charles C Thomas, 1964.

Grobman, H. Some comments on the evaluation program findings and their implications. *Biological Sciences Curriculum Study Newsletter,* 1962, *19,* 25-29.

Guglielmino, L.M. *Self-directed learning readiness scale.* Boca Raton, Fla.: Author, 1977.

Guidance Associates. *Teaching training in values education: A workshop* (sound filmstrip). White Plains, N.Y.: Author, 1976. (a)

Guidance Associates. *Values in American history: Conscience in conflict* (sound filmstrip). Mount Kisco, N.Y.: Author, 1976. (b)

Guidance Associates. *Values in a democracy: Making ethical decisions.* Mount Kisco, N.Y.: Author, 1976. (c)

Guilford, J.P. Three faces of intellect. *American Psychologist,* 1959, *14,* 469-479.

Guilford, J.P. Factorial angles to psychology. *Psychological Review,* 1961, *68,* 1-20.

Guilford, J.P. *The nature of human intelligence.* New York, N.Y.: McGraw-Hill, 1967.

Guilford, J.P. Intellect and the gifted. *The Gifted Child Quarterly,* 1972, *16,* 175-243.

Guilford, J.P. Varieties of creative giftedness, their measurement and development. *The Gifted Child Quarterly,* 1975, *19,* 107-121.

Guilford, J.P. *Way beyond the IQ.* Buffalo, N.Y.: Creative Education Foundation, Inc., 1977.

Hanley, J.P., Whitla, D.K., Moo, E.W., & Walter, A.S. *Man: A course of study: An evaluation.* Cambridge, Mass.: Education Development Center, 1970.

Hartshorne, J., & May, M. A summary of the work of the character inquiry. *Religious Education,* 1930, *25,* 607-619.

Hays, B.M., & Pereira, E.R. Effect of visual memory training on reading ability of kindergarten and first grade children. *The Journal of Experimental Education,* 1972, *41,*

Holland, J.G. Response contingencies in teaching-machine programs. *Journal of Programmed Instruction,* 1965, *5,* 474-482.

Hoyt, D.P. *The relationship between college grades and adult achievement: A review of the literature* (Research Report No. 7). Iowa City, Ia.: American Testing Program, 1965.

Hunt, D.E. Person-environment interaction: A challenge found wanting before it was tried. *Review of Educational Research,* 1975, *45,* 209-230.

Institute for Staff Development (Eds.). *Hilda Taba teaching strategies program: Unit 1.* Miami, Fla.: Author, 1971. (a)

Institute for Staff Development (Eds.). *Hilda Taba teaching strategies program: Unit 2.* Miami, Fla.: Author, 1971. (b)

Institute for Staff Development (Eds.). *Hilda Taba teaching strategies program: Unit 3.* Miami, Fla.: Author, 1971. (c)

Institute for Staff Development (Eds.). *Hilda Taba teaching strategies program: Unit 4.* Miami, Fla.: Author, 1971. (d)

Joyce, B., & Weil, B. *Models of teaching.* Englewood Cliffs, N.J.: Prentice-Hall, Inc., 1972.

Jung, C.G. *Psychological types.* London: Rutledge & Kegan Paul, 1923.

Kant, I. [*Critique of pure reason*] (N.K. Smith, trans.). New York, N.Y.: St. Martin's Press, 1965. (Originally published, 1929.)

Karnes, F.A., & Brown, K.E. Moral development and the gifted: An initial investigation. *Roeper Report,* 1981, *3,* 8-10.

Kohlberg, L. *The development of modes of moral thinking in the years 10 to 16.* Unpublished doctoral dissertation, University of Chicago, 1958.

Kohlberg, L. Moral education in the schools: A developmental view. *The School Review,* 1966, *74,* 1-29.

Kohlberg, L. Stages of moral development as the basis for moral education. In C.M. Beck, B.S. Crittenden, & E.V. Sullivan (Eds.), *Moral education: Interdisciplinary approaches.* New York, N.Y.: Newman Press, 1971.

Kohlberg, L., & Mayer, R. Development as the aim of education. *Harvard Educational Review,* 1972, *42,* 449-496.

Krathwohl, D.R., Bloom, B.S., & Masia, B.B. *Taxonomy of educational objectives: The classification of educational goals. Handbook II: Affective domain.* New York, N.Y.: David McKay Co., 1964.

Kurtines, W., & Greif, E.B. The development of moral thought: Review and evaluation of Kohlberg's approach. *Psychological Bulletin,* 1974, *81,* 453-470.

Lessinger, L.M. Test building and test banks through the use of The Taxonomy of Educational Objectives. *California Journal of Educational Research,* 1963, *14,* 195-201.

Lowman, L.M. An experimental evaluation of two curriculum designs for teaching first year algebra in a ninth grade class (Doctoral dissertation, University of Oklahoma, 1961). *Dissertation Abstracts,* 1961, *22,* 502. (University Microfilms No. 61-2864)

Lundy, R.A. *Dimensions of learning for the highly gifted student*. Palo Alto, Calif.: Palo Alto Unified School District, 1978. (ERIC Document Reproduction Service No. ED 155 864)

Lüscher, M. *The Lüscher color test*. New York, N.Y.: Random House, 1969.

MacKinnon, D.W. The nature and nurture of creative talent. *American Psychologist*, 1962, *17*, 484-495.

MacKinnon, D.W. Personality and the realization of creative potential. *American Psychologist*, 1965, *20*, 273-281.

Maehr, M.L. Continuing motivation: An analysis of a seldom considered educational outcome. *Review of Educational Research*, 1976, *46*, 443-462.

Maker, C.J. *Training teachers for the gifted and talented: A comparison of models*. Reston, Va.: The Council for Exceptional Children, 1975.

Maker, C.J. Developing multiple talents in exceptional children. *Teaching Exceptional Children*, 1979, *11*, 120-124.

Maker, C.J. *Curriculum development for the gifted*. Rockville, Md.: Aspen Systems Corporation, 1982.

Maker, C.J., Redden, M.R., Tonelson, S., & Howell, R.M. *The self-perceptions of successful handicapped scientists* (BEH Grant No. G00-7701-905. Albuquerque, New Mexico: University of New Mexico, 1978.

Makovic, M.V. The gifted child. In W.F. Jenks (Ed.), *Special education of the exceptional child*. Washington, D.C.: Catholic University Press, 1953.

Mansfield, R.S., Busse, F.V., & Krepelka, E.J. The effectiveness of creativity training. *Review of Educational Research*, 1978, *48*, 517-536.

Maslow, A. *Motivation and personality* (2nd. ed.). New York, N.Y.: Harper & Row, 1970.

Mayor, J. *The University of Maryland mathematics project* (Progress Report No. 11). College Park, Md.: College of Education, University of Maryland, 1966.

McGuire, C. Research in the process approach to the construction and to analysis of medical examinations. *National Council on Measurement in Education Yearbook*, 1963, *20*, 7-16.

McKenzie, G.R. Some effects of frequent quizzes on inferential thinking. *American Educational Research Journal*, 1972, *9*, 231-240.

McLachlan, J.F., & Hunt, D.E. Differential effects of discovery learning as a function of student conceptual level. *Canadian Journal of Behavioral Science*, 1973, *5*, 152-160.

Meeker, M.N. *The structure of intellect: Its interpretation and uses*. Columbus, Oh.: Charles E. Merrill, 1969.

Meeker, M. *Advanced SOI divergent production sourcebook*. El Segundo, Calif.: SOI Institute, 1969.

Meeker, M. *SOI group memory test and training model*. El Segundo, Calif.: SOI Institute, 1973.

Meeker, M. *Learning to plan, judge and make decisions, advanced: A structure of intellect evaluation workbook*. El Segundo, Calif. SOI Institute, 1976.

Meeker, M., & Meeker, R. *SOI learning abilities test* (Rev. ed.). El Segundo, Calif.: SOI Institute, 1979.

Morris, G.C. *Educational objectives of higher secondary school science*. Melbourne, Australia: Australian Council on Educational Research, 1961.

Mosston, M. *Teaching: From command to discovery*. Belmont, Calif.: Wadsworth, 1972.

Mourad, S.A. Relationship of grade level, sex, and creativity to readiness for self-directed learning among intellectually gifted students (Doctoral dissertation, University of Georgia, 1979). *Dissertation Abstracts International*, 1979, *40*, 2002A. (University Microfilms No. 7923138).

Muson, H. Moral thinking: Can it be taught? *Psychology Today,* February 1979, 48-58; 67-68; 92.

Noller, R.B., Treffinger, D.J., & Houseman, E.D. *It's a gas to be gifted or CPS for the gifted and talented.* Buffalo, N.Y.: D.O.K. Publishers, 1979.

Osborn, A. *Applied imagination.* New York, N.Y.: Scribners, 1963.

Osler, S.F., & Fivel, M.W. Concept attainment: I. The role of age and intelligence in concept attainment by induction. *Journal of Experimental Psychology,* 1961, *62,* 1-8.

Osler, S.F., & Troutman, G.E. Concept attainment: II. The effect of stimulus upon concept attainment at two levels of intelligence. *Journal of Experimental Psychology,* 1961, *62,* 9-13.

Parnes, S.J. *Programming creative behavior.* Buffalo, N.Y.: State University of New York at Buffalo, 1966.

Parnes, S.J. *Creative potential and the education experience* (Occasional Paper No. 2). Buffalo, N.Y.: Creative Education Foundation, 1967.

Parnes, S.J. Guiding creative action. *The Gifted Child Quarterly,* 1977, *21,* 460-472.

Parnes, S.J., Noller, R., & Biondi, A. *Guide to creative action.* New York, N.Y.: Scribners, 1967.

Phenix, P.H. *Realms of meaning.* New York, N.Y.: McGraw-Hill, 1964.

Piaget, J. *The origins of intelligence in children.* New York, N.Y.: Norton, 1963.

Piaget, J. *The moral development of the child.* Glencoe, Ill.: Free Press, 1948.

Piaget, J., & Inhelder, B. *The psychology of the child.* New York, N.Y.: Basic Books, 1969.

Porter, N., & Taylor, N. *How to assess the moral reasoning of students.* Toronto, Ontario: The Ontario Institute for Studies in Education, 1972.

Proviss, M. Ability grouping in arithmetic. *Elementary School Journal,* 1960, *60,* 391-398.

Raths, L.E. Clarifying values. In R.S. Fleming (Ed.), *Curriculum for today's boys and girls.* Columbus, Oh.: Charles E. Merrill, 1963.

Raths, L.E., Harmin, M., & Simon, S.B. *Values and teaching.* Columbus, Oh.: Charles E. Merrill, 1966.

Rawls, J. *A theory of justice.* Cambridge, Mass.: Harvard University Press, 1971.

Renzulli, J.S. *New directions in creativity.* New York, N.Y.: Harper & Row, 1976.

Renzulli, J.S. *The enrichment triad model: A guide for developing defensible programs for the gifted and talented.* Wethersfield, Conn.: Creative Learning Press, 1977.

Renzulli, J.S. What makes giftedness? *Phi Delta Kappan,* 1978, *60,* 180-184; 261.

Renzulli, J.S., & Gable, R.K. A factorial study of the attitudes of gifted students toward independent study. *The Gifted Child Quarterly,* 1976, *20,* 91-99.

Renzulli, J.S., Smith, F.H., White. A.J., Callahan, C.M., & Hartman, R.K. *Scales for rating the behavioral characteristics of superior students* (SRBCSS). Wethersfield, Conn.: Creative Learning Press, 1976.

Renzulli, J.S., & Smith, L.H. *Learning styles inventory: A measure of student preference for instructional techniques.* Mansfield Center, Conn.: Creative Learning Press, 1978.

Rest, J. *Defining issues test.* Minneapolis, Minn.: University of Minnesota, 1972.

Rest, J. Developmental psychology as a guide to value education: A review of "Kohlbergian" programs. *Review of Educational Research,* 1974, *44,* 241-257.

Roe, A. *The making of a scientist.* New York, N.Y.: Dodd & Mead, 1952.

Ross, J.D., & Ross, C.M. *The Ross test of higher cognitive processes.* Novato, Calif.: Academic Therapy Publications, 1976.

Selman, R. The relation of the role-taking to the development of moral judgment in children. *Child Development,* 1971, *42,* 79-91.

Stanley, J.C., & Bolton, D.T. Book reviews. *Psychological Measurement*, 1957, *17*, 631-634.

Stevenson, G., Seghini, J.B., Timothy, K., Brown, K., Lloyd, B.C., Zimmerman, M.A., Maxfield, S., & Buchanan, J. *Project implode: Igniting creative potential*. Salt Lake City, Ut.: Bella-Vista-Institute for Behavioral Research in Creativity, 1971.

Stewart, E.D. Learning styles among gifted/talented students: Preferences for instructional techniques (Doctoral dissertation, University of Connecticut, 1979). *Dissertation Abstracts International*, 1980, *40*, 4503A-4504A. (University Microfilms No. 8003762).

Stoker, H.W., & Kropp, R.P. Measurement of cognitive processes. *Journal of Educational Measurement*, 1964, *1*, 39-42.

Suchman, R. Inquiry and education. In J. Gallagher (Ed.), *Teaching gifted students: A book of readings*. Boston: Allyn & Bacon, 1965.

Sullivan, E.V. *Moral learning: Some findings, issues and questions*. New York, N.Y.: Paulist Press, 1975.

Suppes, P. *Sets and numbers: Teacher's handbook for book 1* (Rev. ed.). New York, N.Y.: Random House, 1969.

Taba, H. *Curriculum development: Theory and practice*. New York, N.Y.: Harcourt, Brace & World, Inc., 1962.

Taba, H. *Thinking in elementary school children* (U.S.O.E. Cooperative Research Project, No. 1574). San Francisco: San Francisco State College, 1964. (ERIC Document Reproduction Service No. ED 003 285)

Taba, H. *Teaching strategies and cognitive functioning in elementary school children* (U.S.O.E. Cooperative Research Project No. 2404). San Francisco: San Francisco State College, 1966.

Tatsuoka, M.M., & Easley, J.A., Jr. *Comparison of UICSM vs traditional algebra classes on COOP algebra test scores* (Research Report No. 1). Urbana, Ill.: University of Illinois Committee on School Mathematics, 1963.

Taylor, C.W. The multiple talent approach. *The Instructor*, 1968, *77*, 27; 142; 144; 146. (a)

Taylor, C.W. Be talent developers as well as knowledge dispensers. *Today's Education*, 1968, *57*, 67-69. (b)

Terman, L.M. (Ed.). *Genetic studies of genius* (Vol. 1): *Mental and physical traits of a thousand gifted children*. Palo Alto, Calif.: Stanford University Press, 1959.

Terman, L.M., & Oden, M. *Genetic studies of genius* (Vol. 5): *The gifted group at mid-life*. Palo Alto, Calif.: Stanford University Press, 1959.

Torrance, E.P. *Rewarding creative behavior*. Englewood Cliffs, N.J.: Prentice-Hall, 1965.

Torrance, E.P. *The search for satori and creativity*. Buffalo, N.Y.: Creative Education Foundation, 1979.

Torrance, E.P., & Mourad, S. Self-directed learning readiness skills of gifted students and their relationship to thinking creatively about the future. *The Gifted Child Quarterly*, 1978, *22*, 180-186.

Treffinger, D.J. Teaching for self-directed learning: A priority for the gifted and talented. *The Gifted Child Quarterly*, 1975, *19*, 46-59.

Treffinger, D.J., & Barton, B.L. *Fostering independent learning*. *G/C/T*, 1979, *7*, 3-6; 54.

Tyler, L.L. The taxonomy of educational objectives: Cognitive domain—It's use in evaluating programmed instruction. *California Journal of Educational Research*, 1966, *17*, 26-32.

Wallace, W.L. The BSCS 1961-62 evaluation program—A statistical report. *Biological Sciences Curriculum Study Newsletter*, 1962, *19*, 22-24.

Wallach, M.A. Tests tell us little about talent. *American Scientist*, 1976, *44*, 57-63.

Wallach, M.A., & Kogan, N. *Modes of thinking in young children*. New York, N.Y.: Holt, Rinehart and Winston, 1965.

Wallen, N.E., Durkin, M.C., Fraenkel, J.R., McNaughton, A.J., & Sawin, E.I. *The Taba curriculum development project in social studies*. Menlo Park, Calif.: Addison-Wesley, 1969.

Watts, G.H., & Anderson, R.C. Effects of three types of inserted questions on learning from prose. *Journal of Educational Psychology*, 1971, *62*, 387-394.

Ward, V.S. *Educating the gifted: An axiomatic approach*. Columbus, Oh.: Charles E. Merrill, 1961.

Williams, F.E. *Classroom ideas for encouraging thinking and feeling* (2nd ed). Buffalo, N.Y.: D.O.K. Publishers, 1970.

Williams, F.E. Models for encouraging creativity in the classroom. In J.C. Gowan & E.P. Torrance (Eds.), *Educating the ablest: A book of readings on the education of gifted children*. Itasca, Ill.: F.E. Peacock Publishers, Inc., 1971.

Williams, F.E. *A total creativity program for individualizing and humanizing the learning process* (Instructional Materials). Englewood Cliffs, N.J.: Educational Technology Publications, 1972.

Williams, F.E. Assessing creativity across Williams "cube" model. *The Gifted Child Quarterly*, 1979, *23*, 748-756. (a)

Williams, F.E. *Creativity assessment packet*. Buffalo, N.Y.: D.O.K. Publishers, 1979. (b)

Wilson, S.H., Greer, J.F., & Johnson, R.M. Syntectics, a creative problem-solving technique for the gifted. *The Gifted Child Quarterly*, 1973, *17*, 260-267.

Index